SURPRISE!

You may be reading the wrong way!

It's true: In keeping with the original Japanese comic format, this book reads from right to left—so action, sound effects, and word balloons are completely reversed. This preserves the orientation of the original artwork—plus, it's fun! Check out the diagram shown here to get the hang of things, and then turn to the other side of the book to get started!

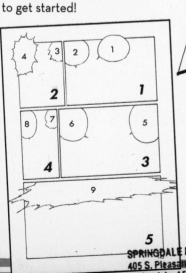

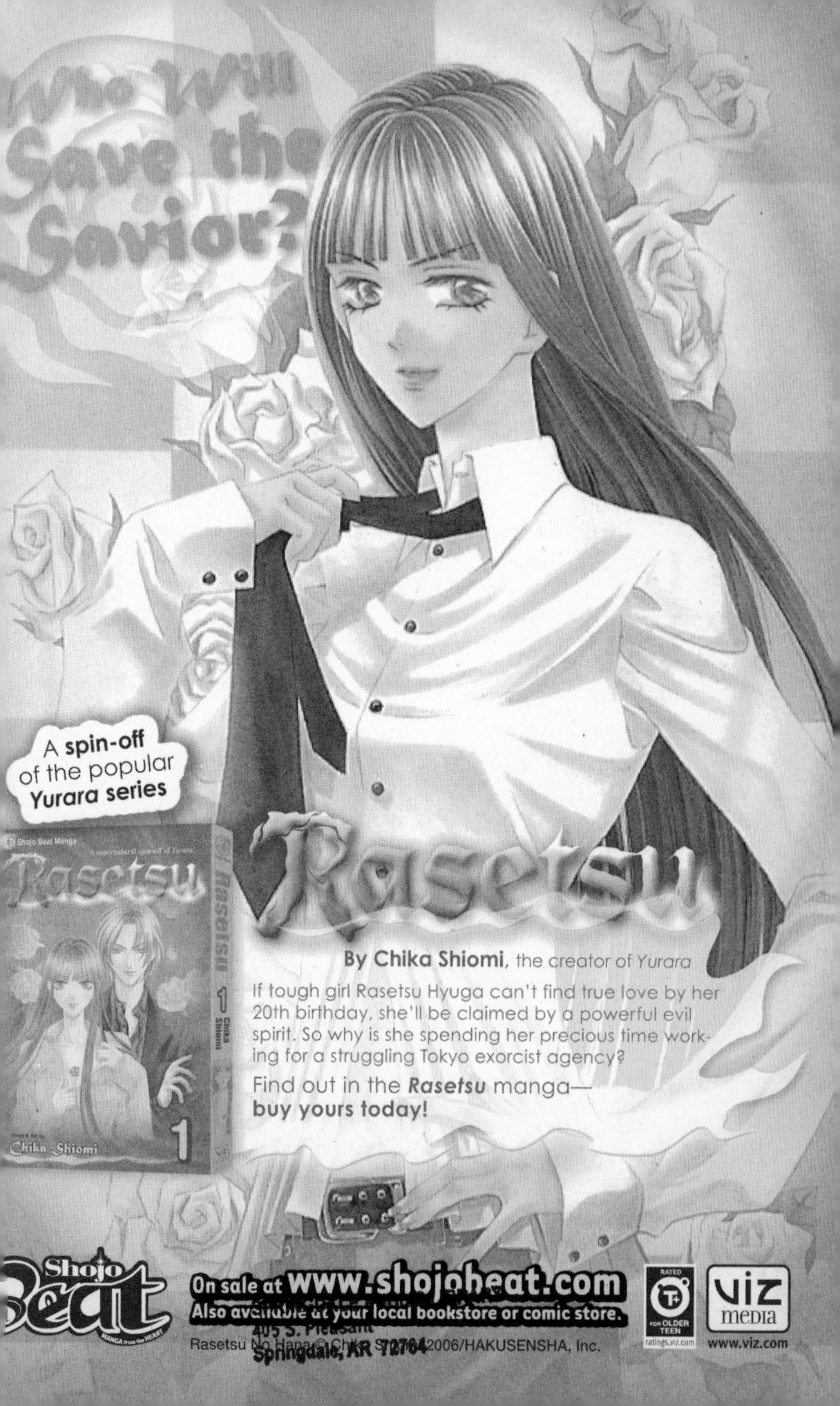
Who Will Save the Savior?
A spin-off of the popular Yurara series
Shojo Beat Manga
Rasetsu
1
Chika Shiomi
Rasetsu
By Chika Shiomi, the creator of Yurara
If tough girl Rasetsu Hyuga can't find true love by her 20th birthday, she'll be claimed by a powerful evil spirit. So why is she spending her precious time working for a struggling Tokyo exorcist agency?
Find out in the Rasetsu manga—buy yours today!
Shojo Beat
MANGA from the HEART
On sale at www.shojobeat.com
Also available at your local bookstore or comic store.
405 S. Pleasant
Springdale, AR 72764
RATED T+ FOR OLDER TEEN
ratings.viz.com
VIZ media
www.viz.com
2006/HAKUSENSHA, Inc.

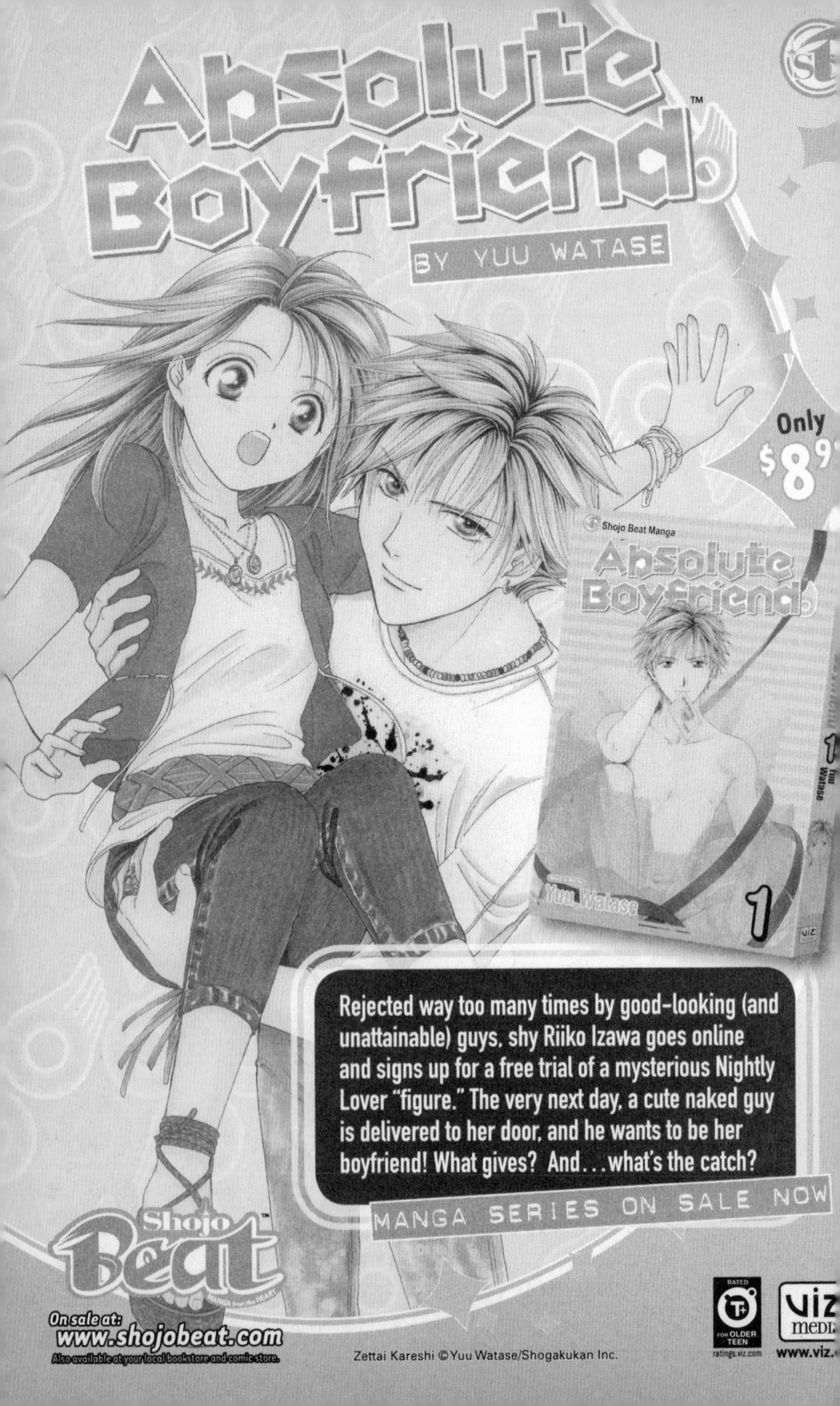

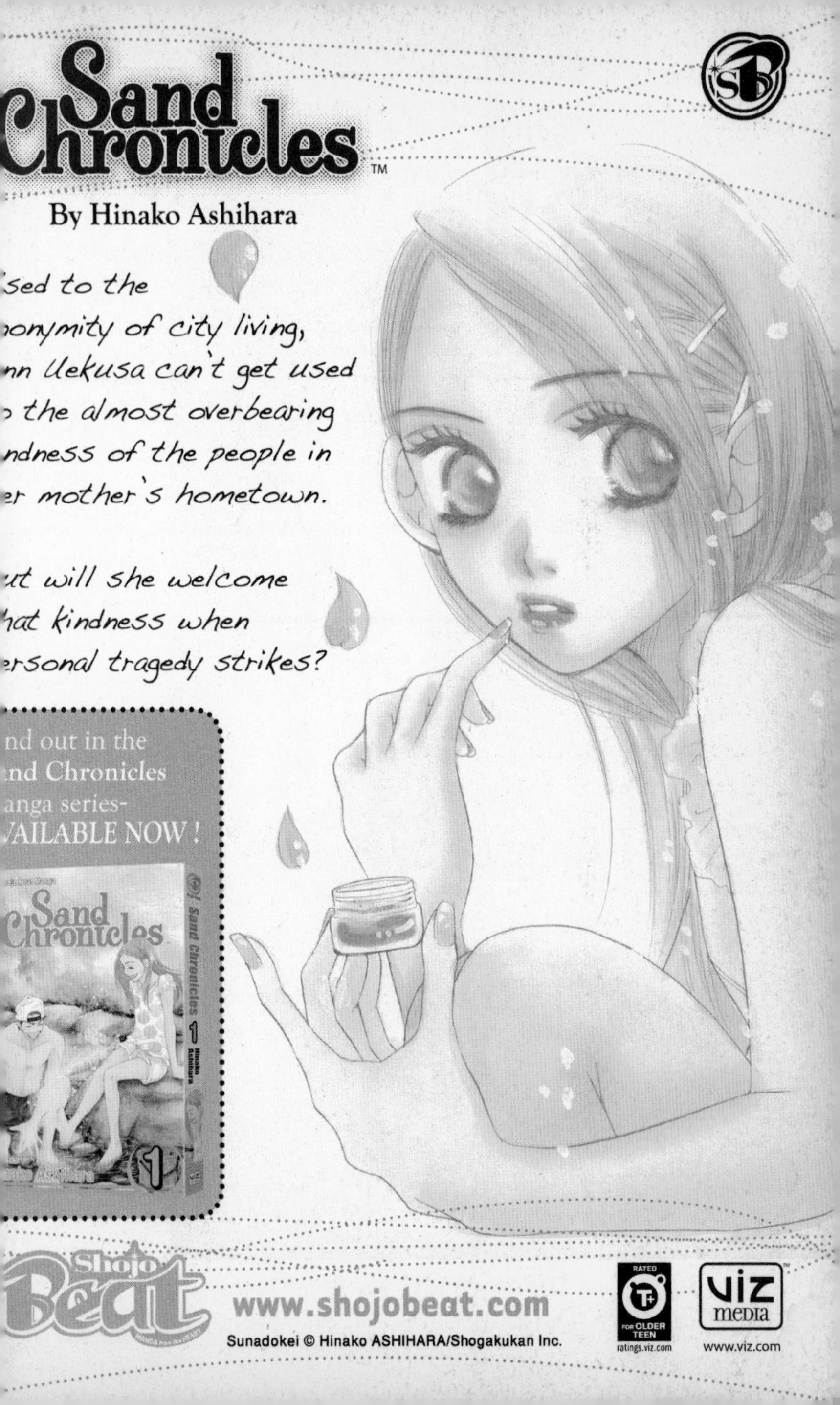
Sand Chronicles™
By Hinako Ashihara
sed to the
nonymity of city living,
nn Uekusa can't get used
the almost overbearing
ndness of the people in
er mother's hometown.
ut will she welcome
hat kindness when
ersonal tragedy strikes?
nd out in the
nd Chronicles
anga series-
VAILABLE NOW!
Sand Chronicles
Sand Chronicles 1
www.shojobeat.com
Sunadokei © Hinako ASHIHARA/Shogakukan Inc.
RATED T+ FOR OLDER TEEN
ratings.viz.com
VIZ media
www.viz.com

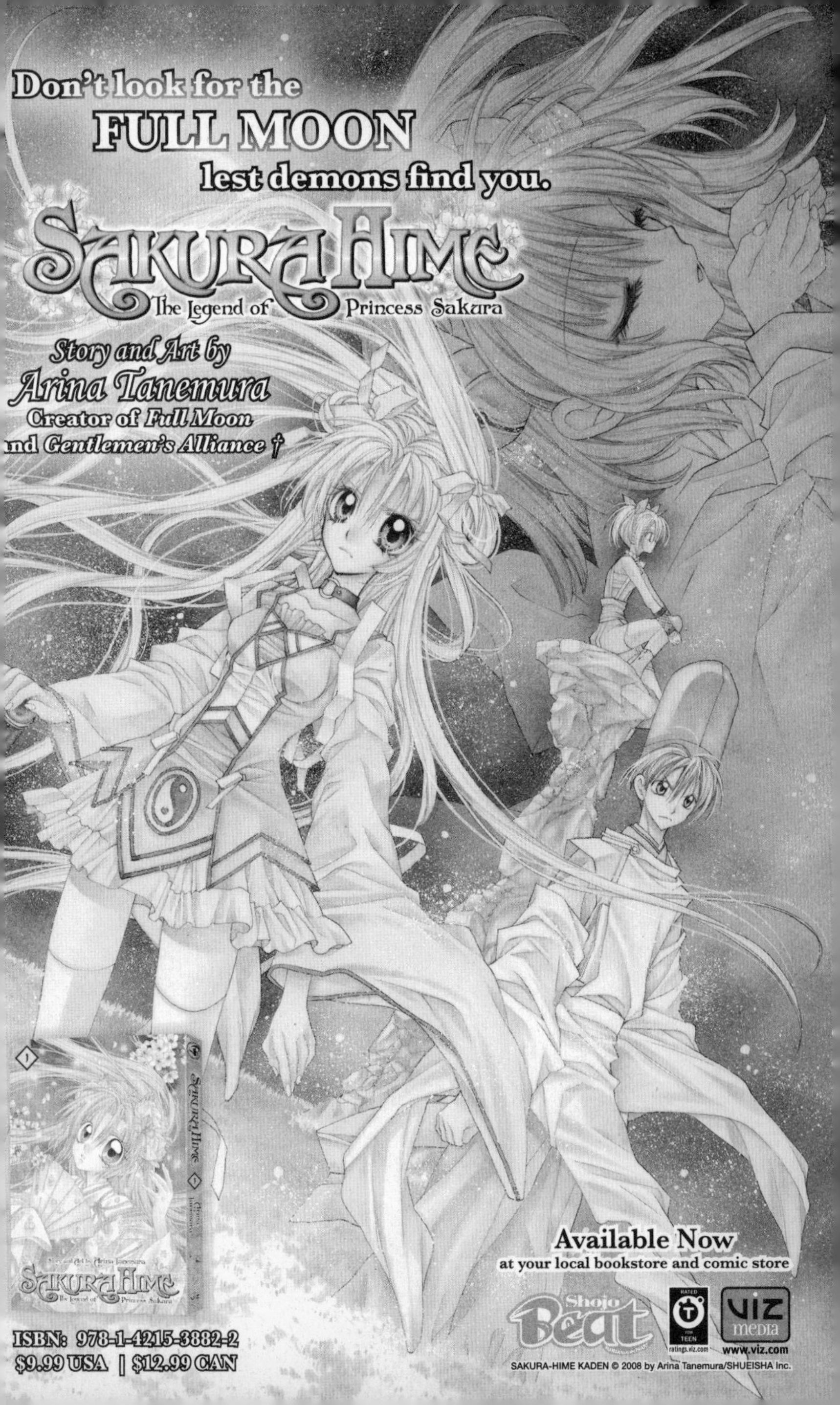

Don't look for the
FULL MOON
lest demons find you.
SAKURA HIME
The Legend of Princess Sakura
Story and Art by
Arina Tanemura
Creator of Full Moon
and Gentlemen's Alliance †
Available Now
at your local bookstore and comic store
Shojo Beat
RATED T TEEN ratings.viz.com
VIZ media
www.viz.com
ISBN: 978-1-4215-3882-2
$9.99 USA | $12.99 CAN
SAKURA-HIME KADEN © 2008 by Arina Tanemura/SHUEISHA Inc.

THE GENTLEMEN'S ALLIANCE †
CROSS

Story & Art by
Arina Tanemura

Vol. 3

CONTENTS

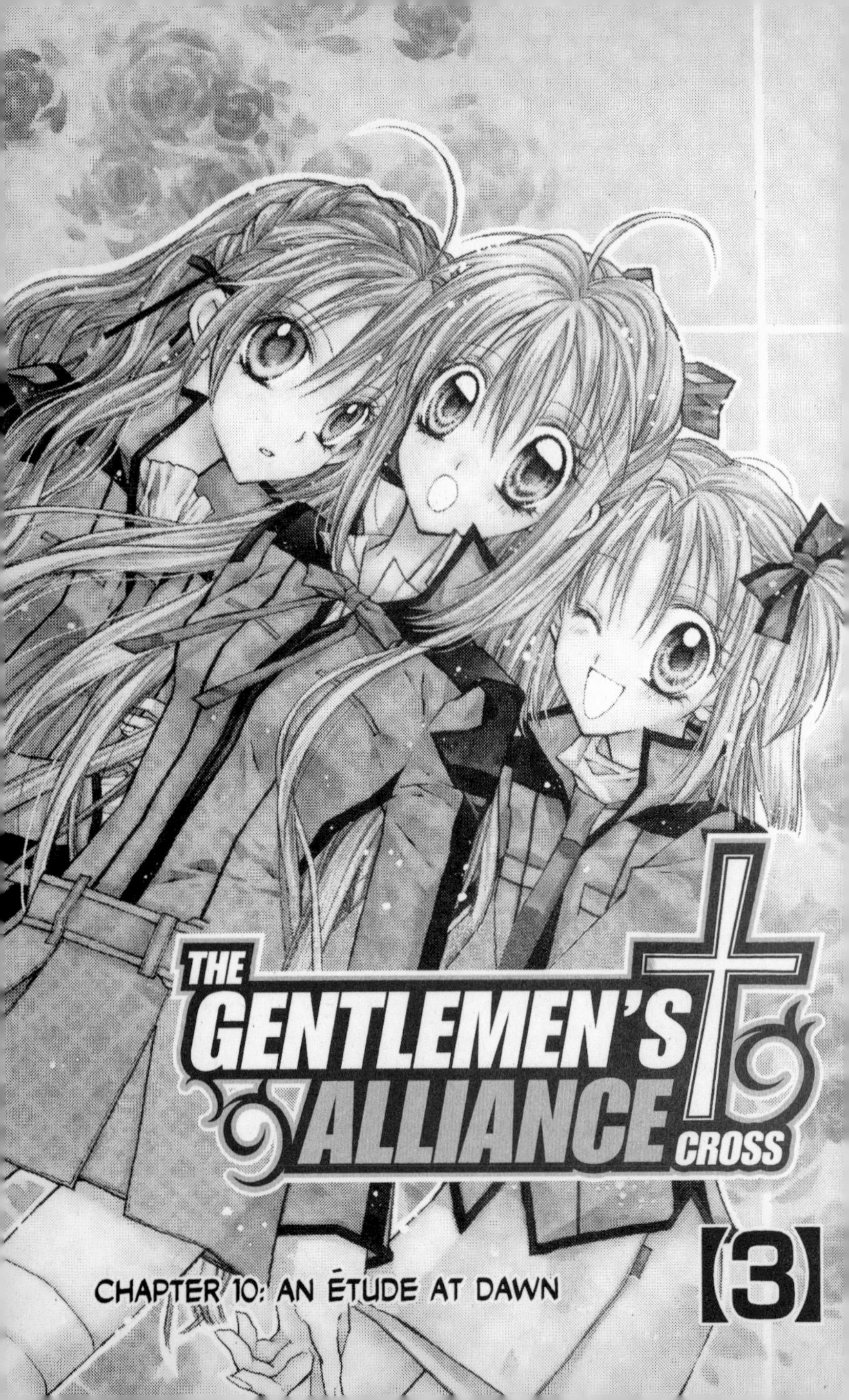
THE GENTLEMEN'S ALLIANCE CROSS
[3]
CHAPTER 10: AN ÉTUDE AT DAWN

CHARACTER INTRODUCTIONS

USHIO AMAMIYA

Clerk

Haine's friend. She's beautiful.

HAINE OTOMIYA

Bodyguard & General Affairs

A cheerful girl who is in love with Shizumasa-sama. Former juvenile delinquent. Adopted into the Otomiya family in fourth grade.

SHIZUMASA TOGU

Student Council President

The richest person in school. Referred to as "the Emperor."

MAORA

Planning Events & Accounting

Childhood friend of Maguri.

MAGURI TSUJIMIYA

Vice President

In love with the Emperor.

THE GENTLEMEN'S ALLIANCE CROSS

Haine Otomiya is a former juvenile delinquent who attends Imperial Academy. She is in love with Shizumasa Togu, aka "The Emperor." He is the richest and most powerful person at the academy.

Imperial Academy is famous for being a school for the wealthy. The students are divided into Gold, Silver, and Bronze, depending on how rich they are. Haine is a Bronze student. She is the adopted daughter of the Otomiya family, which is on the verge of bankruptcy. After finding the "kidnapped" Emperor, she was allowed on the student council. To help Shizumasa ward off girls, she becomes his fake girlfriend and is given the rank of Platinum.

Shizumsasa asks Haine to come to his private room, and there she finds him and Ushio in a compromising position. Haine realizes Shizumasa has hurt her on purpose; he hates people who get close to him, and he hates himself most of all.

Shizumasa has distanced himself from Haine , and the complicated situation in Shizumasa's life is making it even harder for her to close the gap between them.

Having been rejected by him, Haine recalls the second time they met…

STORY THUS FAR

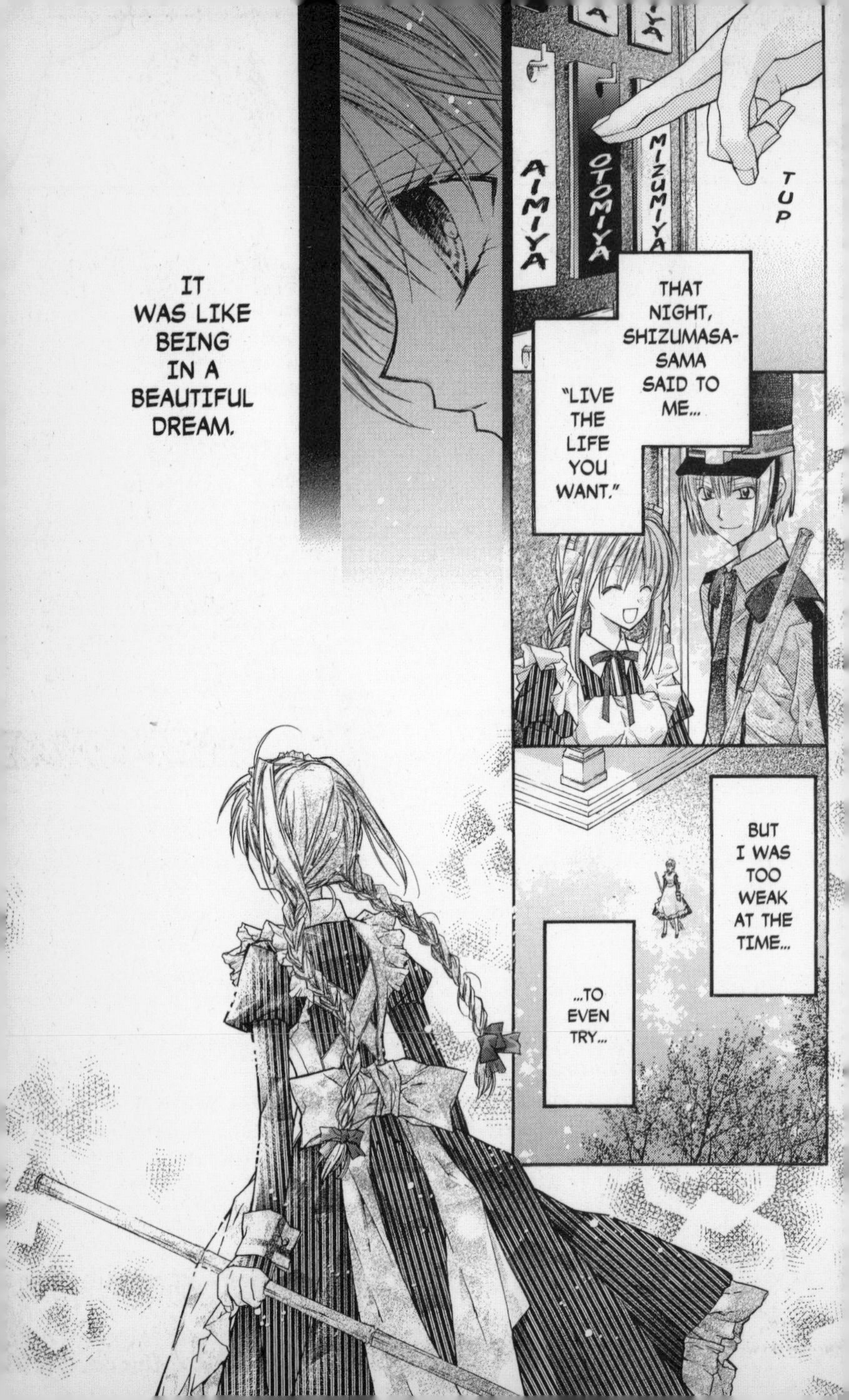
TUP
MIZUMIYA
OTOMIYA
AIMIYA
THAT NIGHT, SHIZUMASA-SAMA SAID TO ME...
"LIVE THE LIFE YOU WANT."
BUT I WAS TOO WEAK AT THE TIME...
...TO EVEN TRY...
IT WAS LIKE BEING IN A BEAUTIFUL DREAM.

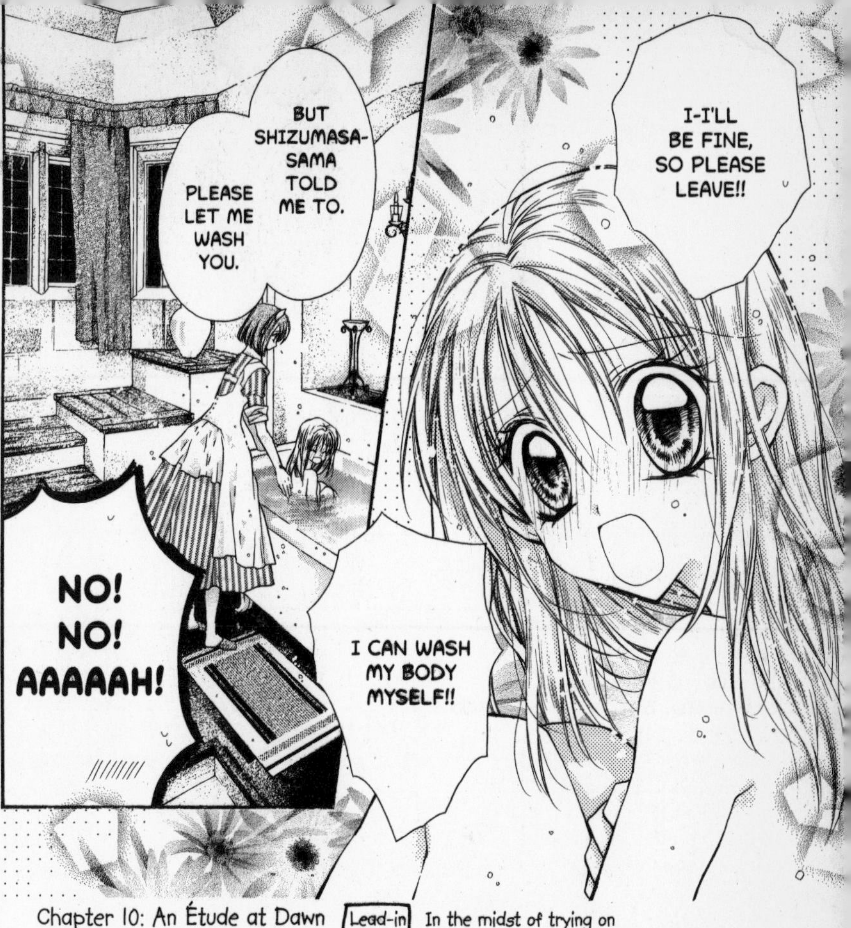
I-I'LL BE FINE, SO PLEASE LEAVE!!
I CAN WASH MY BODY MYSELF!!
BUT SHIZUMASA-SAMA TOLD ME TO.
PLEASE LET ME WASH YOU.
NO! NO! AAAAAH!

Chapter 10: An Étude at Dawn
※I'm giving away some of the story.

Lead-in
In the midst of trying on my winter clothes... How does it look?

Stories about the past... I love writing about them... //// Sorry. (Like Fin, Moe-san, etc.) I had come up with a lot of this chapter before I started writing this series, so I'm happy to see it finally come into being...!

Having a bed inside a greenhouse has always been a fancy of mine. (And there's water flowing inside the greenhouse too...), but I don't have any source material to draw it from (it's all in my mind). I'm indebted to my assistants who molded it into shape from my rough sketches!!

I believe that Shizumasa's feelings for Haine are actually even stronger than Haine's feelings for Shizumasa. He may be the type of person who cannot live as "himself"... In some ways, he's very much like Mao-chan to me. They both don't seem to be enjoying life. On the other hand, Haine is the exact opposite, so that may be why they can't leave her alone.

This is when Ushio changes after being left alone for a while. I can't wait to see what's going on inside her... I'd be very happy if you would wait patiently for that time to come...

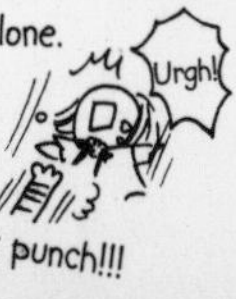
Urgh!
Cat punch!!!

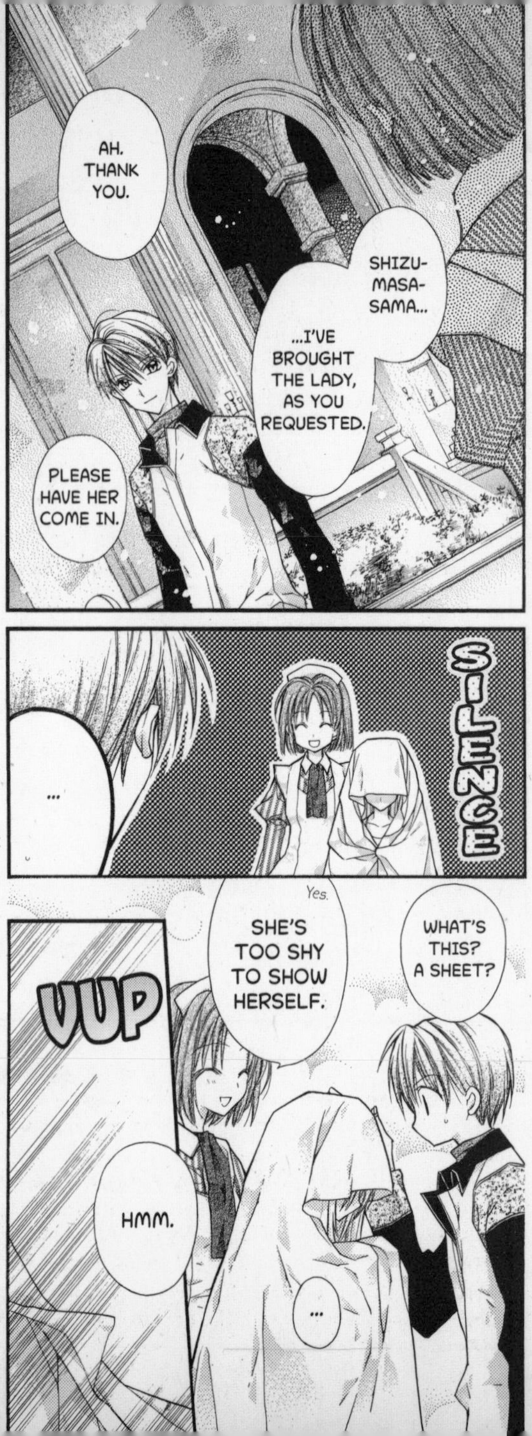
SHIZU-MASA-SAMA...
...I'VE BROUGHT THE LADY, AS YOU REQUESTED.
AH. THANK YOU.
PLEASE HAVE HER COME IN.
SILENCE
...
WHAT'S THIS? A SHEET?
Yes.
SHE'S TOO SHY TO SHOW HERSELF.
VUP
HMM.
...

Greetings.

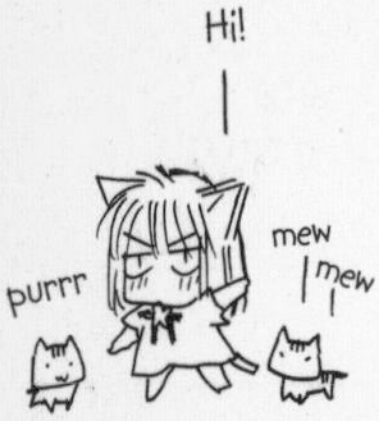
Hi!
mew
mew
purrr

✿ Hello! It's Arina Tanemura. We're already at volume 3 for the *Gentleman's Alliance*!! The excursion chapter, which is the main part of this volume, is one of my favorites, so I'm glad to see it come out.

✿ I'm very sorry, but please wait a little bit more for the character profiles. (I don't want to rush through them too quickly...;)

✿ The cover illustration for this volume is of Ushio-chan. She hasn't been in the story a lot, but she's extremely popular.✧ Ushio fans, please wait a little longer; to see her more often in the story...;;

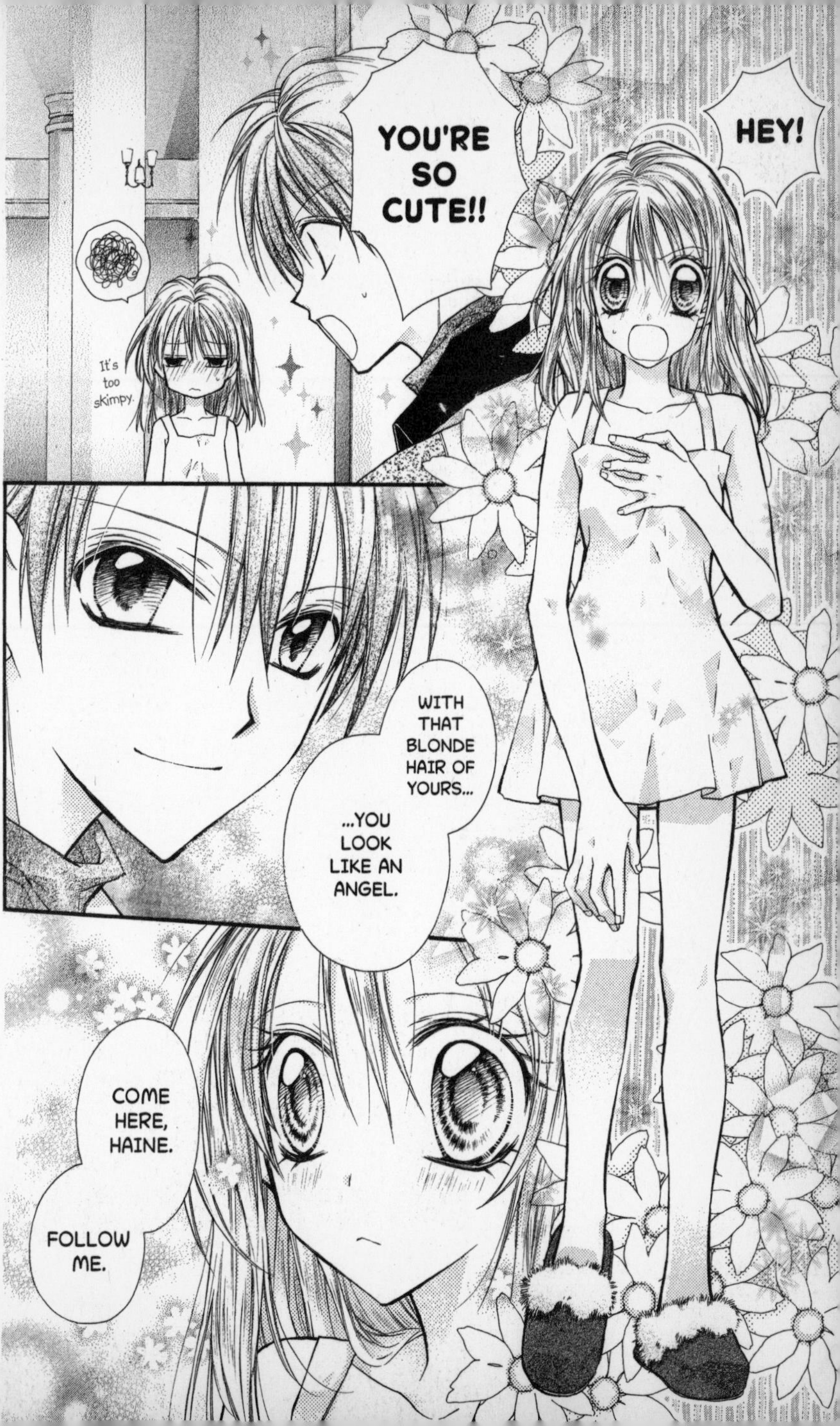

HEY!
YOU'RE SO CUTE!!
It's too skimpy.
WITH THAT BLONDE HAIR OF YOURS...
...YOU LOOK LIKE AN ANGEL.
COME HERE, HAINE.
FOLLOW ME.

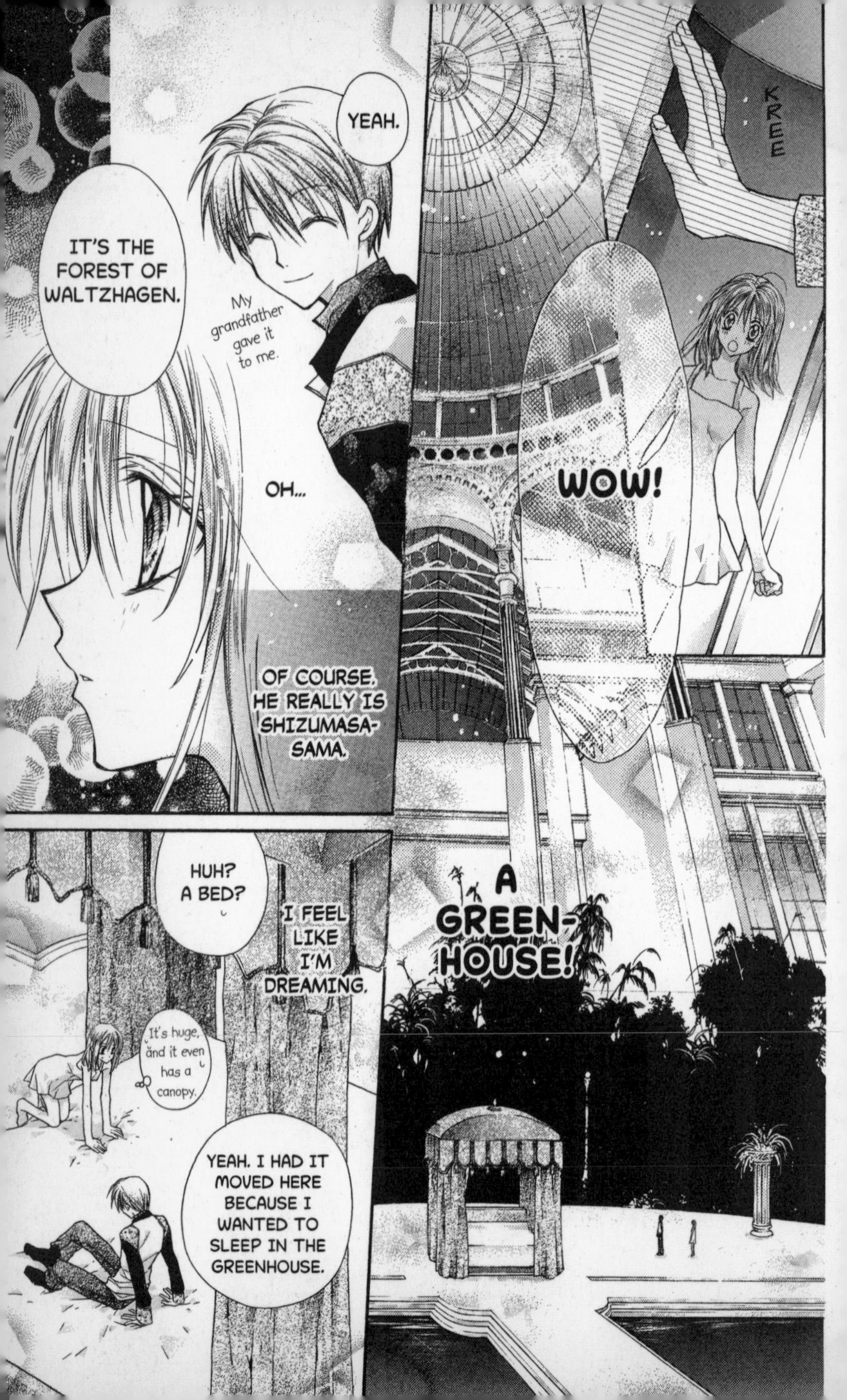
KREE
WOW!
A GREEN-HOUSE!
YEAH.
IT'S THE FOREST OF WALTZHAGEN.
My grandfather gave it to me.
OH...
OF COURSE. HE REALLY IS SHIZUMASA-SAMA.
HUH? A BED?
I FEEL LIKE I'M DREAMING.
It's huge, and it even has a canopy.
YEAH. I HAD IT MOVED HERE BECAUSE I WANTED TO SLEEP IN THE GREENHOUSE.

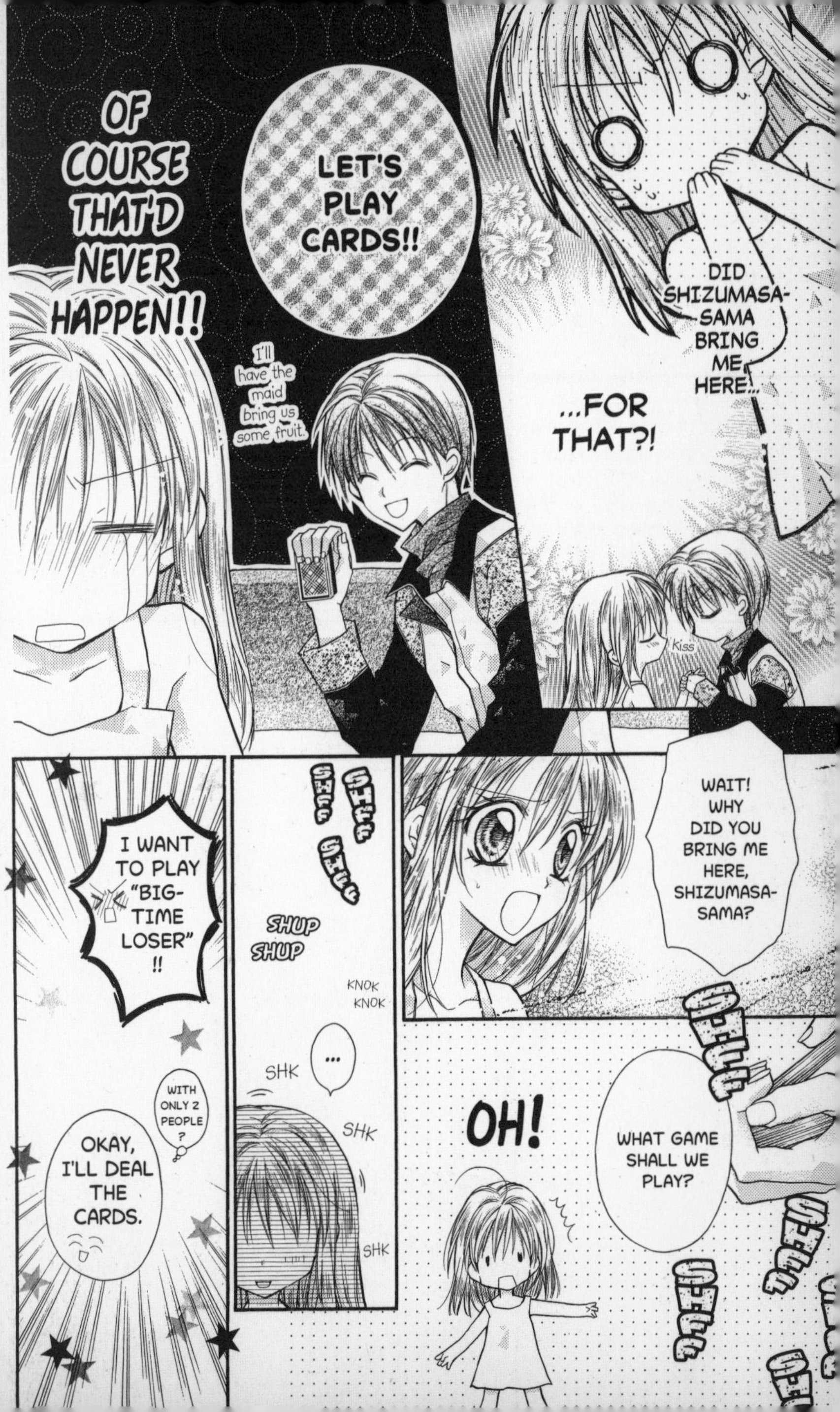
DID SHIZUMASA-SAMA BRING ME HERE...
...FOR THAT?!
Kiss
LET'S PLAY CARDS!!
I'll have the maid bring us some fruit.
OF COURSE THAT'D NEVER HAPPEN!!
WAIT! WHY DID YOU BRING ME HERE, SHIZUMASA-SAMA?
WHAT GAME SHALL WE PLAY?
OH!
SHUP SHUP
KNOK KNOK
...
SHK
SHK
SHK
I WANT TO PLAY "BIG-TIME LOSER"!!
WITH ONLY 2 PEOPLE?
OKAY, I'LL DEAL THE CARDS.

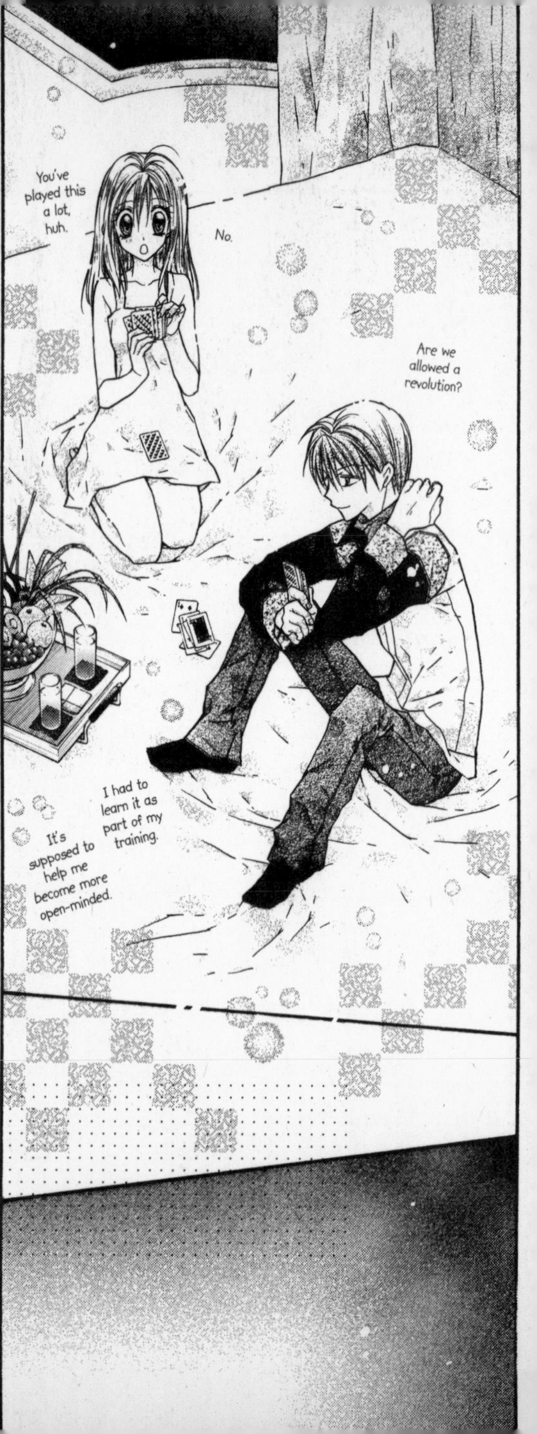
You've played this a lot, huh.
No.
Are we allowed a revolution?
I had to learn it as part of my training.
It's supposed to help me become more open-minded.

Full Moon Final Live

✿The "Full Moon Final Live" (TOCT-25818) is now on sale, and I, Tanemura, much to our surprise, sing on the bonus track! ////

✿It all happened months ago when I was playing with myco-chan and we happened to start talking about the CD. "Is there anything we can do to get everyone talking about this CD?" For some reason or other, the words, "I could sing on it," popped out of my mouth. ////

✿I admit there was a part of me that wanted to try it, but the major reason is because I didn't want to come up with a huge project since that would bother a lot of people. The easiest way was to do it myself...

✿Anyway, I agreed. (Or did I force them to let me sing?) The song is my very, very favorite song, "SMILE." ← It's a great song.

✿I started by listening to "SMILE," sung by myco-chan, included in the CD single of "Eternal Snow," but...

The song is unbelievably hard...||||

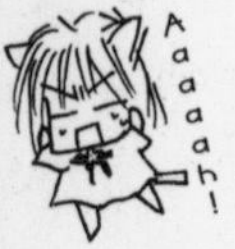
Aaaaah!

What should I do?! What will happen to the CD?!

(continues)

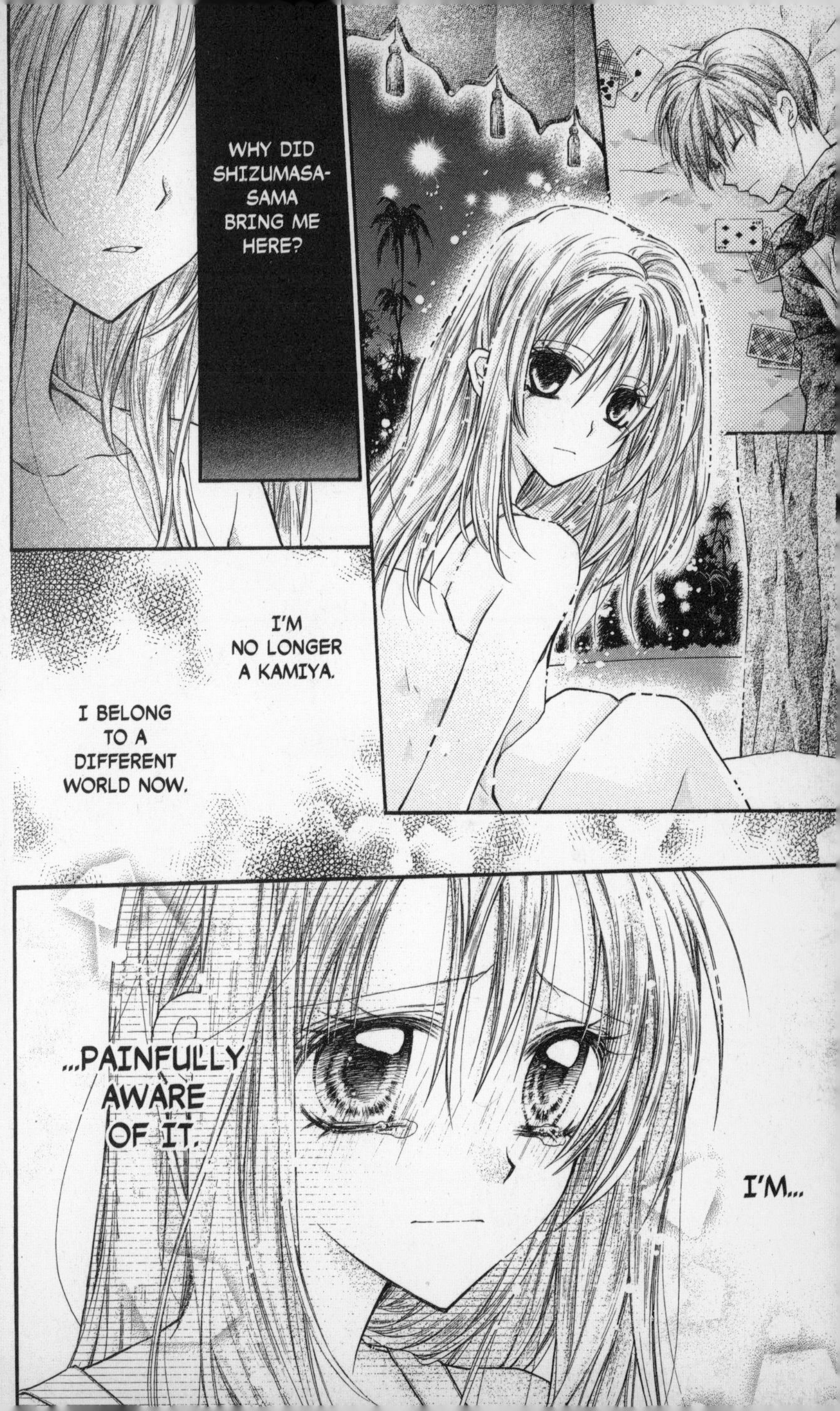
WHY DID SHIZUMASA-SAMA BRING ME HERE?
I'M NO LONGER A KAMIYA.
I BELONG TO A DIFFERENT WORLD NOW.
I'M...
...PAINFULLY AWARE OF IT.

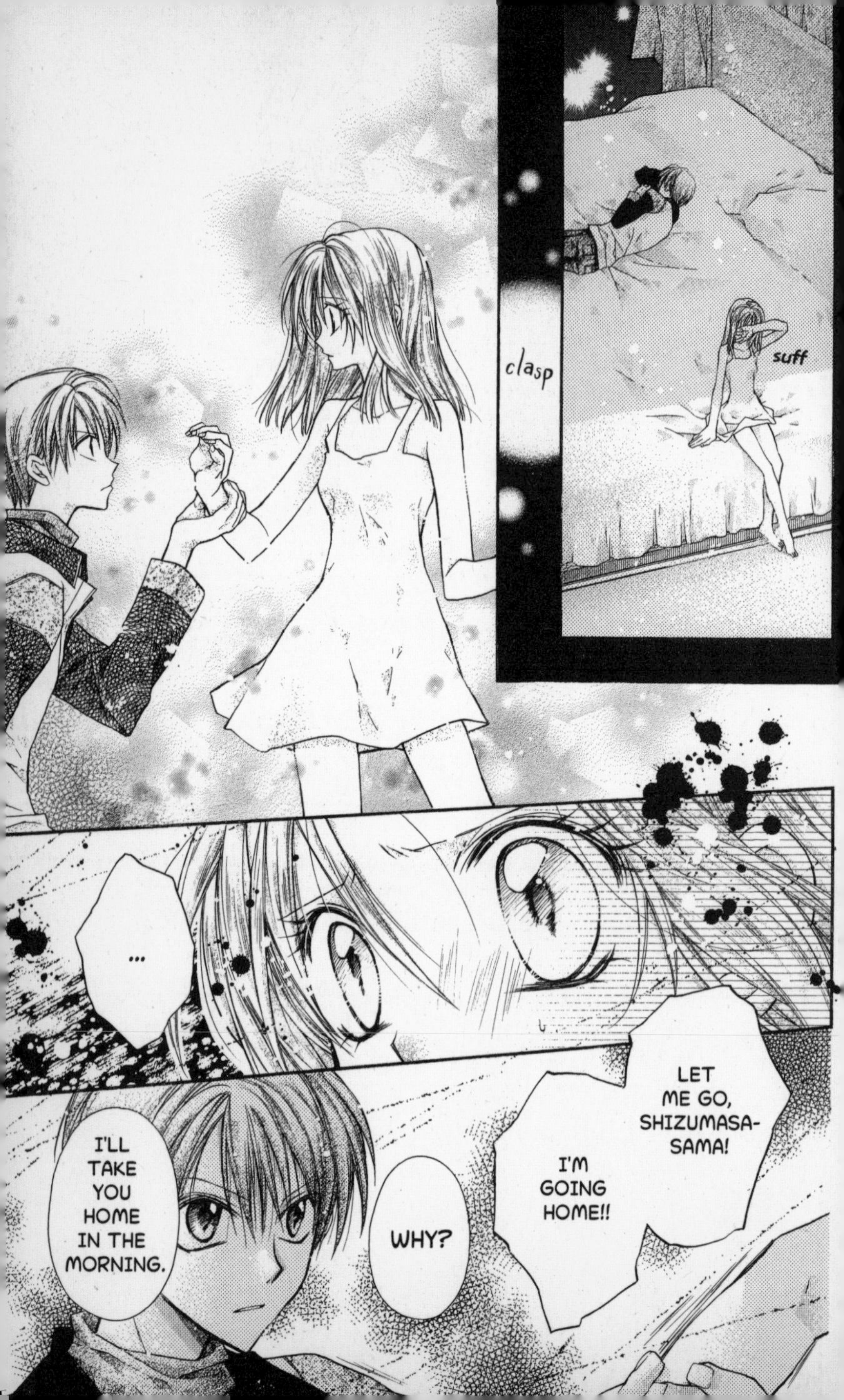
suff
clasp
...
LET ME GO, SHIZUMASA-SAMA!
I'M GOING HOME!!
WHY?
I'LL TAKE YOU HOME IN THE MORNING.

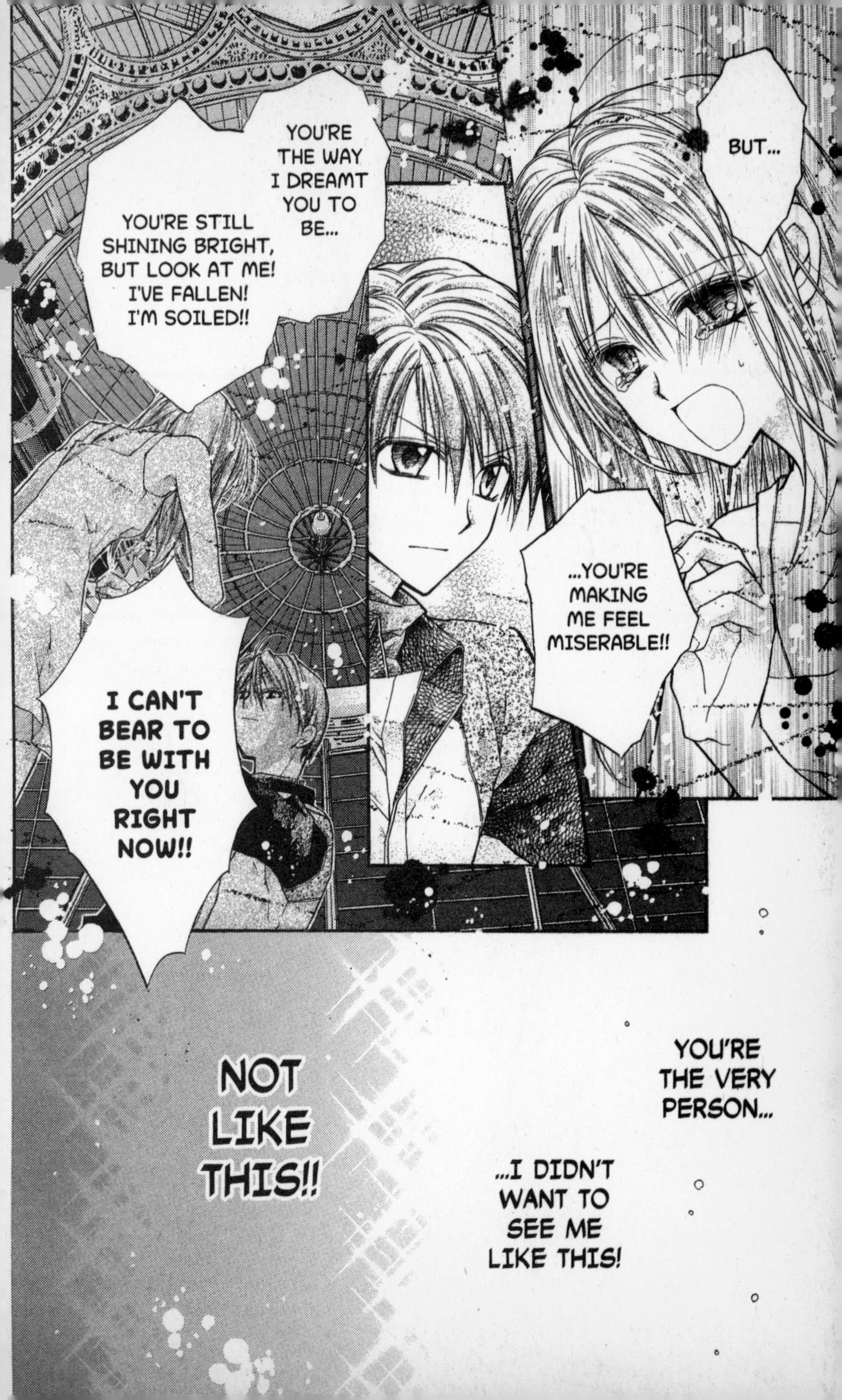
BUT...
YOU'RE THE WAY I DREAMT YOU TO BE...
YOU'RE STILL SHINING BRIGHT, BUT LOOK AT ME! I'VE FALLEN! I'M SOILED!!
...YOU'RE MAKING ME FEEL MISERABLE!!
I CAN'T BEAR TO BE WITH YOU RIGHT NOW!!
YOU'RE THE VERY PERSON...
...I DIDN'T WANT TO SEE ME LIKE THIS!
NOT LIKE THIS!!

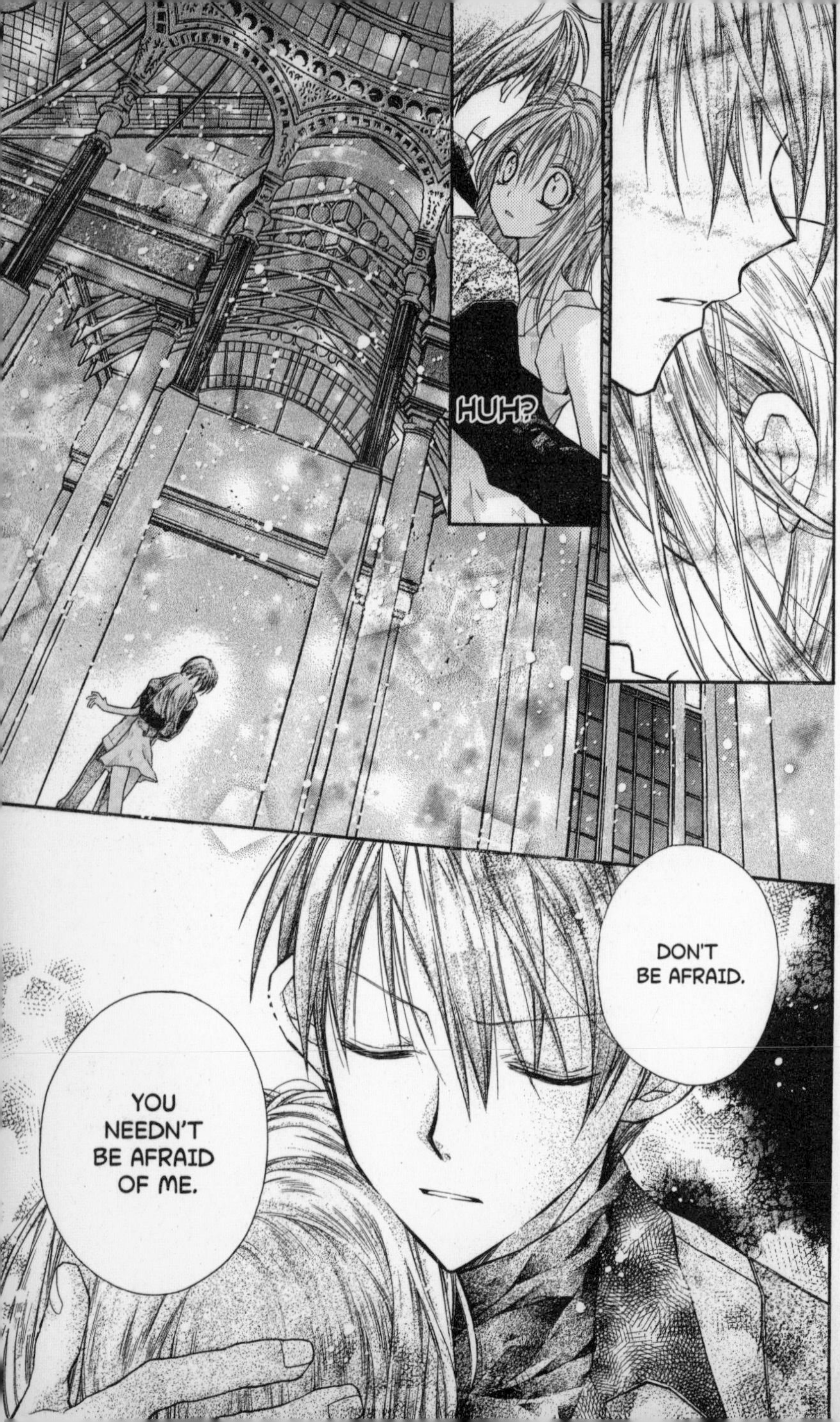
HUH?
DON'T BE AFRAID.
YOU NEEDN'T BE AFRAID OF ME.

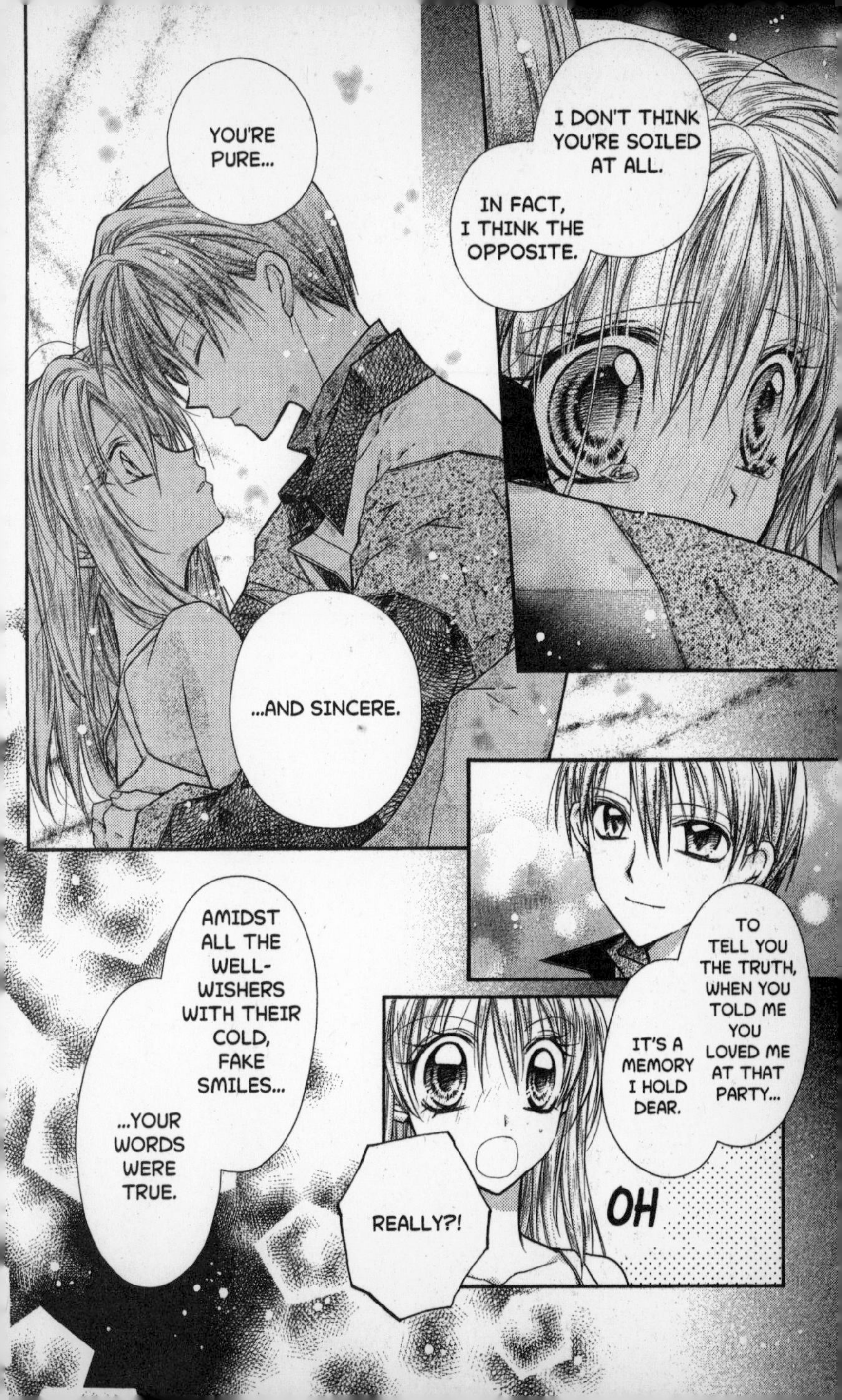
I DON'T THINK YOU'RE SOILED AT ALL.
IN FACT, I THINK THE OPPOSITE.
YOU'RE PURE...
...AND SINCERE.
TO TELL YOU THE TRUTH, WHEN YOU TOLD ME YOU LOVED ME AT THAT PARTY...
IT'S A MEMORY I HOLD DEAR.
OH
REALLY?!
AMIDST ALL THE WELL-WISHERS WITH THEIR COLD, FAKE SMILES...
...YOUR WORDS WERE TRUE.

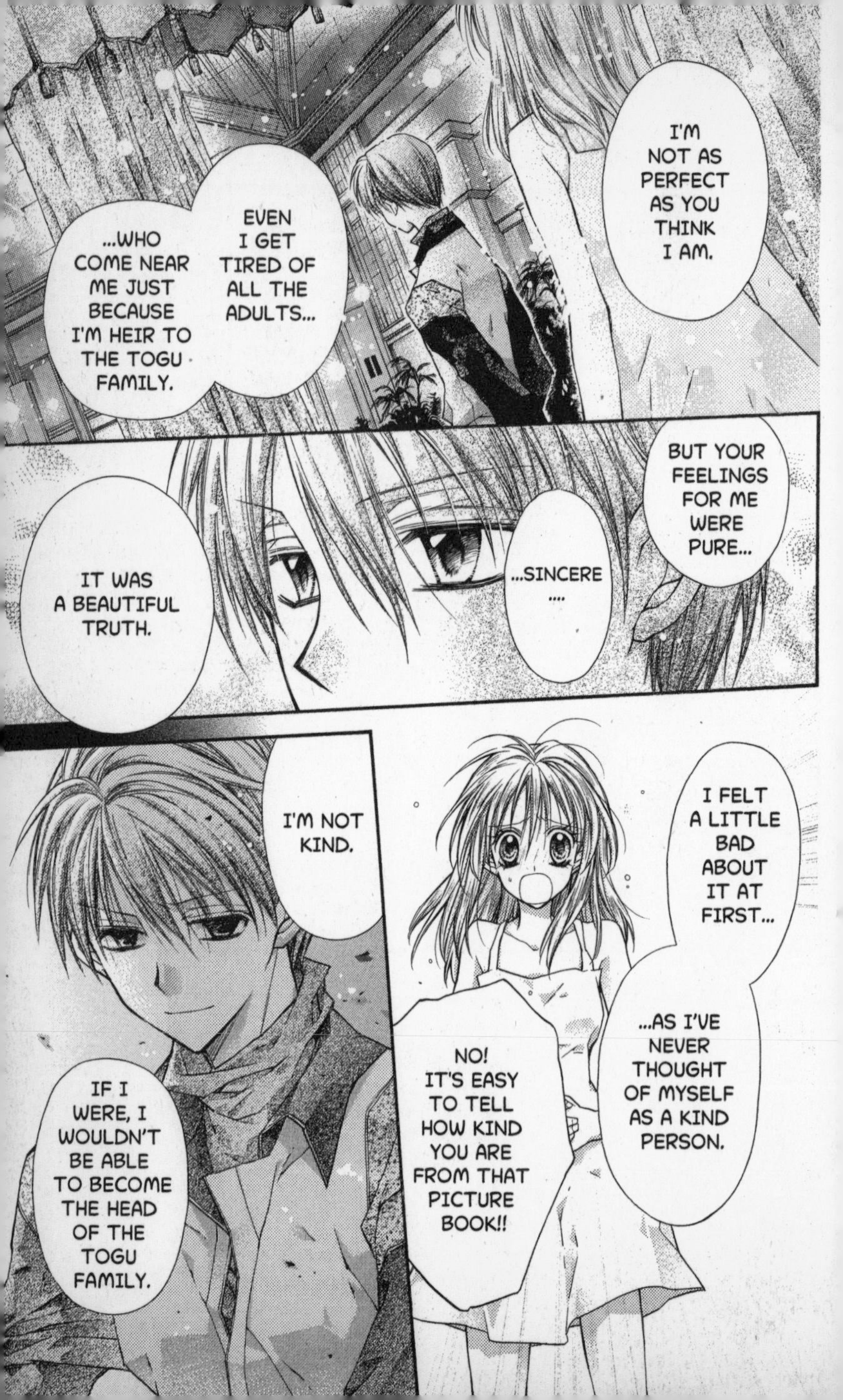
I'M NOT AS PERFECT AS YOU THINK I AM.
EVEN I GET TIRED OF ALL THE ADULTS...
...WHO COME NEAR ME JUST BECAUSE I'M HEIR TO THE TOGU FAMILY.
BUT YOUR FEELINGS FOR ME WERE PURE...
...SINCERE ....
IT WAS A BEAUTIFUL TRUTH.
I FELT A LITTLE BAD ABOUT IT AT FIRST...
...AS I'VE NEVER THOUGHT OF MYSELF AS A KIND PERSON.
NO! IT'S EASY TO TELL HOW KIND YOU ARE FROM THAT PICTURE BOOK!!
I'M NOT KIND.
IF I WERE, I WOULDN'T BE ABLE TO BECOME THE HEAD OF THE TOGU FAMILY.

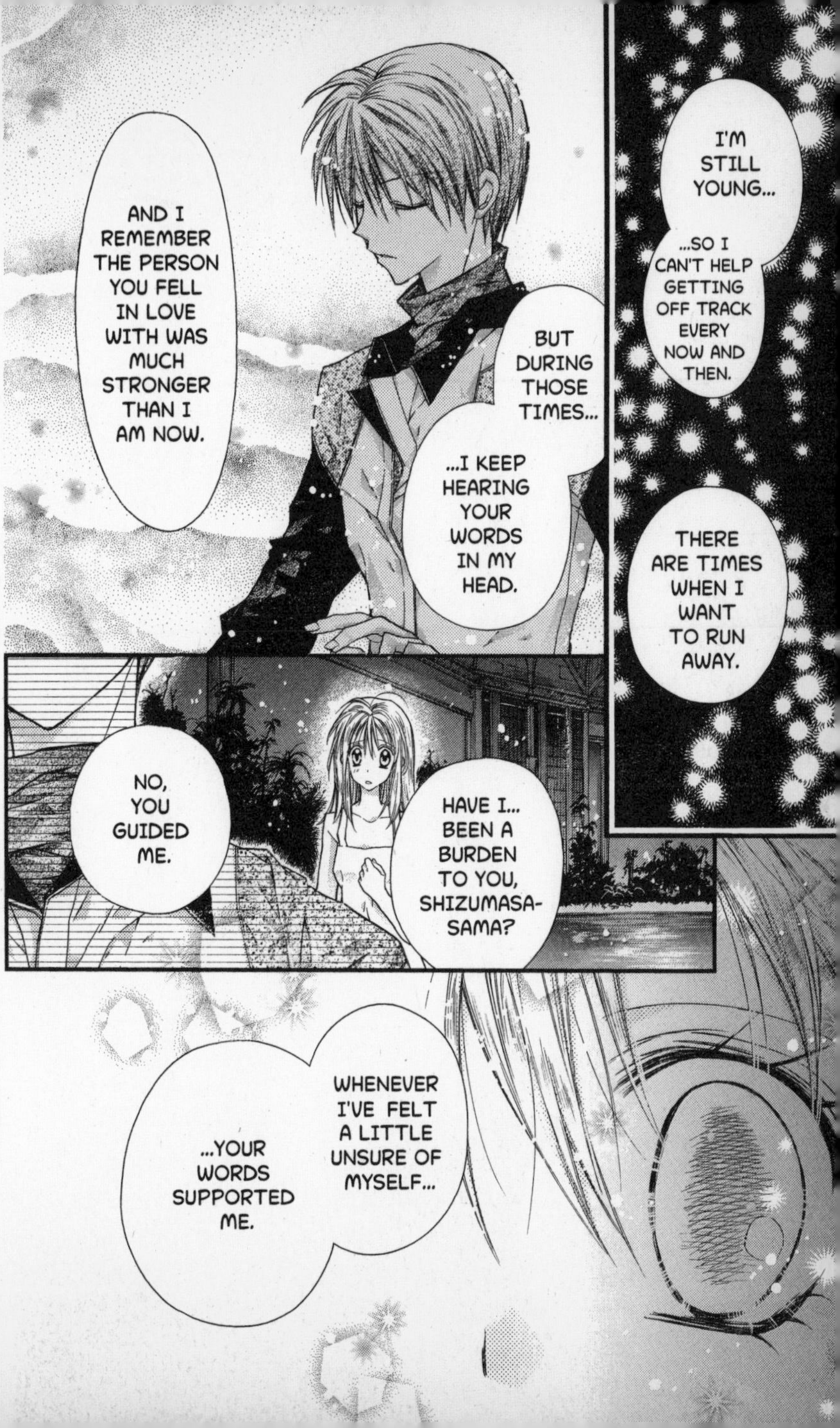
I'M STILL YOUNG...
...SO I CAN'T HELP GETTING OFF TRACK EVERY NOW AND THEN.
THERE ARE TIMES WHEN I WANT TO RUN AWAY.
BUT DURING THOSE TIMES...
...I KEEP HEARING YOUR WORDS IN MY HEAD.
AND I REMEMBER THE PERSON YOU FELL IN LOVE WITH WAS MUCH STRONGER THAN I AM NOW.
HAVE I... BEEN A BURDEN TO YOU, SHIZUMASA-SAMA?
NO, YOU GUIDED ME.
WHENEVER I'VE FELT A LITTLE UNSURE OF MYSELF...
...YOUR WORDS SUPPORTED ME.

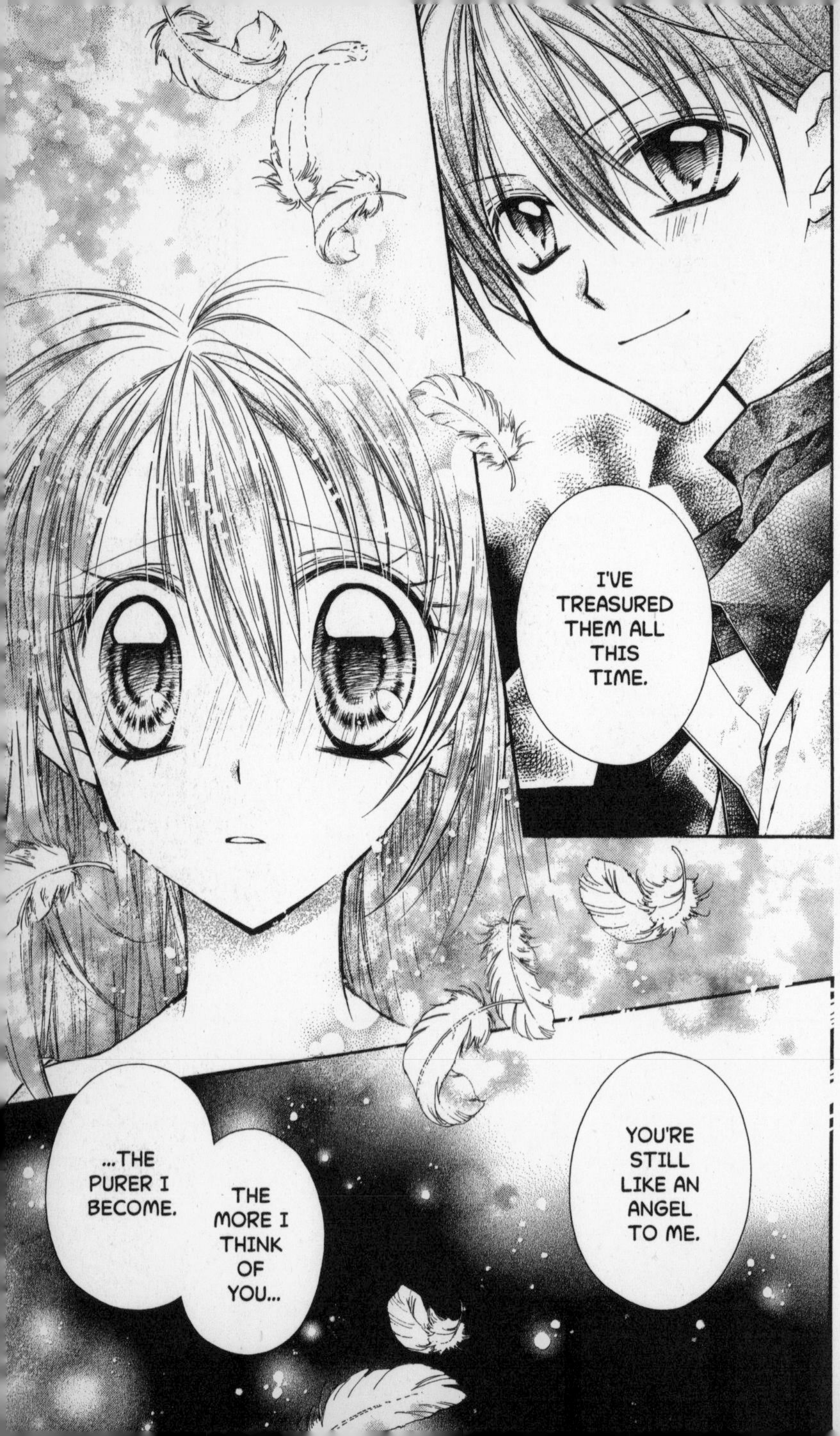
I'VE TREASURED THEM ALL THIS TIME.
YOU'RE STILL LIKE AN ANGEL TO ME.
THE MORE I THINK OF YOU...
...THE PURER I BECOME.

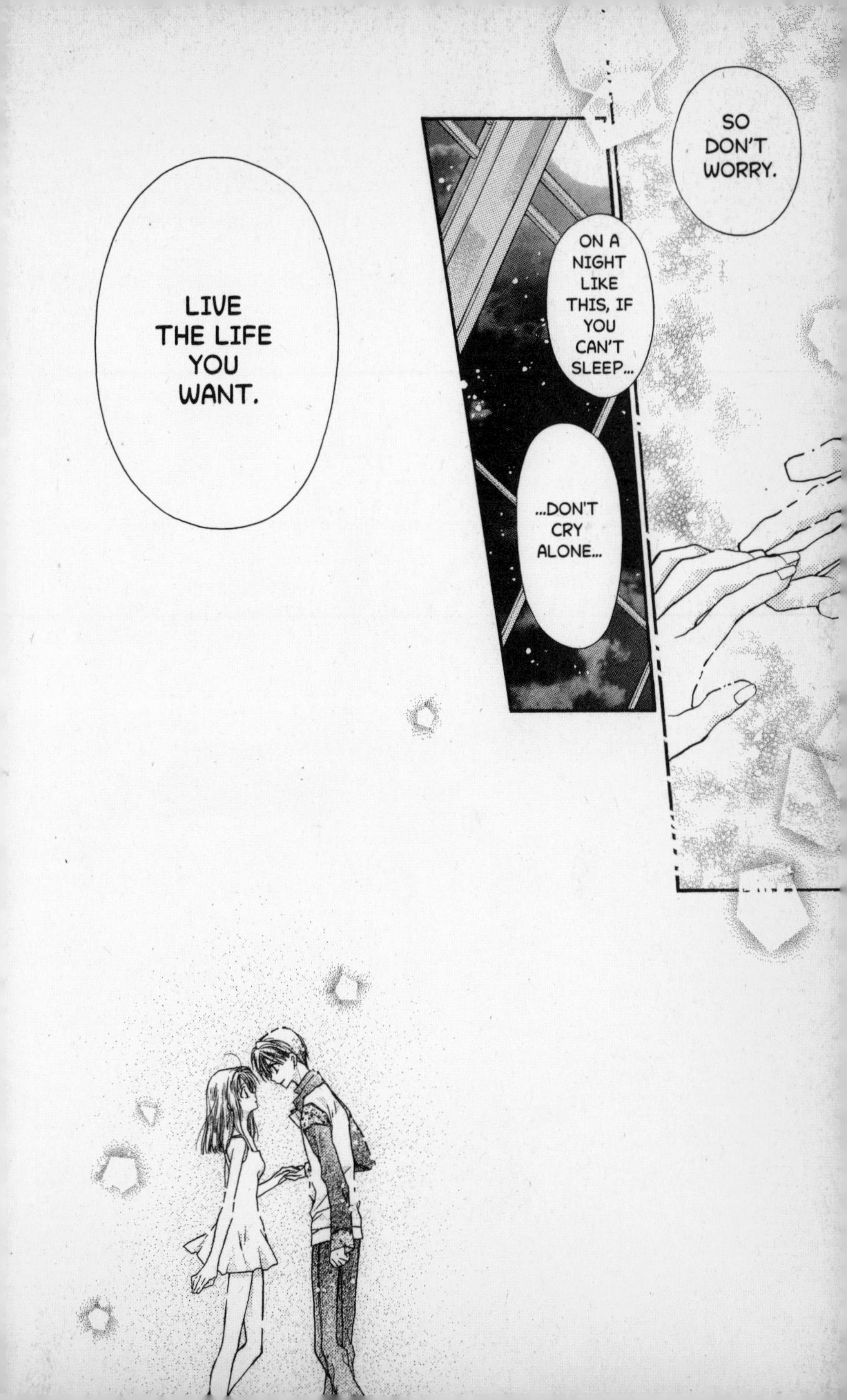
SO DON'T WORRY.
ON A NIGHT LIKE THIS, IF YOU CAN'T SLEEP...
...DON'T CRY ALONE...
LIVE THE LIFE YOU WANT.

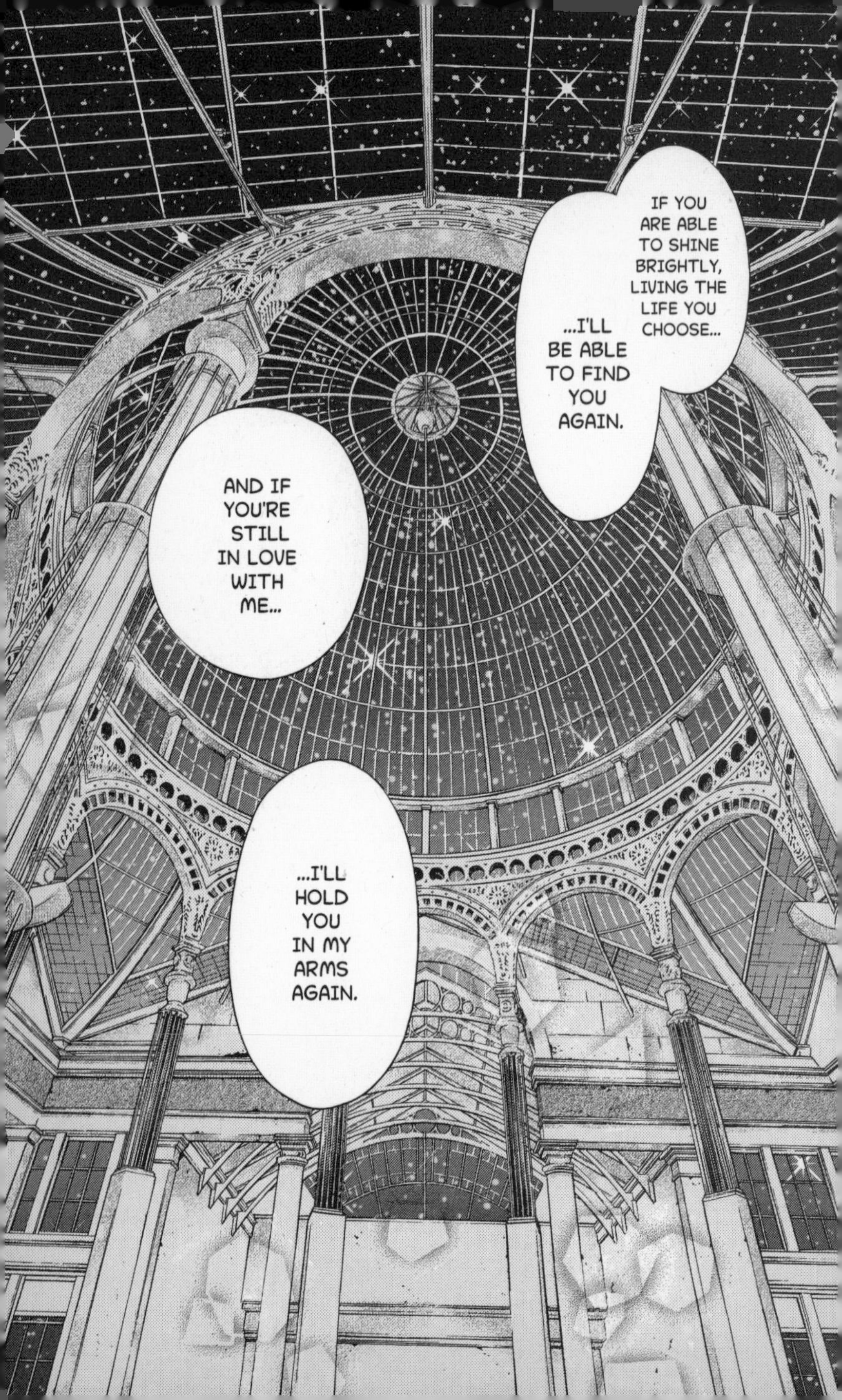
IF YOU ARE ABLE TO SHINE BRIGHTLY, LIVING THE LIFE YOU CHOOSE...
...I'LL BE ABLE TO FIND YOU AGAIN.
AND IF YOU'RE STILL IN LOVE WITH ME...
...I'LL HOLD YOU IN MY ARMS AGAIN.

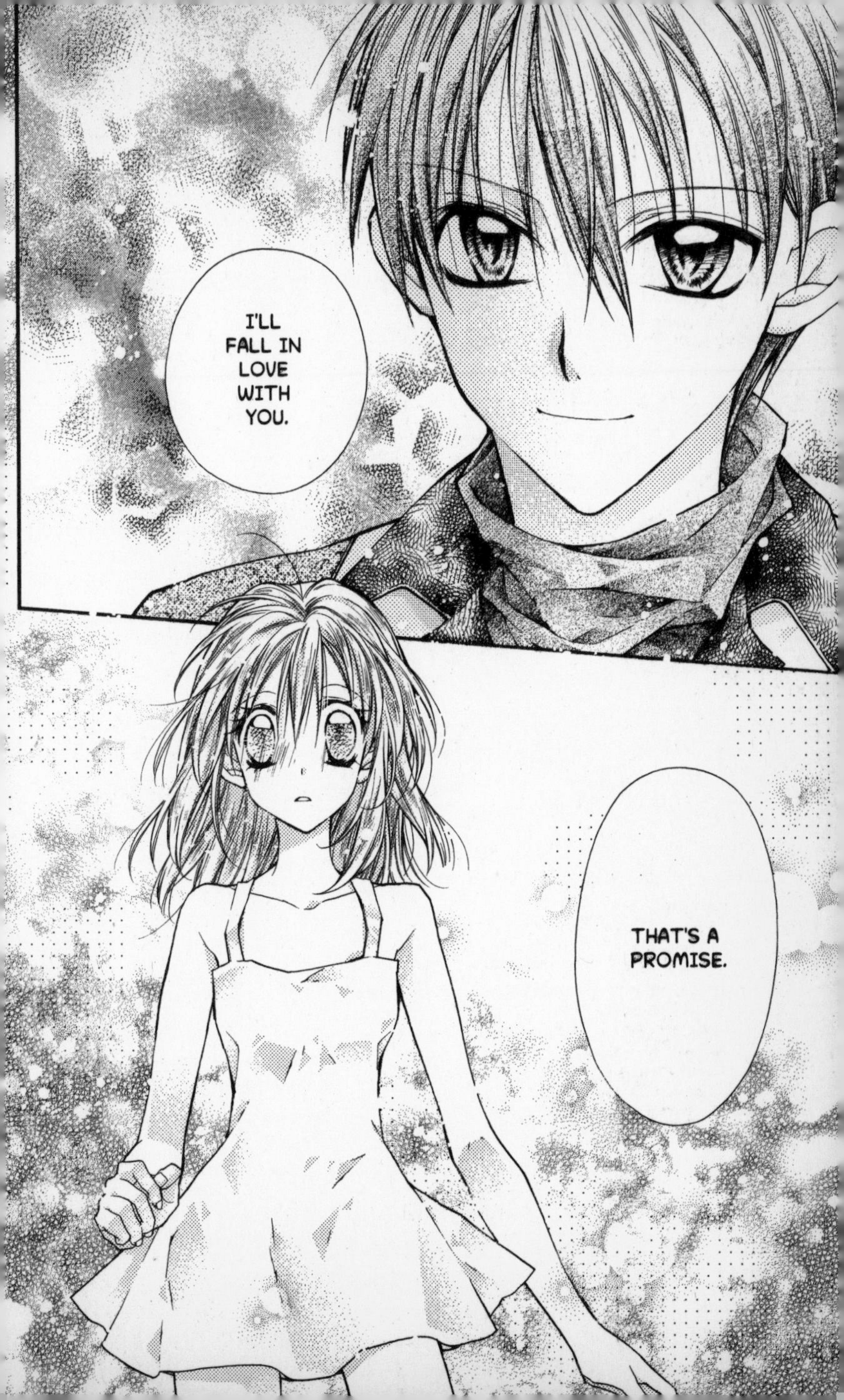
I'LL FALL IN LOVE WITH YOU.
THAT'S A PROMISE.

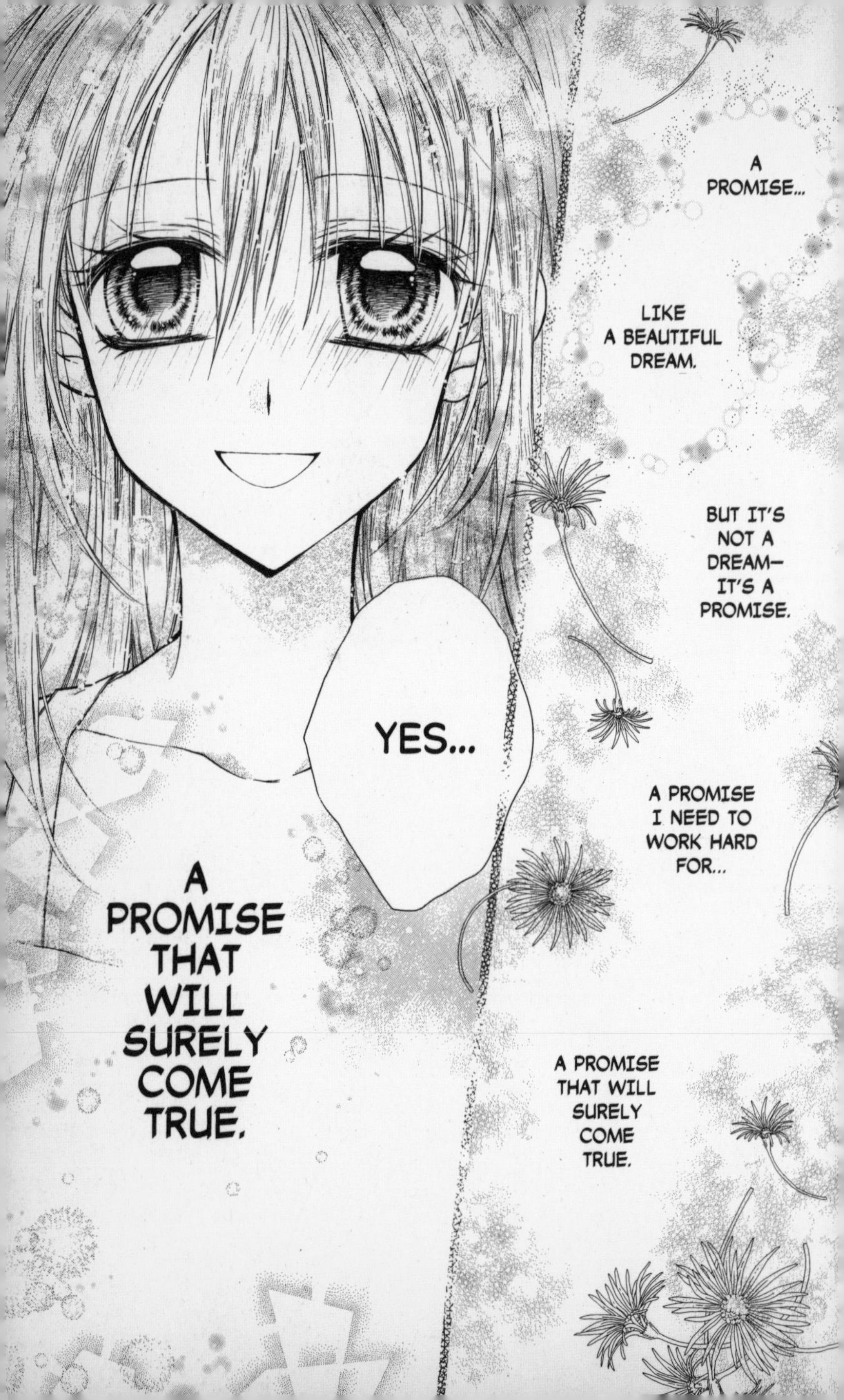
A PROMISE...
LIKE A BEAUTIFUL DREAM.
BUT IT'S NOT A DREAM— IT'S A PROMISE.
A PROMISE I NEED TO WORK HARD FOR...
A PROMISE THAT WILL SURELY COME TRUE.
YES...
A PROMISE THAT WILL SURELY COME TRUE.

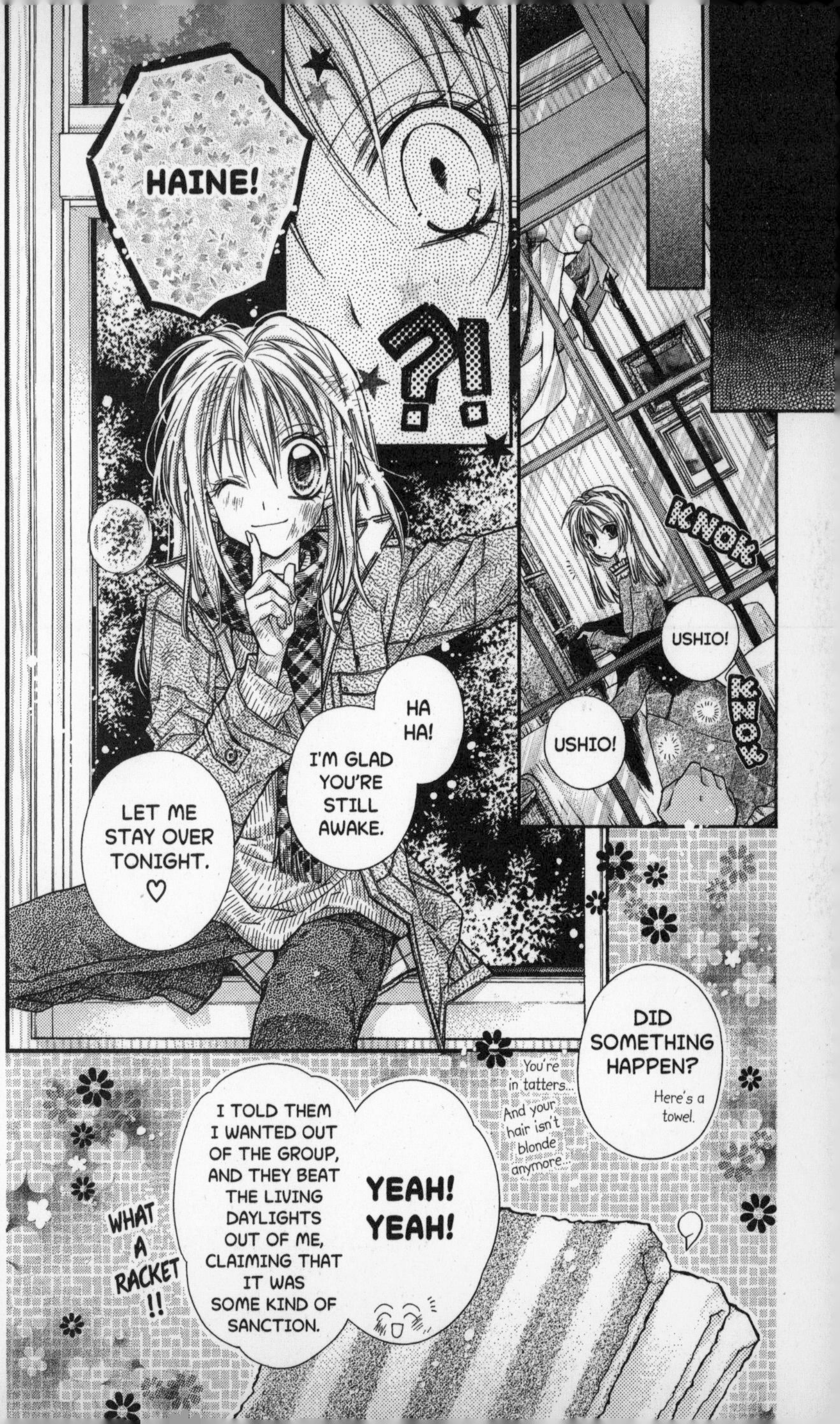
KNOK
USHIO!
KNOK
USHIO!
HAINE!
?!
HA HA! I'M GLAD YOU'RE STILL AWAKE.
LET ME STAY OVER TONIGHT. ♡
DID SOMETHING HAPPEN?
Here's a towel.
You're in tatters... And your hair isn't blonde anymore...
?
YEAH! YEAH!
I TOLD THEM I WANTED OUT OF THE GROUP, AND THEY BEAT THE LIVING DAYLIGHTS OUT OF ME, CLAIMING THAT IT WAS SOME KIND OF SANCTION.
WHAT A RACKET!!

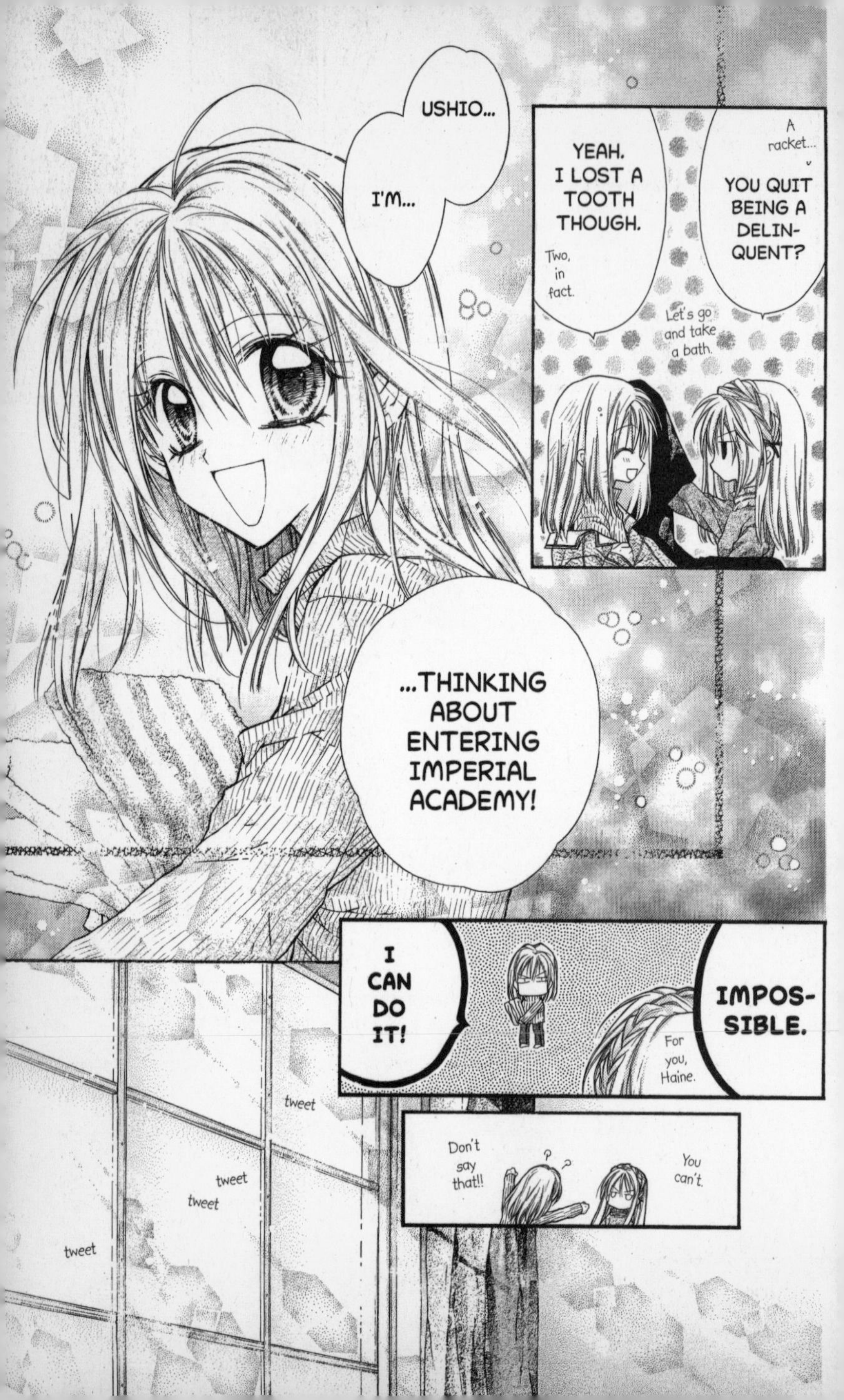
YOU QUIT BEING A DELIN-QUENT?
A racket...
YEAH. I LOST A TOOTH THOUGH.
Two, in fact.
Let's go and take a bath.
USHIO...
I'M...
...THINKING ABOUT ENTERING IMPERIAL ACADEMY!
IMPOS-SIBLE.
For you, Haine.
I CAN DO IT!
You can't.
Don't say that!!
tweet
tweet
tweet
tweet

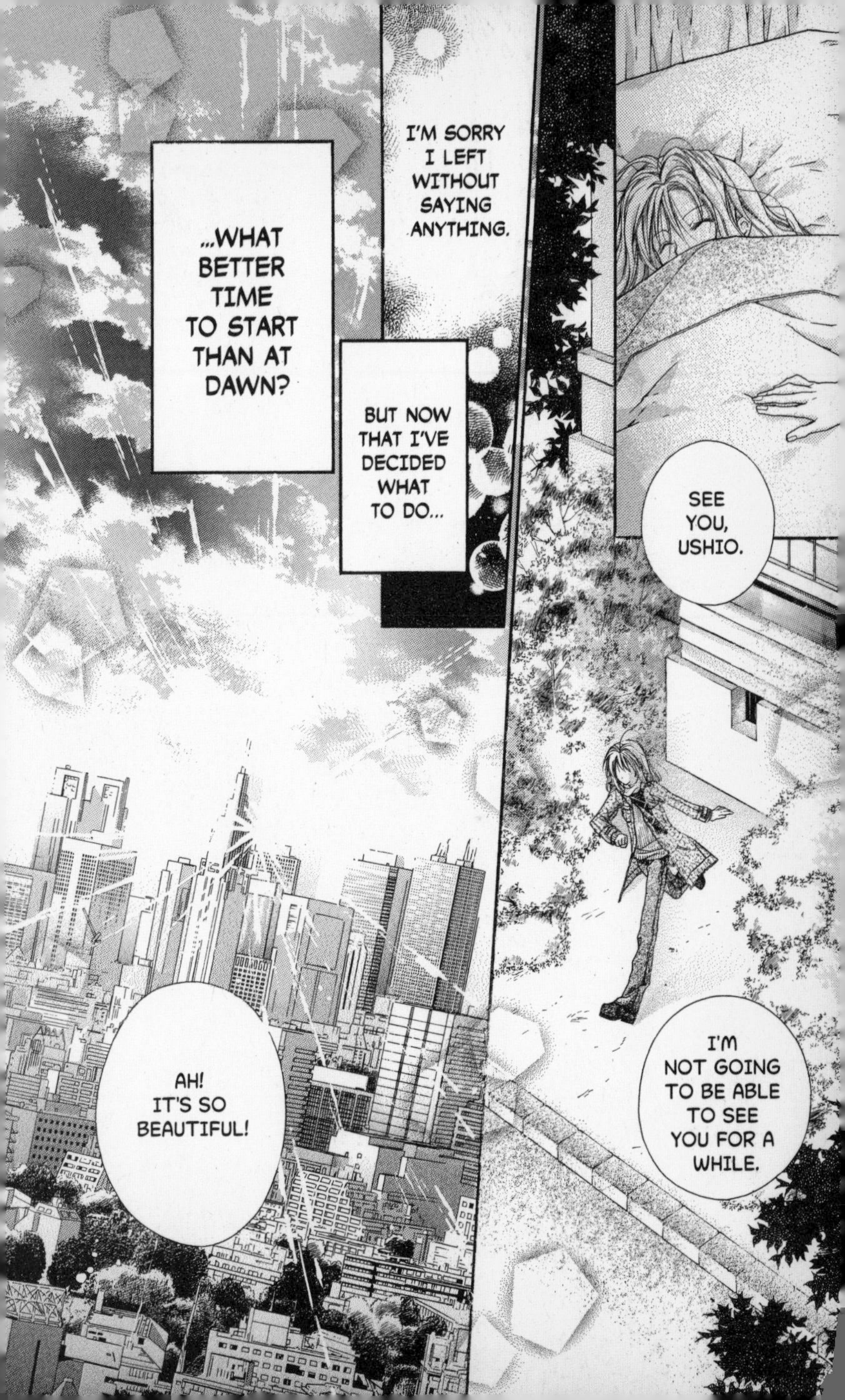
SEE YOU, USHIO.
I'M NOT GOING TO BE ABLE TO SEE YOU FOR A WHILE.
I'M SORRY I LEFT WITHOUT SAYING ANYTHING.
BUT NOW THAT I'VE DECIDED WHAT TO DO...
...WHAT BETTER TIME TO START THAN AT DAWN?
AH! IT'S SO BEAUTIFUL!

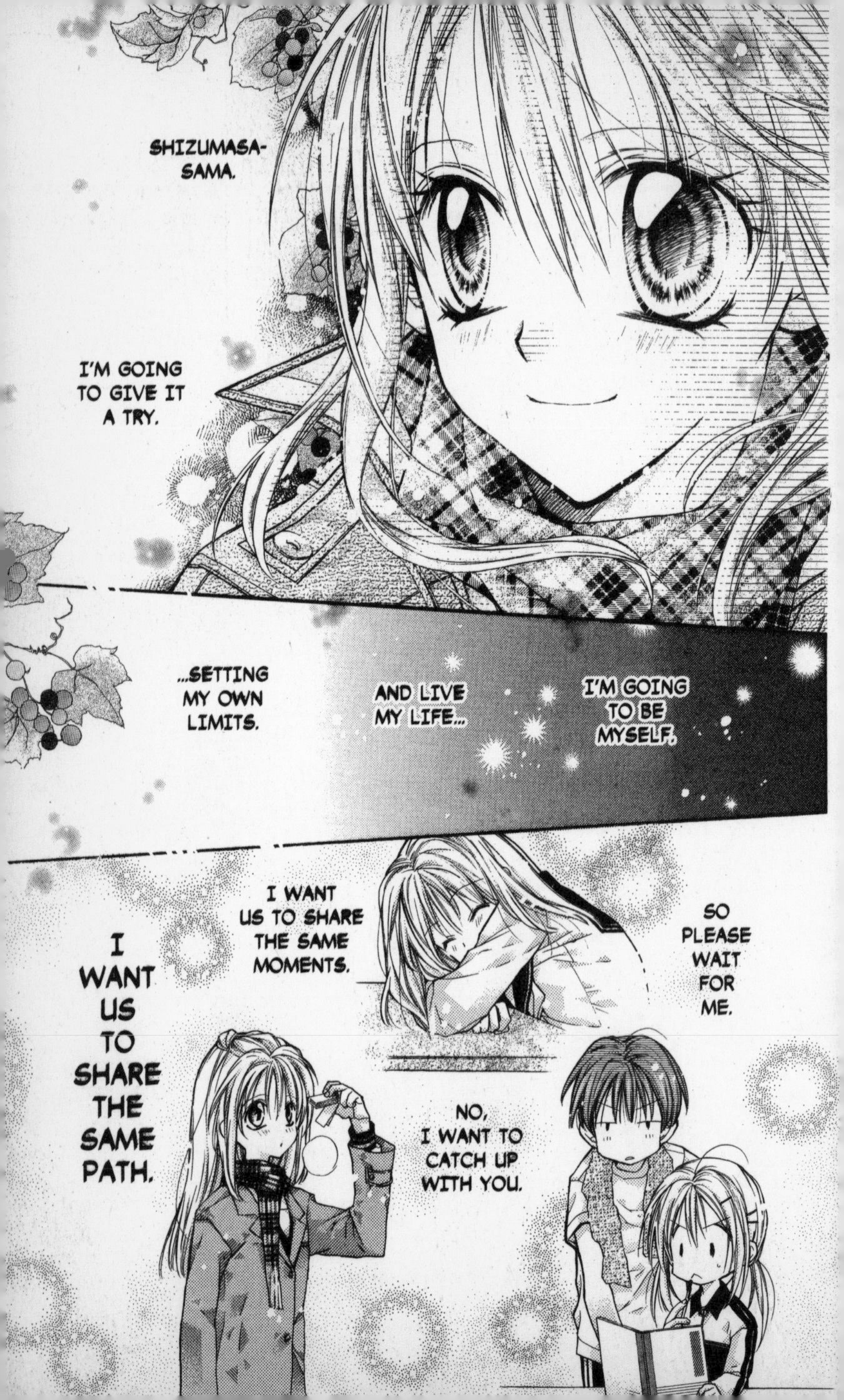
SHIZUMASA-SAMA.
I'M GOING TO GIVE IT A TRY.
I'M GOING TO BE MYSELF.
AND LIVE MY LIFE...
...SETTING MY OWN LIMITS.
SO PLEASE WAIT FOR ME.
I WANT US TO SHARE THE SAME MOMENTS.
NO, I WANT TO CATCH UP WITH YOU.
I WANT US TO SHARE THE SAME PATH.

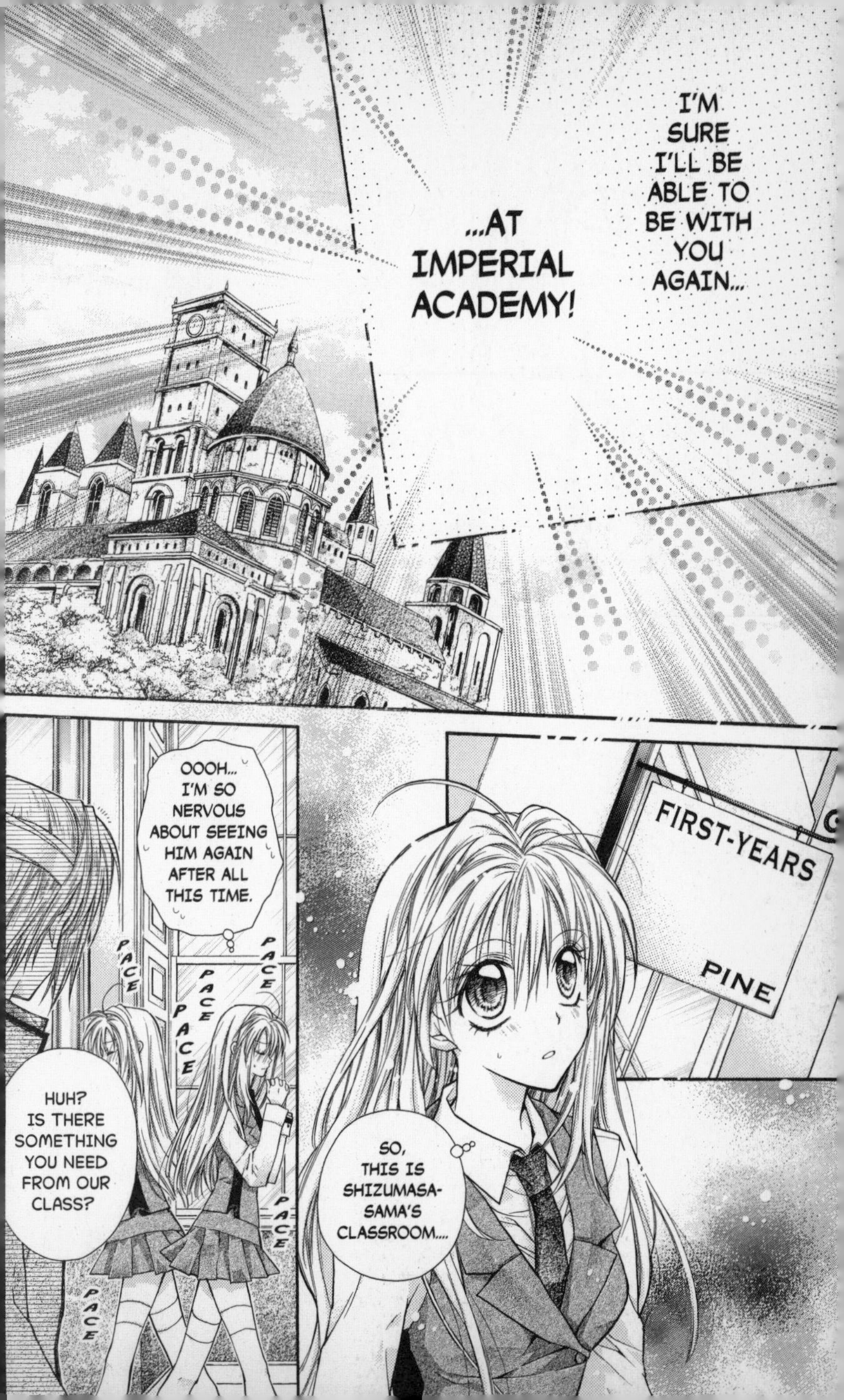
I'M SURE I'LL BE ABLE TO BE WITH YOU AGAIN...
...AT IMPERIAL ACADEMY!
FIRST-YEARS
PINE
SO, THIS IS SHIZUMASA-SAMA'S CLASSROOM....
OOOH... I'M SO NERVOUS ABOUT SEEING HIM AGAIN AFTER ALL THIS TIME.
PACE
PACE
PACE
PACE
PACE
PACE
HUH? IS THERE SOMETHING YOU NEED FROM OUR CLASS?

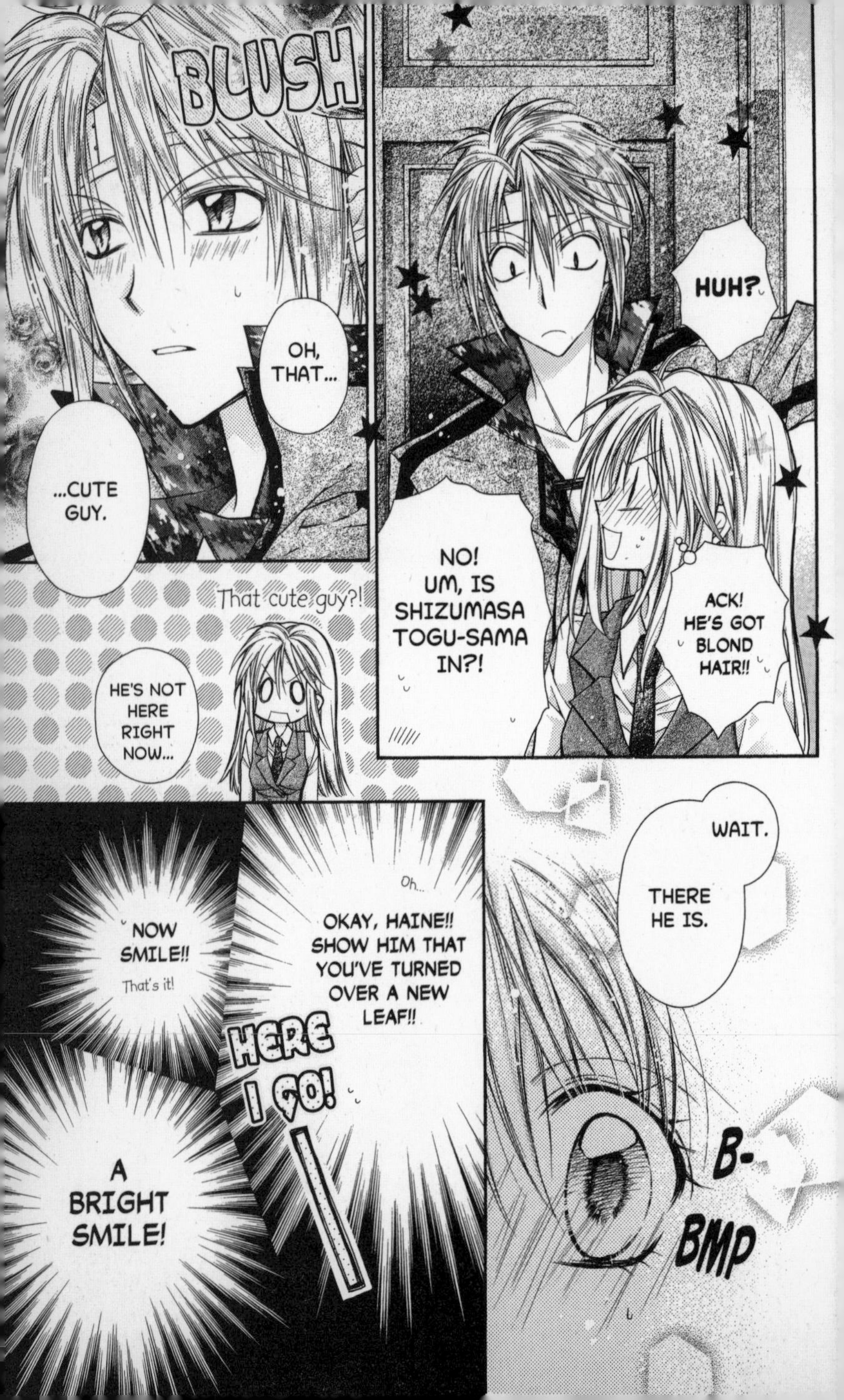
HUH?
ACK! HE'S GOT BLOND HAIR!!
NO! UM, IS SHIZUMASA TOGU-SAMA IN?!
BLUSH
OH, THAT...
...CUTE GUY.
That cute guy?!
HE'S NOT HERE RIGHT NOW...
WAIT.
THERE HE IS.
B-BMP
Oh...
OKAY, HAINE!! SHOW HIM THAT YOU'VE TURNED OVER A NEW LEAF!!
HERE I GO!
NOW SMILE!!
That's it!
A BRIGHT SMILE!

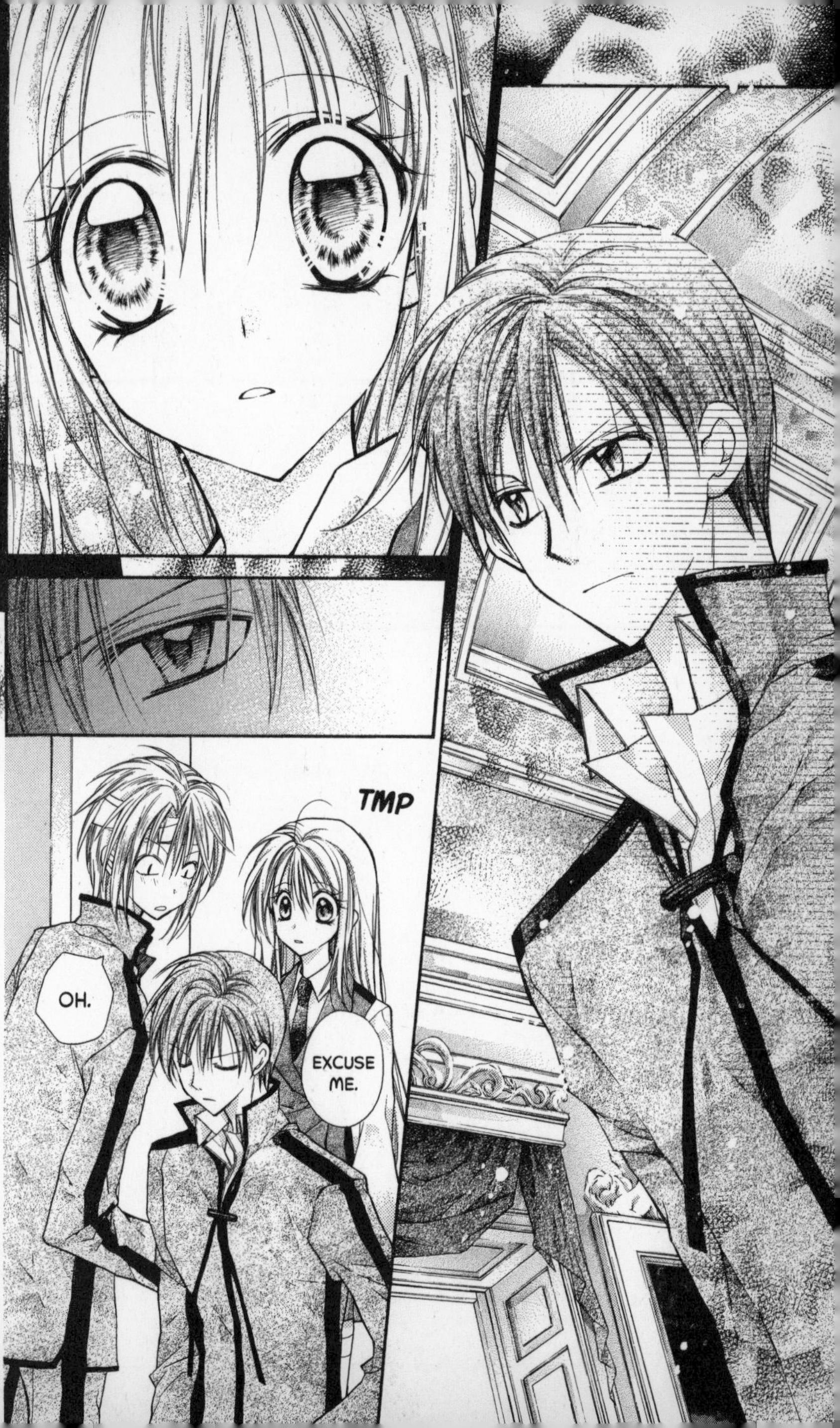
TMP
EXCUSE ME.
OH.

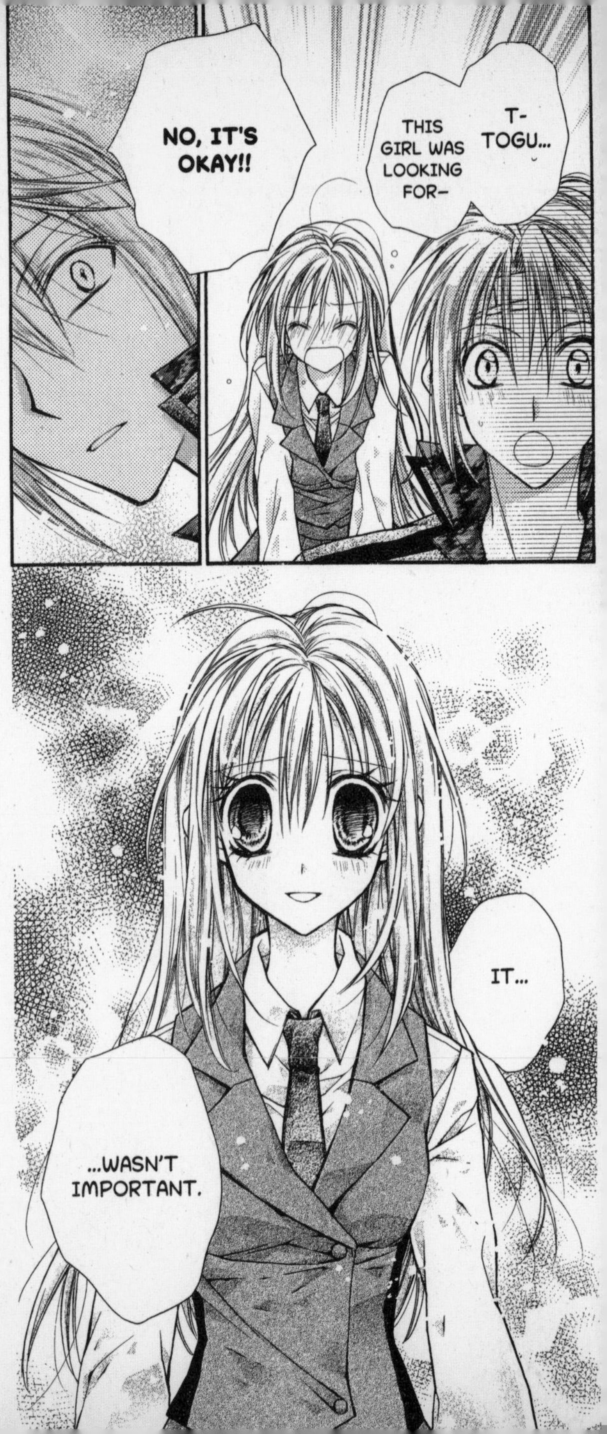
T-TOGU...
THIS GIRL WAS LOOKING FOR-
NO, IT'S OKAY!!
IT...
...WASN'T IMPORTANT.

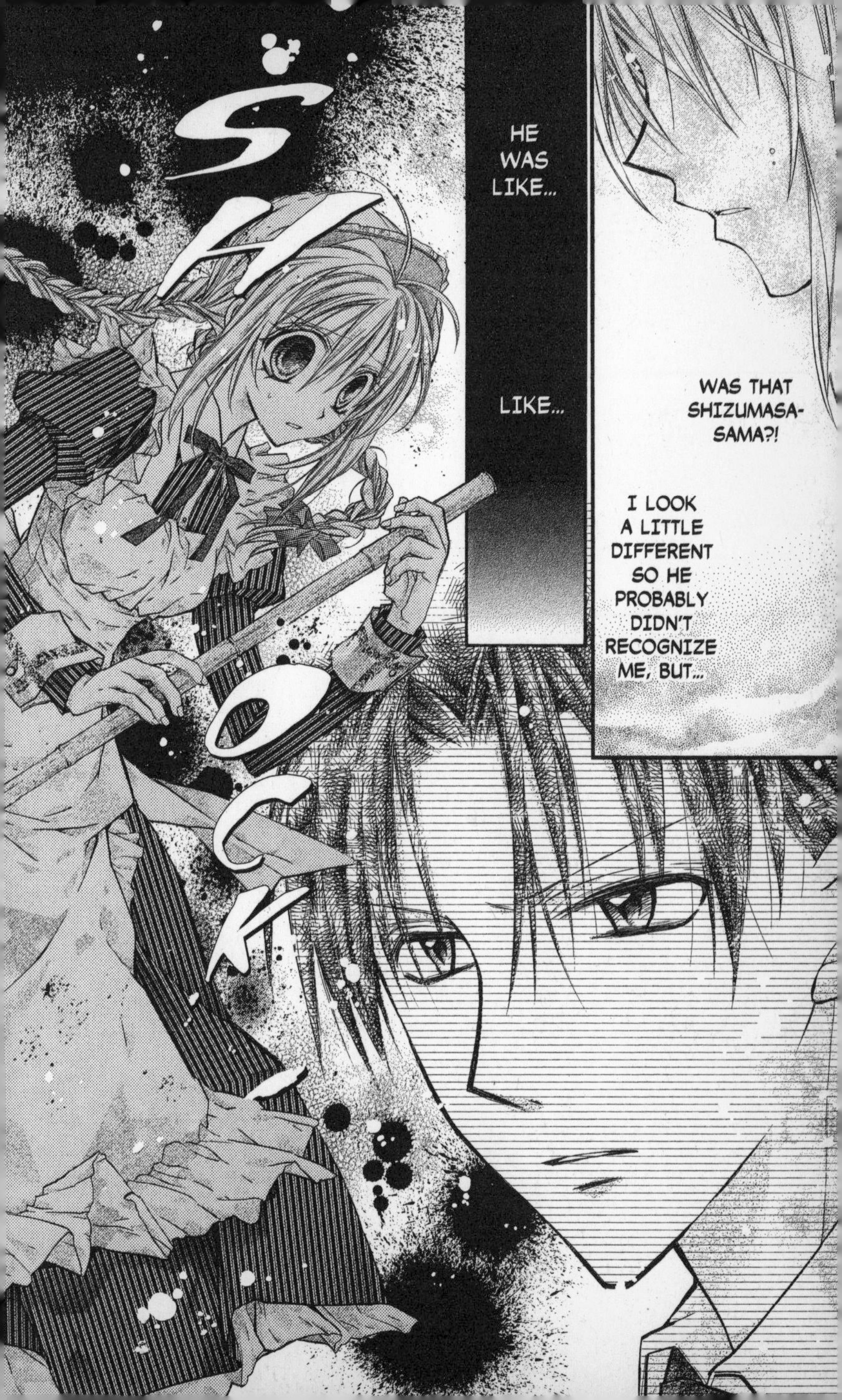
WAS THAT SHIZUMASA-SAMA?!
I LOOK A LITTLE DIFFERENT SO HE PROBABLY DIDN'T RECOGNIZE ME, BUT...
HE WAS LIKE...
LIKE...
SHOCK

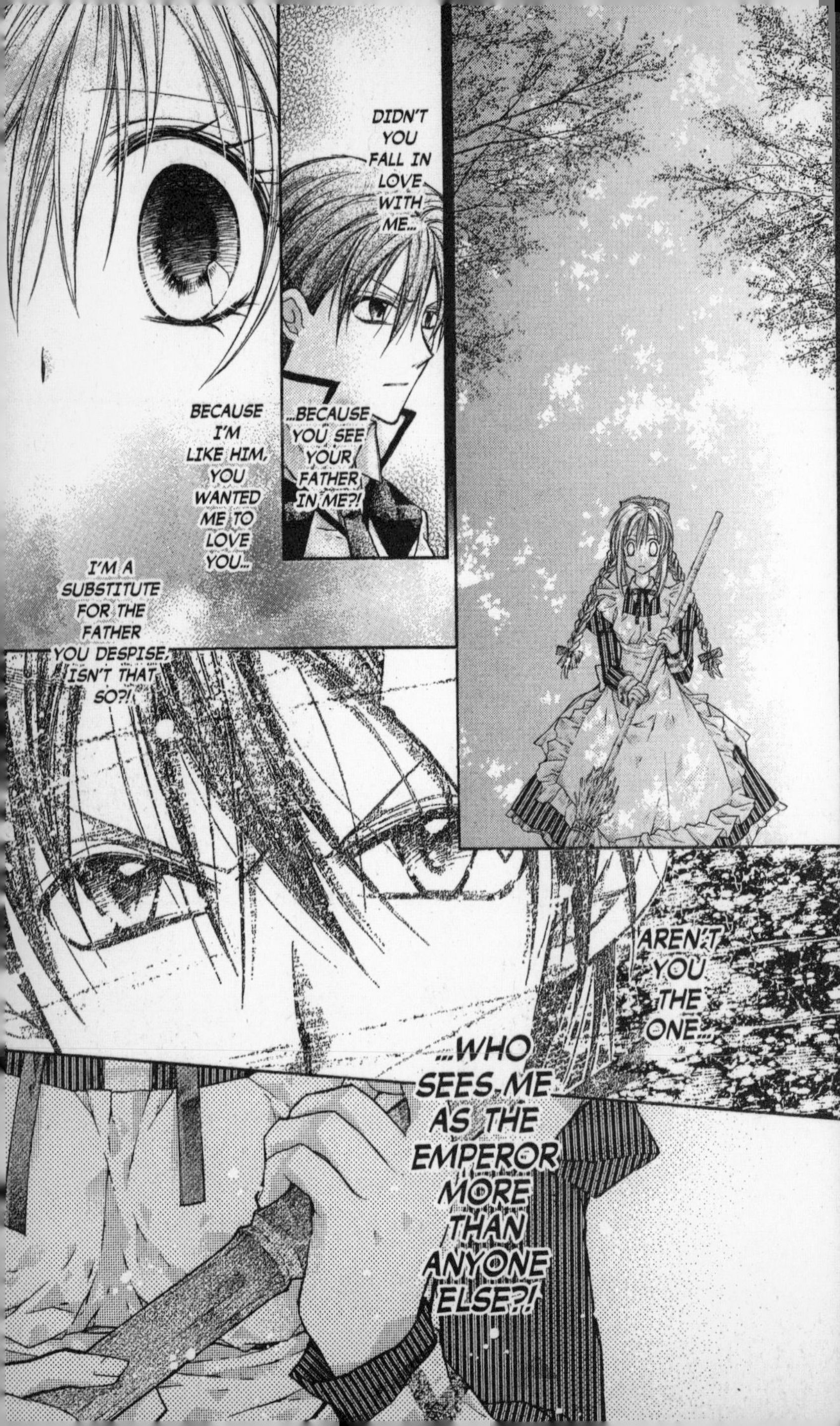
DIDN'T YOU FALL IN LOVE WITH ME...
...BECAUSE YOU SEE YOUR FATHER IN ME?!
BECAUSE I'M LIKE HIM, YOU WANTED ME TO LOVE YOU...
I'M A SUBSTITUTE FOR THE FATHER YOU DESPISE, ISN'T THAT SO?!
AREN'T YOU THE ONE...
...WHO SEES ME AS THE EMPEROR MORE THAN ANYONE ELSE?!

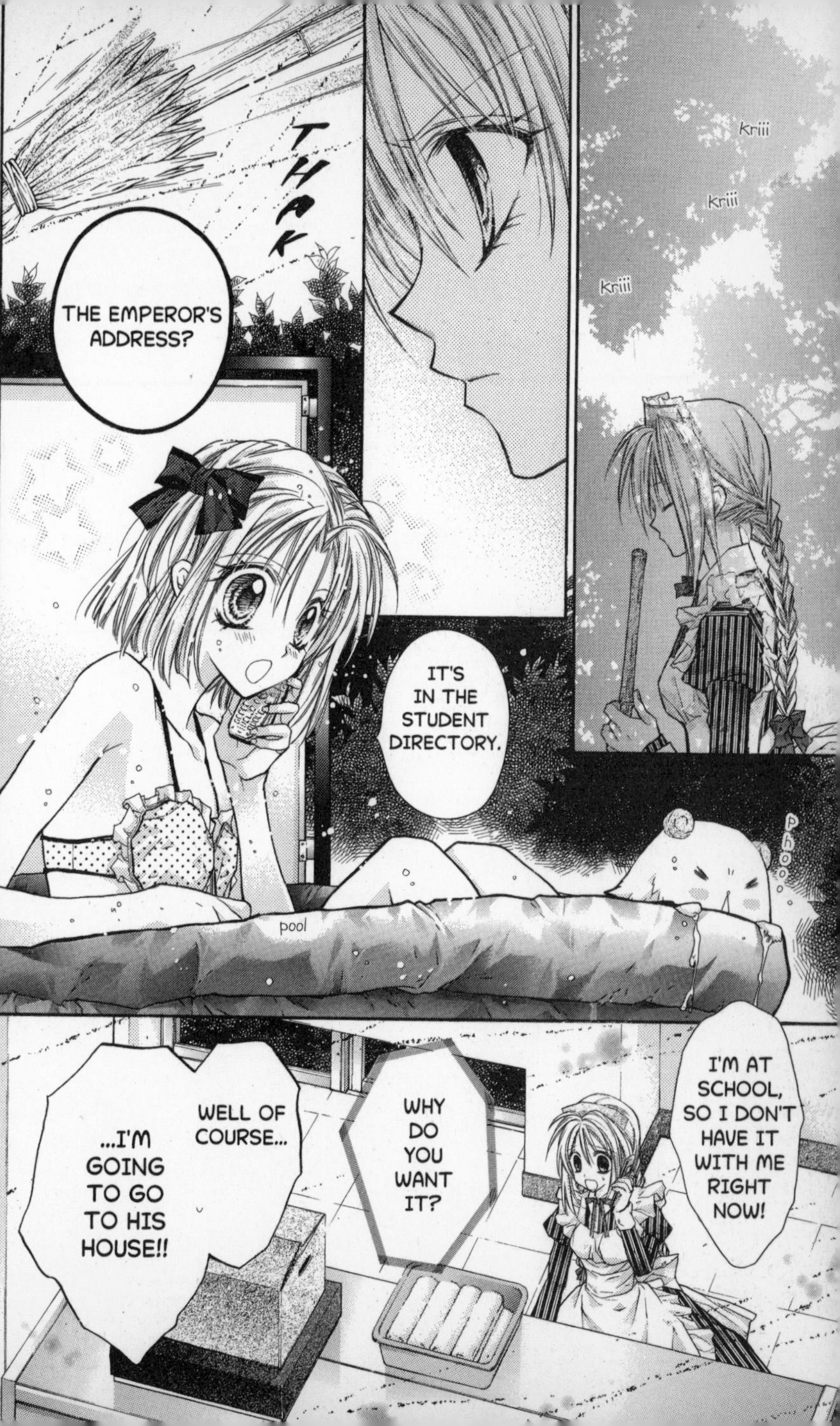
kriii
kriii
kriii
THAK
THE EMPEROR'S ADDRESS?
IT'S IN THE STUDENT DIRECTORY.
Phooo
pool
I'M AT SCHOOL, SO I DON'T HAVE IT WITH ME RIGHT NOW!
WHY DO YOU WANT IT?
WELL OF COURSE...
...I'M GOING TO GO TO HIS HOUSE!!

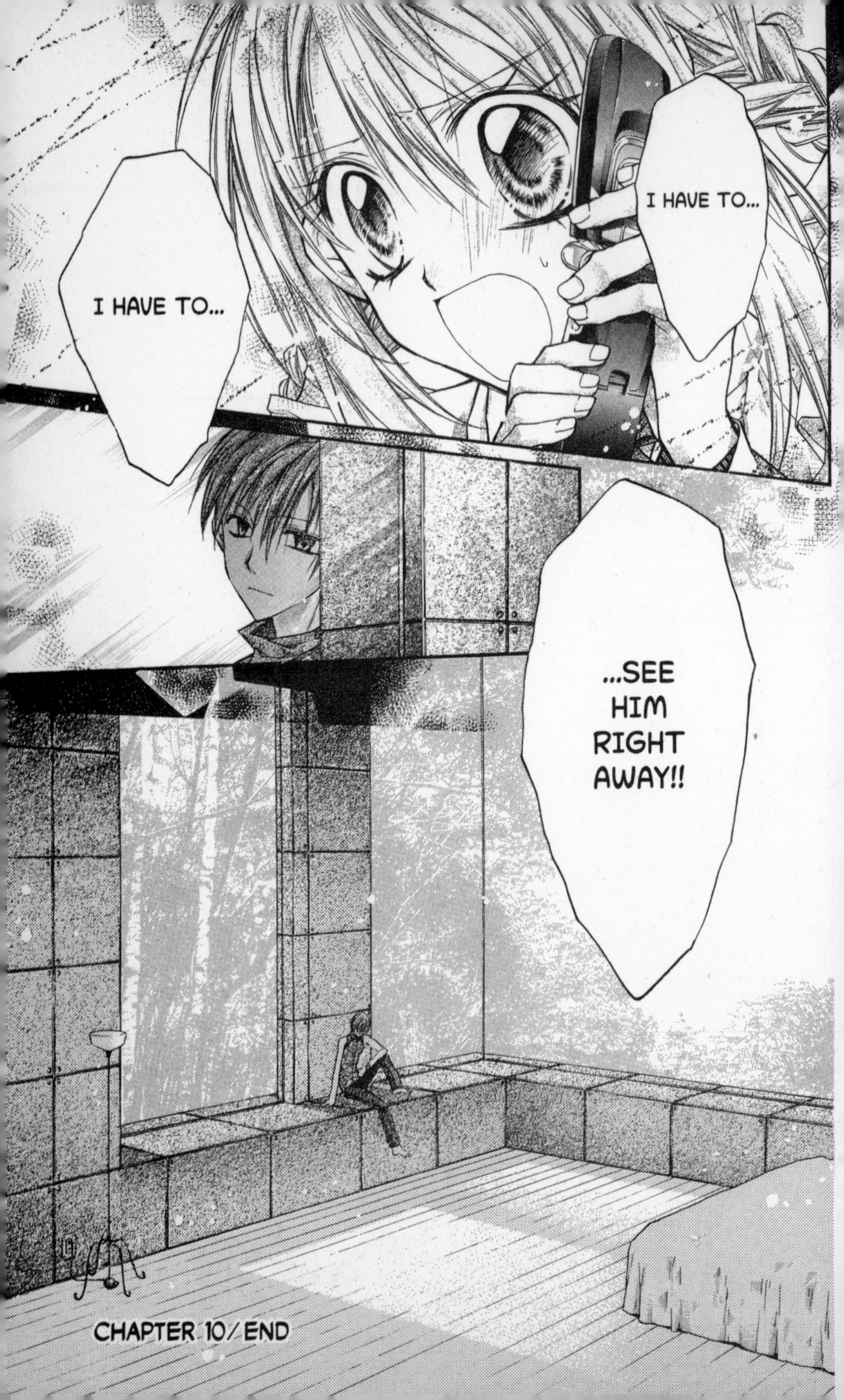
I HAVE TO...
I HAVE TO...
...SEE HIM RIGHT AWAY!!
CHAPTER 10/END

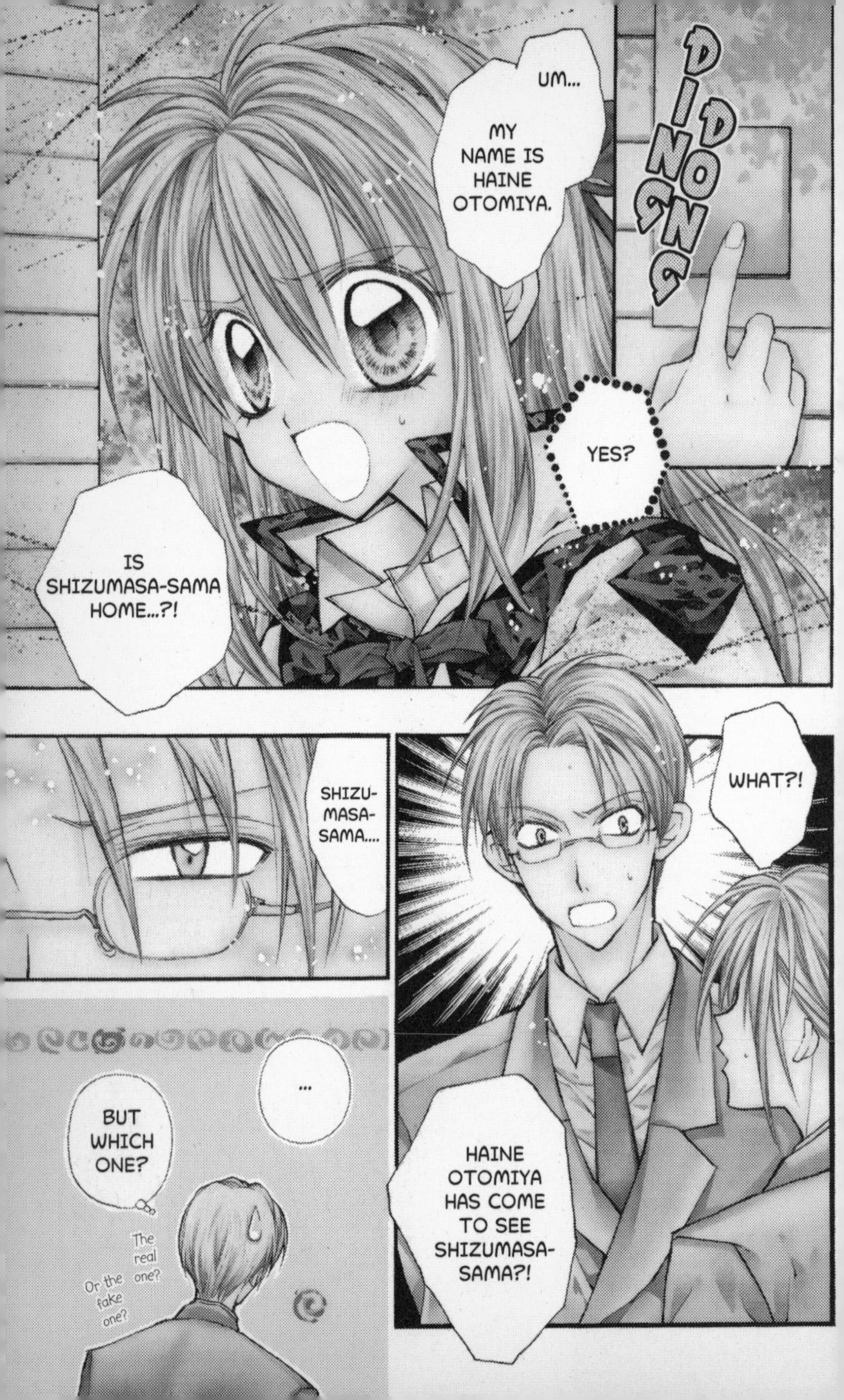
DING DONG
UM...
MY NAME IS HAINE OTOMIYA.
YES?
IS SHIZUMASA-SAMA HOME...?!
WHAT?!
HAINE OTOMIYA HAS COME TO SEE SHIZUMASA-SAMA?!
SHIZU-MASA-SAMA....
...
BUT WHICH ONE?
The real one?
Or the fake one?

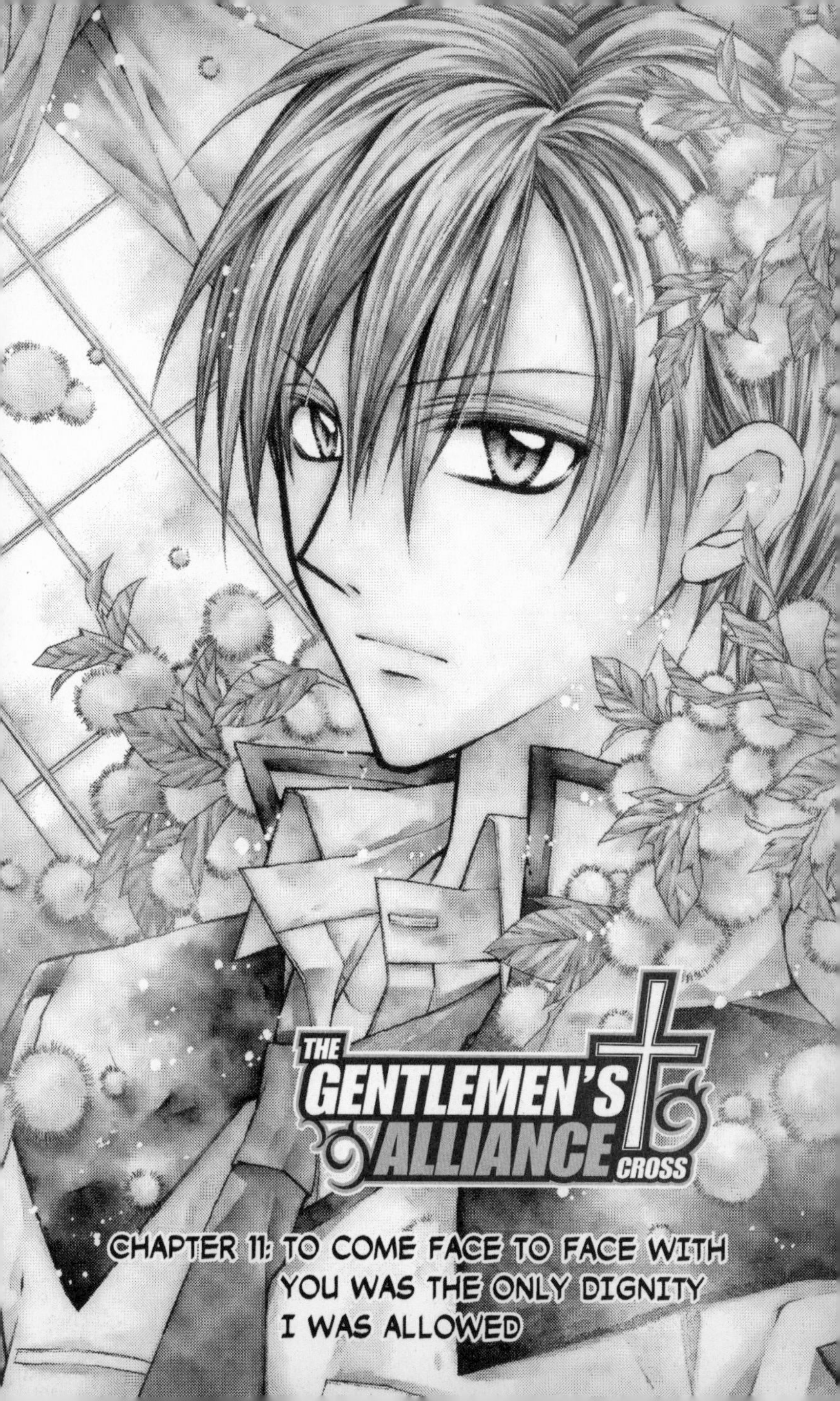
THE GENTLEMEN'S ALLIANCE CROSS
CHAPTER 11: TO COME FACE TO FACE WITH YOU WAS THE ONLY DIGNITY I WAS ALLOWED

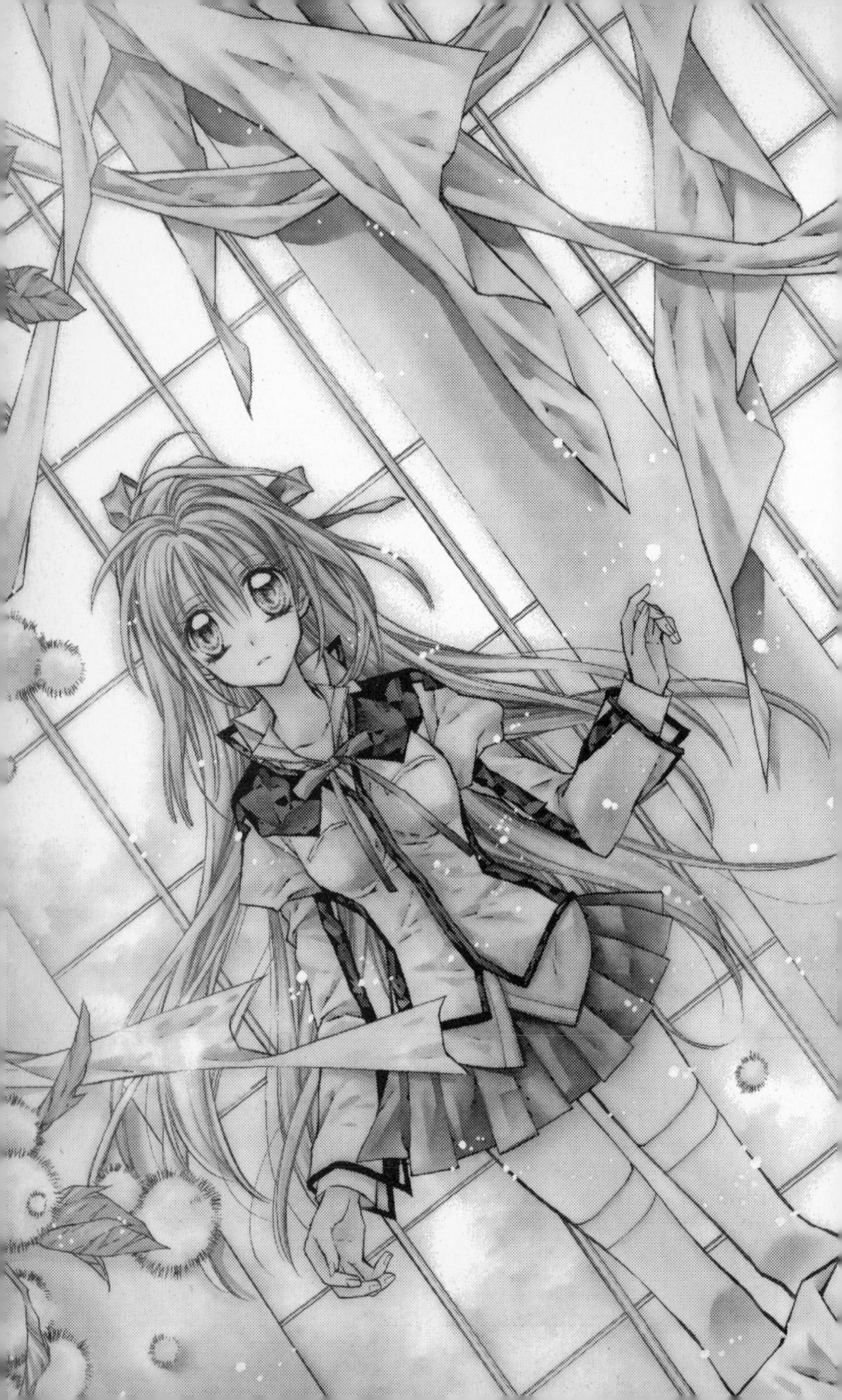

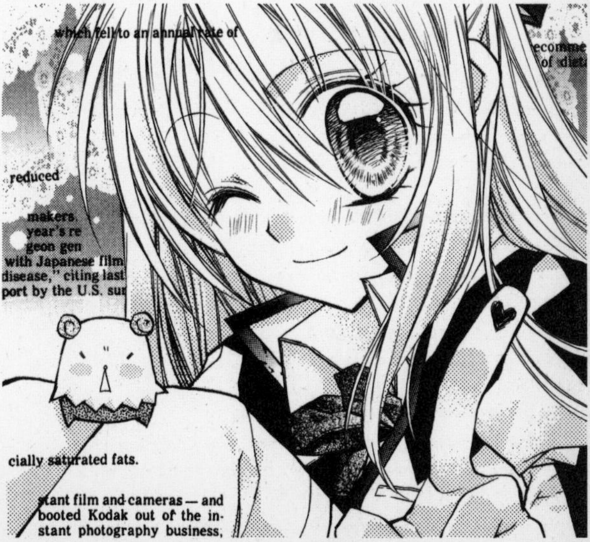
which fell to an annual rate of
ecomme
of dieta
reduced
makers.
year's re
geon gen
with Japanese film
disease," citing last
port by the U.S. sur
cially saturated fats.
stant film and cameras — and
booted Kodak out of the in-
stant photography business,

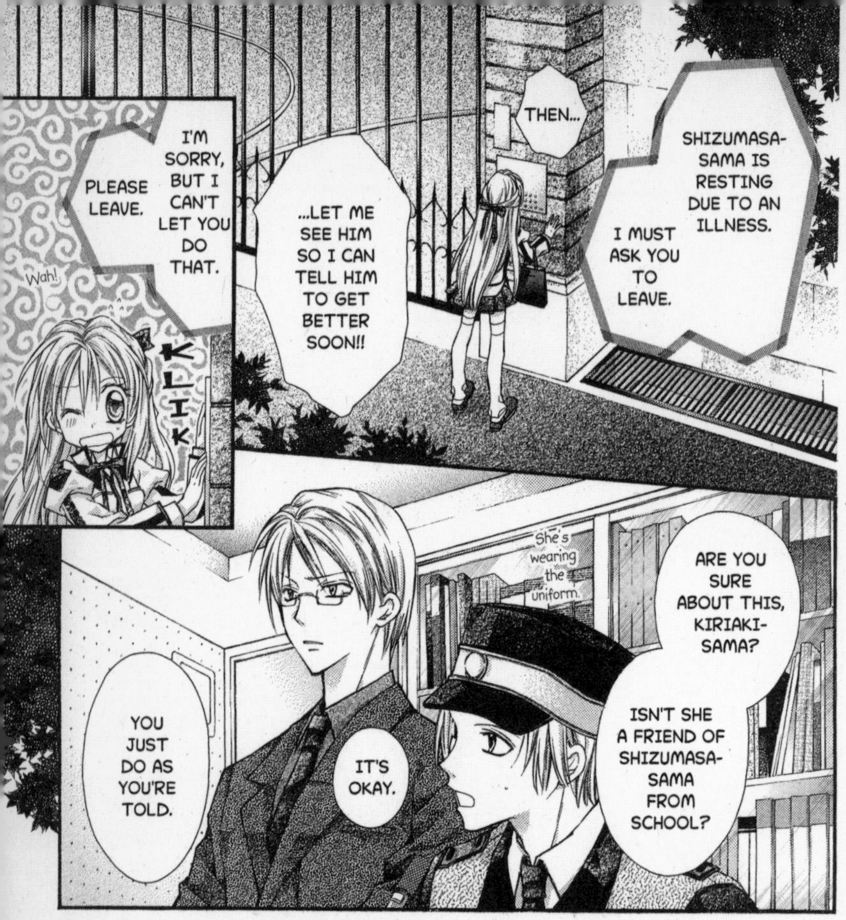
SHIZUMASA-SAMA IS RESTING DUE TO AN ILLNESS.
I MUST ASK YOU TO LEAVE.
THEN...
...LET ME SEE HIM SO I CAN TELL HIM TO GET BETTER SOON!!
I'M SORRY, BUT I CAN'T LET YOU DO THAT.
PLEASE LEAVE.
Wah!
KLIK
ARE YOU SURE ABOUT THIS, KIRIAKI-SAMA?
She's wearing the uniform.
ISN'T SHE A FRIEND OF SHIZUMASA-SAMA FROM SCHOOL?
IT'S OKAY.
YOU JUST DO AS YOU'RE TOLD.

Chapter 11: To Come Face to Face with You Was the Only Dignity I Was Allowed

Lead-in I want to talk to you about... My feelings, the picture book, my father, and...you...

※I'm giving away some of the story.

I'm actually pretty fond of the title and the lead-in for chapter 11. This chapter was placed at the very front of the magazine, and it came with colored pages, so I felt motivated to do something special. I included Haine's love declaration for Shizumasa, and an explanation of the first chapter.

I like the people from the Togu family too. Senri started working for them when he was 16.

Kiriaki finds it hard to get along with foolhardy Senri, but he gets good results. Senri probably shocks him, but then he thinks, "No! I will follow proper methods! That's the way it should be!" It must be hard for him to watch Senri, who is a bit dicey...

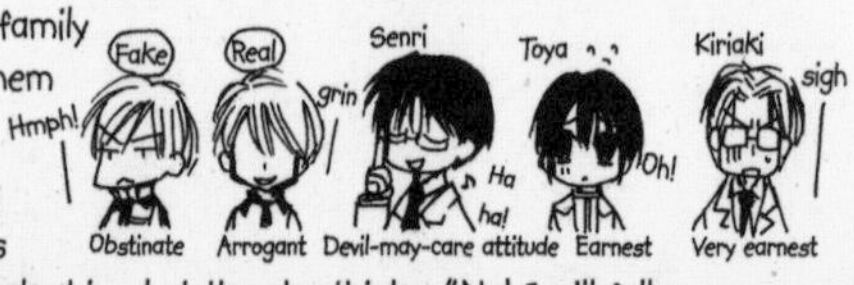
Fake
Real
Senri
Toya
Kiriaki
Hmph!
grin
Ha ha!
Oh!
sigh
Obstinate
Arrogant
Devil-may-care attitude
Earnest
Very earnest

I hadn't thought up Mao-chan's inner character when I created him, so I'm not too sure about that yet... I'm gradually getting the hang of it, but...who knows how it's going to turn out...

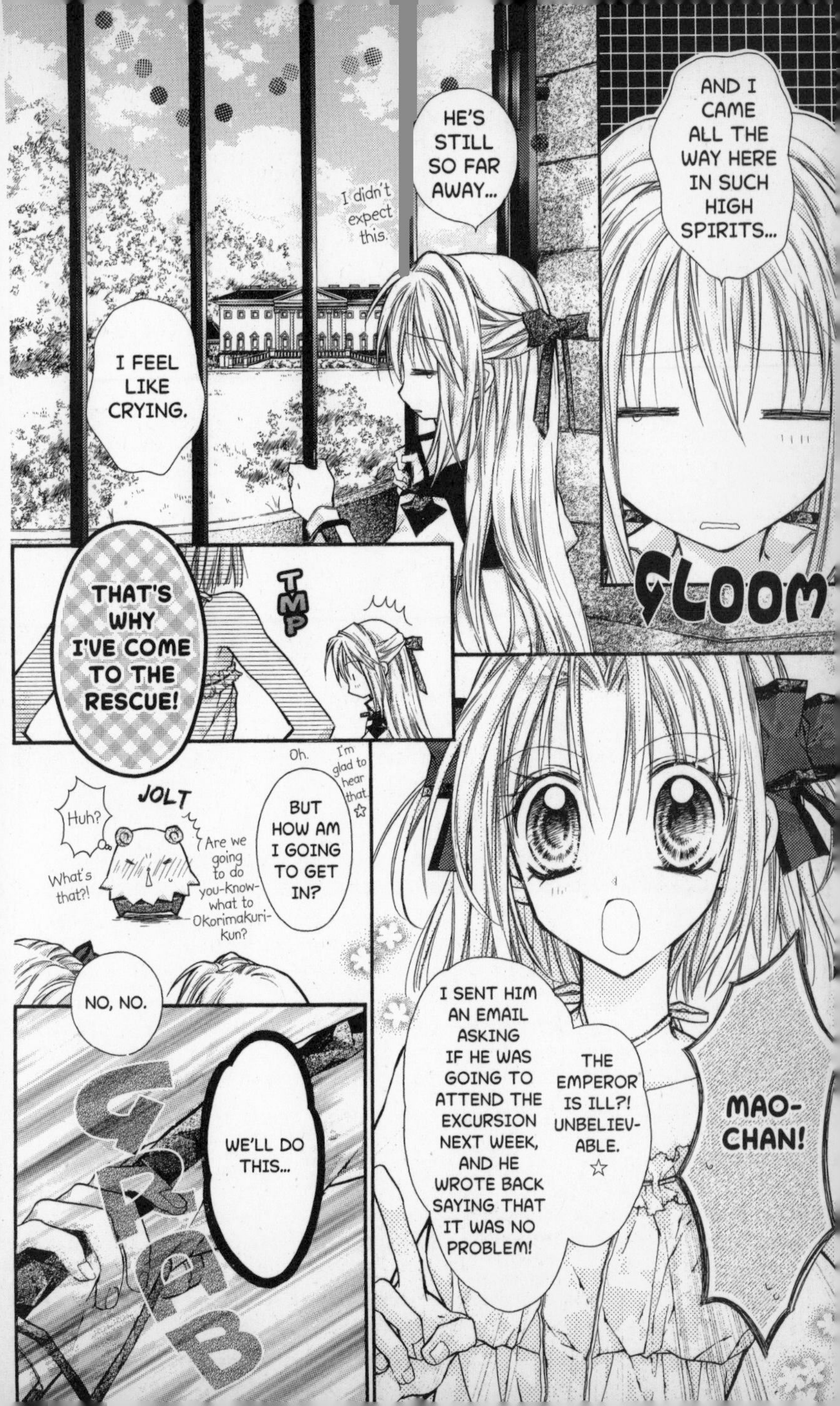
AND I CAME ALL THE WAY HERE IN SUCH HIGH SPIRITS...
GLOOM
HE'S STILL SO FAR AWAY...
I didn't expect this.
I FEEL LIKE CRYING.
MAO-CHAN!
THE EMPEROR IS ILL?! UNBELIEV-ABLE. ☆
I SENT HIM AN EMAIL ASKING IF HE WAS GOING TO ATTEND THE EXCURSION NEXT WEEK, AND HE WROTE BACK SAYING THAT IT WAS NO PROBLEM!
TMP
THAT'S WHY I'VE COME TO THE RESCUE!
I'm glad to hear that. ☆
Oh.
BUT HOW AM I GOING TO GET IN?
Are we going to do you-know-what to Okorimakuri-kun?
JOLT
Huh?
What's that?!
NO, NO.
WE'LL DO THIS...
GRAB

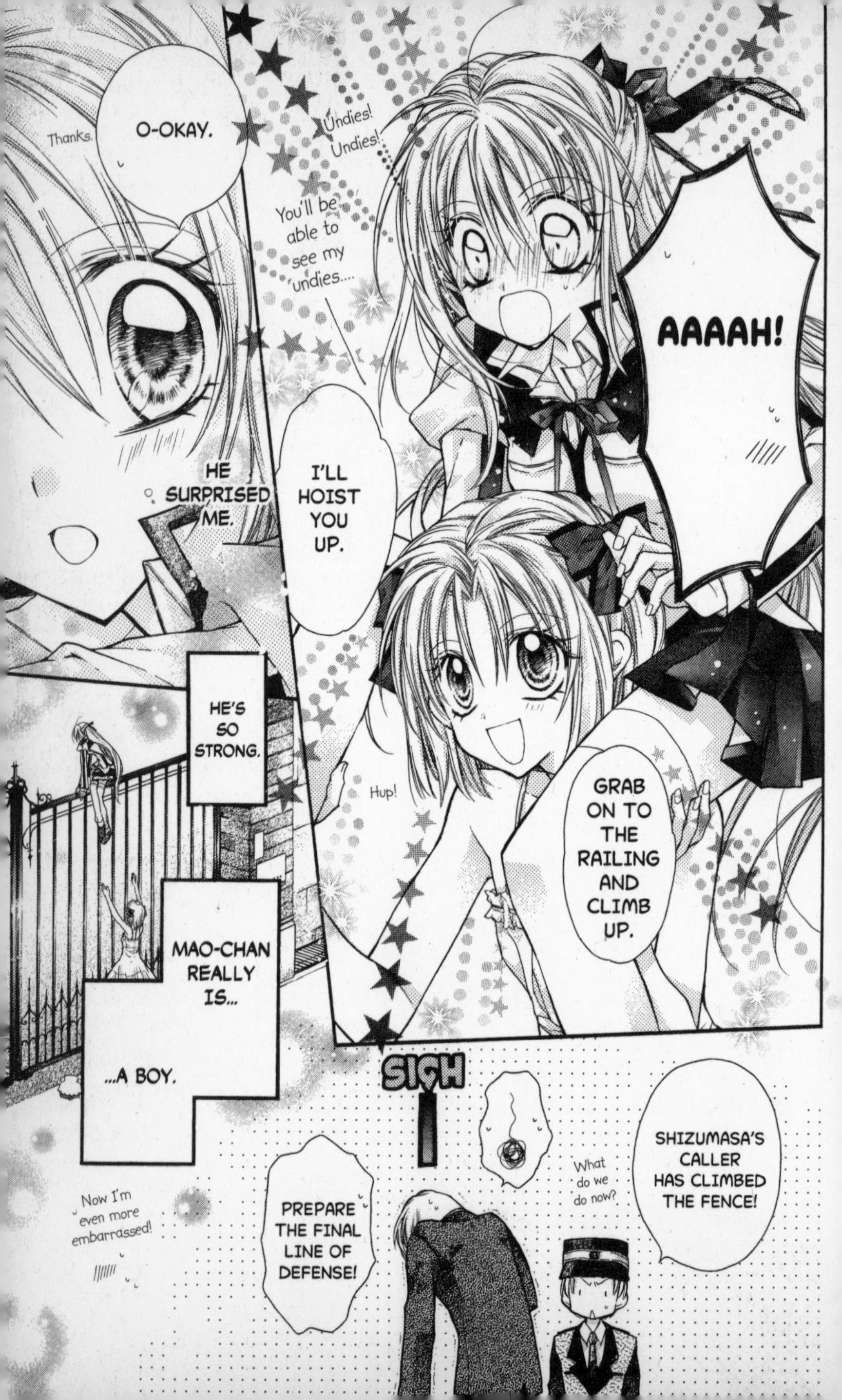
AAAAH!
Undies! Undies!
You'll be able to see my undies....
I'LL HOIST YOU UP.
GRAB ON TO THE RAILING AND CLIMB UP.
Hup!
O-OKAY.
Thanks.
HE SURPRISED ME.
HE'S SO STRONG.
MAO-CHAN REALLY IS...
...A BOY.
Now I'm even more embarrassed!
SHIZUMASA'S CALLER HAS CLIMBED THE FENCE!
What do we do now?
SIGH
PREPARE THE FINAL LINE OF DEFENSE!

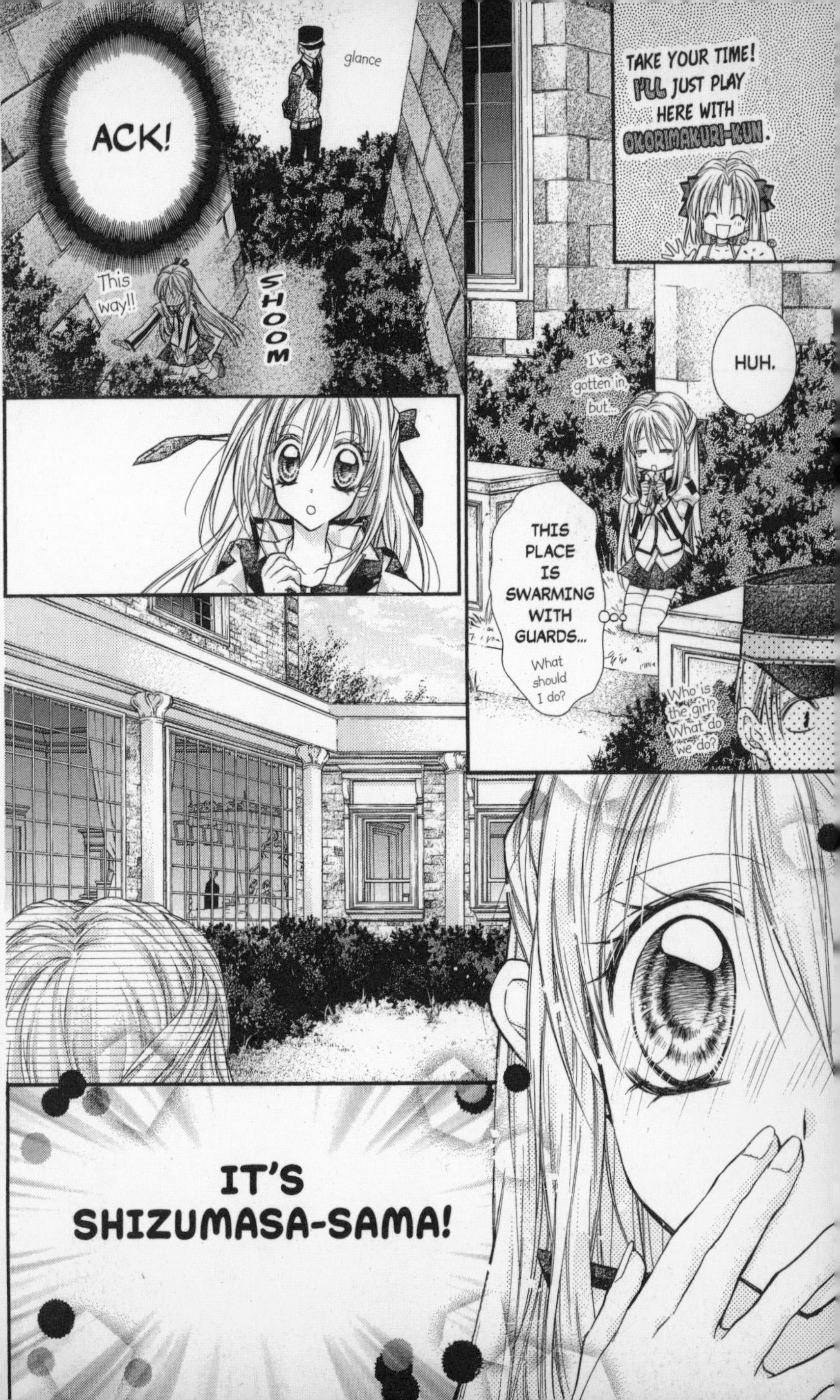
TAKE YOUR TIME! I'LL JUST PLAY HERE WITH OKORIMAKURI-KUN.
glance
ACK!
This way!!
SHOOM
HUH.
I've gotten in, but...
THIS PLACE IS SWARMING WITH GUARDS...
What should I do?
Who is the girl? What do we do?
IT'S SHIZUMASA-SAMA!

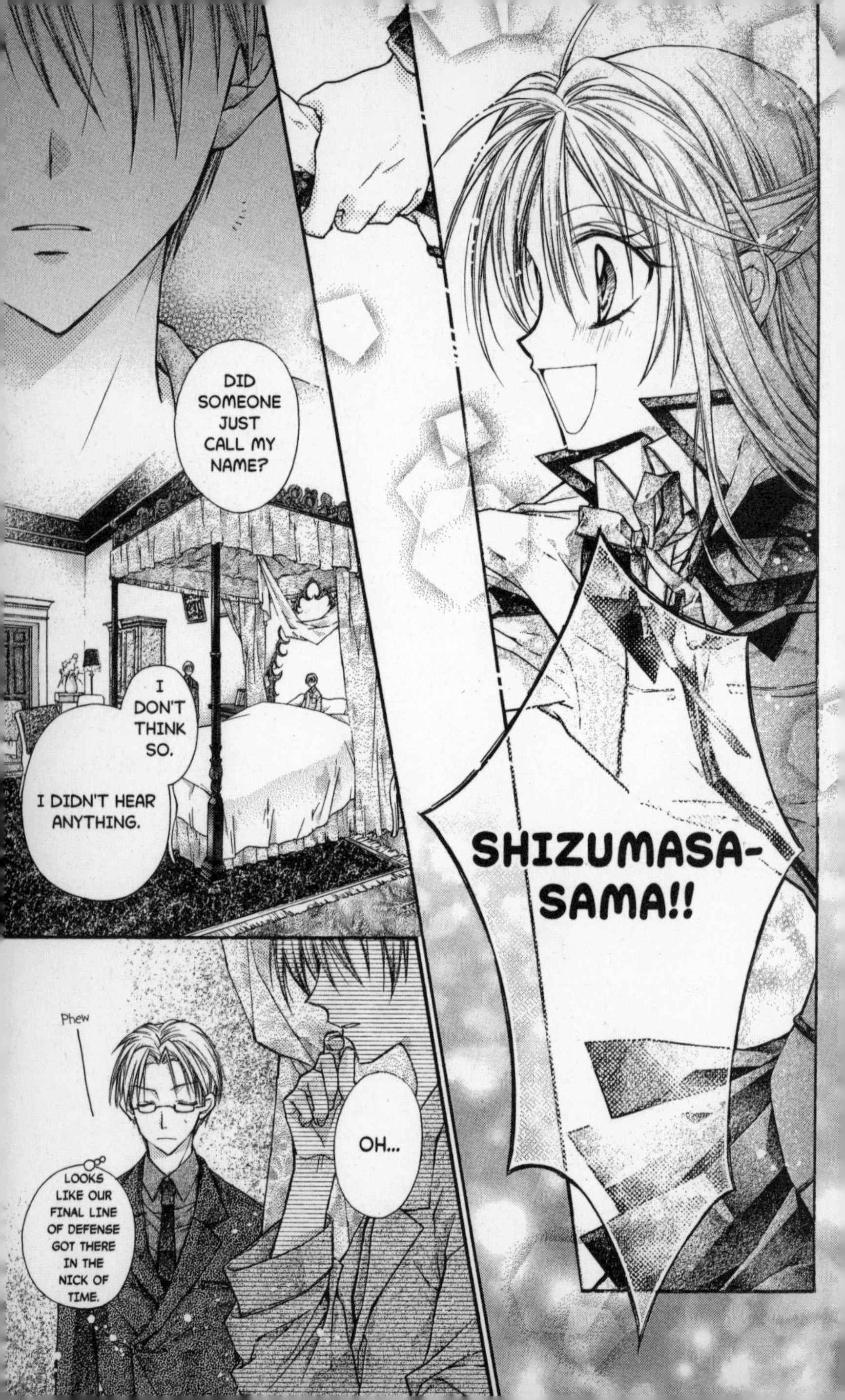
SHIZUMASA-SAMA!!
DID SOMEONE JUST CALL MY NAME?
I DON'T THINK SO.
I DIDN'T HEAR ANYTHING.
OH...
Phew
LOOKS LIKE OUR FINAL LINE OF DEFENSE GOT THERE IN THE NICK OF TIME.

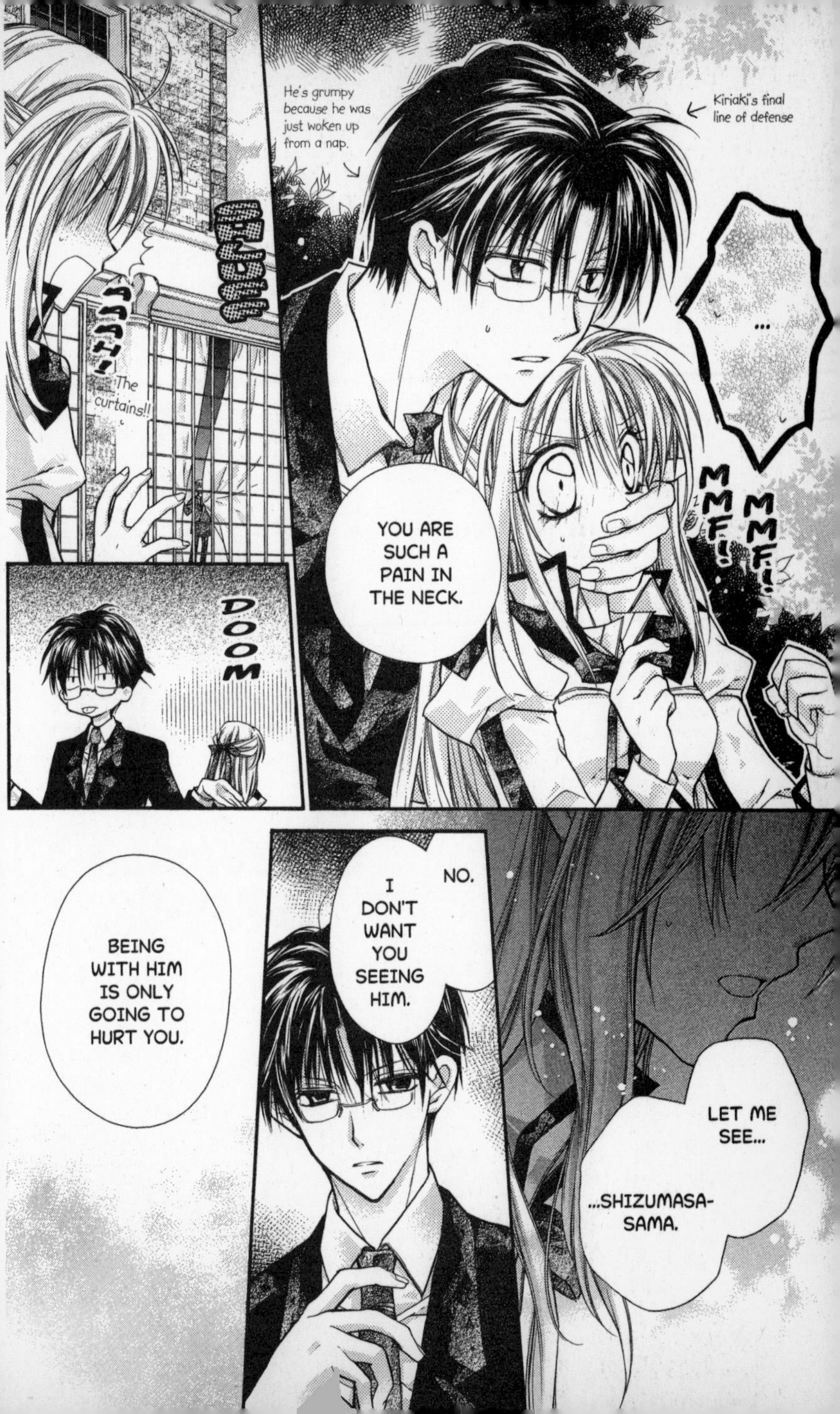
He's grumpy because he was just woken up from a nap.
Kiriaki's final line of defense
...
MMF! MMF!
YOU ARE SUCH A PAIN IN THE NECK.
AAAH!
The curtains!!
DOOM
LET ME SEE...
...SHIZUMASA-SAMA.
NO.
I DON'T WANT YOU SEEING HIM.
BEING WITH HIM IS ONLY GOING TO HURT YOU.

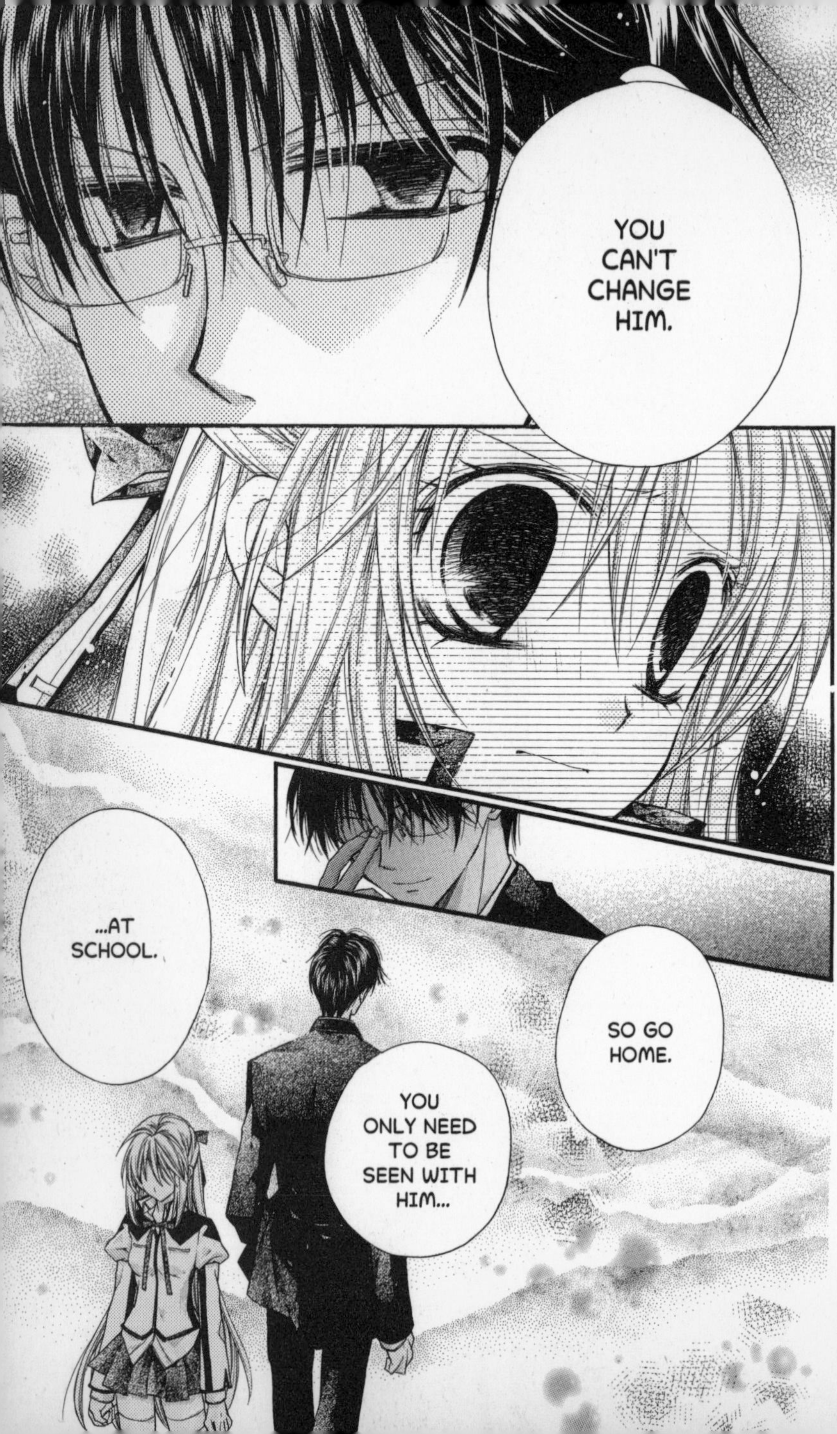
YOU CAN'T CHANGE HIM.
SO GO HOME.
YOU ONLY NEED TO BE SEEN WITH HIM...
...AT SCHOOL.

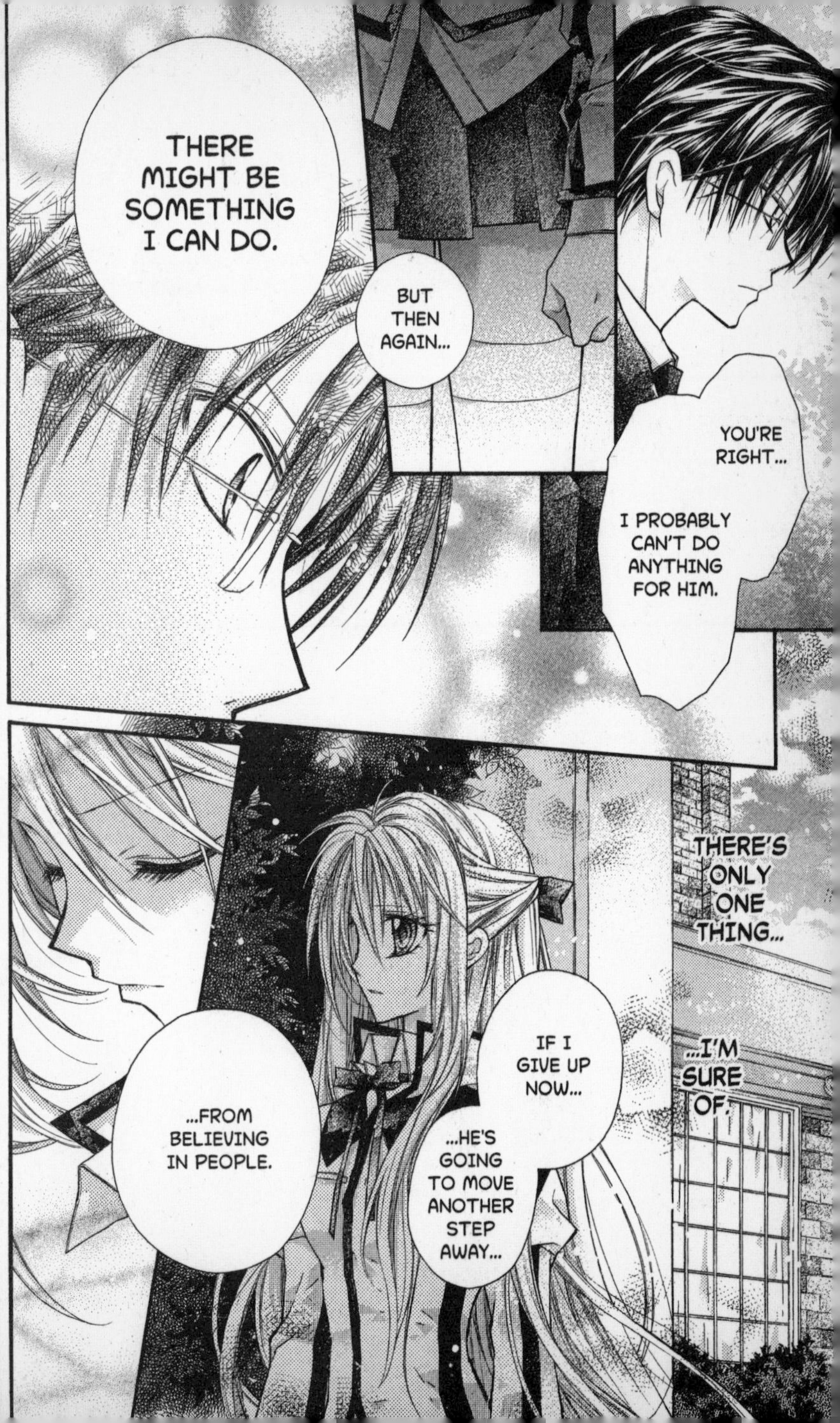
YOU'RE RIGHT...
I PROBABLY CAN'T DO ANYTHING FOR HIM.
BUT THEN AGAIN...
THERE MIGHT BE SOMETHING I CAN DO.
THERE'S ONLY ONE THING...
...I'M SURE OF.
IF I GIVE UP NOW...
...HE'S GOING TO MOVE ANOTHER STEP AWAY...
...FROM BELIEVING IN PEOPLE.

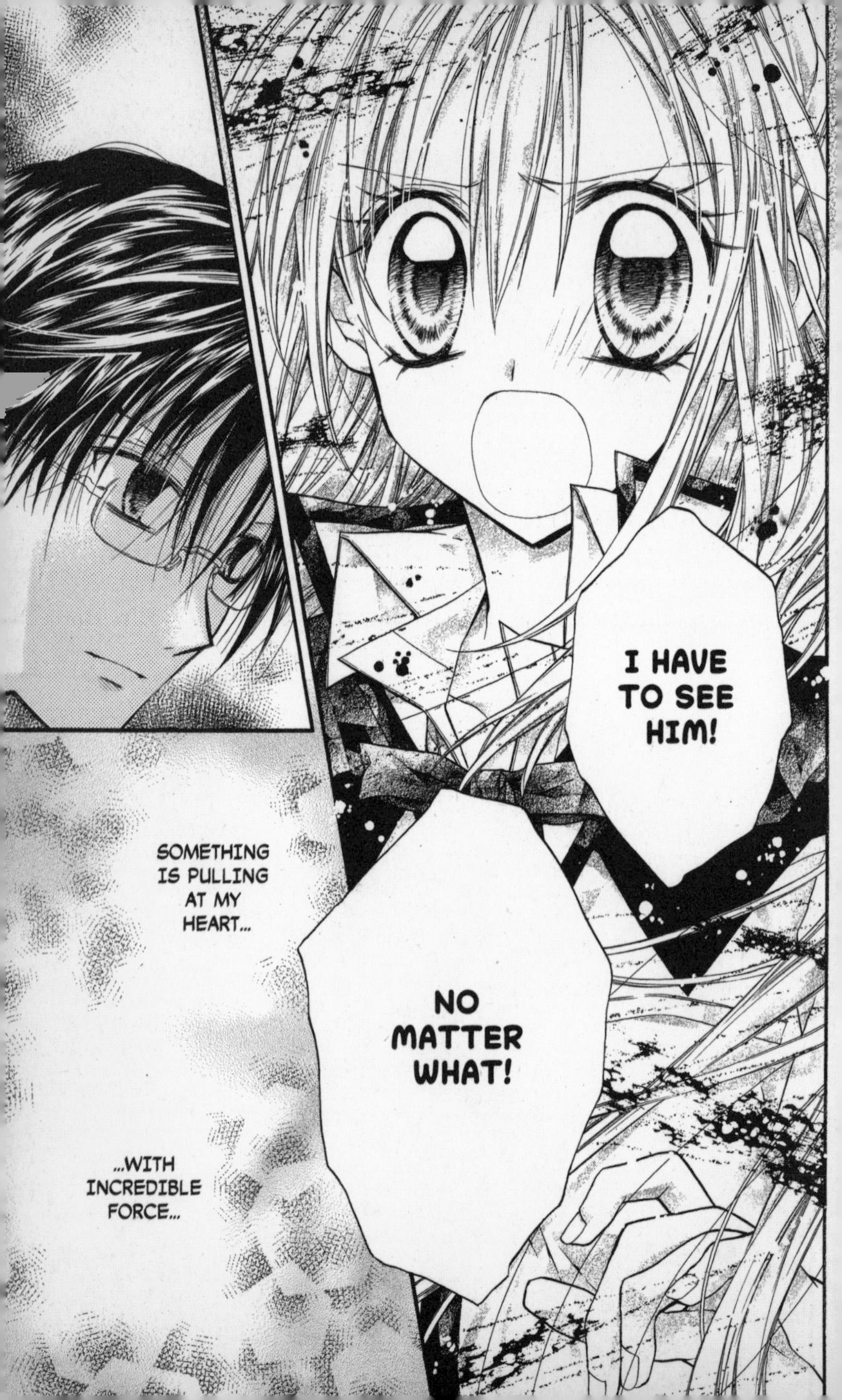
I HAVE TO SEE HIM!
NO MATTER WHAT!
SOMETHING IS PULLING AT MY HEART...
...WITH INCREDIBLE FORCE...

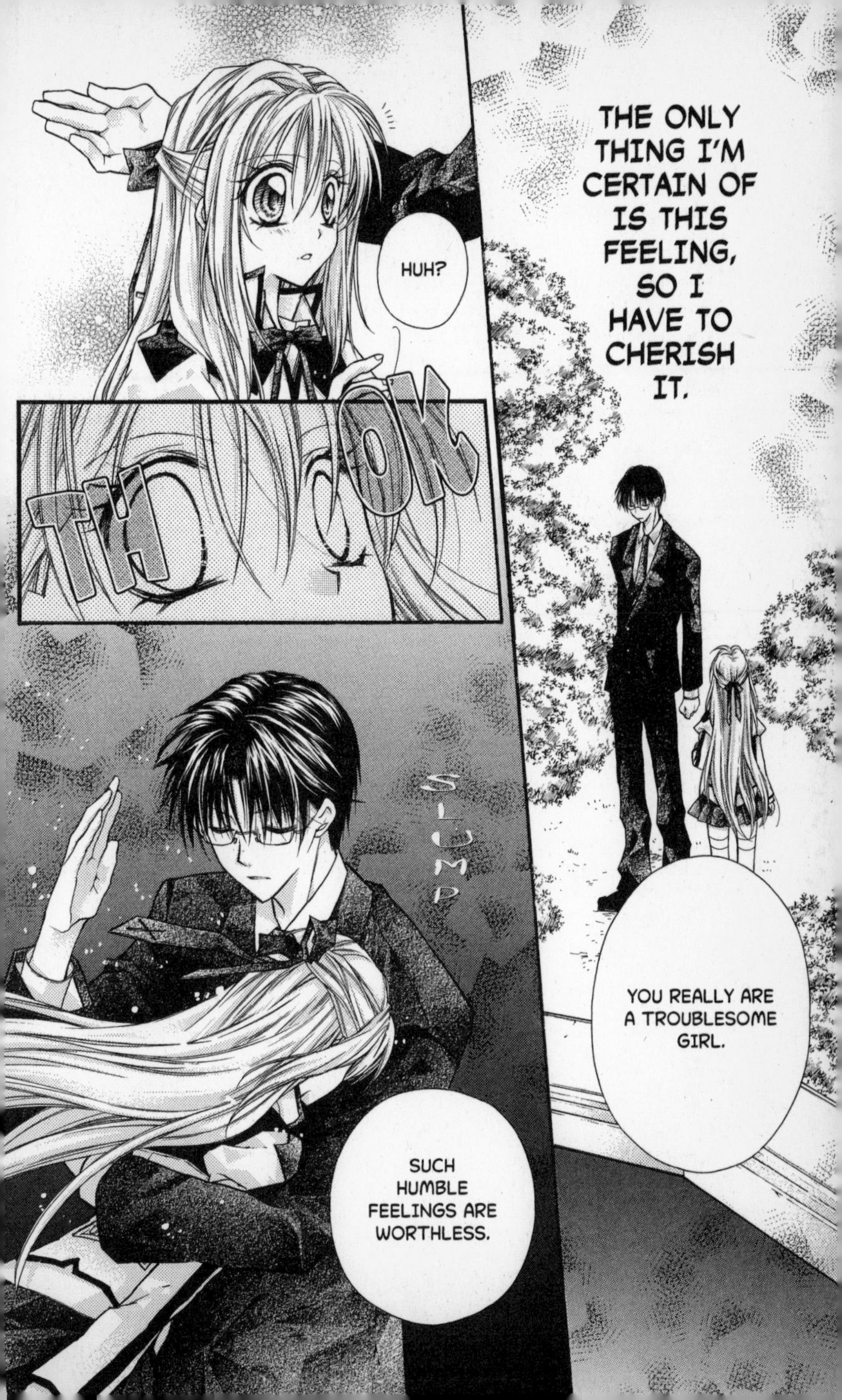
THE ONLY THING I'M CERTAIN OF IS THIS FEELING, SO I HAVE TO CHERISH IT.
YOU REALLY ARE A TROUBLESOME GIRL.
HUH?
TH
OK
SLUMP
SUCH HUMBLE FEELINGS ARE WORTHLESS.

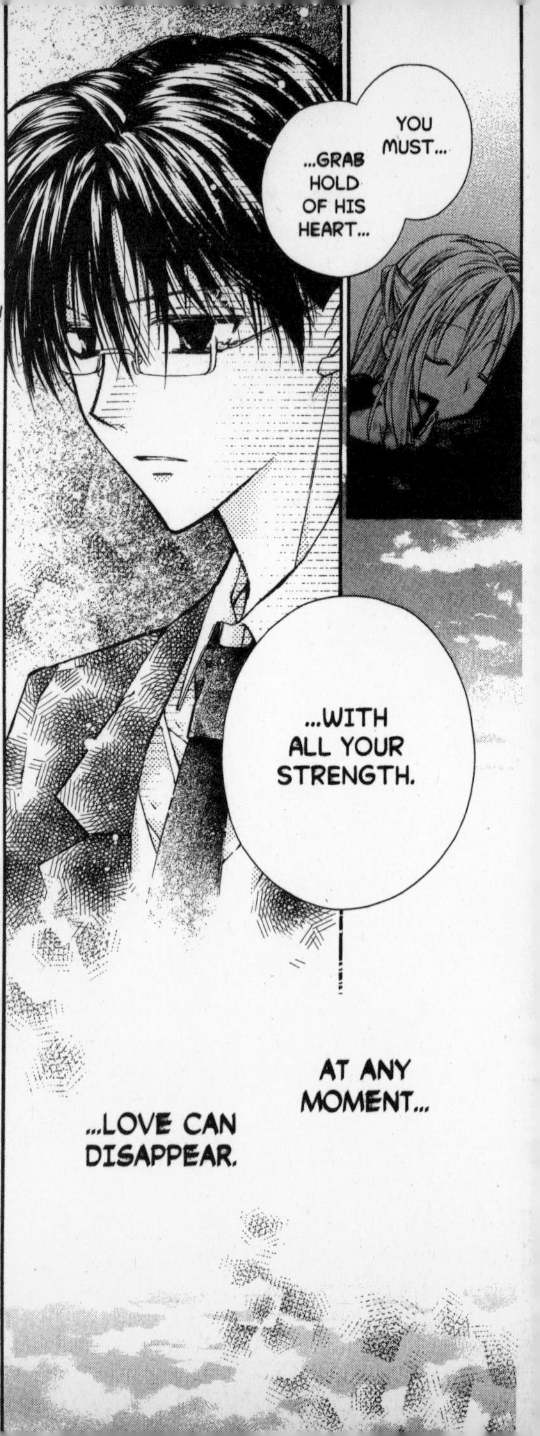
YOU MUST...
...GRAB HOLD OF HIS HEART...
...WITH ALL YOUR STRENGTH.
AT ANY MOMENT...
...LOVE CAN DISAPPEAR.

Full Moon Final Live 2 **2**

✿ I had my assistants listen to me sing.

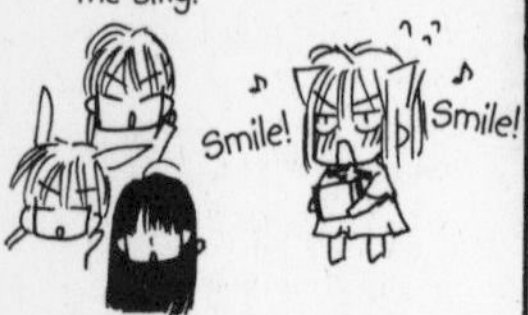
Smile!
Smile!

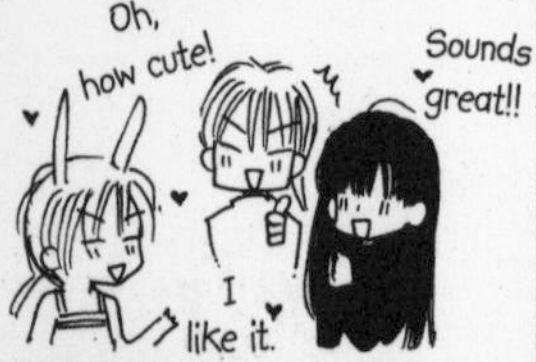
Oh, how cute!
Sounds great!!
I like it.

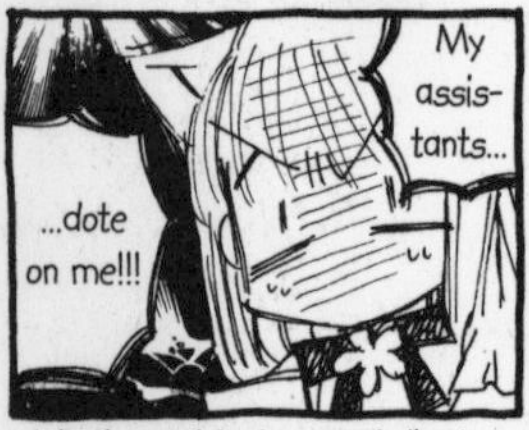
My assis-tants...
...dote on me!!!

※ Doting assistants → Similar to doting parents. (Assistants who don't realize that Sensei is making a fool of herself when she sings.)

I'm sorry, everyone.

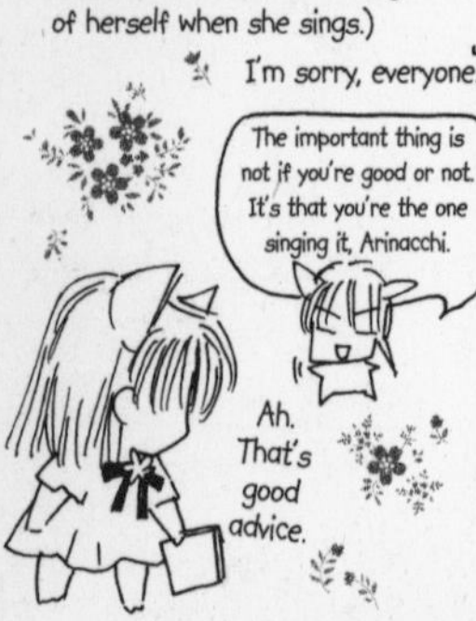
The important thing is not if you're good or not. It's that you're the one singing it, Arinacchi.
Ah. That's good advice.

(continues)

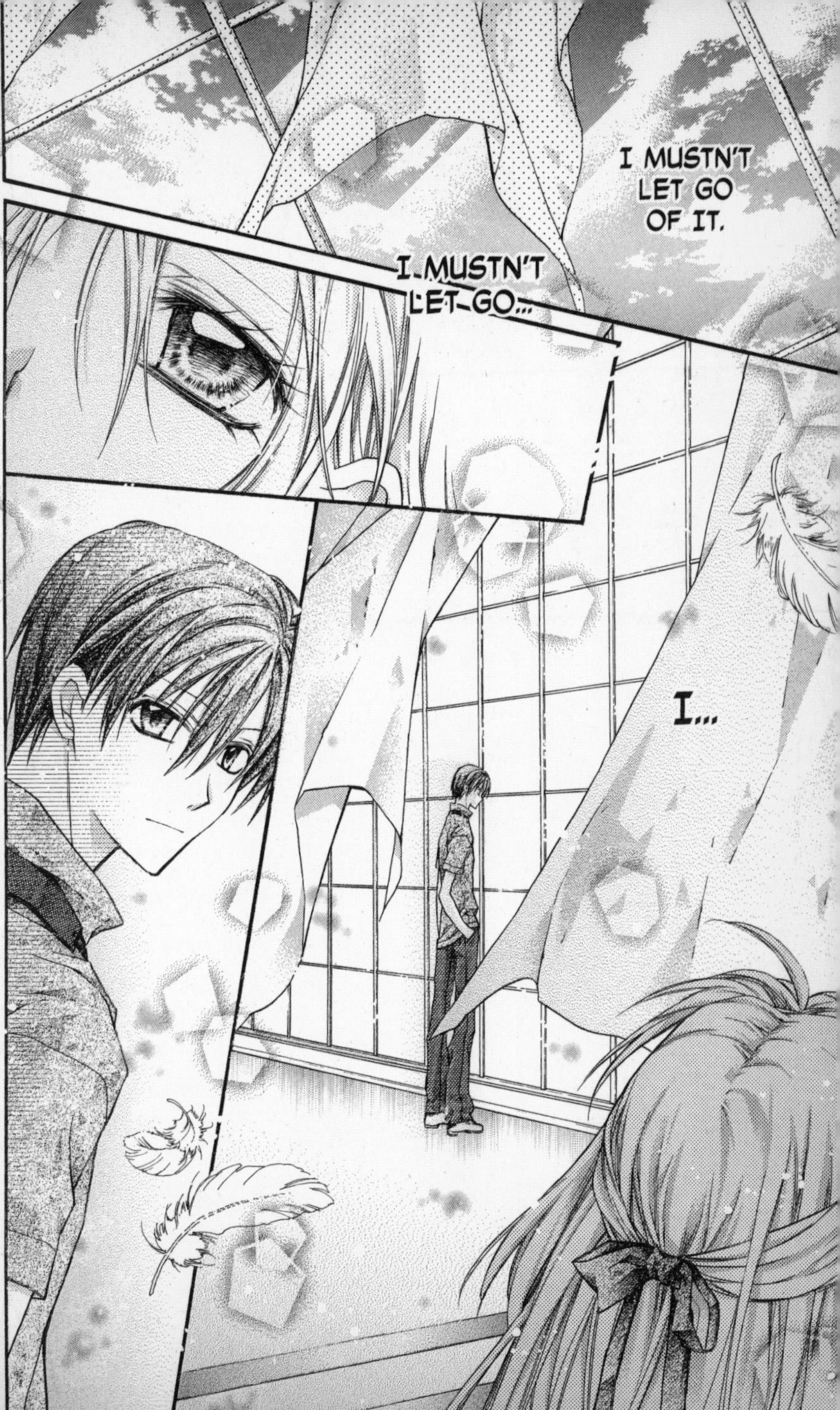
I MUSTN'T LET GO OF IT.
I MUSTN'T LET GO...
I...

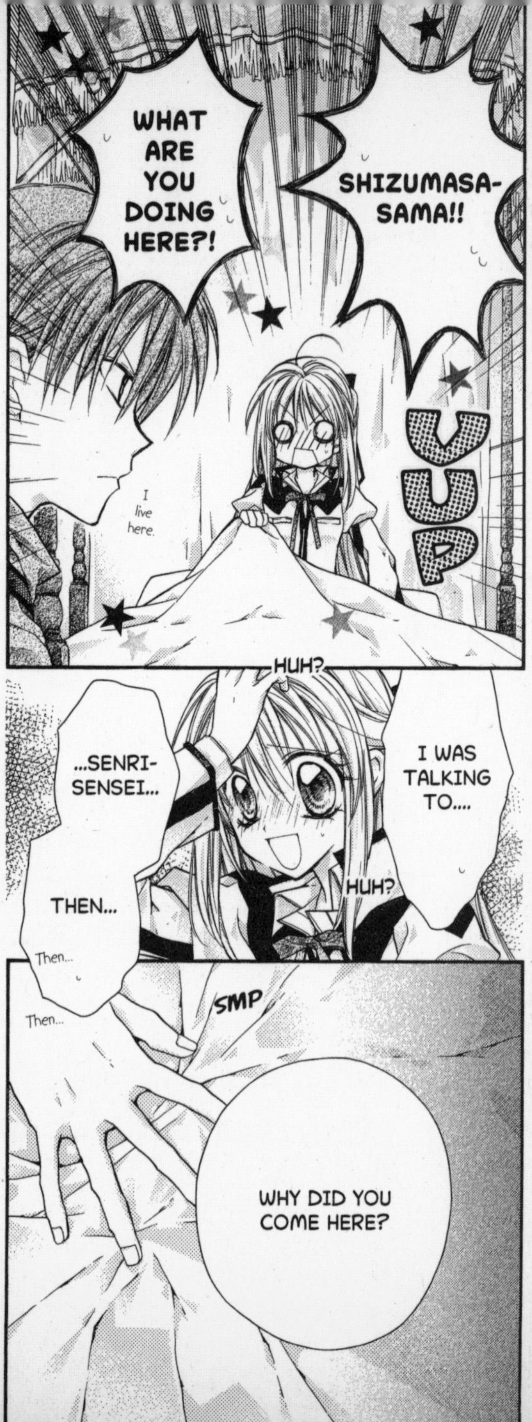
WHAT ARE YOU DOING HERE?!
SHIZUMASA-SAMA!!
VUP
I live here.
HUH?
I WAS TALKING TO....
...SENRI-SENSEI...
HUH?
THEN...
Then...
Then...
SMP
WHY DID YOU COME HERE?

Full Moon Final Live 3

✿ I went to Toshiba EMI.

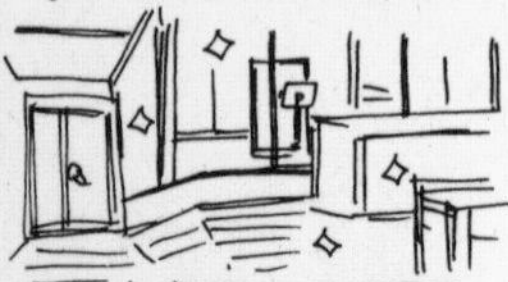

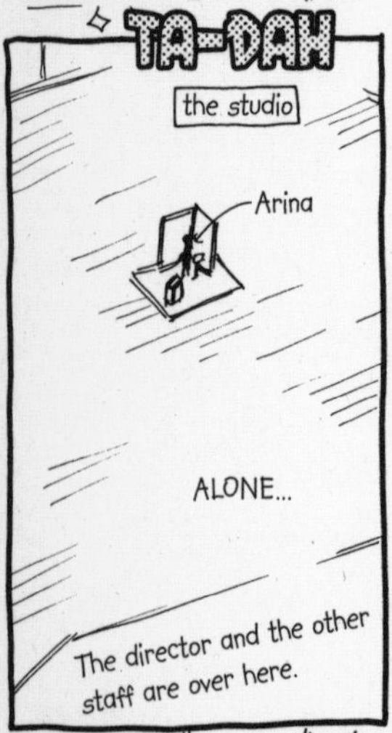
TA-DAH
the studio
Arina
ALONE...
The director and the other staff are over here.

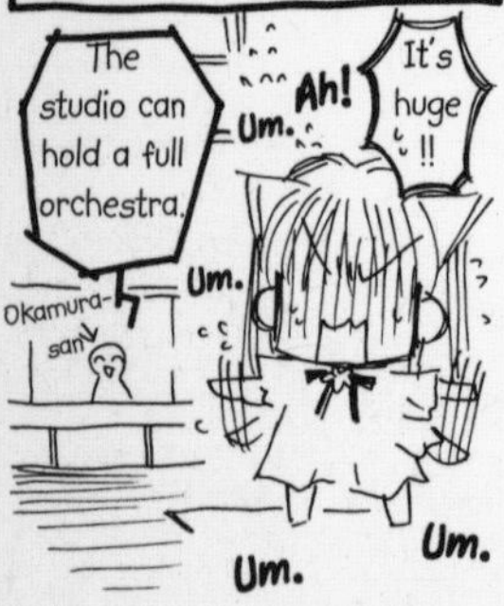
The studio can hold a full orchestra.
Ah!
It's huge !!
Um.
Um.
Okamura-san
Um.
Um.

I thought the studio would be small, so I was really surprised.

(continues)

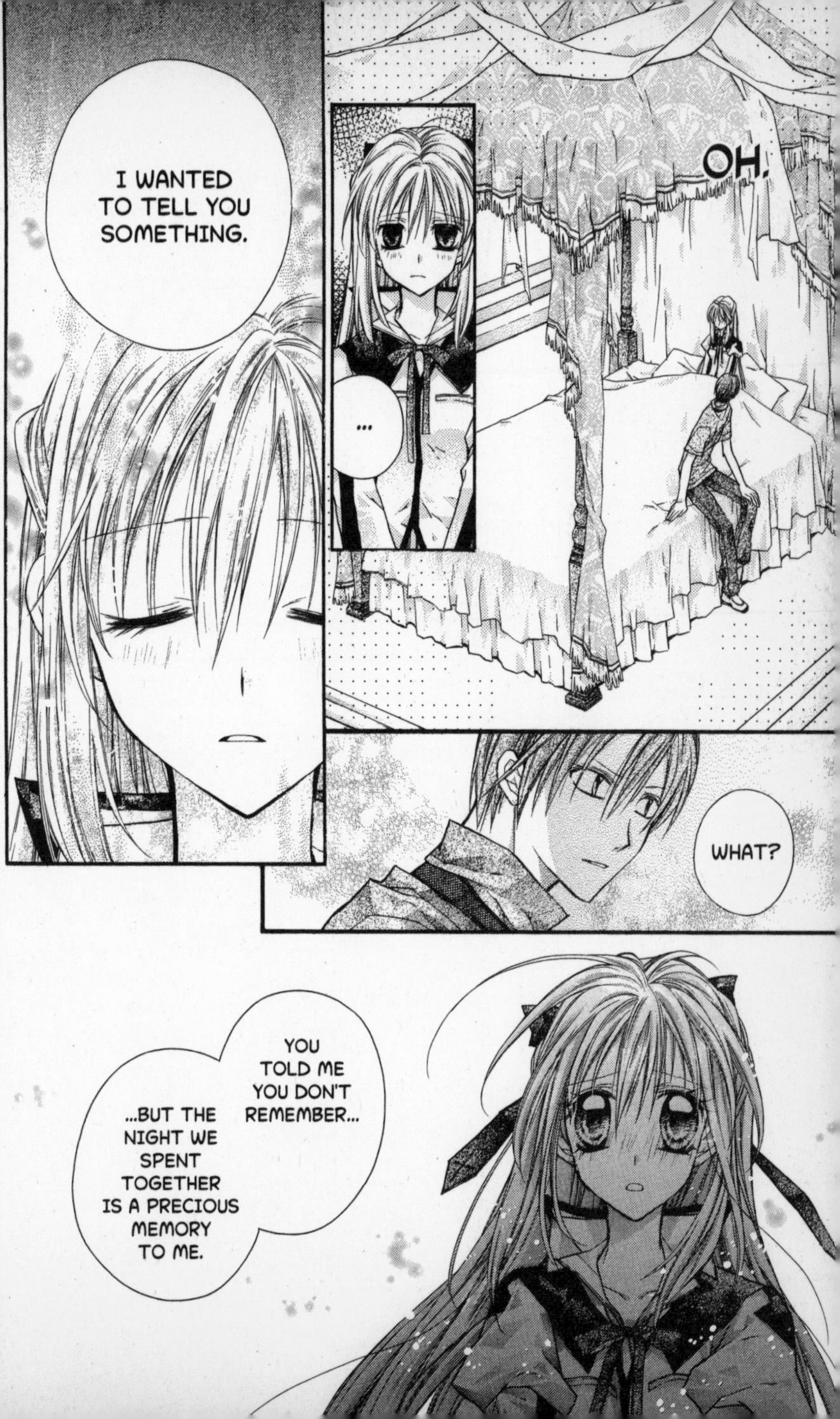
OH.
...
WHAT?
I WANTED TO TELL YOU SOMETHING.
YOU TOLD ME YOU DON'T REMEMBER...
...BUT THE NIGHT WE SPENT TOGETHER IS A PRECIOUS MEMORY TO ME.

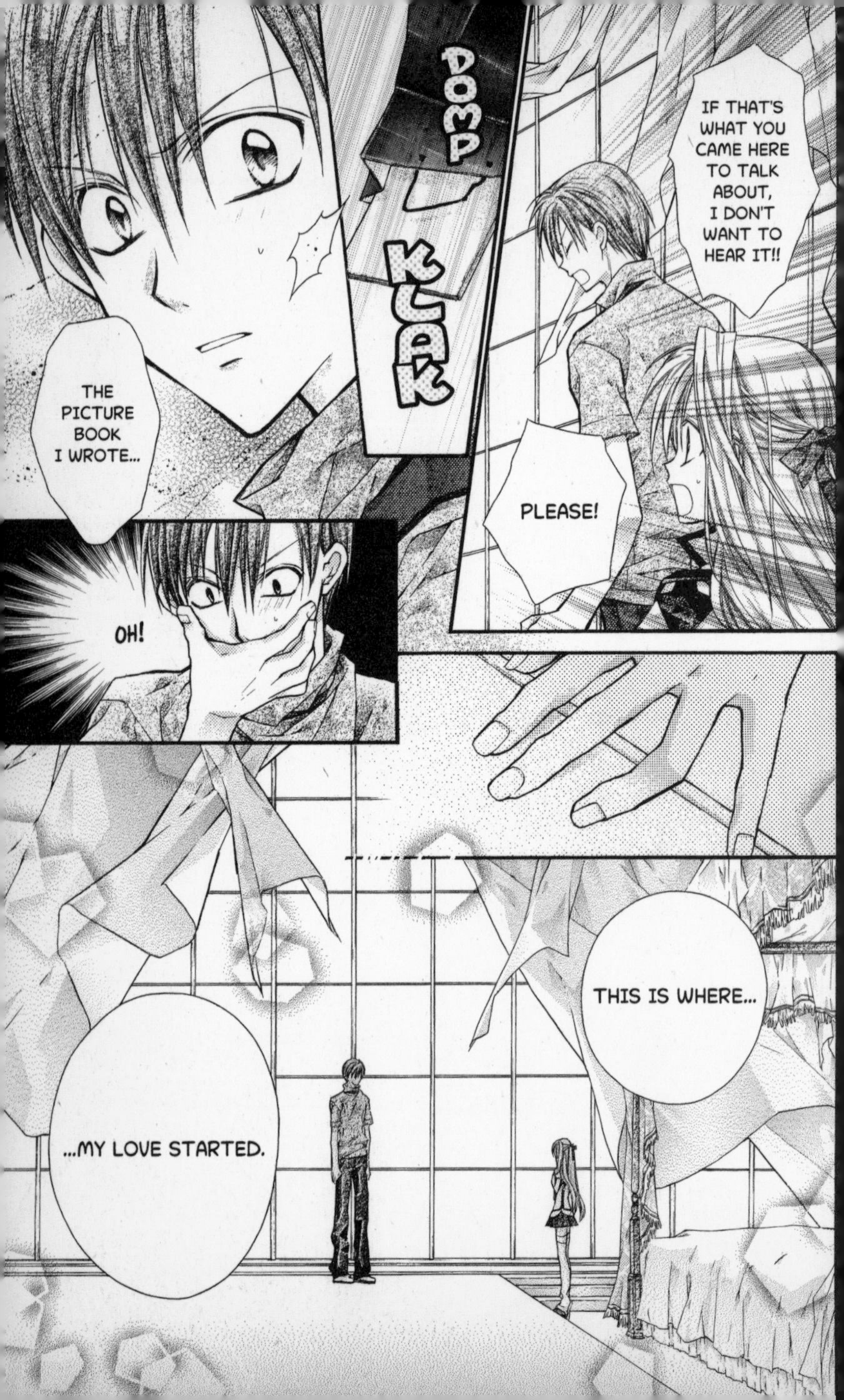
IF THAT'S WHAT YOU CAME HERE TO TALK ABOUT, I DON'T WANT TO HEAR IT!!
PLEASE!
DOMP
KLAK
THE PICTURE BOOK I WROTE...
OH!
THIS IS WHERE...
...MY LOVE STARTED.

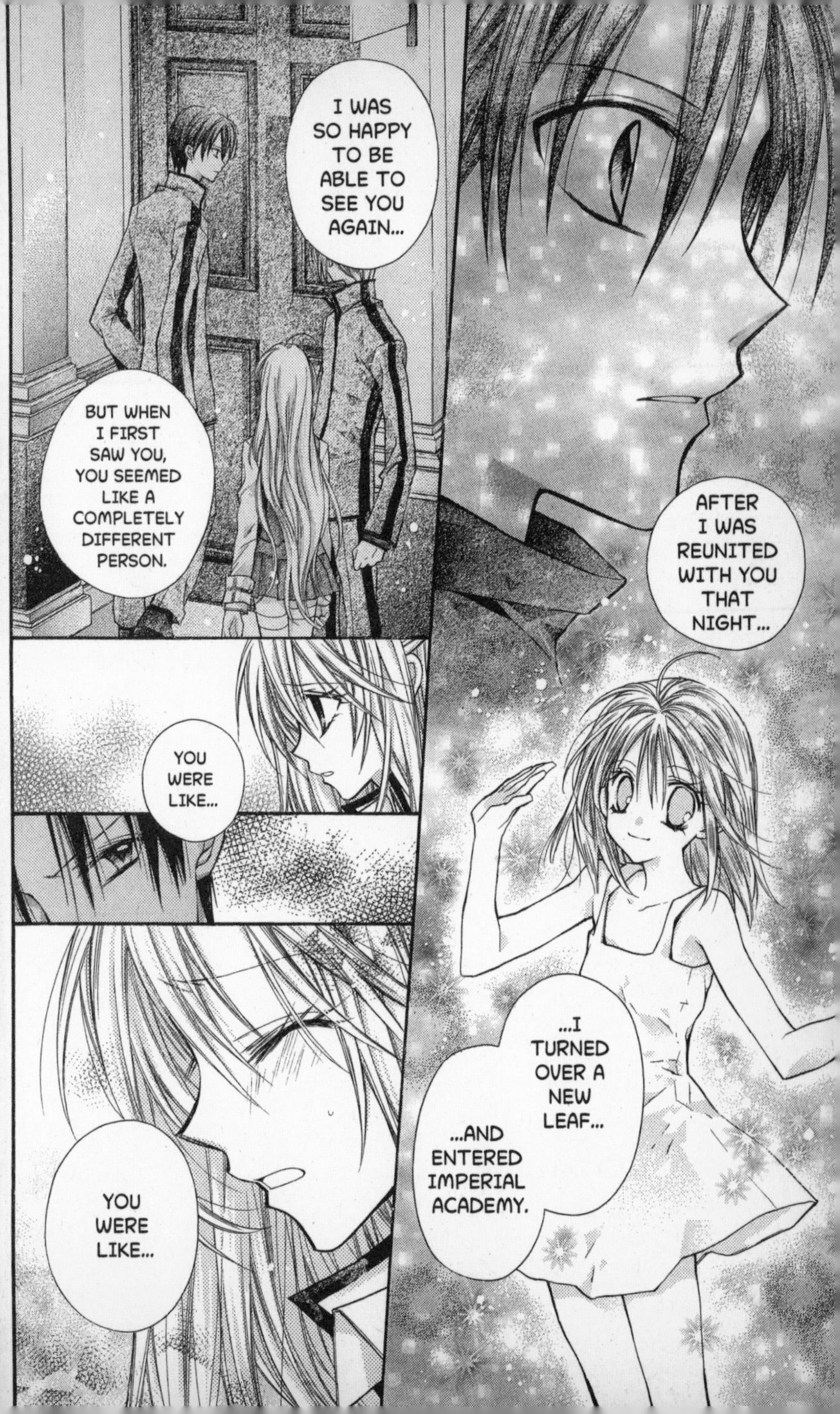
AFTER I WAS REUNITED WITH YOU THAT NIGHT...
...I TURNED OVER A NEW LEAF...
...AND ENTERED IMPERIAL ACADEMY.
I WAS SO HAPPY TO BE ABLE TO SEE YOU AGAIN...
BUT WHEN I FIRST SAW YOU, YOU SEEMED LIKE A COMPLETELY DIFFERENT PERSON.
YOU WERE LIKE...
YOU WERE LIKE...

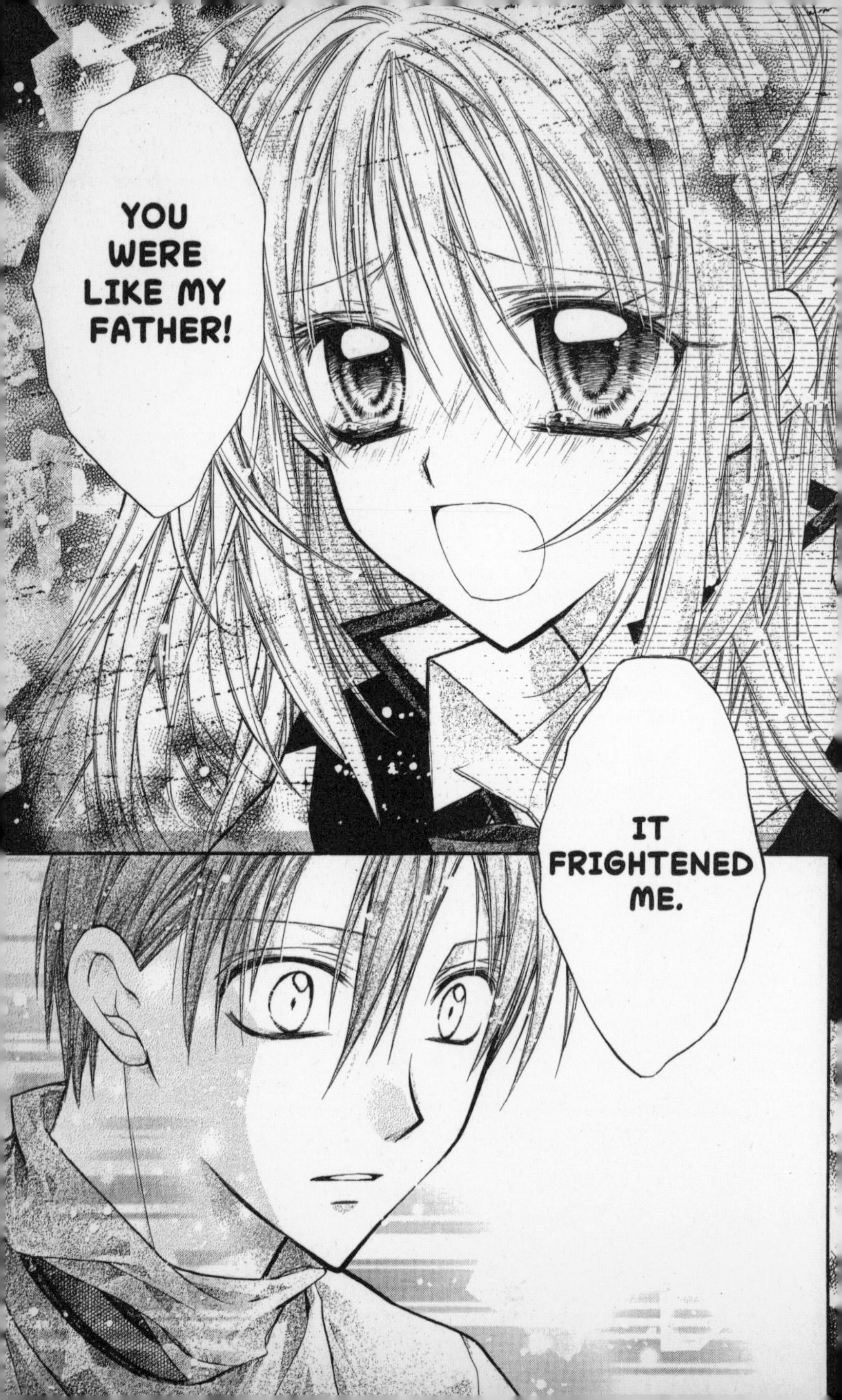
YOU WERE LIKE MY FATHER!
IT FRIGHTENED ME.

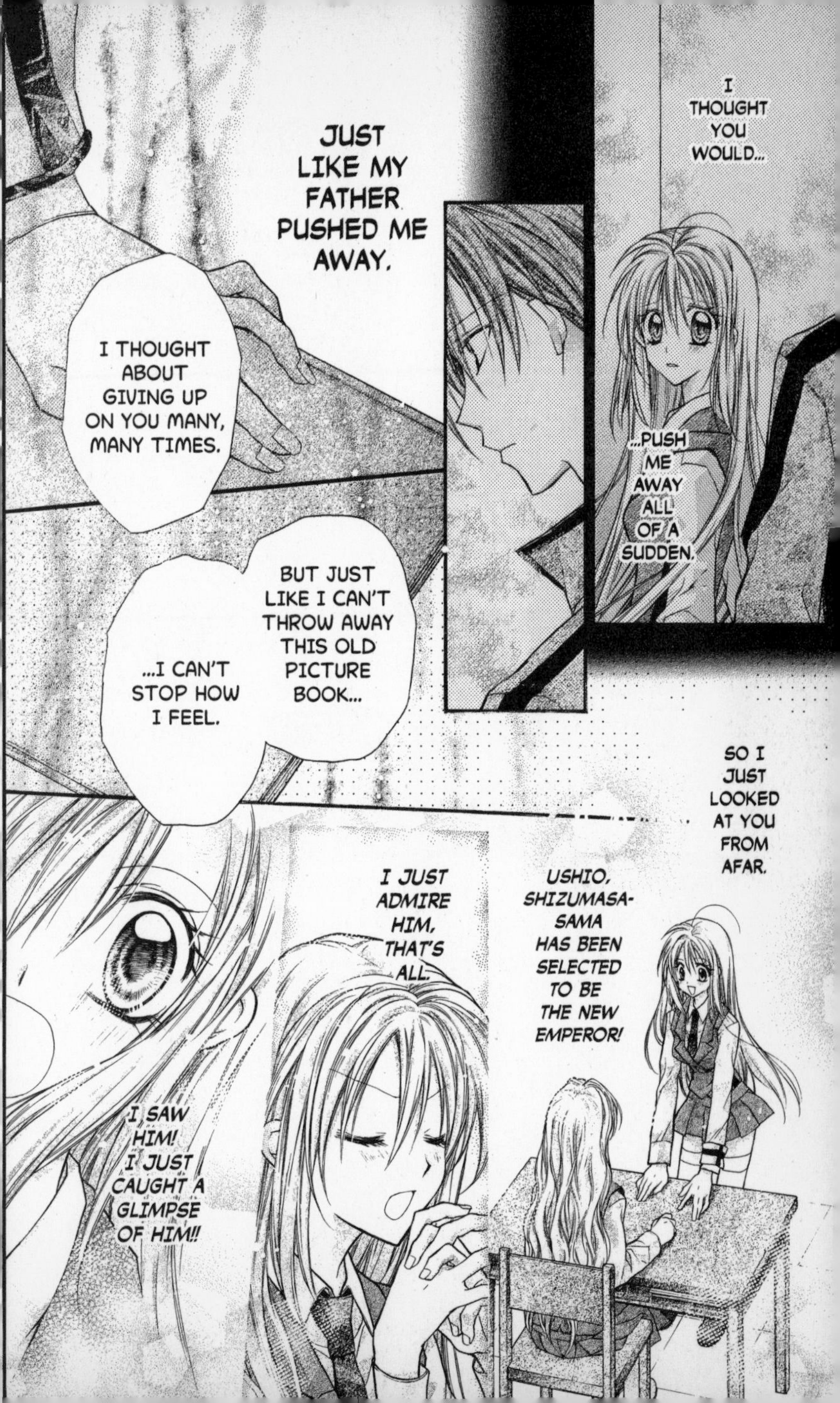
I THOUGHT YOU WOULD...
...PUSH ME AWAY ALL OF A SUDDEN.
JUST LIKE MY FATHER PUSHED ME AWAY.
I THOUGHT ABOUT GIVING UP ON YOU MANY, MANY TIMES.
BUT JUST LIKE I CAN'T THROW AWAY THIS OLD PICTURE BOOK...
...I CAN'T STOP HOW I FEEL.
SO I JUST LOOKED AT YOU FROM AFAR.
USHIO, SHIZUMASA-SAMA HAS BEEN SELECTED TO BE THE NEW EMPEROR!
I JUST ADMIRE HIM, THAT'S ALL.
I SAW HIM! I JUST CAUGHT A GLIMPSE OF HIM!!

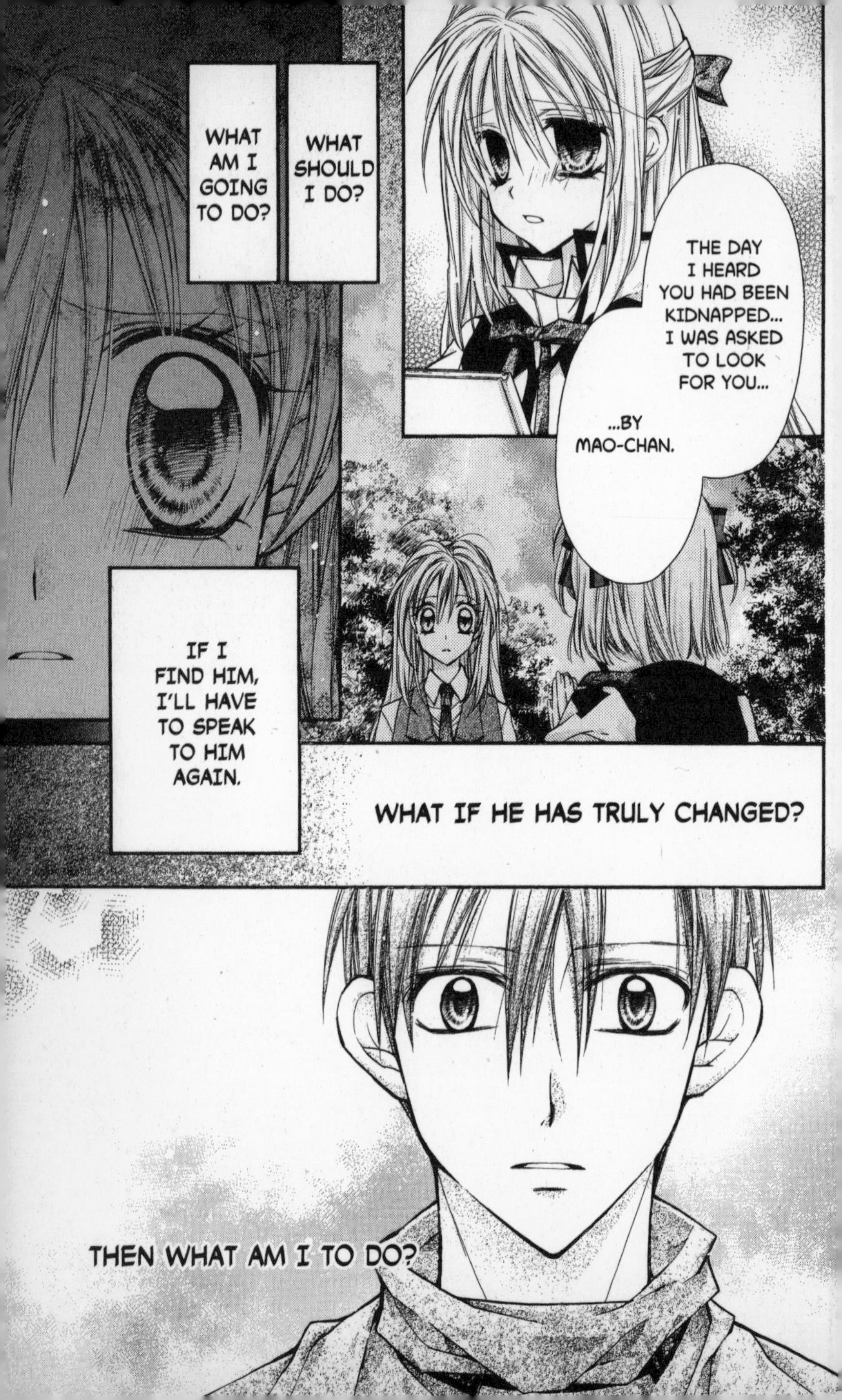
THE DAY I HEARD YOU HAD BEEN KIDNAPPED... I WAS ASKED TO LOOK FOR YOU...
...BY MAO-CHAN.
WHAT SHOULD I DO?
WHAT AM I GOING TO DO?
IF I FIND HIM, I'LL HAVE TO SPEAK TO HIM AGAIN.
WHAT IF HE HAS TRULY CHANGED?
THEN WHAT AM I TO DO?

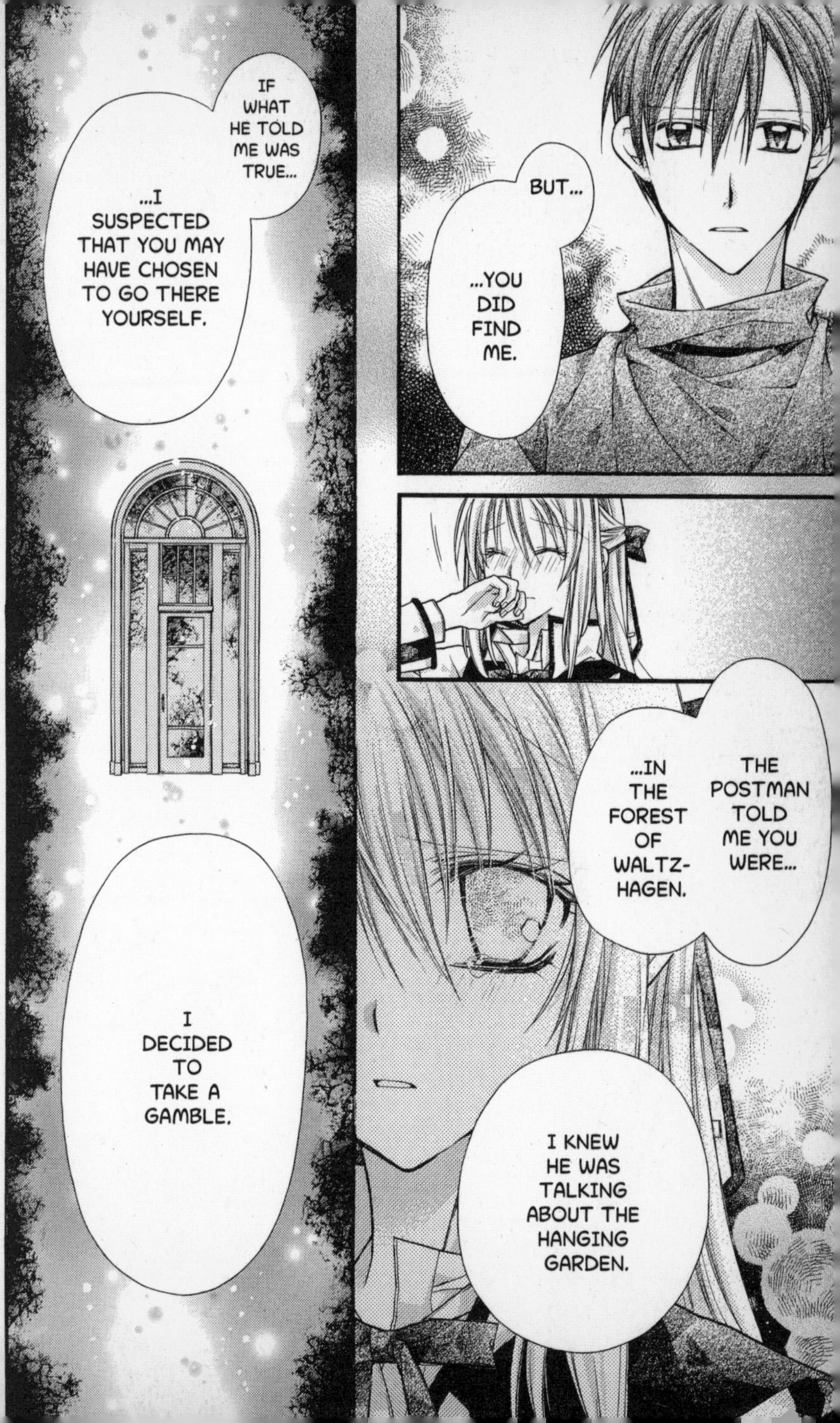
BUT...
...YOU DID FIND ME.
THE POSTMAN TOLD ME YOU WERE...
...IN THE FOREST OF WALTZ-HAGEN.
I KNEW HE WAS TALKING ABOUT THE HANGING GARDEN.
IF WHAT HE TOLD ME WAS TRUE...
...I SUSPECTED THAT YOU MAY HAVE CHOSEN TO GO THERE YOURSELF.
I DECIDED TO TAKE A GAMBLE.

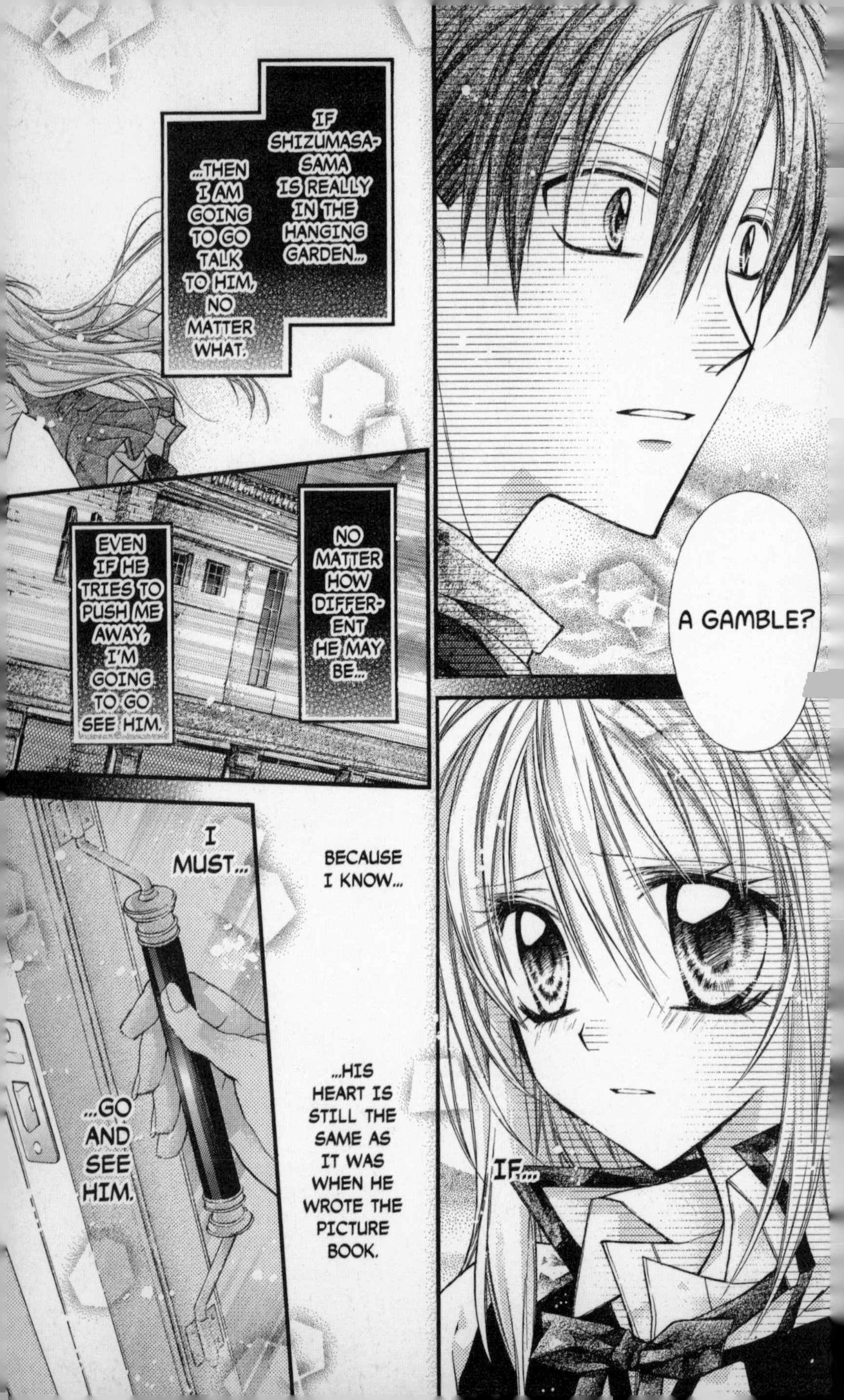
A GAMBLE?
IF SHIZUMASA-SAMA IS REALLY IN THE HANGING GARDEN...
...THEN I AM GOING TO GO TALK TO HIM, NO MATTER WHAT.
NO MATTER HOW DIFFERENT HE MAY BE...
EVEN IF HE TRIES TO PUSH ME AWAY, I'M GOING TO GO SEE HIM.
IF...
BECAUSE I KNOW...
...HIS HEART IS STILL THE SAME AS IT WAS WHEN HE WROTE THE PICTURE BOOK.
I MUST...
...GO AND SEE HIM.

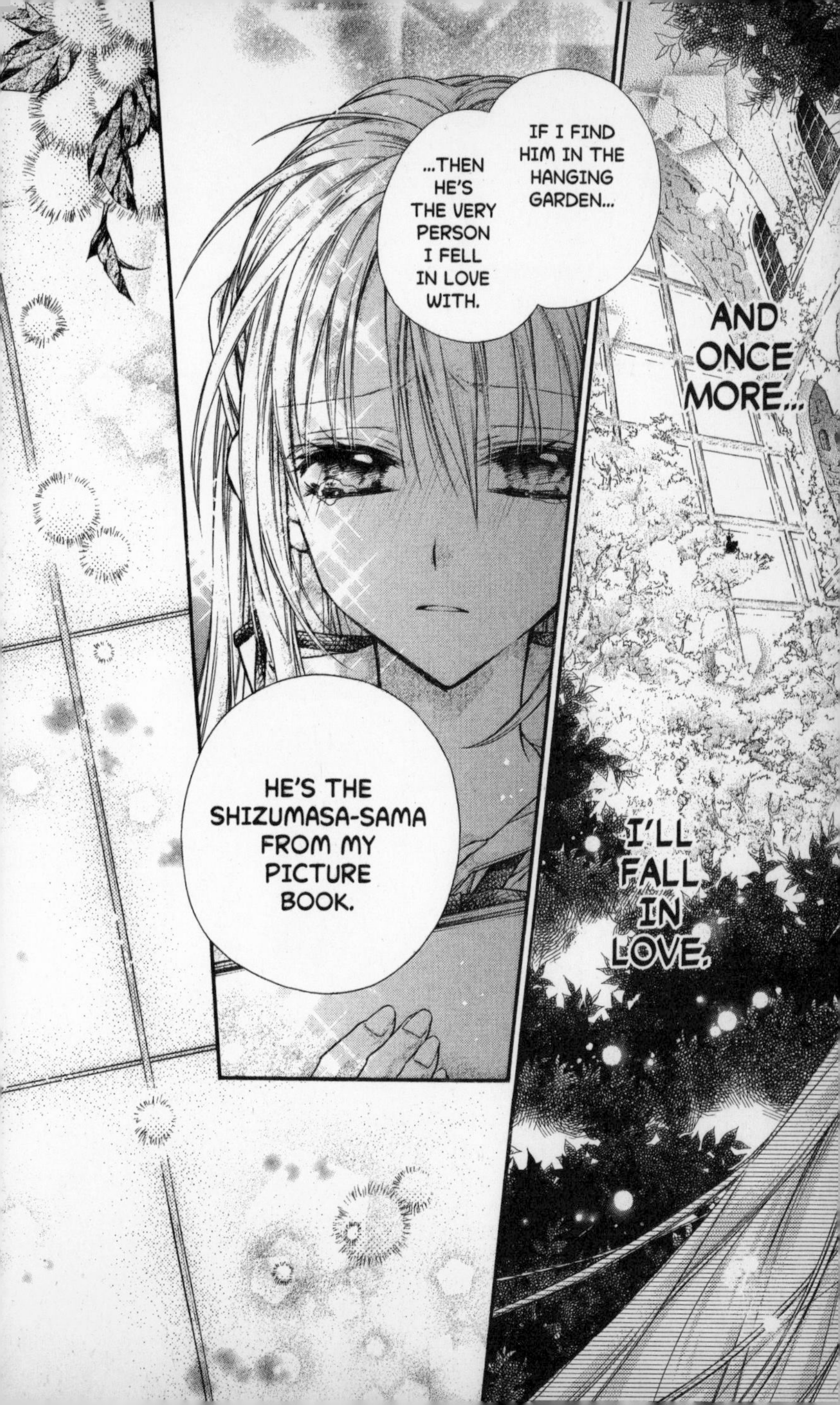
IF I FIND HIM IN THE HANGING GARDEN...
...THEN HE'S THE VERY PERSON I FELL IN LOVE WITH.
HE'S THE SHIZUMASA-SAMA FROM MY PICTURE BOOK.
AND ONCE MORE...
I'LL FALL IN LOVE.

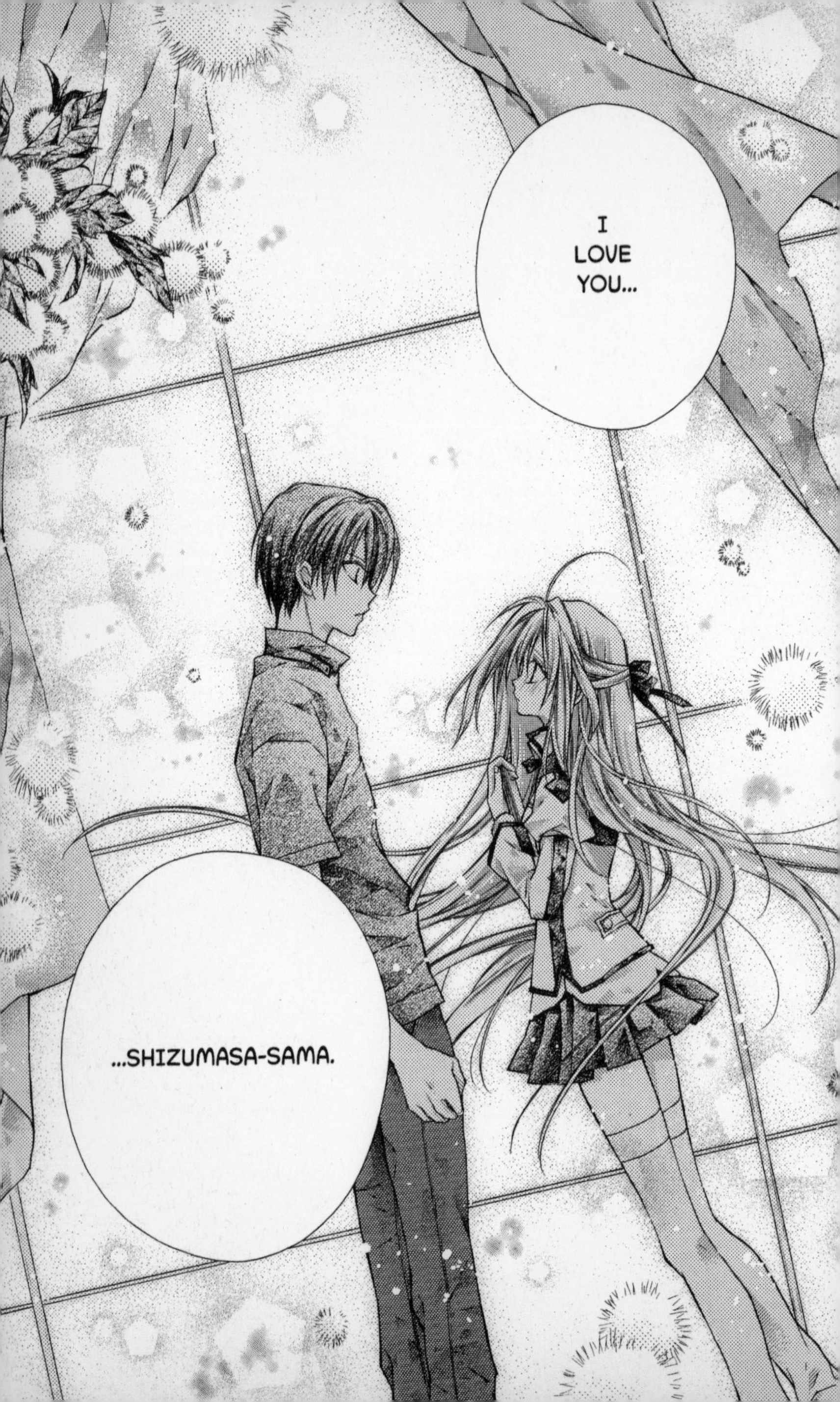
I LOVE YOU...
...SHIZUMASA-SAMA.

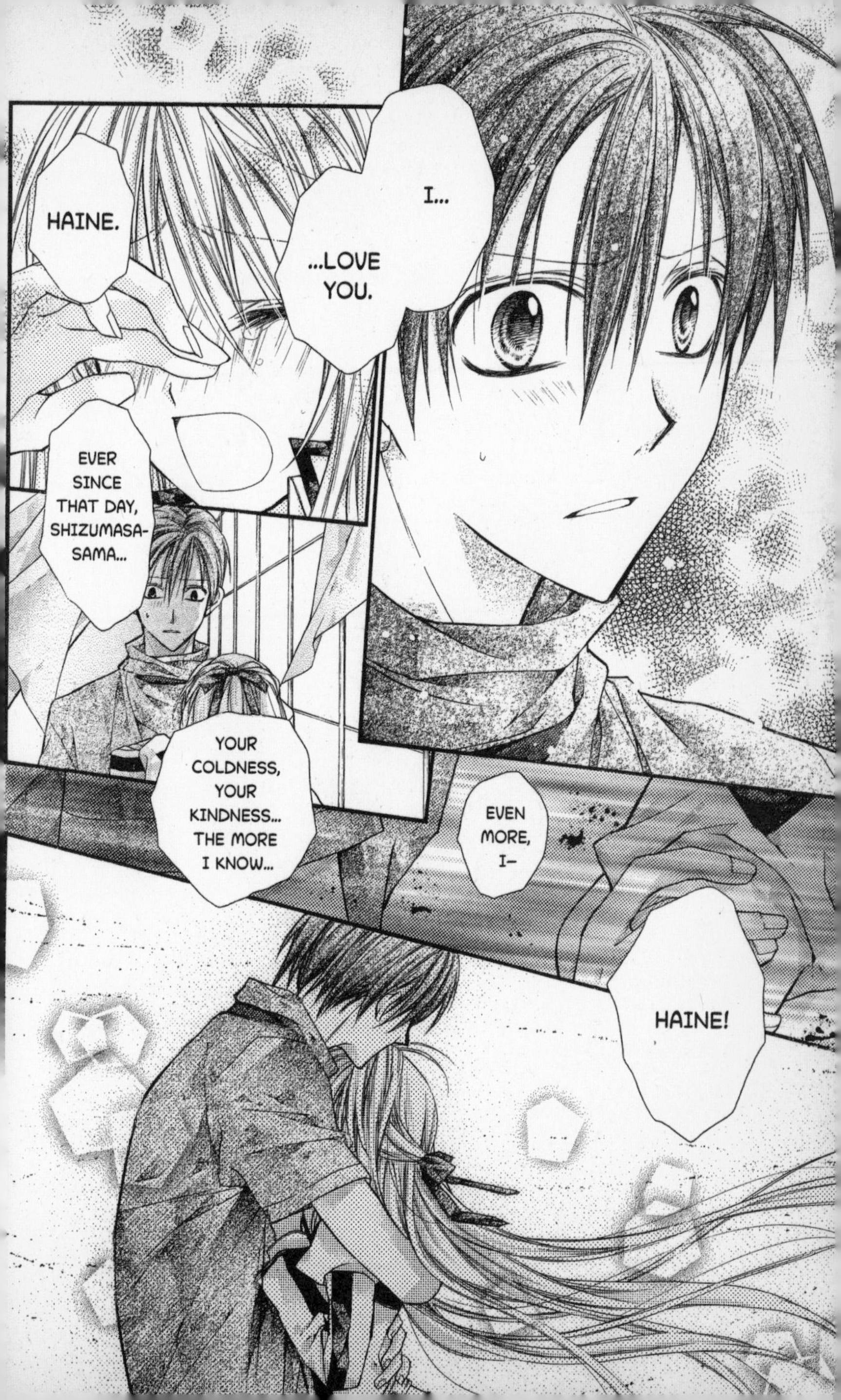
I...
...LOVE YOU.
HAINE.
EVER SINCE THAT DAY, SHIZUMASA-SAMA...
YOUR COLDNESS, YOUR KINDNESS... THE MORE I KNOW...
EVEN MORE, I—
HAINE!

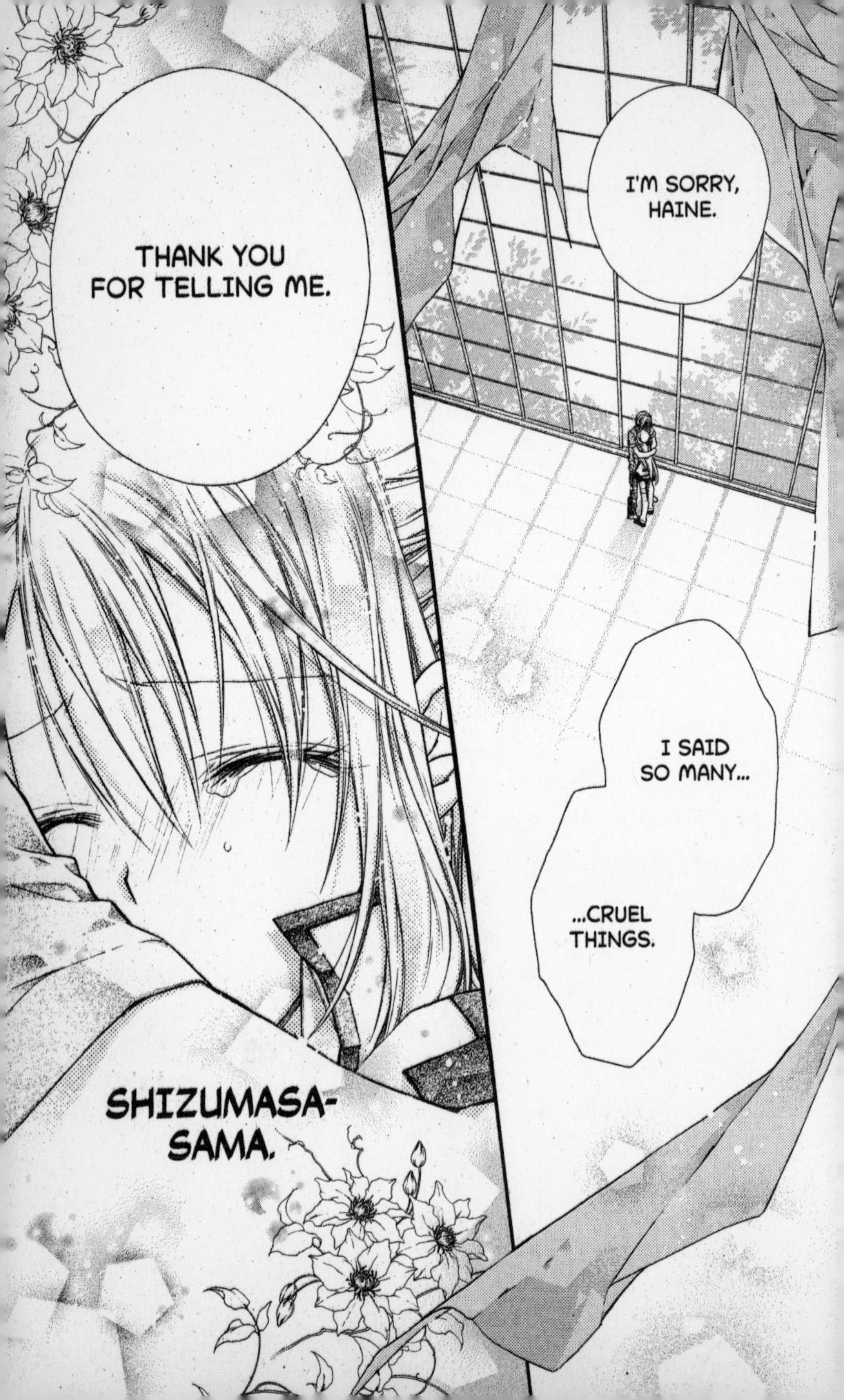
I'M SORRY, HAINE.
I SAID SO MANY...
...CRUEL THINGS.
THANK YOU FOR TELLING ME.
SHIZUMASA-SAMA.

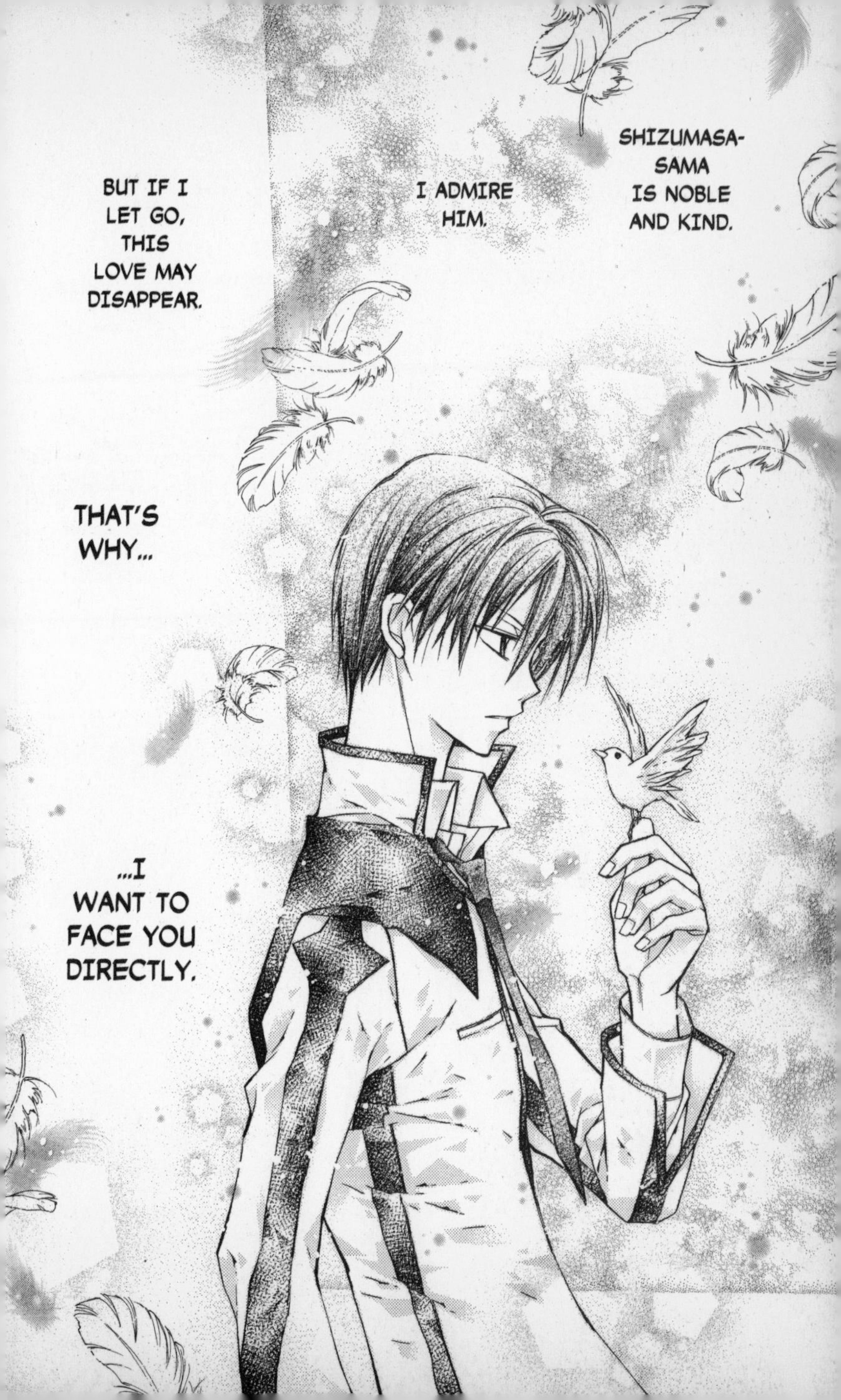
SHIZUMASA-SAMA IS NOBLE AND KIND.
I ADMIRE HIM.
BUT IF I LET GO, THIS LOVE MAY DISAPPEAR.
THAT'S WHY...
...I WANT TO FACE YOU DIRECTLY.

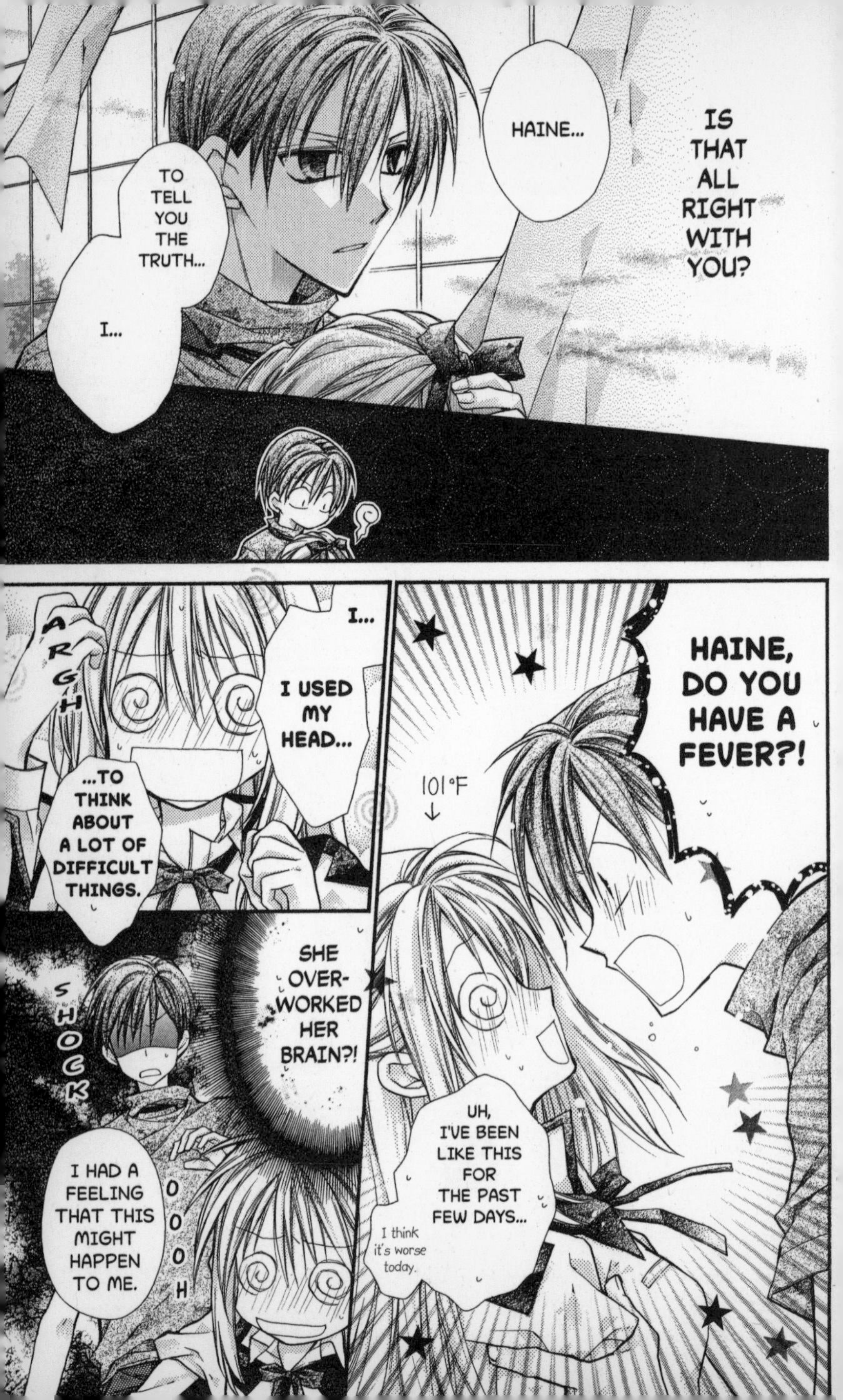
IS THAT ALL RIGHT WITH YOU?
HAINE...
TO TELL YOU THE TRUTH...
I...
HAINE, DO YOU HAVE A FEVER?!
101°F ↓
UH, I'VE BEEN LIKE THIS FOR THE PAST FEW DAYS...
I think it's worse today.
I...
I USED MY HEAD...
ARGH
...TO THINK ABOUT A LOT OF DIFFICULT THINGS.
SHE OVER-WORKED HER BRAIN?!
SHOCK
OOOOH
I HAD A FEELING THAT THIS MIGHT HAPPEN TO ME.

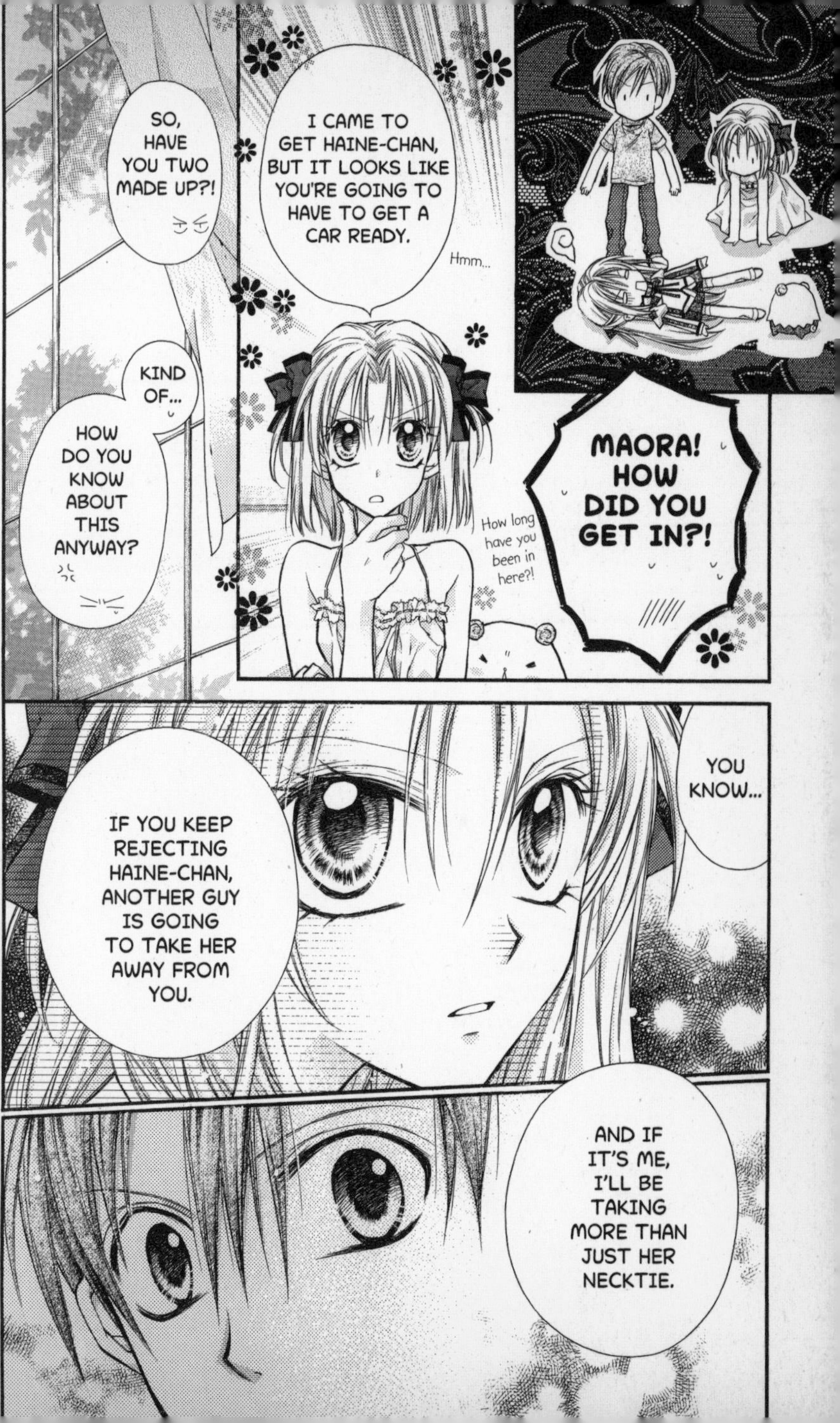
MAORA! HOW DID YOU GET IN?!
How long have you been in here?!
I CAME TO GET HAINE-CHAN, BUT IT LOOKS LIKE YOU'RE GOING TO HAVE TO GET A CAR READY.
Hmm...
SO, HAVE YOU TWO MADE UP?!
KIND OF...
HOW DO YOU KNOW ABOUT THIS ANYWAY?
YOU KNOW...
IF YOU KEEP REJECTING HAINE-CHAN, ANOTHER GUY IS GOING TO TAKE HER AWAY FROM YOU.
AND IF IT'S ME, I'LL BE TAKING MORE THAN JUST HER NECKTIE.

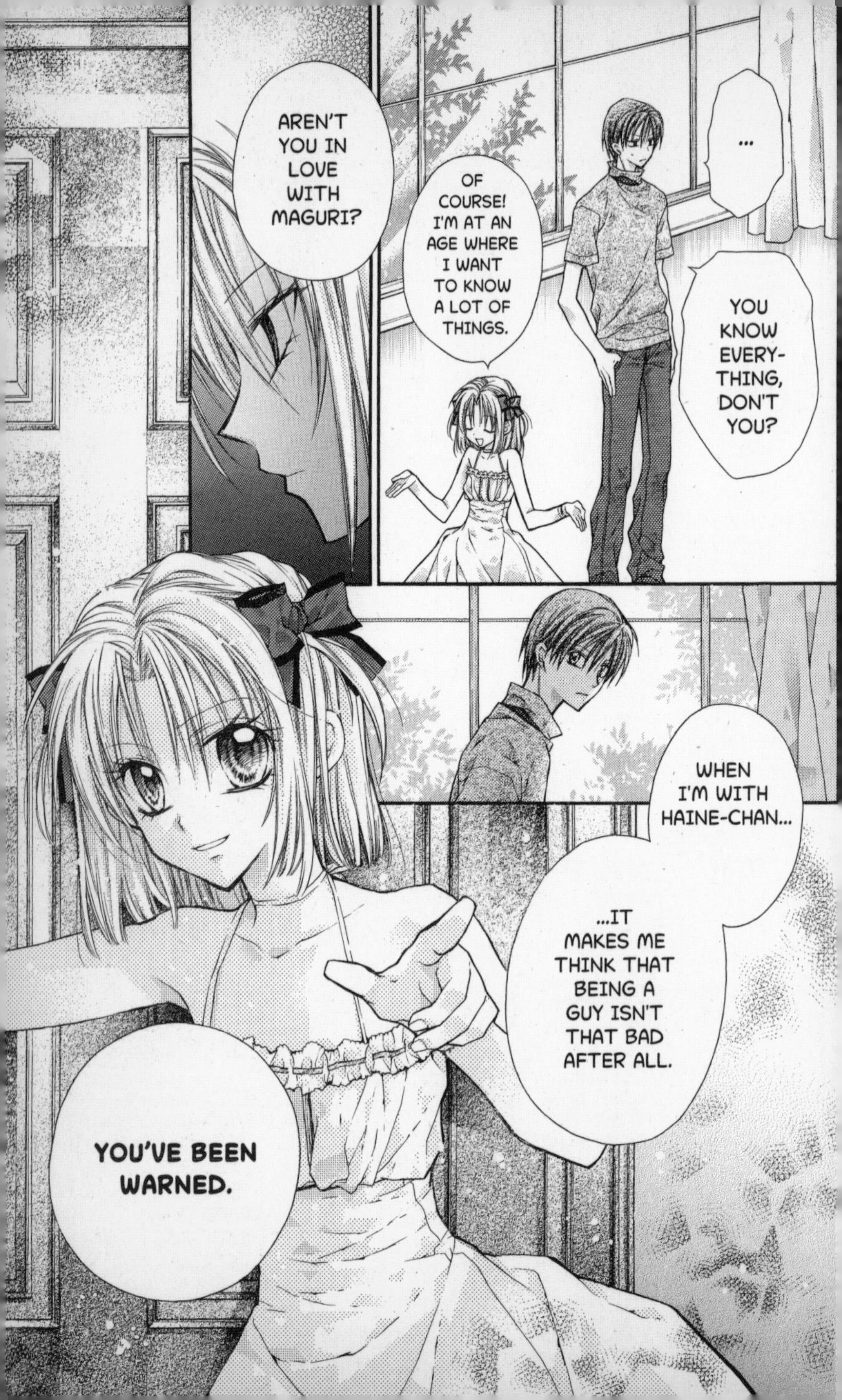
...
YOU KNOW EVERY-THING, DON'T YOU?
OF COURSE! I'M AT AN AGE WHERE I WANT TO KNOW A LOT OF THINGS.
AREN'T YOU IN LOVE WITH MAGURI?
WHEN I'M WITH HAINE-CHAN...
...IT MAKES ME THINK THAT BEING A GUY ISN'T THAT BAD AFTER ALL.
YOU'VE BEEN WARNED.

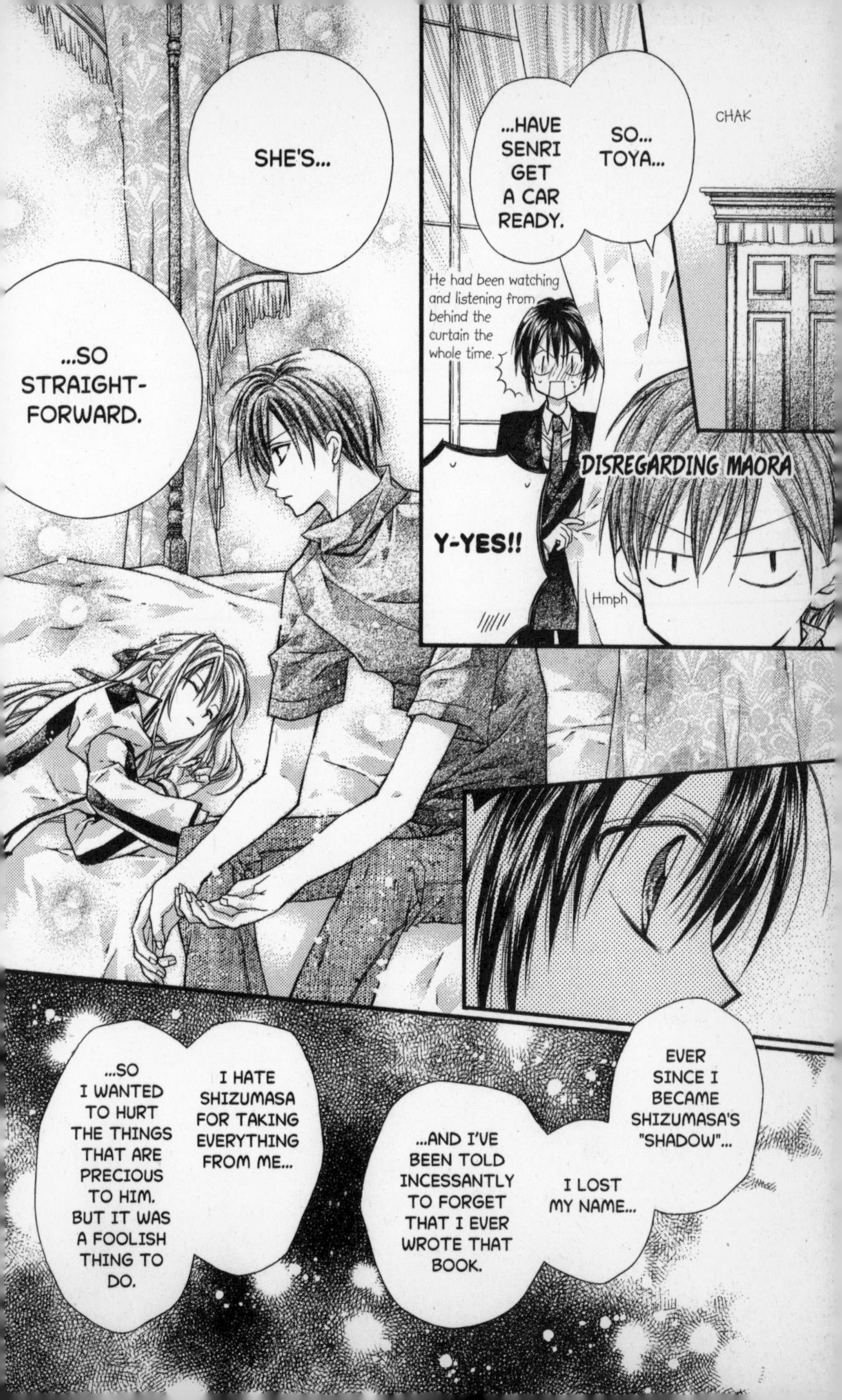
CHAK
SO... TOYA...
...HAVE SENRI GET A CAR READY.
DISREGARDING MAORA
Hmph
He had been watching and listening from behind the curtain the whole time.
Y-YES!!
SHE'S...
...SO STRAIGHT-FORWARD.
EVER SINCE I BECAME SHIZUMASA'S "SHADOW"...
I LOST MY NAME...
...AND I'VE BEEN TOLD INCESSANTLY TO FORGET THAT I EVER WROTE THAT BOOK.
I HATE SHIZUMASA FOR TAKING EVERYTHING FROM ME...
...SO I WANTED TO HURT THE THINGS THAT ARE PRECIOUS TO HIM. BUT IT WAS A FOOLISH THING TO DO.

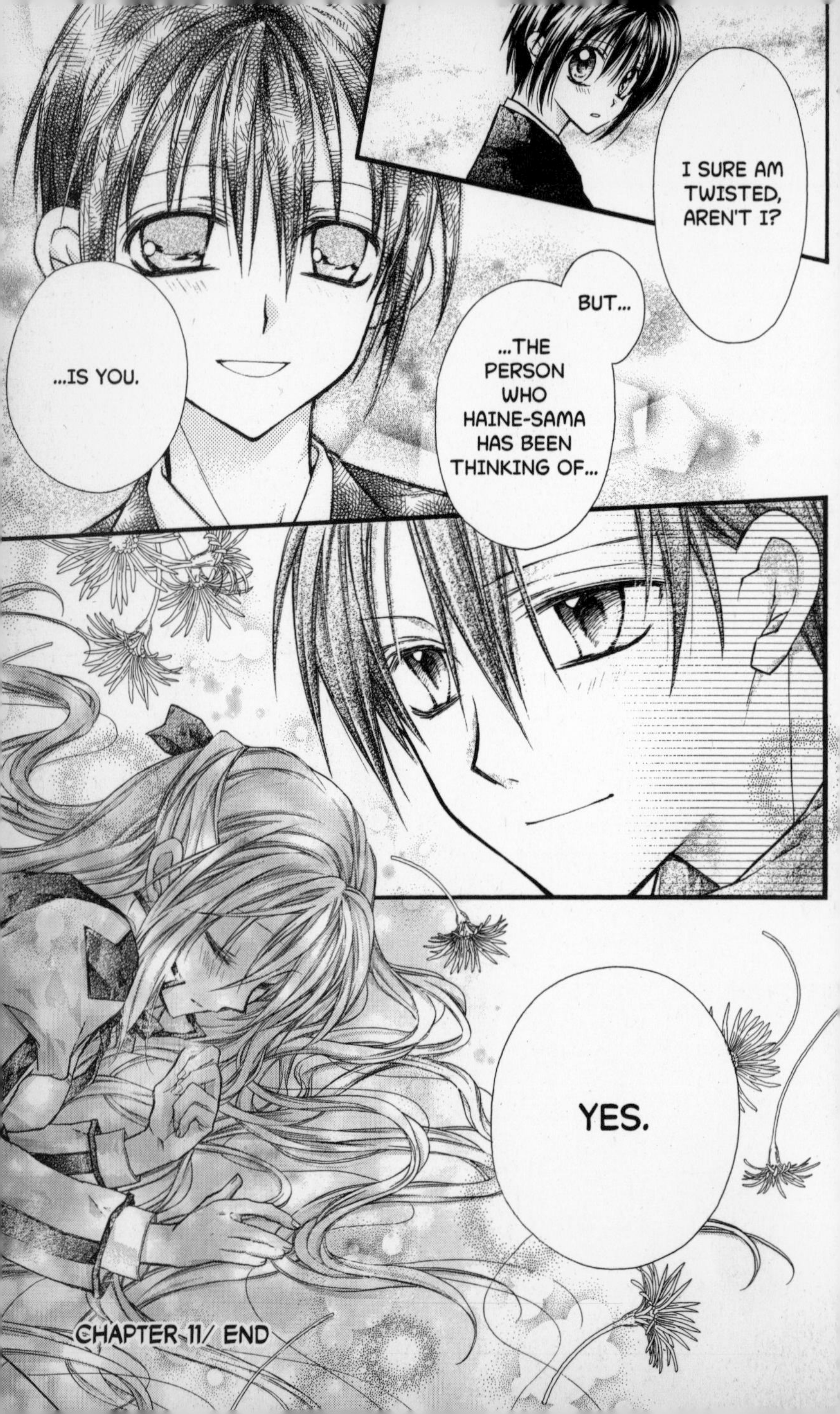
I SURE AM TWISTED, AREN'T I?
BUT...
...THE PERSON WHO HAINE-SAMA HAS BEEN THINKING OF...
...IS YOU.
YES.
CHAPTER 11/ END

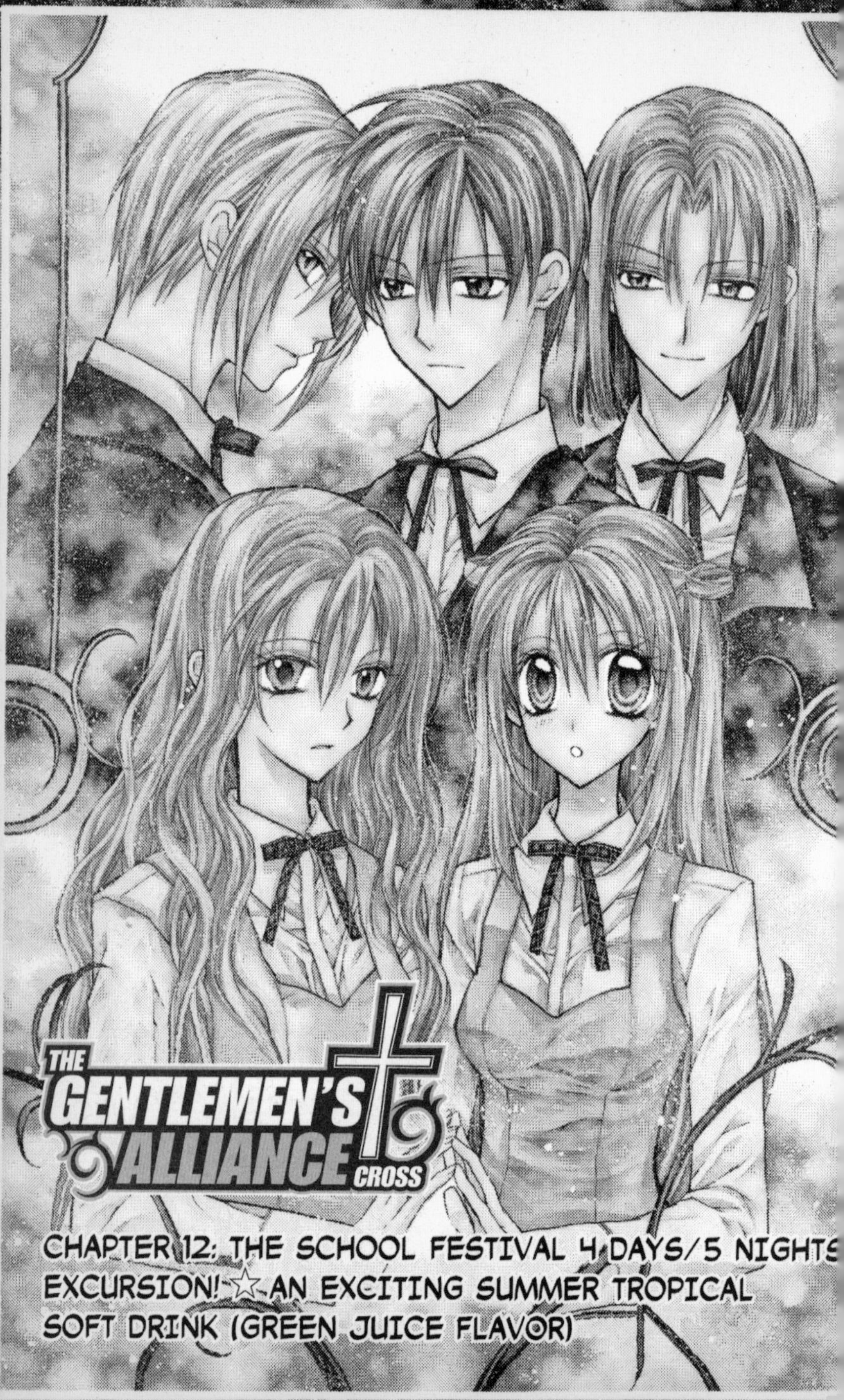
THE GENTLEMEN'S ALLIANCE CROSS
CHAPTER 12: THE SCHOOL FESTIVAL 4 DAYS/5 NIGHTS EXCURSION! ☆ AN EXCITING SUMMER TROPICAL SOFT DRINK (GREEN JUICE FLAVOR)

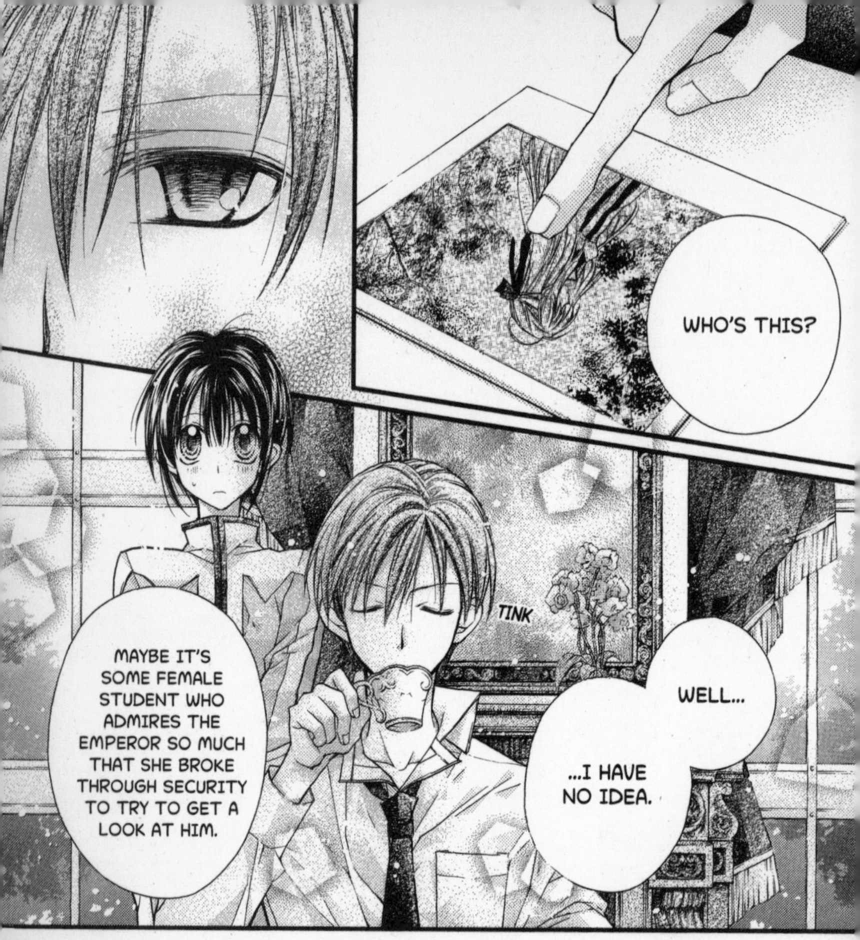
WHO'S THIS?
TINK
WELL...
...I HAVE NO IDEA.
MAYBE IT'S SOME FEMALE STUDENT WHO ADMIRES THE EMPEROR SO MUCH THAT SHE BROKE THROUGH SECURITY TO TRY TO GET A LOOK AT HIM.

Chapter 12: The School Festival 4 Days/5 Nights Excursion! ☆ Lead-in An Exciting Summer Tropical Soft Drink (Green Juice Flavor)

A love triangle or square?!

This excursion episode was very popular. And the Kamiya siblings. I love them! But it was a pain to ink their black hair... Tachibana was intended to be like a mini-Kazuhito-sama so that's why he's like that. Komaki-chan (I took the name "Komaki" from the name of a place near my house) is the perfect personification of everything I like. The part I put most of my effort into was her uniform!!

↑ Many people may think that my characters are filled with everything I like, but there's a lot of characters who turn out to be different once I draw them!! ...It happens a lot to me. So I'm really happy when I get the exact character I envisioned.

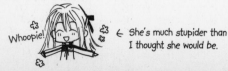

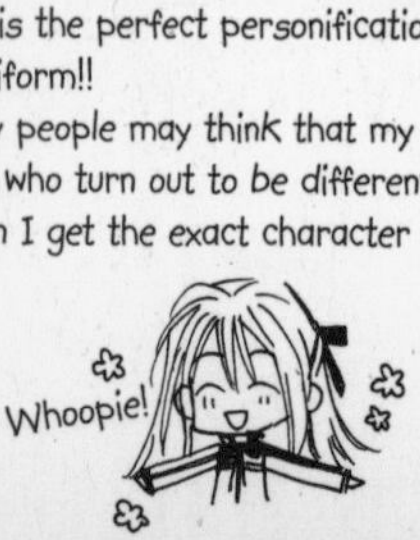
Whoopie!

← She's much stupider than I thought she would be.

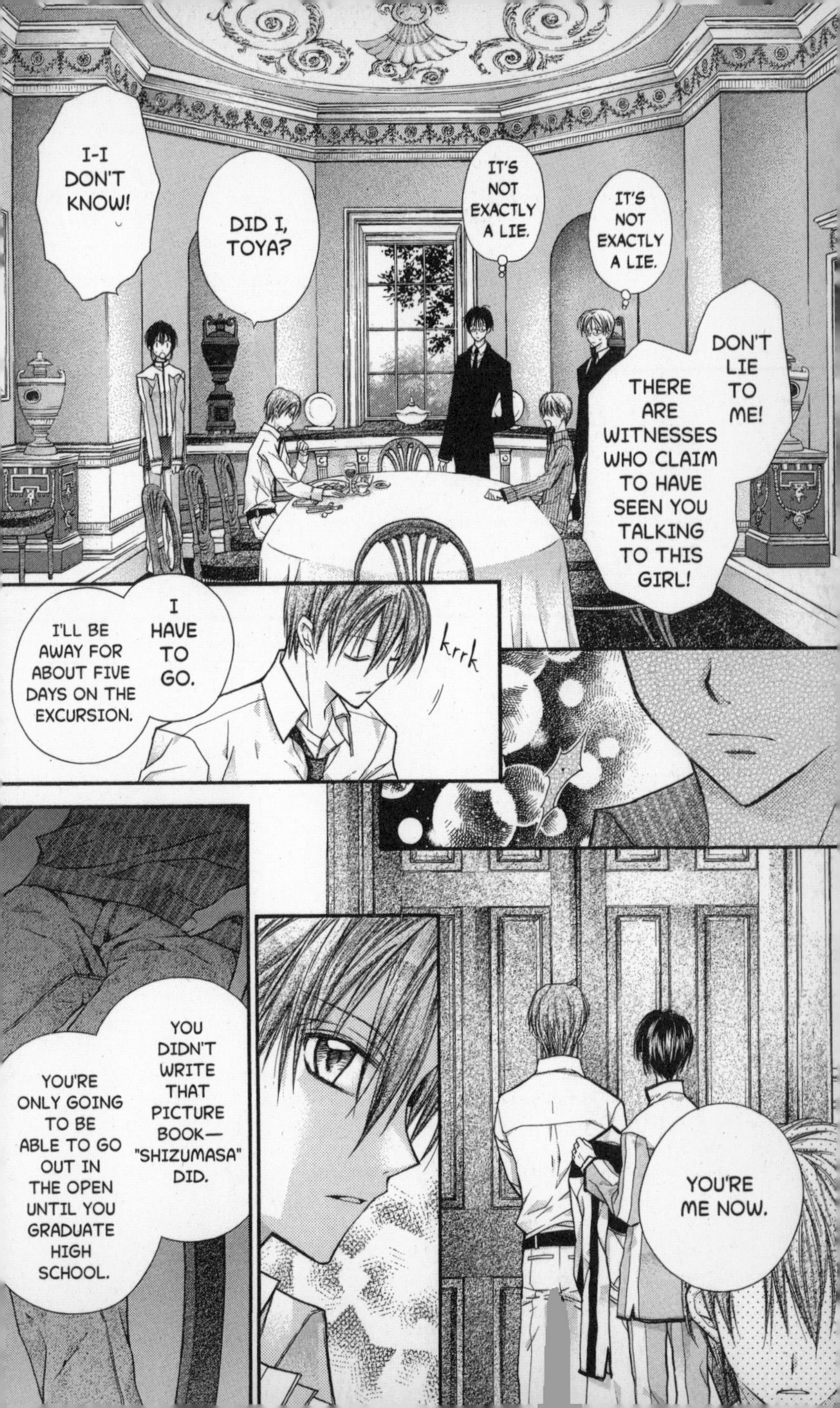
DON'T LIE TO ME!
THERE ARE WITNESSES WHO CLAIM TO HAVE SEEN YOU TALKING TO THIS GIRL!
IT'S NOT EXACTLY A LIE.
IT'S NOT EXACTLY A LIE.
DID I, TOYA?
I-I DON'T KNOW!
krrk
I HAVE TO GO.
I'LL BE AWAY FOR ABOUT FIVE DAYS ON THE EXCURSION.
YOU'RE ME NOW.
YOU DIDN'T WRITE THAT PICTURE BOOK— "SHIZUMASA" DID.
YOU'RE ONLY GOING TO BE ABLE TO GO OUT IN THE OPEN UNTIL YOU GRADUATE HIGH SCHOOL.

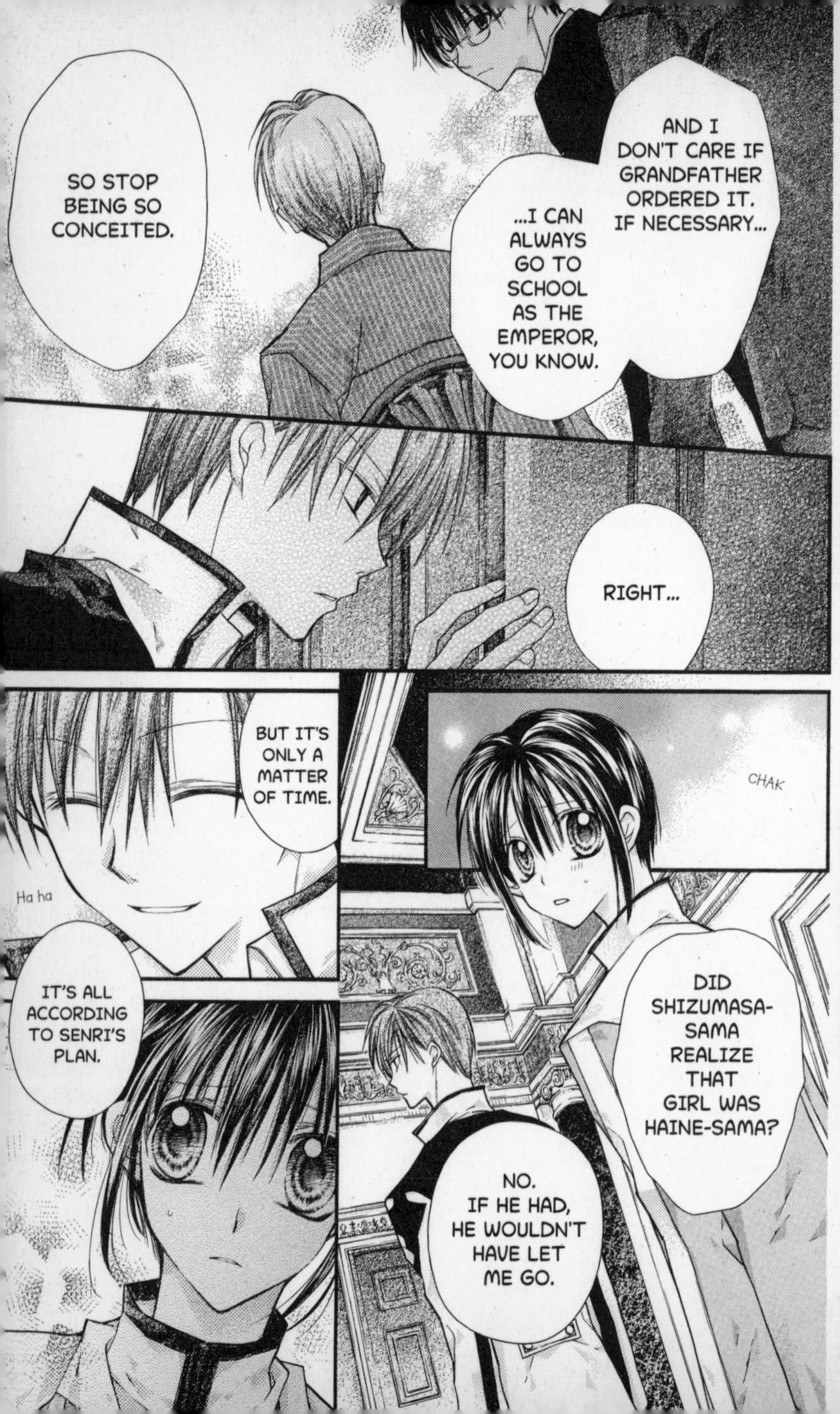
AND I DON'T CARE IF GRANDFATHER ORDERED IT. IF NECESSARY...
...I CAN ALWAYS GO TO SCHOOL AS THE EMPEROR, YOU KNOW.
SO STOP BEING SO CONCEITED.
RIGHT...
CHAK
DID SHIZUMASA-SAMA REALIZE THAT GIRL WAS HAINE-SAMA?
NO. IF HE HAD, HE WOULDN'T HAVE LET ME GO.
BUT IT'S ONLY A MATTER OF TIME.
Ha ha
IT'S ALL ACCORDING TO SENRI'S PLAN.

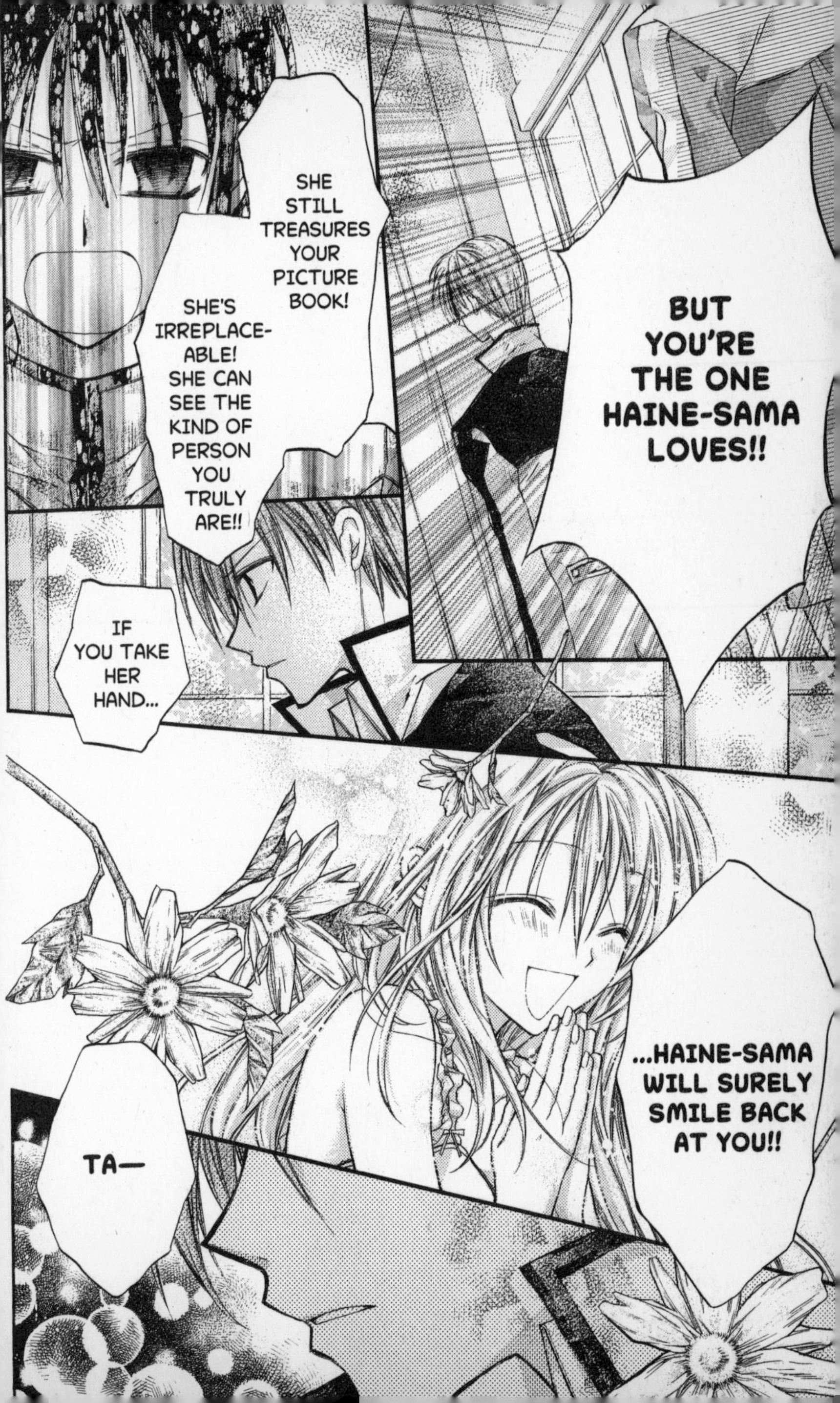
BUT YOU'RE THE ONE HAINE-SAMA LOVES!!
SHE STILL TREASURES YOUR PICTURE BOOK!
SHE'S IRREPLACE-ABLE! SHE CAN SEE THE KIND OF PERSON YOU TRULY ARE!!
IF YOU TAKE HER HAND...
...HAINE-SAMA WILL SURELY SMILE BACK AT YOU!!
TA—

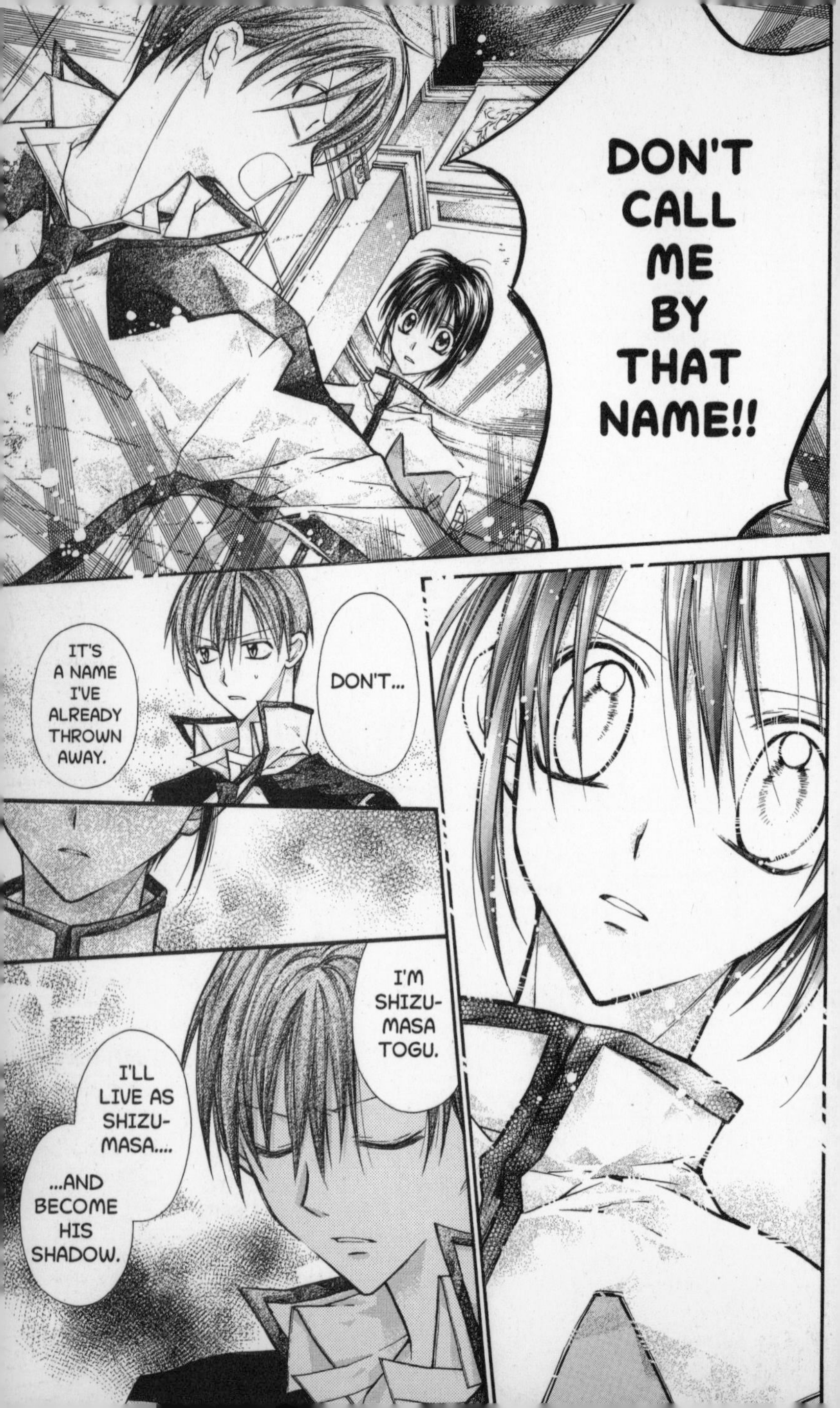
DON'T CALL ME BY THAT NAME!!
DON'T...
IT'S A NAME I'VE ALREADY THROWN AWAY.
I'M SHIZU-MASA TOGU.
I'LL LIVE AS SHIZU-MASA....
...AND BECOME HIS SHADOW.

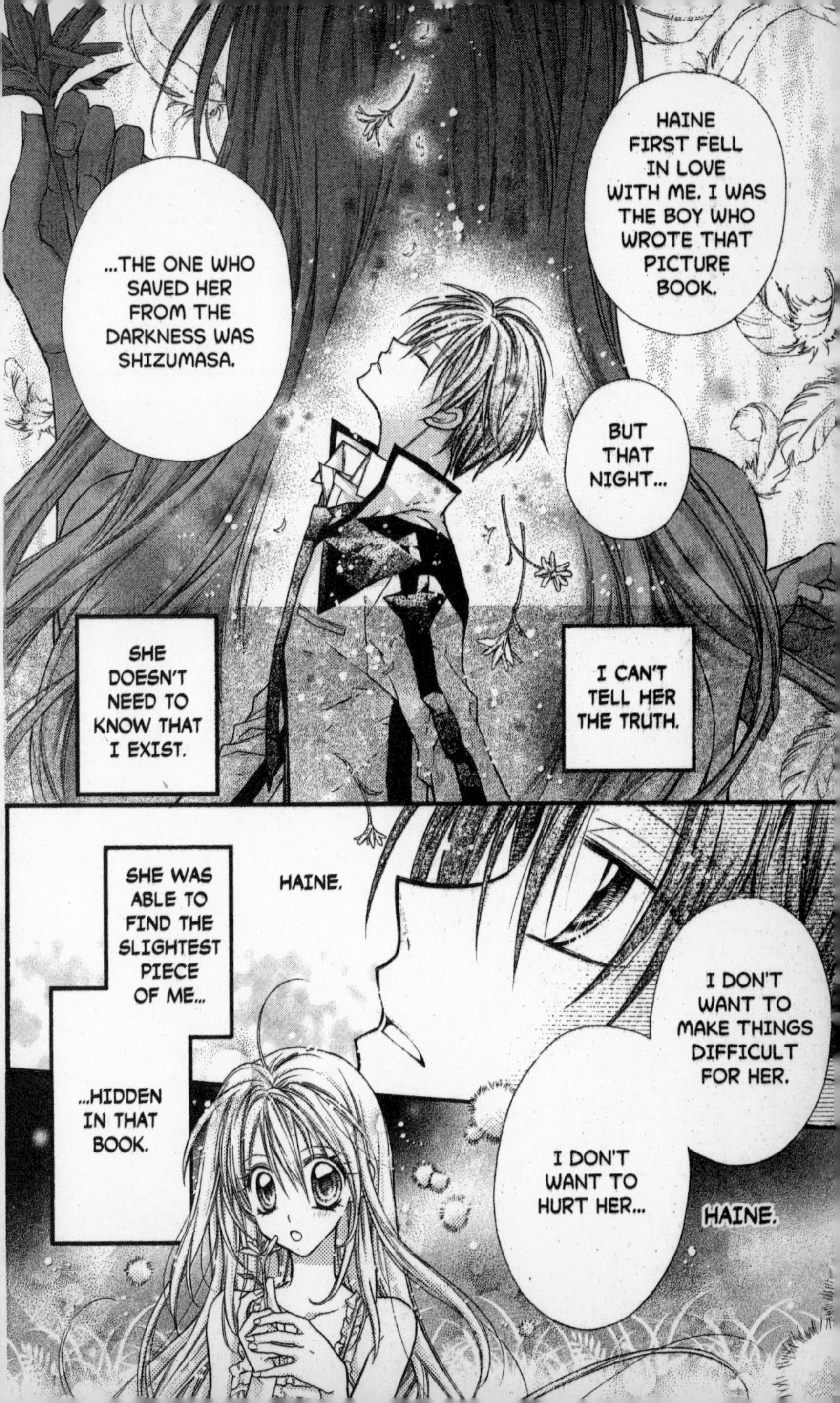
HAINE FIRST FELL IN LOVE WITH ME. I WAS THE BOY WHO WROTE THAT PICTURE BOOK.
BUT THAT NIGHT...
...THE ONE WHO SAVED HER FROM THE DARKNESS WAS SHIZUMASA.
I CAN'T TELL HER THE TRUTH.
SHE DOESN'T NEED TO KNOW THAT I EXIST.
I DON'T WANT TO MAKE THINGS DIFFICULT FOR HER.
I DON'T WANT TO HURT HER...
HAINE.
HAINE.
SHE WAS ABLE TO FIND THE SLIGHTEST PIECE OF ME...
...HIDDEN IN THAT BOOK.

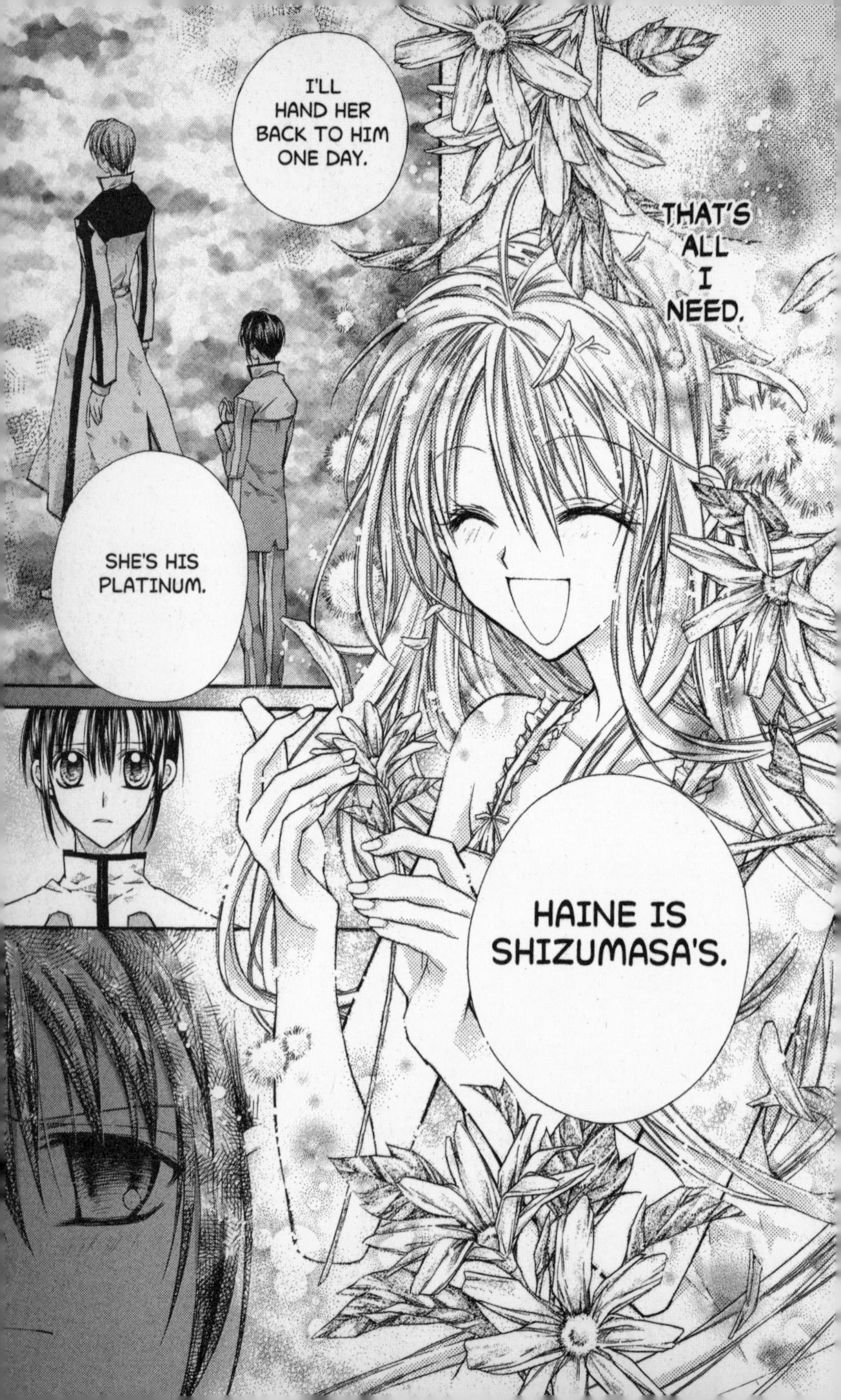
THAT'S ALL I NEED.
HAINE IS SHIZUMASA'S.
I'LL HAND HER BACK TO HIM ONE DAY.
SHE'S HIS PLATINUM.

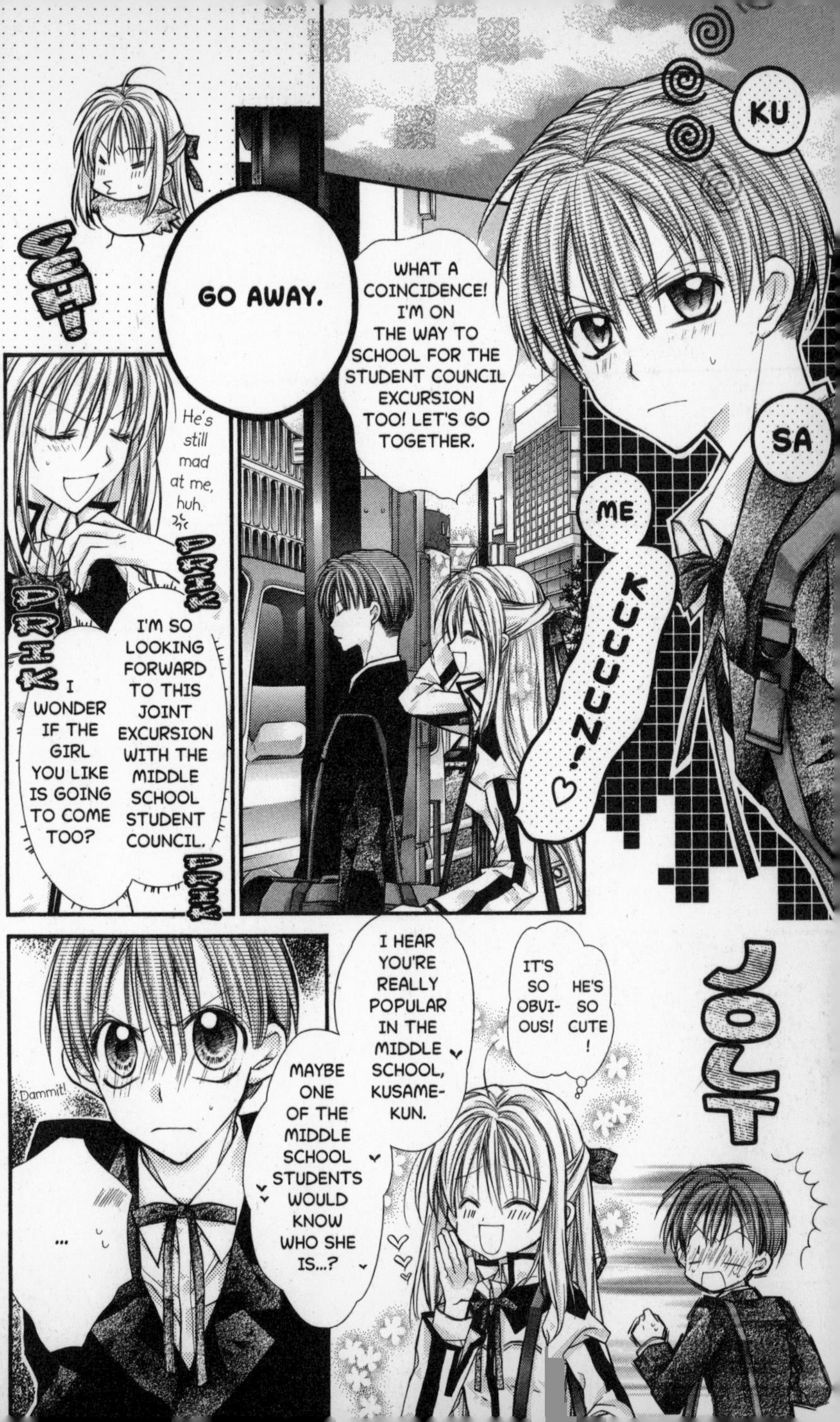
KU
SA
ME
KUUUUN!♡
WHAT A COINCIDENCE! I'M ON THE WAY TO SCHOOL FOR THE STUDENT COUNCIL EXCURSION TOO! LET'S GO TOGETHER.
GO AWAY.
He's still mad at me, huh.
I'M SO LOOKING FORWARD TO THIS JOINT EXCURSION WITH THE MIDDLE SCHOOL STUDENT COUNCIL.
I WONDER IF THE GIRL YOU LIKE IS GOING TO COME TOO?
PRIK
JOLT
IT'S SO OBVIOUS!
HE'S SO CUTE!
I HEAR YOU'RE REALLY POPULAR IN THE MIDDLE SCHOOL, KUSAME-KUN.
MAYBE ONE OF THE MIDDLE SCHOOL STUDENTS WOULD KNOW WHO SHE IS...?
Dammit!
...

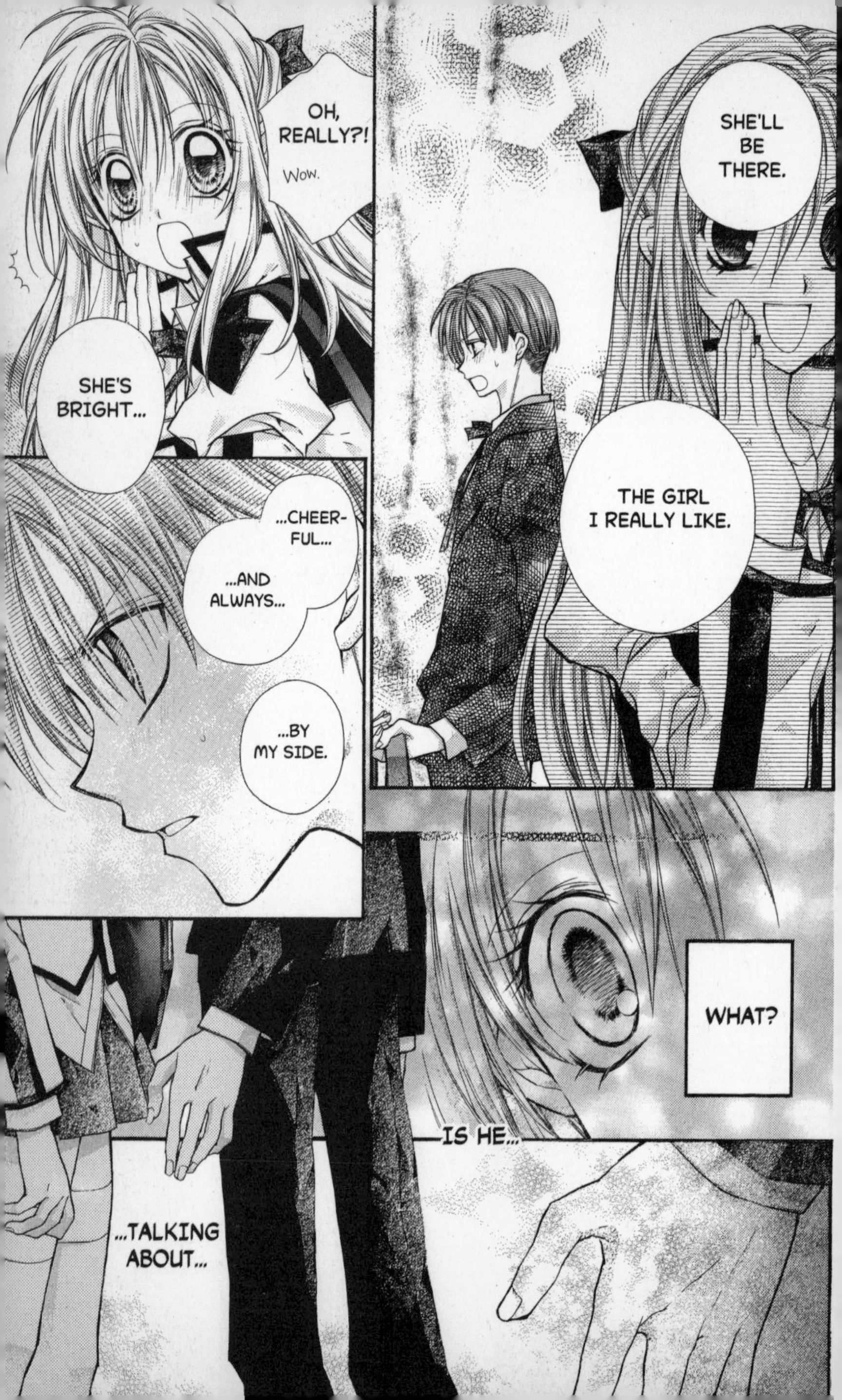
SHE'LL BE THERE.
THE GIRL I REALLY LIKE.
OH, REALLY?!
Wow.
SHE'S BRIGHT...
...CHEERFUL...
...AND ALWAYS...
...BY MY SIDE.
WHAT?
IS HE...
...TALKING ABOUT...

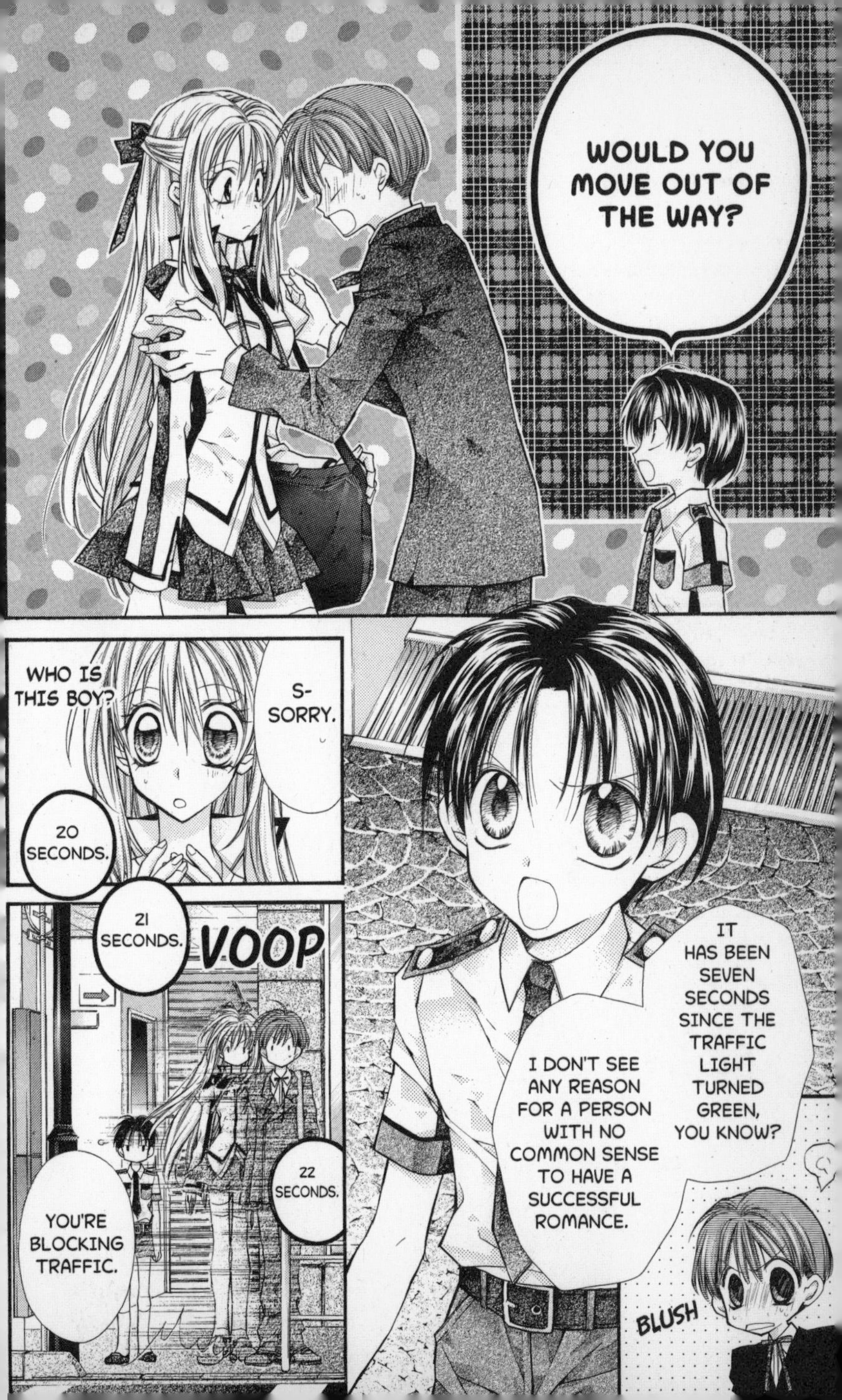
WOULD YOU MOVE OUT OF THE WAY?
IT HAS BEEN SEVEN SECONDS SINCE THE TRAFFIC LIGHT TURNED GREEN, YOU KNOW?
I DON'T SEE ANY REASON FOR A PERSON WITH NO COMMON SENSE TO HAVE A SUCCESSFUL ROMANCE.
BLUSH
S-SORRY.
WHO IS THIS BOY?
20 SECONDS.
21 SECONDS.
VOOP
22 SECONDS.
YOU'RE BLOCKING TRAFFIC.

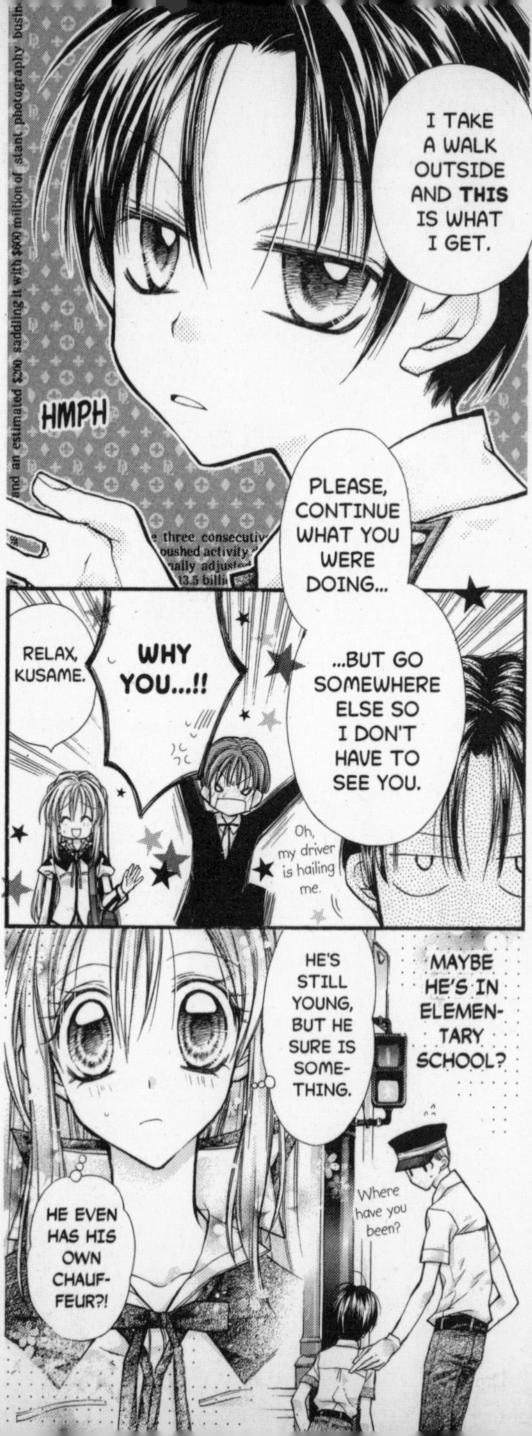
I TAKE A WALK OUTSIDE AND **THIS** IS WHAT I GET.
HMPH
PLEASE, CONTINUE WHAT YOU WERE DOING...
...BUT GO SOMEWHERE ELSE SO I DON'T HAVE TO SEE YOU.
Oh, my driver is hailing me.
WHY YOU...!!
RELAX, KUSAME.
MAYBE HE'S IN ELEMENTARY SCHOOL?
HE'S STILL YOUNG, BUT HE SURE IS SOMETHING.
Where have you been?
HE EVEN HAS HIS OWN CHAUFFEUR?!

Full Moon Final Live 4

To tell you the truth... I was concentrating so much on singing that I don't remember much. (I'm sorry.)

I'll be glad if you'd not think too much about whether I'm good at singing or not, and just enjoy the differences between myco's song and my song. (Mine's just an added bonus...You know, a little fun on my part. Really.) ← ////

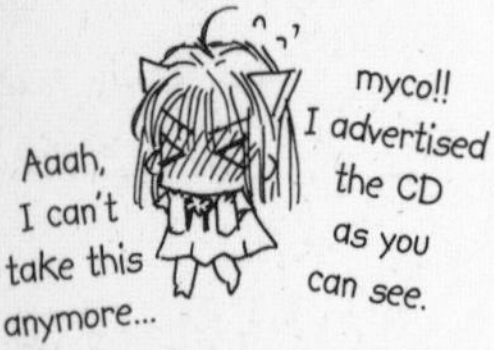
Aaah, I can't take this anymore...
myco!! I advertised the CD as you can see.

All the Changin' My Life songs that were used in *Full Moon* are included in this CD, and it even includes a special drama track. There's also a cover by Meroko and Takuto, so it truly is the *Full Moon* greatest hits album!! Please give it a listen when you have the chance.

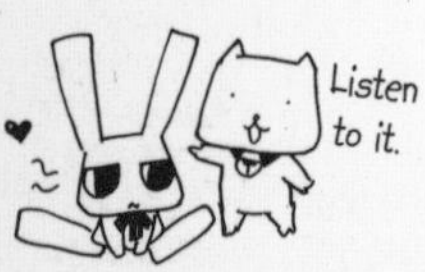
Listen to it.

●END●

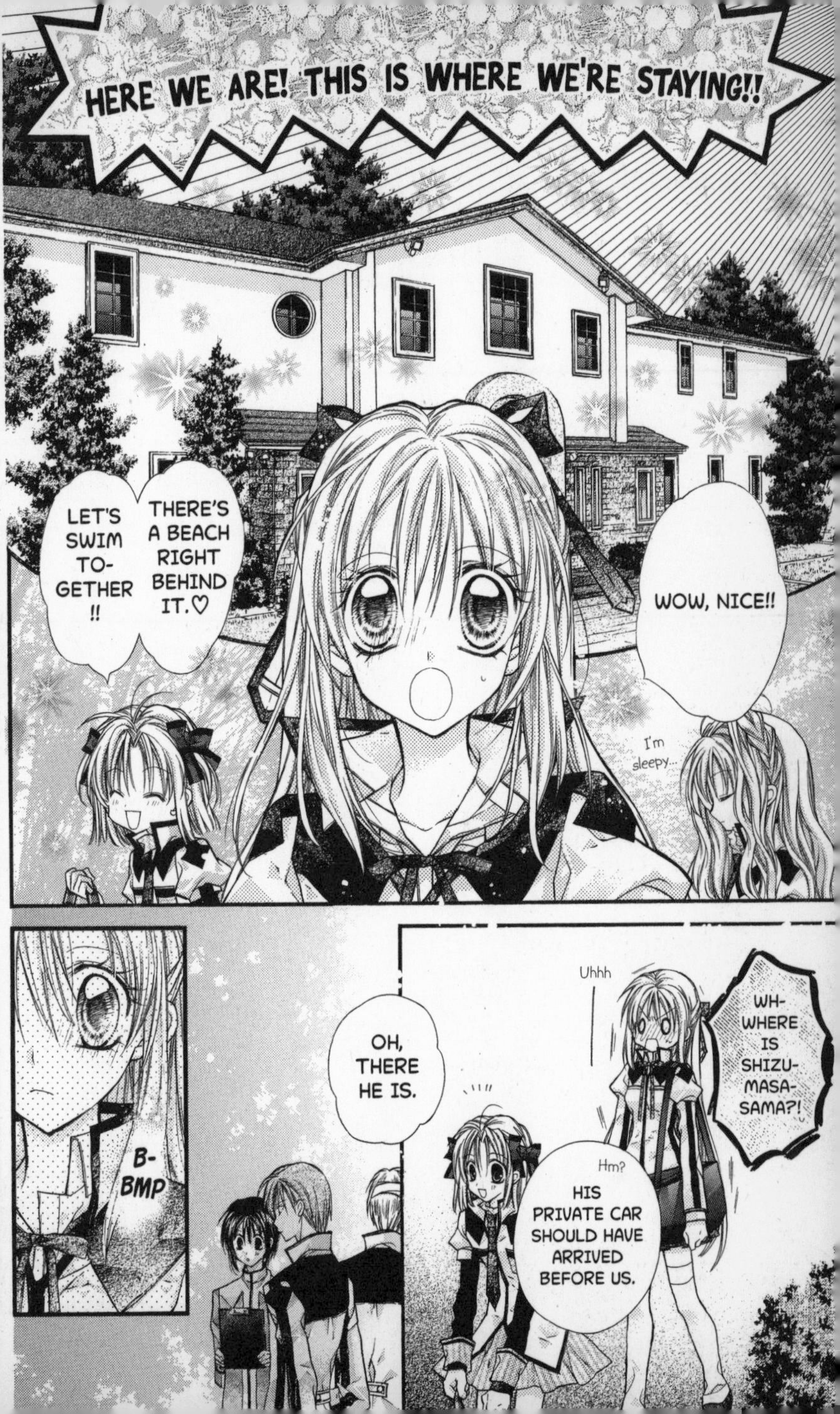
HERE WE ARE! THIS IS WHERE WE'RE STAYING!!
WOW, NICE!!
I'm sleepy...
THERE'S A BEACH RIGHT BEHIND IT.♡
LET'S SWIM TO-GETHER!!
WH-WHERE IS SHIZU-MASA-SAMA?!
Uhhh
Hm?
HIS PRIVATE CAR SHOULD HAVE ARRIVED BEFORE US.
OH, THERE HE IS.
B-BMP

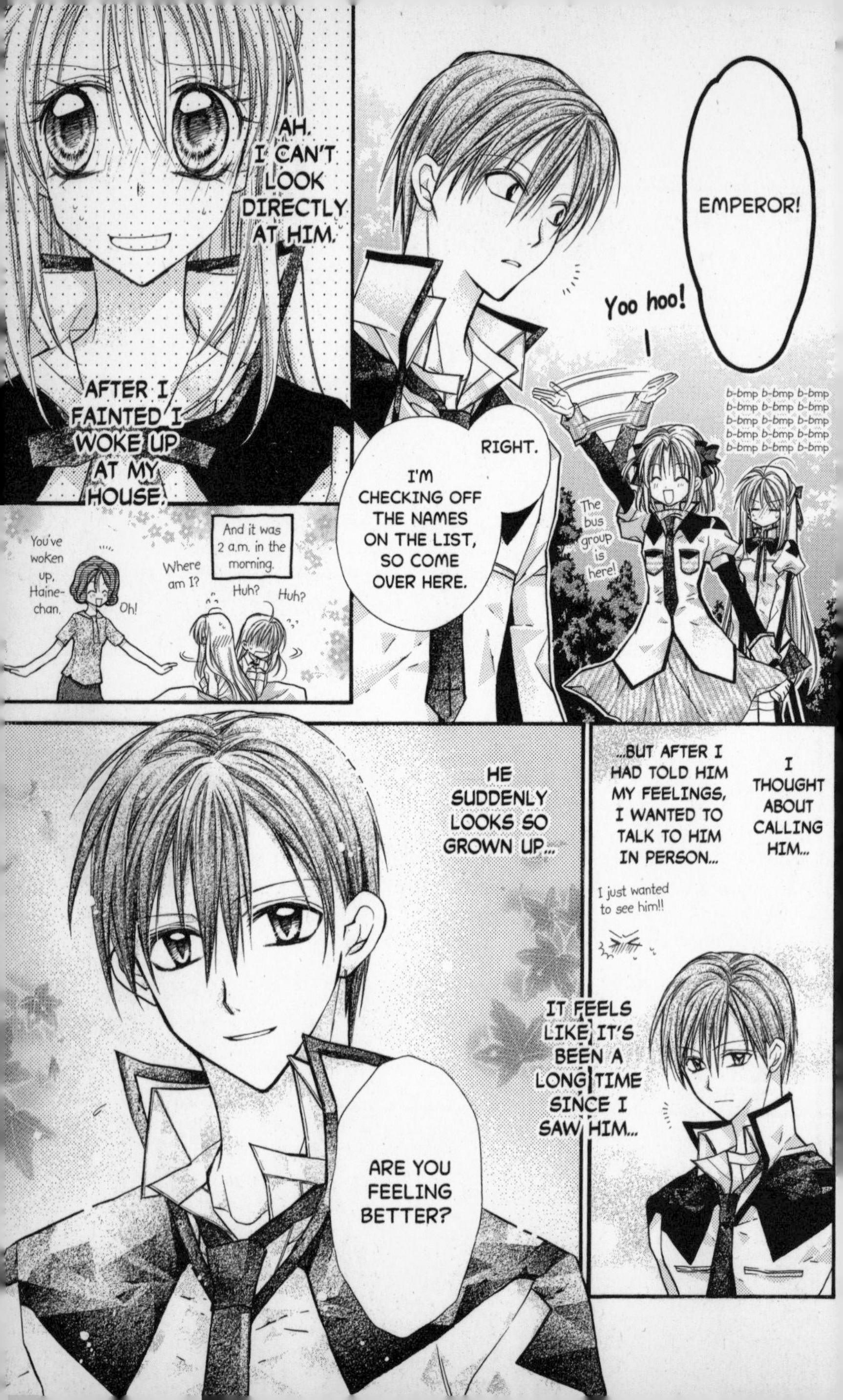

EMPEROR!
Yoo hoo!
b-bmp b-bmp b-bmp b-bmp b-bmp b-bmp b-bmp b-bmp b-bmp b-bmp b-bmp b-bmp b-bmp b-bmp b-bmp
The bus group is here!
RIGHT.
I'M CHECKING OFF THE NAMES ON THE LIST, SO COME OVER HERE.
AH. I CAN'T LOOK DIRECTLY AT HIM.
AFTER I FAINTED I WOKE UP AT MY HOUSE.
And it was 2 a.m. in the morning.
Where am I?
Huh?
Huh?
You've woken up, Haine-chan.
Oh!
I THOUGHT ABOUT CALLING HIM...
...BUT AFTER I HAD TOLD HIM MY FEELINGS, I WANTED TO TALK TO HIM IN PERSON...
I just wanted to see him!!
IT FEELS LIKE IT'S BEEN A LONG TIME SINCE I SAW HIM...
HE SUDDENLY LOOKS SO GROWN UP...
ARE YOU FEELING BETTER?

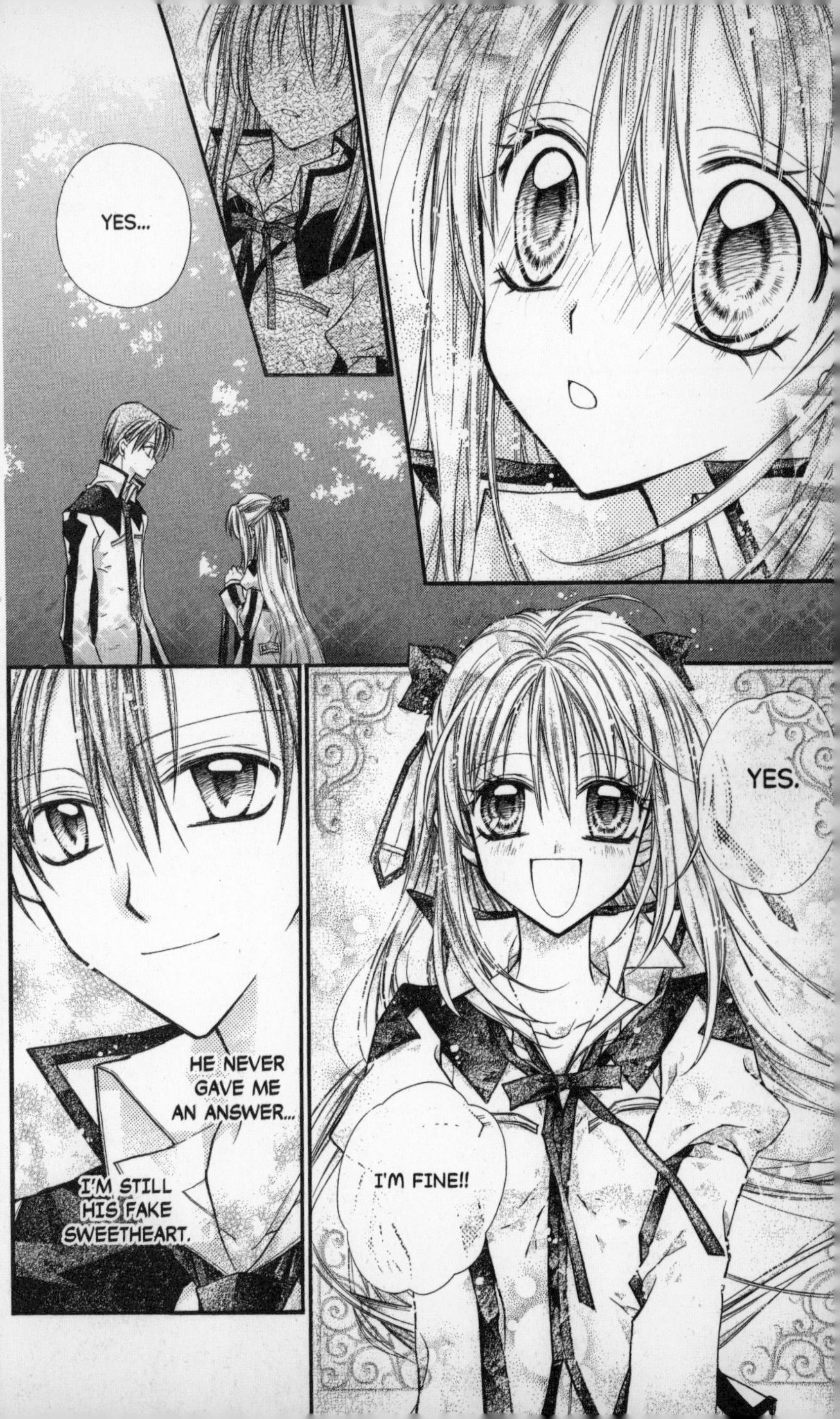
YES...
YES.
I'M FINE!!
HE NEVER GAVE ME AN ANSWER...
I'M STILL HIS FAKE SWEETHEART.

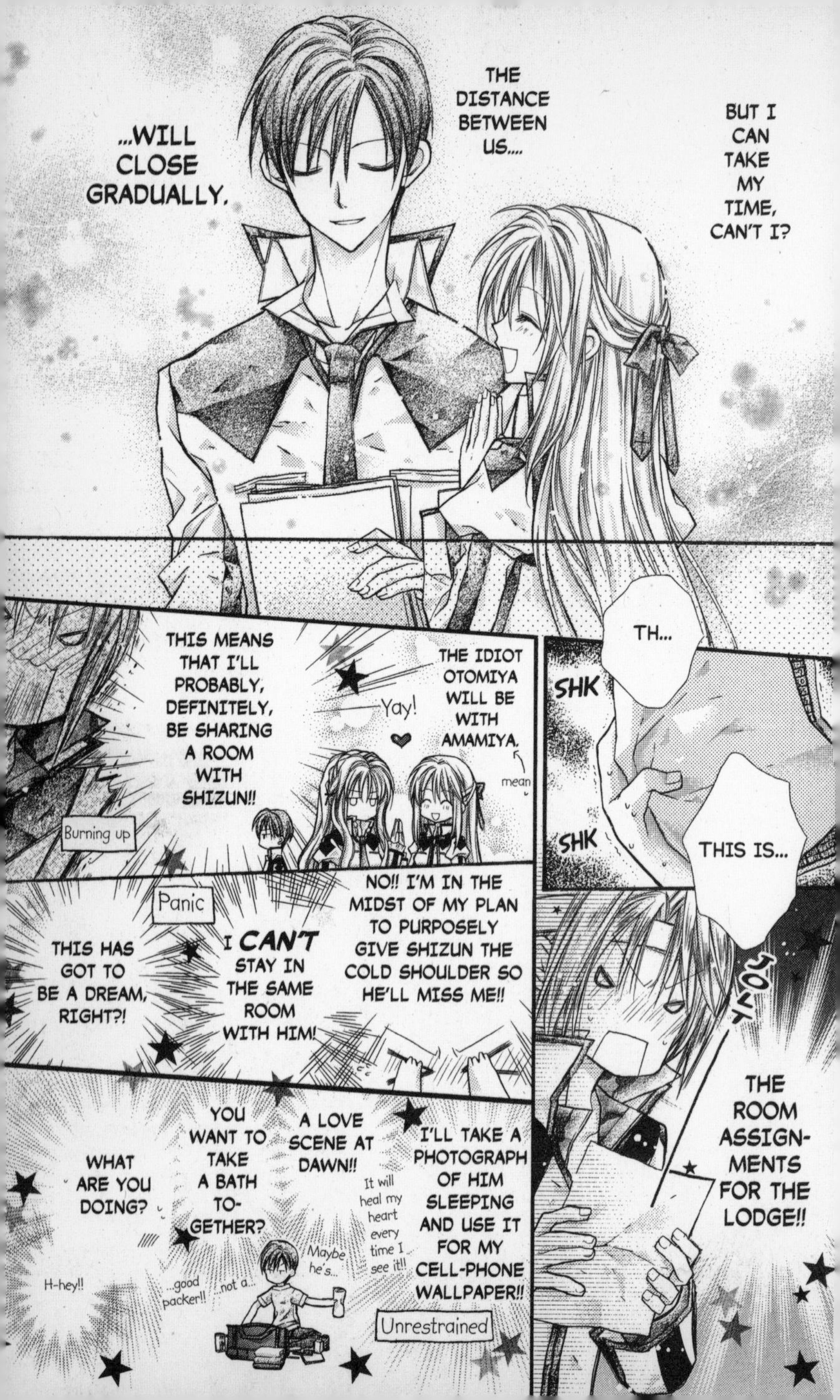

BUT I CAN TAKE MY TIME, CAN'T I?
THE DISTANCE BETWEEN US....
...WILL CLOSE GRADUALLY.
TH...
SHK
SHK
THIS IS...
YOINK
THE ROOM ASSIGNMENTS FOR THE LODGE!!
THIS MEANS THAT I'LL PROBABLY, DEFINITELY, BE SHARING A ROOM WITH SHIZUN!!
THE IDIOT OTOMIYA WILL BE WITH AMAMIYA.
mean
Yay!
Burning up
NO!! I'M IN THE MIDST OF MY PLAN TO PURPOSELY GIVE SHIZUN THE COLD SHOULDER SO HE'LL MISS ME!!
I CAN'T STAY IN THE SAME ROOM WITH HIM!
Panic
THIS HAS GOT TO BE A DREAM, RIGHT?!
I'LL TAKE A PHOTOGRAPH OF HIM SLEEPING AND USE IT FOR MY CELL-PHONE WALLPAPER!!
It will heal my heart every time I see it!!
A LOVE SCENE AT DAWN!!
YOU WANT TO TAKE A BATH TO-GETHER?
WHAT ARE YOU DOING?
Maybe he's...
...not a...
...good packer!!
H-hey!!
Unrestrained

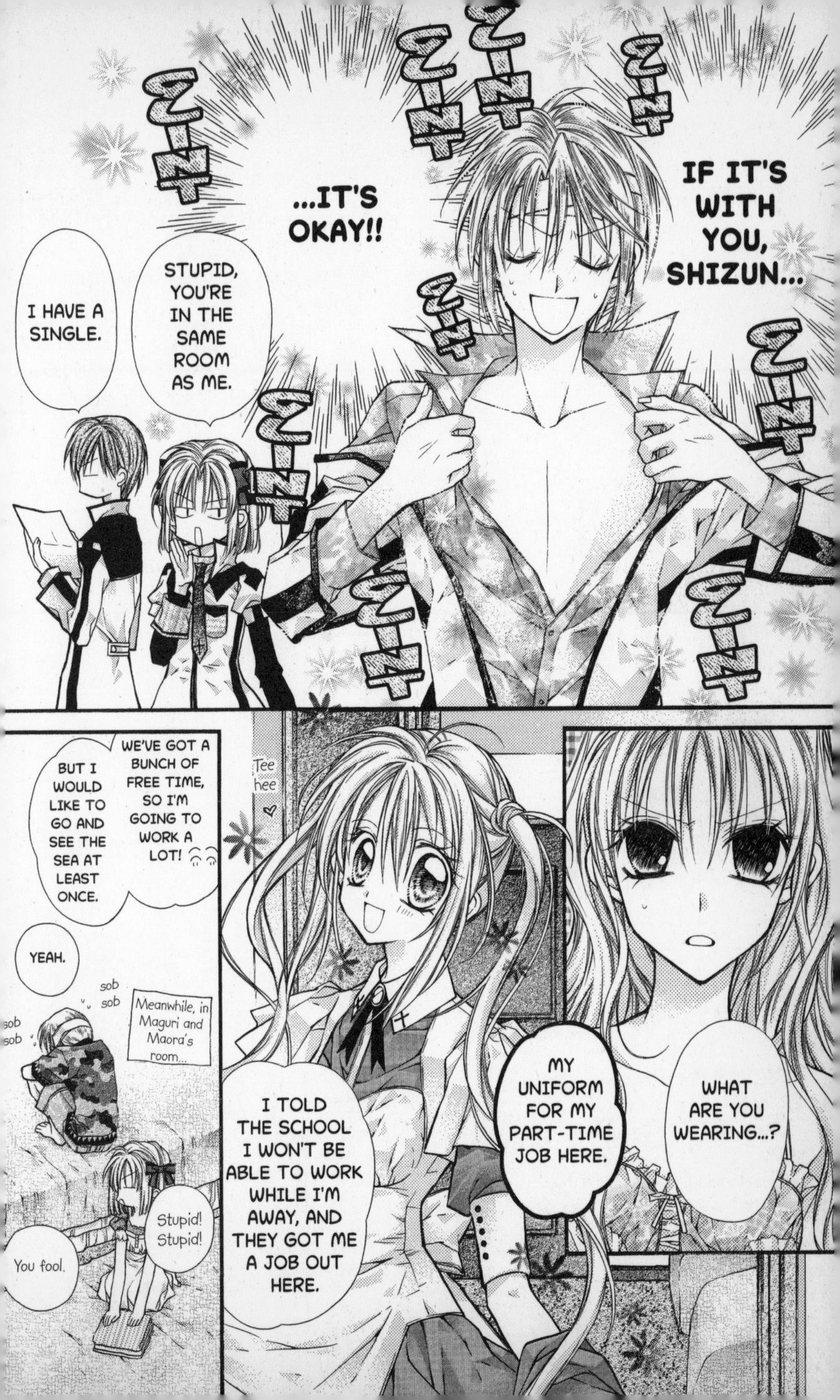
IF IT'S WITH YOU, SHIZUN...
...IT'S OKAY!!
STUPID, YOU'RE IN THE SAME ROOM AS ME.
I HAVE A SINGLE.
WHAT ARE YOU WEARING...?
Tee hee
MY UNIFORM FOR MY PART-TIME JOB HERE.
I TOLD THE SCHOOL I WON'T BE ABLE TO WORK WHILE I'M AWAY, AND THEY GOT ME A JOB OUT HERE.
WE'VE GOT A BUNCH OF FREE TIME, SO I'M GOING TO WORK A LOT!
BUT I WOULD LIKE TO GO AND SEE THE SEA AT LEAST ONCE.
YEAH.
Meanwhile, in Maguri and Maora's room...
sob sob
sob sob
Stupid! Stupid!
You fool.

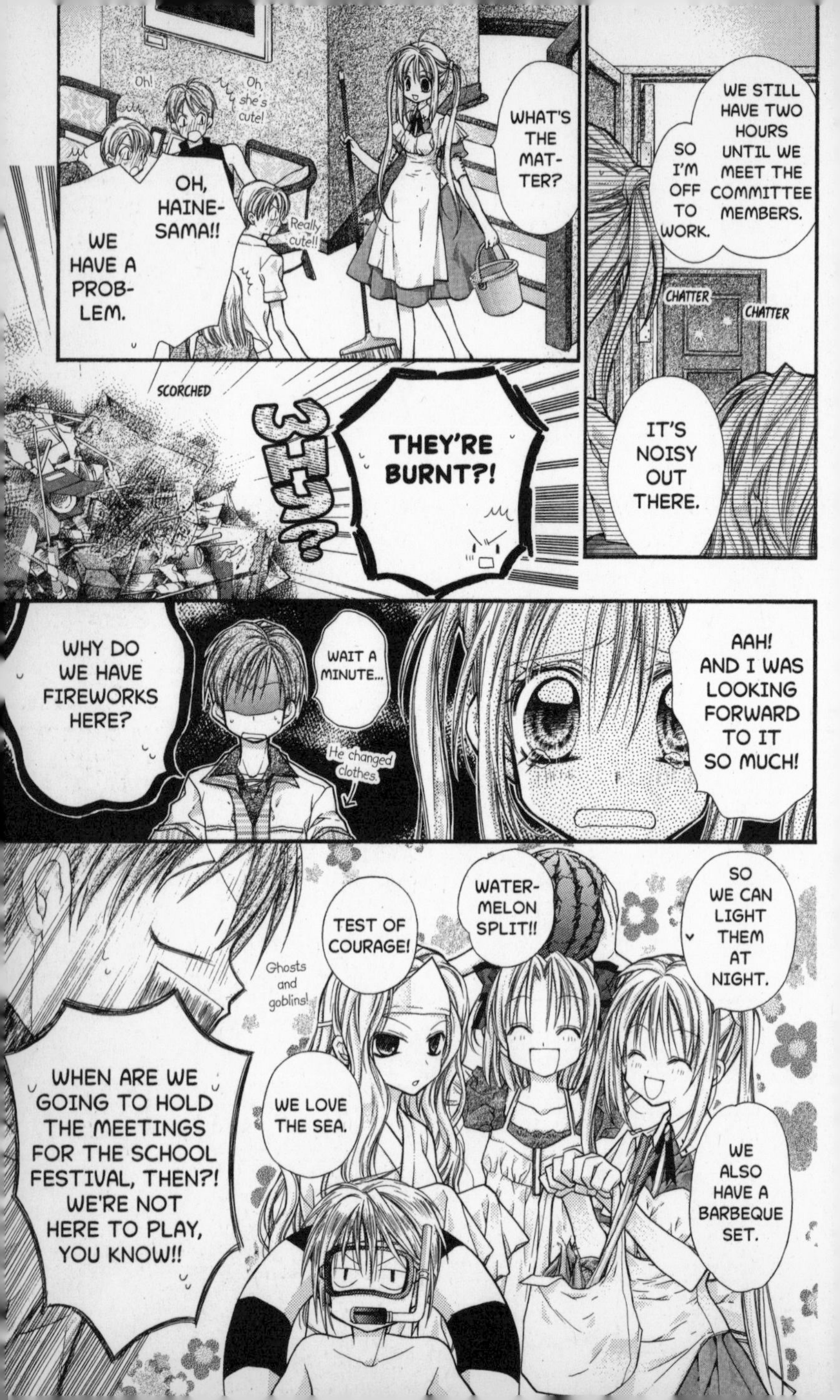
WE STILL HAVE TWO HOURS UNTIL WE MEET THE COMMITTEE MEMBERS.
SO I'M OFF TO WORK.
CHATTER
CHATTER
IT'S NOISY OUT THERE.
WHAT'S THE MAT-TER?
Oh, she's cute!
Oh!
OH, HAINE-SAMA!!
Really cute!!
WE HAVE A PROB-LEM.
THEY'RE BURNT?!
SCORCHED
AAH! AND I WAS LOOKING FORWARD TO IT SO MUCH!
WAIT A MINUTE...
He changed clothes.
WHY DO WE HAVE FIREWORKS HERE?
SO WE CAN LIGHT THEM AT NIGHT.
WATER-MELON SPLIT!!
TEST OF COURAGE!
Ghosts and goblins!
WE ALSO HAVE A BARBEQUE SET.
WE LOVE THE SEA.
WHEN ARE WE GOING TO HOLD THE MEETINGS FOR THE SCHOOL FESTIVAL, THEN?! WE'RE NOT HERE TO PLAY, YOU KNOW!!

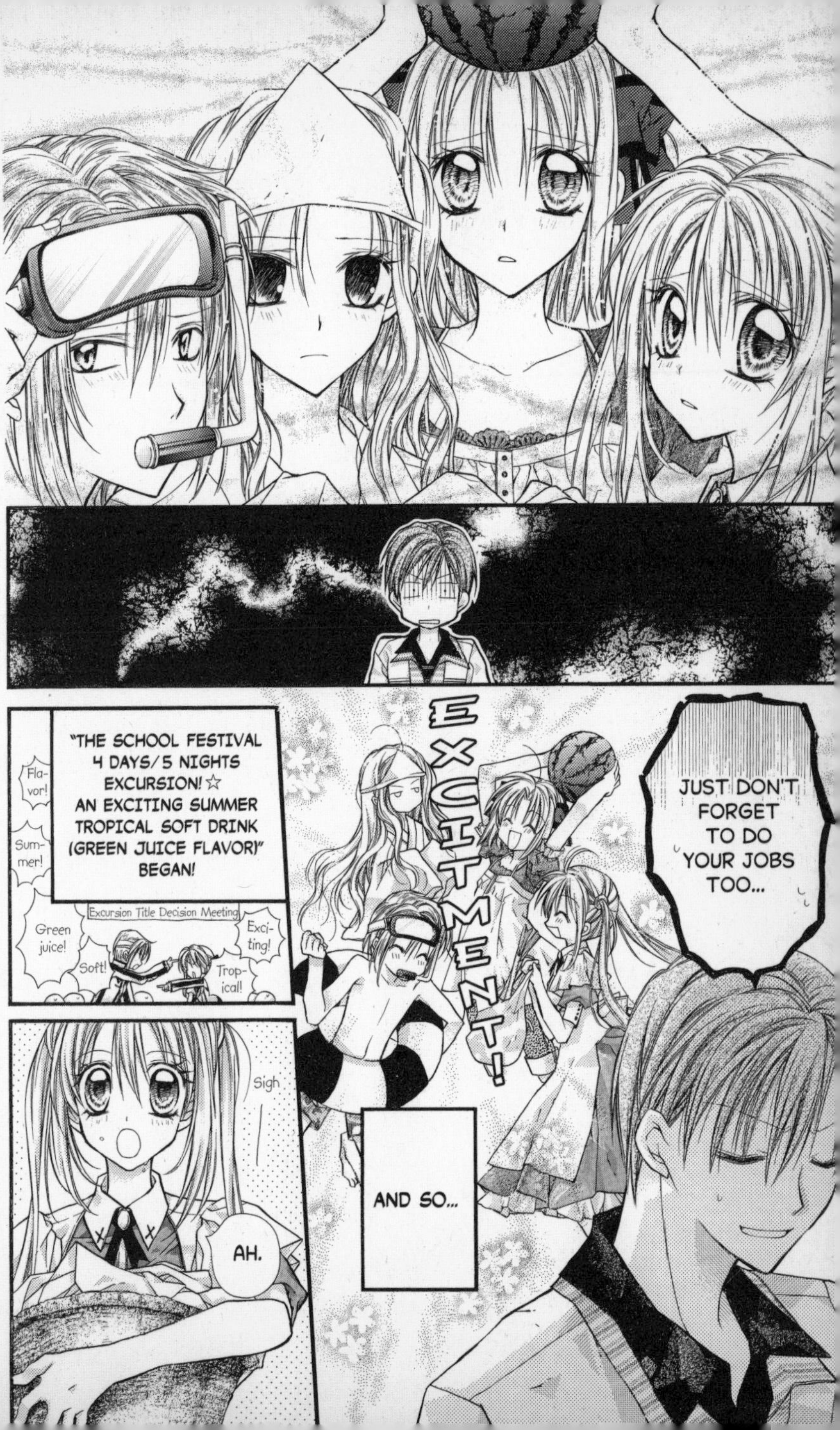
JUST DON'T FORGET TO DO YOUR JOBS TOO...
EXCITEMENT!
"THE SCHOOL FESTIVAL 4 DAYS/5 NIGHTS EXCURSION! ☆ AN EXCITING SUMMER TROPICAL SOFT DRINK (GREEN JUICE FLAVOR)" BEGAN!
Fla-vor!
Sum-mer!
Excursion Title Decision Meeting
Exci-ting!
Trop-ical!
Green juice!
Soft!
AND SO...
Sigh
AH.

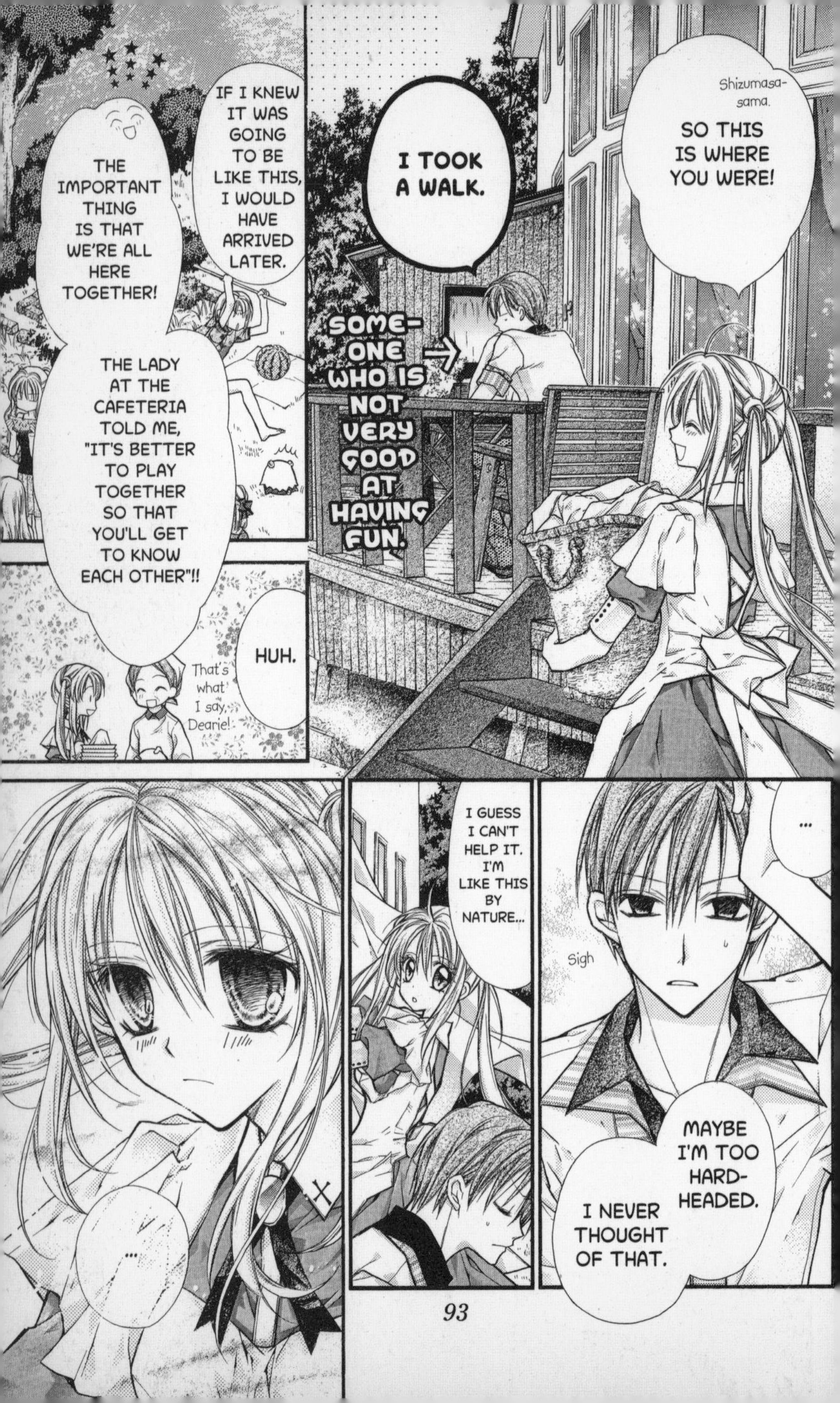
Shizumasa-sama.
SO THIS IS WHERE YOU WERE!
I TOOK A WALK.
SOME-ONE WHO IS NOT VERY GOOD AT HAVING FUN.
IF I KNEW IT WAS GOING TO BE LIKE THIS, I WOULD HAVE ARRIVED LATER.
THE IMPORTANT THING IS THAT WE'RE ALL HERE TOGETHER!
THE LADY AT THE CAFETERIA TOLD ME, "IT'S BETTER TO PLAY TOGETHER SO THAT YOU'LL GET TO KNOW EACH OTHER"!!
HUH.
That's what I say, Dearie!
...
Sigh
MAYBE I'M TOO HARD-HEADED.
I NEVER THOUGHT OF THAT.
I GUESS I CAN'T HELP IT. I'M LIKE THIS BY NATURE...
...

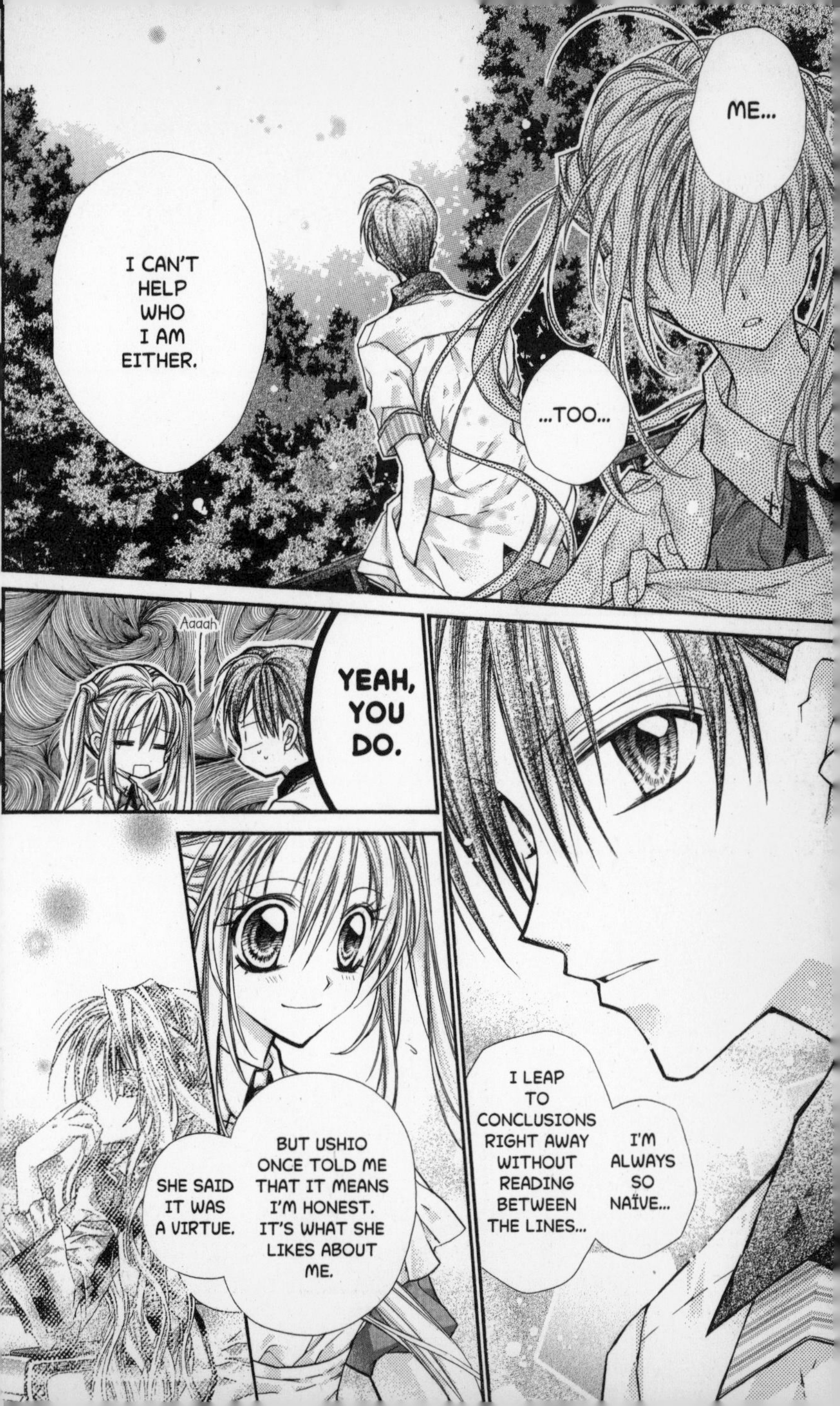
ME...
...TOO...
I CAN'T HELP WHO I AM EITHER.
I'M ALWAYS SO NAÏVE...
I LEAP TO CONCLUSIONS RIGHT AWAY WITHOUT READING BETWEEN THE LINES...
YEAH, YOU DO.
Aaaah
BUT USHIO ONCE TOLD ME THAT IT MEANS I'M HONEST. IT'S WHAT SHE LIKES ABOUT ME.
SHE SAID IT WAS A VIRTUE.

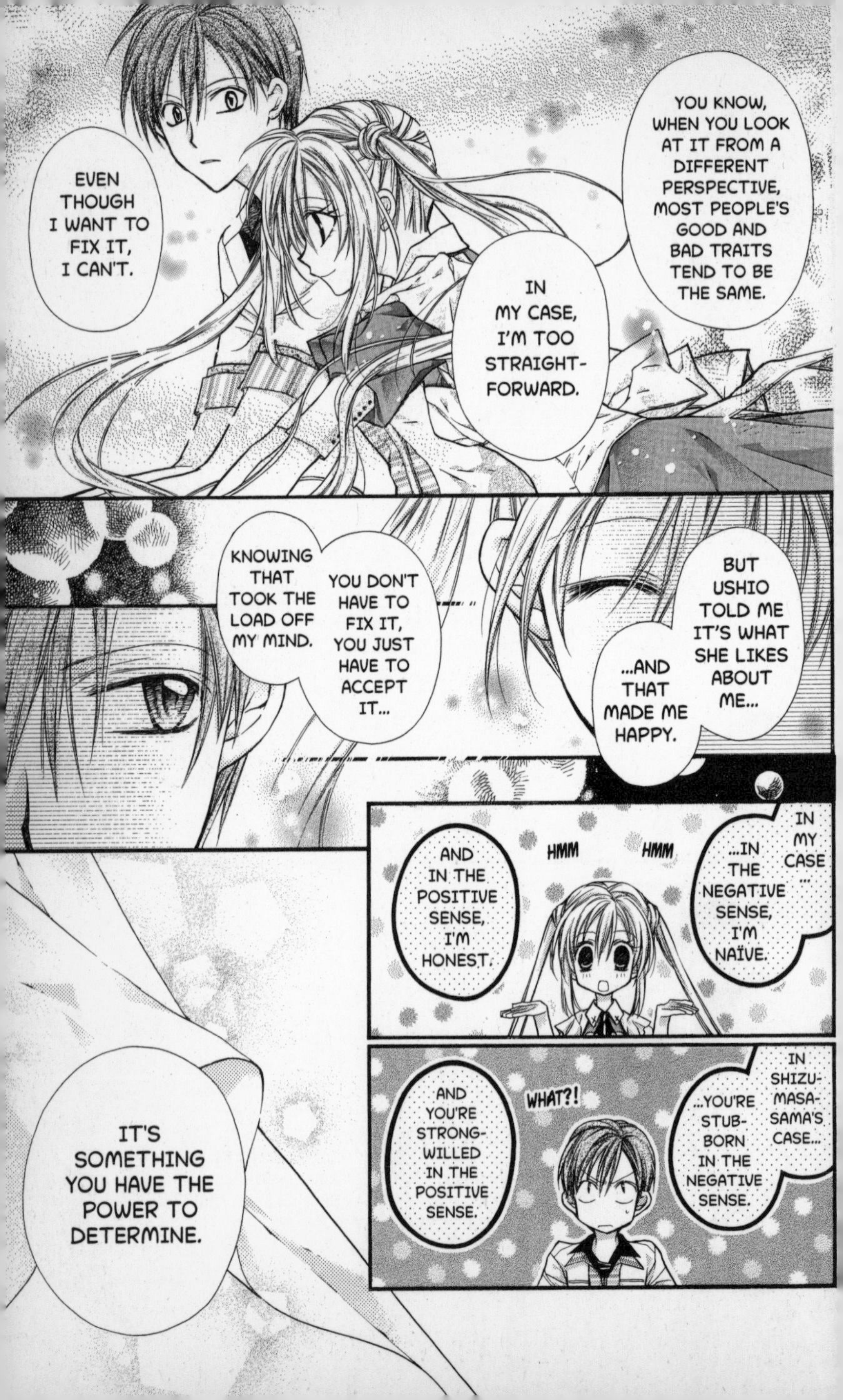
YOU KNOW, WHEN YOU LOOK AT IT FROM A DIFFERENT PERSPECTIVE, MOST PEOPLE'S GOOD AND BAD TRAITS TEND TO BE THE SAME.
IN MY CASE, I'M TOO STRAIGHT-FORWARD.
EVEN THOUGH I WANT TO FIX IT, I CAN'T.
BUT USHIO TOLD ME IT'S WHAT SHE LIKES ABOUT ME...
...AND THAT MADE ME HAPPY.
YOU DON'T HAVE TO FIX IT, YOU JUST HAVE TO ACCEPT IT...
KNOWING THAT TOOK THE LOAD OFF MY MIND.
IN MY CASE...
...IN THE NEGATIVE SENSE, I'M NAÏVE.
HMM
HMM
AND IN THE POSITIVE SENSE, I'M HONEST.
IN SHIZU-MASA-SAMA'S CASE...
...YOU'RE STUB-BORN IN THE NEGATIVE SENSE.
WHAT?!
AND YOU'RE STRONG-WILLED IN THE POSITIVE SENSE.
IT'S SOMETHING YOU HAVE THE POWER TO DETERMINE.

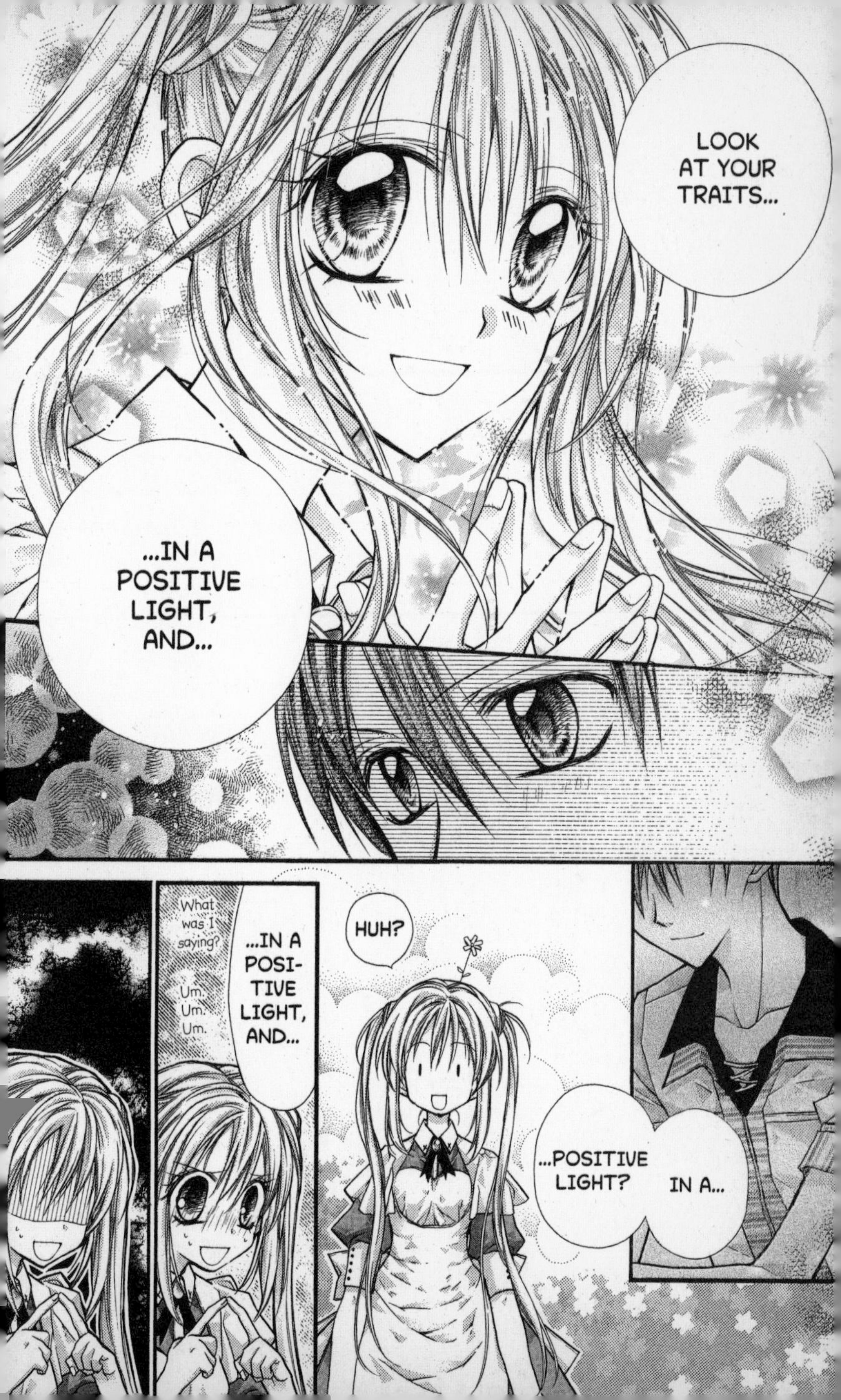
LOOK AT YOUR TRAITS...
...IN A POSITIVE LIGHT, AND...
IN A...
...POSITIVE LIGHT?
HUH?
...IN A POSI-TIVE LIGHT, AND...
What was I saying?
Um. Um. Um.

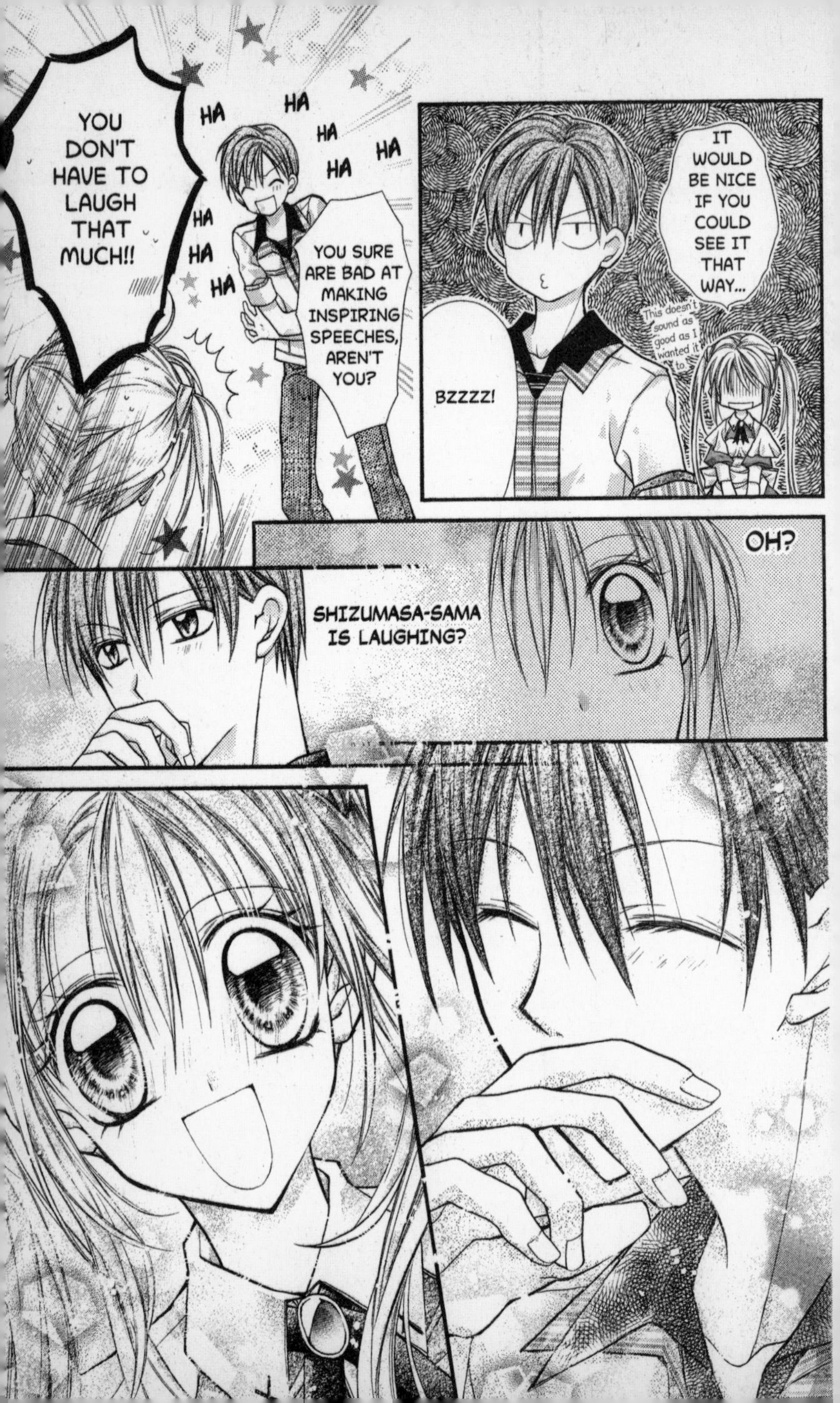
IT WOULD BE NICE IF YOU COULD SEE IT THAT WAY...
BZZZZ!
This doesn't sound as good as I wanted it to.
HA HA HA HA HA HA HA HA
YOU SURE ARE BAD AT MAKING INSPIRING SPEECHES, AREN'T YOU?
YOU DON'T HAVE TO LAUGH THAT MUCH!!
OH?
SHIZUMASA-SAMA IS LAUGHING?

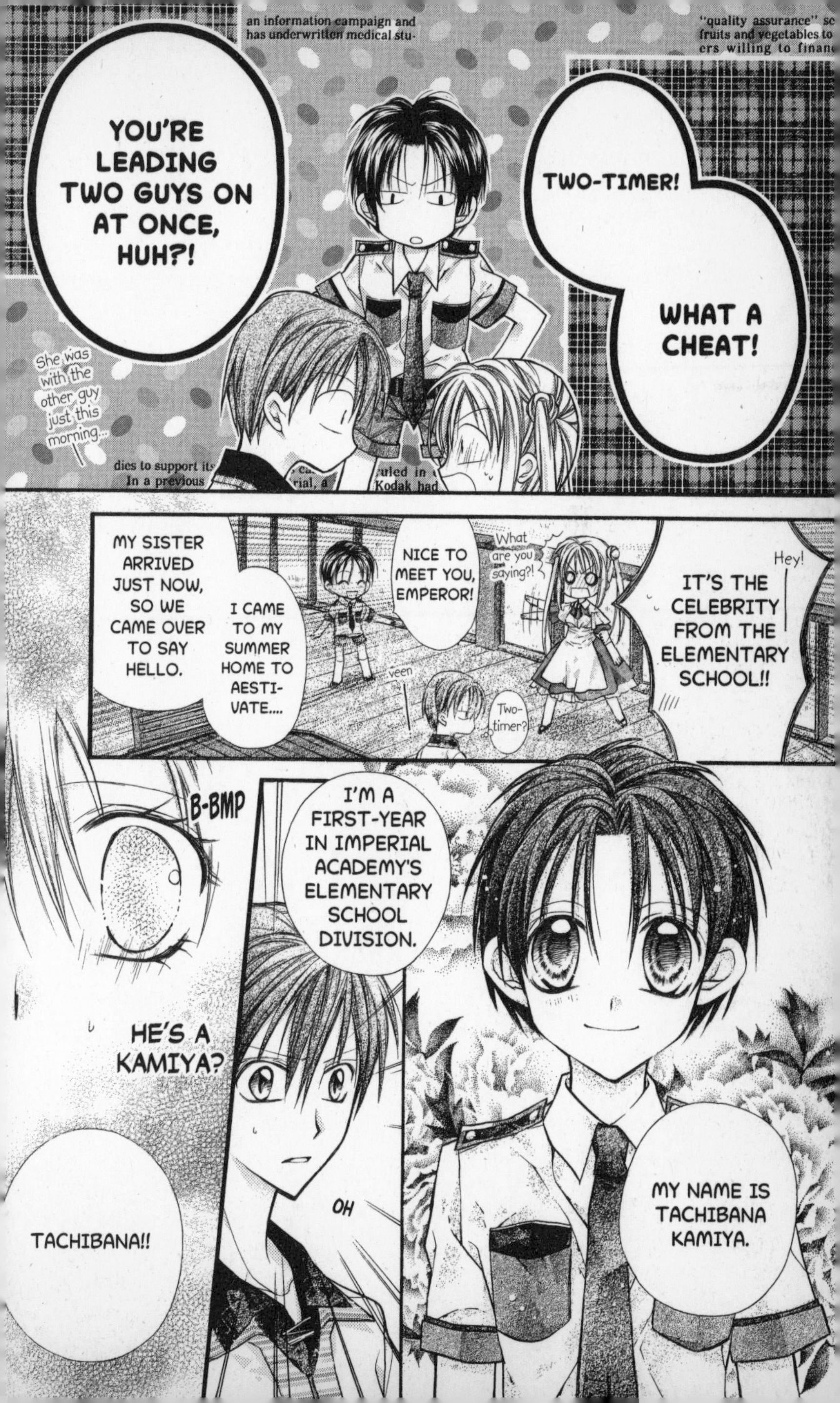
TWO-TIMER!
WHAT A CHEAT!
YOU'RE LEADING TWO GUYS ON AT ONCE, HUH?!
She was with the other guy just this morning...
Hey!
IT'S THE CELEBRITY FROM THE ELEMENTARY SCHOOL!!
What are you saying?!
NICE TO MEET YOU, EMPEROR!
Two-timer?
veen
I CAME TO MY SUMMER HOME TO AESTI-VATE....
MY SISTER ARRIVED JUST NOW, SO WE CAME OVER TO SAY HELLO.
I'M A FIRST-YEAR IN IMPERIAL ACADEMY'S ELEMENTARY SCHOOL DIVISION.
MY NAME IS TACHIBANA KAMIYA.
OH
B-BMP
HE'S A KAMIYA?
TACHIBANA!!

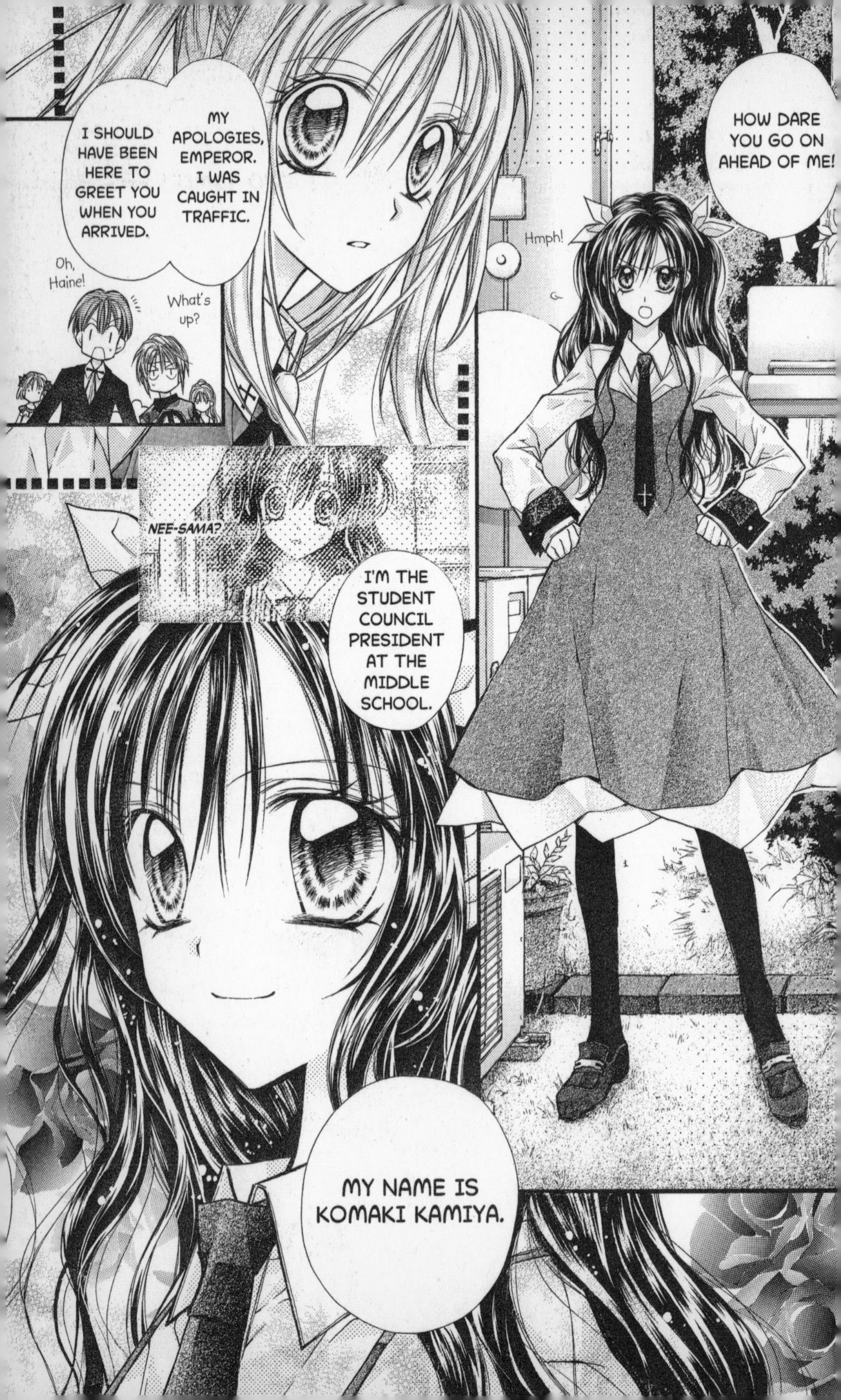
HOW DARE YOU GO ON AHEAD OF ME!
Hmph!
MY APOLOGIES, EMPEROR. I WAS CAUGHT IN TRAFFIC.
I SHOULD HAVE BEEN HERE TO GREET YOU WHEN YOU ARRIVED.
Oh, Haine!
What's up?
NEE-SAMA?
I'M THE STUDENT COUNCIL PRESIDENT AT THE MIDDLE SCHOOL.
MY NAME IS KOMAKI KAMIYA.

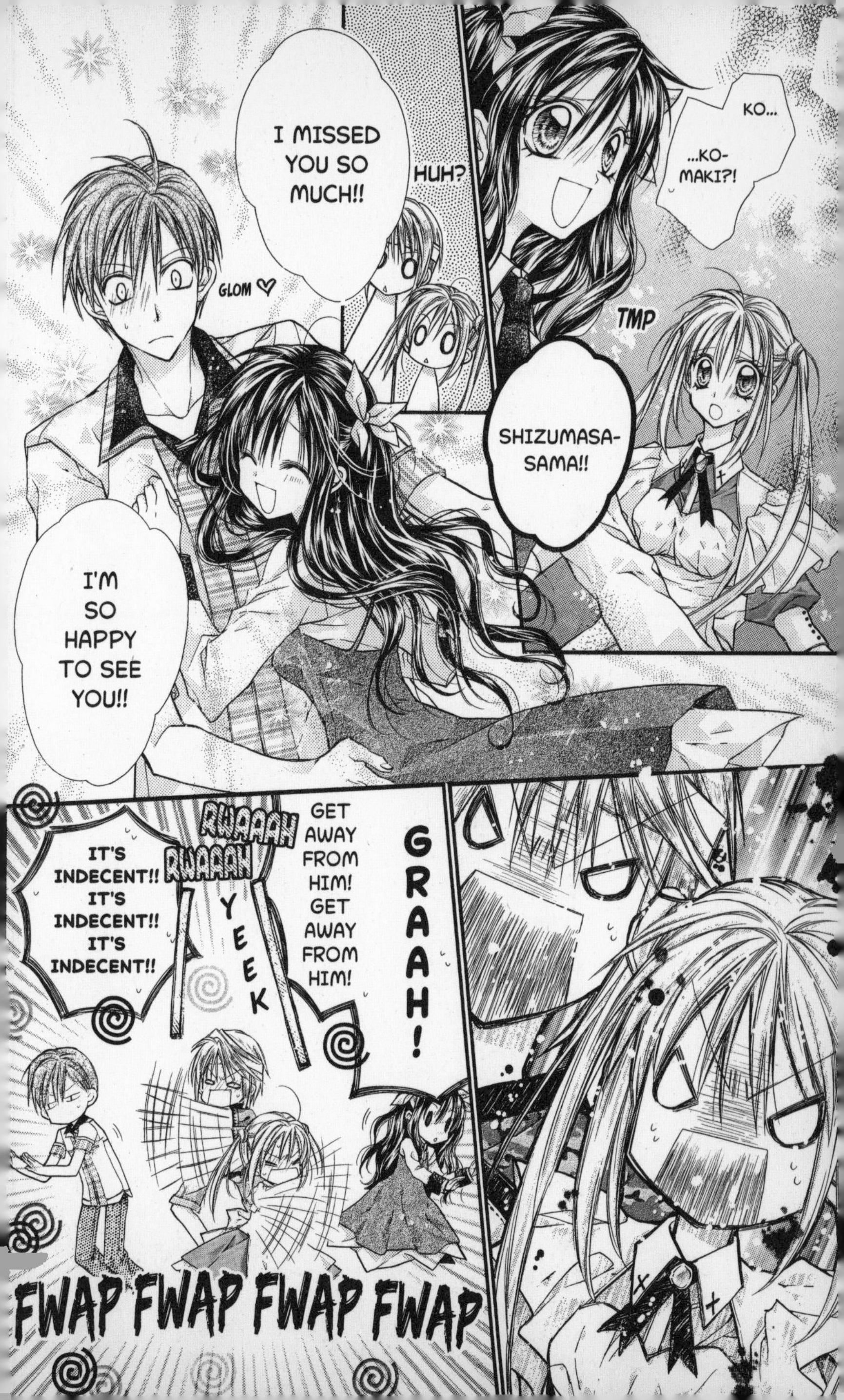
KO...
...KO-MAKI?!
TMP
SHIZUMASA-SAMA!!
HUH?
I MISSED YOU SO MUCH!!
GLOM ♥
I'M SO HAPPY TO SEE YOU!!
GRAAH!
GET AWAY FROM HIM! GET AWAY FROM HIM!
YEEK
RWAAAH RWAAAH
IT'S INDECENT!! IT'S INDECENT!! IT'S INDECENT!!
FWAP FWAP FWAP FWAP

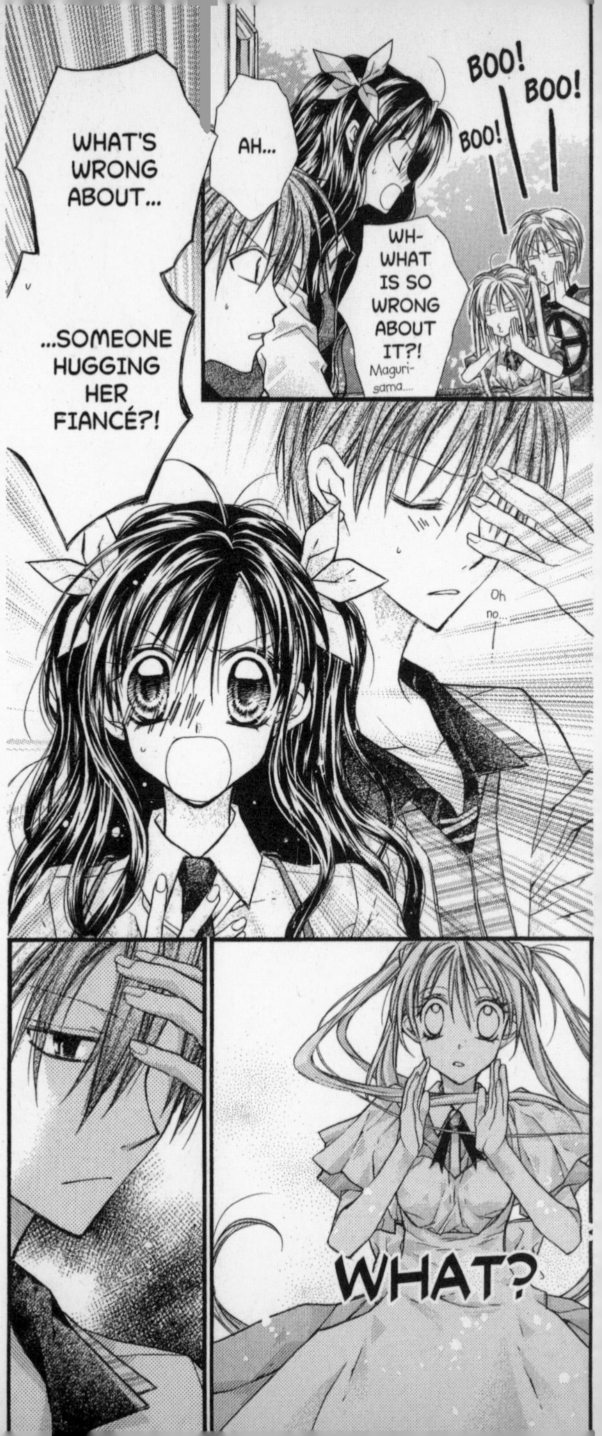
BOO!
BOO!
BOO!
AH...
WH-WHAT IS SO WRONG ABOUT IT?!
Maguri-sama....
WHAT'S WRONG ABOUT...
...SOMEONE HUGGING HER FIANCÉ?!
Oh no...
WHAT?

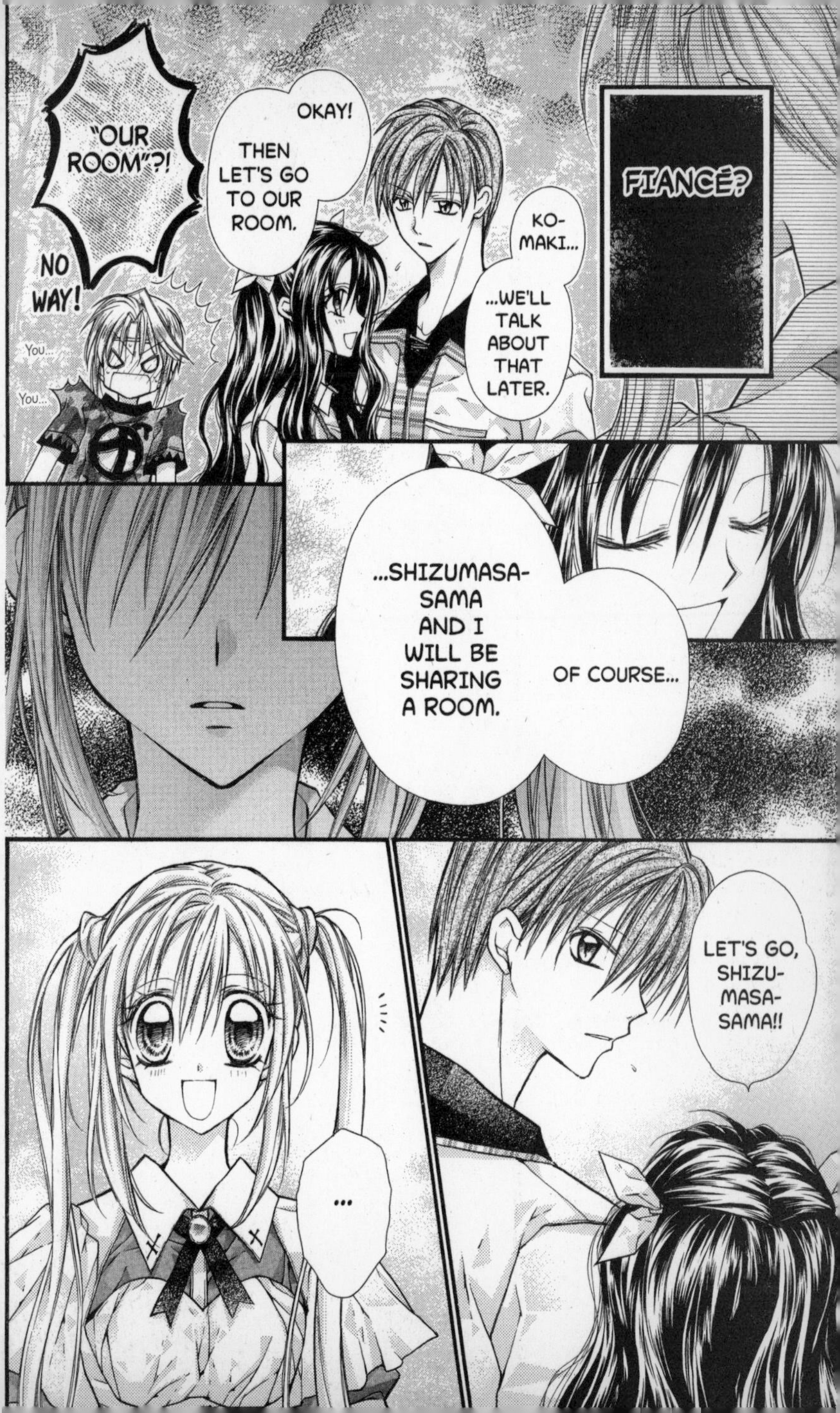
FIANCÉ?
OKAY!
THEN LET'S GO TO OUR ROOM.
KO-MAKI...
...WE'LL TALK ABOUT THAT LATER.
"OUR ROOM"?!
NO WAY!
You...
You...
OF COURSE...
...SHIZUMASA-SAMA AND I WILL BE SHARING A ROOM.
LET'S GO, SHIZU-MASA-SAMA!!
...

Games

Tales of Legendia

I wanted to play some kind of RPG, and I decided to buy this one because I heard it was good.

It really is ☆ **fun** ☆! Of all the *Tales* series I have played, I like this one the most. (Though I like the battles in *Symphonia* the best.) Actually, I'm still in the midst of playing it (I had gone as far as Chloe's Character Quest when Saori-san deleted my save file...)

The stories in the Character Quests are really good, and I'm often surprised, thinking, "Wow, you've taken it this far!"

As for the characters, my favorites are Chloe, Jay, and Grune. (Well, I like all of them.)

While I was playing the Character Quests, it really made me feel like I lived at Werites myself!

I even bought the original sound track for this, which is very rare for me! I usually listen to music when I'm working, but I start falling asleep if it doesn't have vocals. So I don't buy many CDs with background music. (But I have the sound tracks for FF10, ICO, and //hack...♥ because I like them!!) ♥♥♥

I really like "Chasing Shirley." It's great. "A Firefly's Light" (with vocals ♥) and "The Bird Chirps, I Sing" are also my favorites. ♥♥♥

↑This one has vocals too. ♥

I highly recommend *Legendia*!! It's a great RPG!

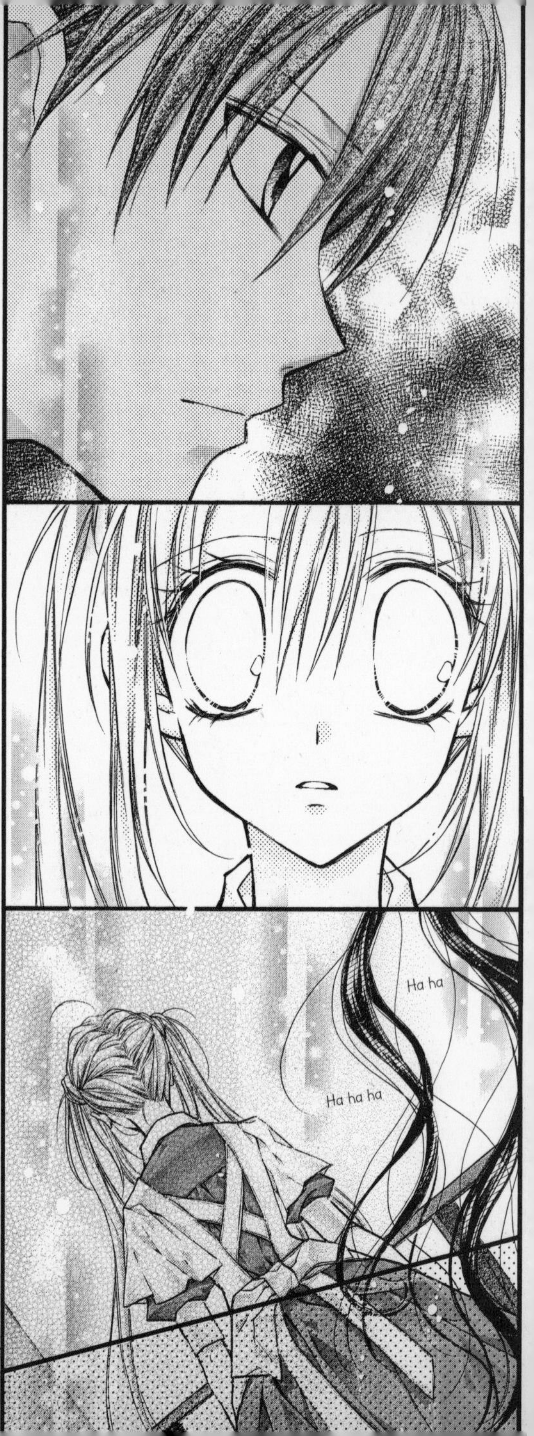
Ha ha
Ha ha ha

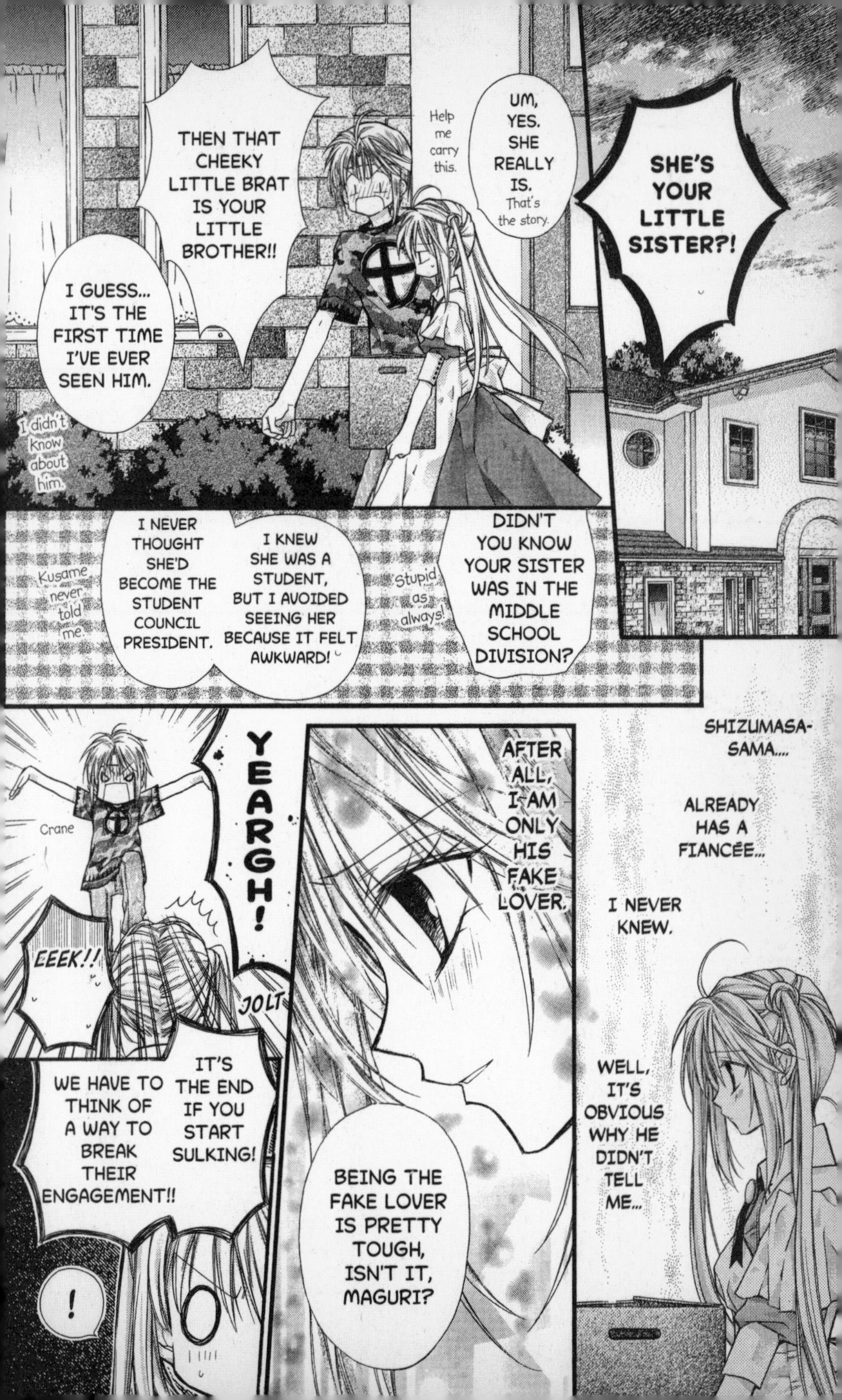
SHE'S YOUR LITTLE SISTER?!
UM, YES. SHE REALLY IS.
That's the story.
Help me carry this.
THEN THAT CHEEKY LITTLE BRAT IS YOUR LITTLE BROTHER!!
I GUESS... IT'S THE FIRST TIME I'VE EVER SEEN HIM.
I didn't know about him.
DIDN'T YOU KNOW YOUR SISTER WAS IN THE MIDDLE SCHOOL DIVISION?
Stupid as always!
I KNEW SHE WAS A STUDENT, BUT I AVOIDED SEEING HER BECAUSE IT FELT AWKWARD!
I NEVER THOUGHT SHE'D BECOME THE STUDENT COUNCIL PRESIDENT.
Kusame never told me.
SHIZUMASA-SAMA....
ALREADY HAS A FIANCÉE...
I NEVER KNEW.
WELL, IT'S OBVIOUS WHY HE DIDN'T TELL ME...
AFTER ALL, I AM ONLY HIS FAKE LOVER.
BEING THE FAKE LOVER IS PRETTY TOUGH, ISN'T IT, MAGURI?
YEARGH!
Crane
EEEK!!
JOLT
IT'S THE END IF YOU START SULKING!
WE HAVE TO THINK OF A WAY TO BREAK THEIR ENGAGEMENT!!
!

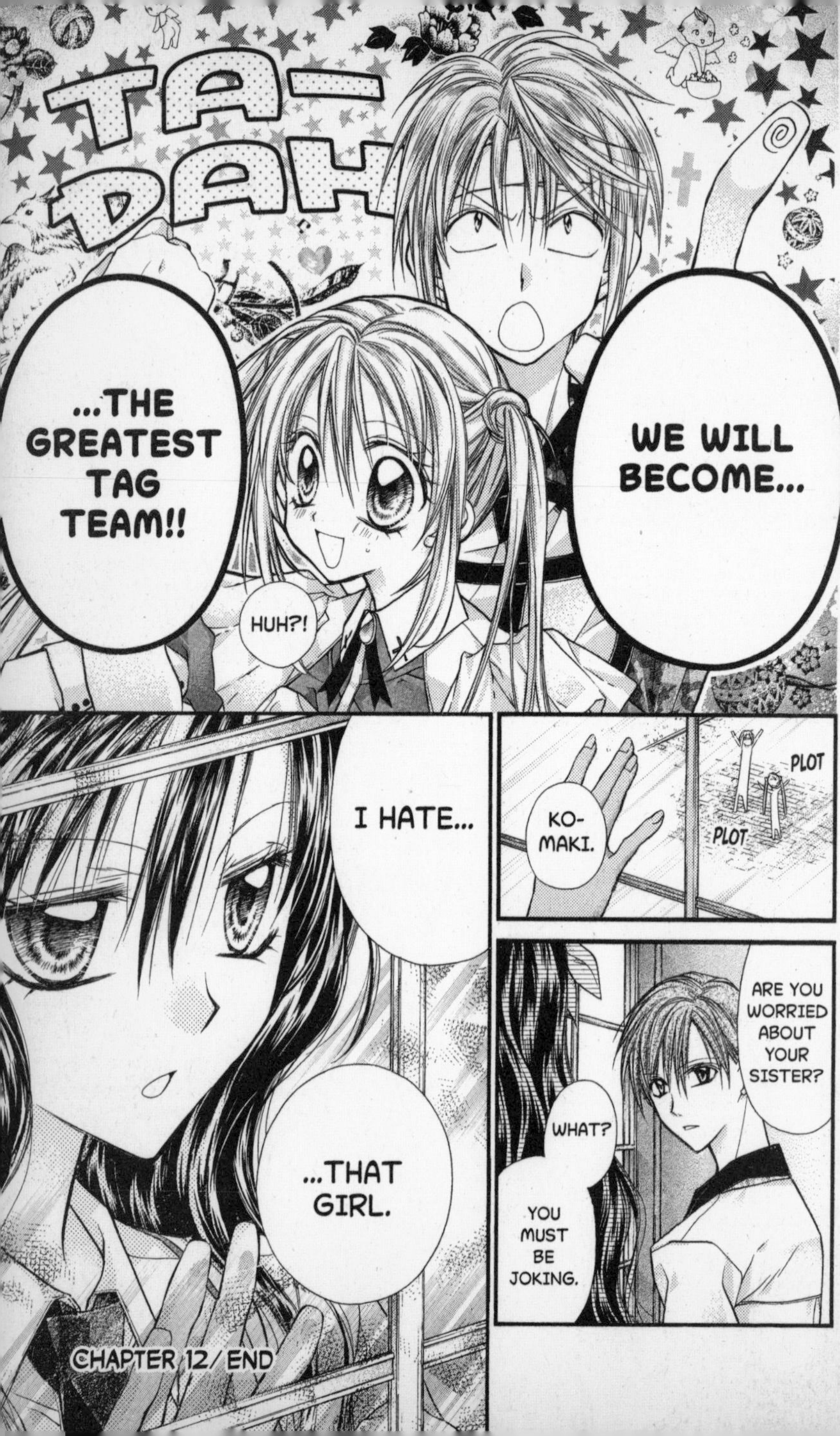

WE WILL BECOME...
...THE GREATEST TAG TEAM!!
TA-DAH
HUH?!
PLOT
PLOT
KO-MAKI.
ARE YOU WORRIED ABOUT YOUR SISTER?
WHAT?
YOU MUST BE JOKING.
I HATE...
...THAT GIRL.
CHAPTER 12/ END

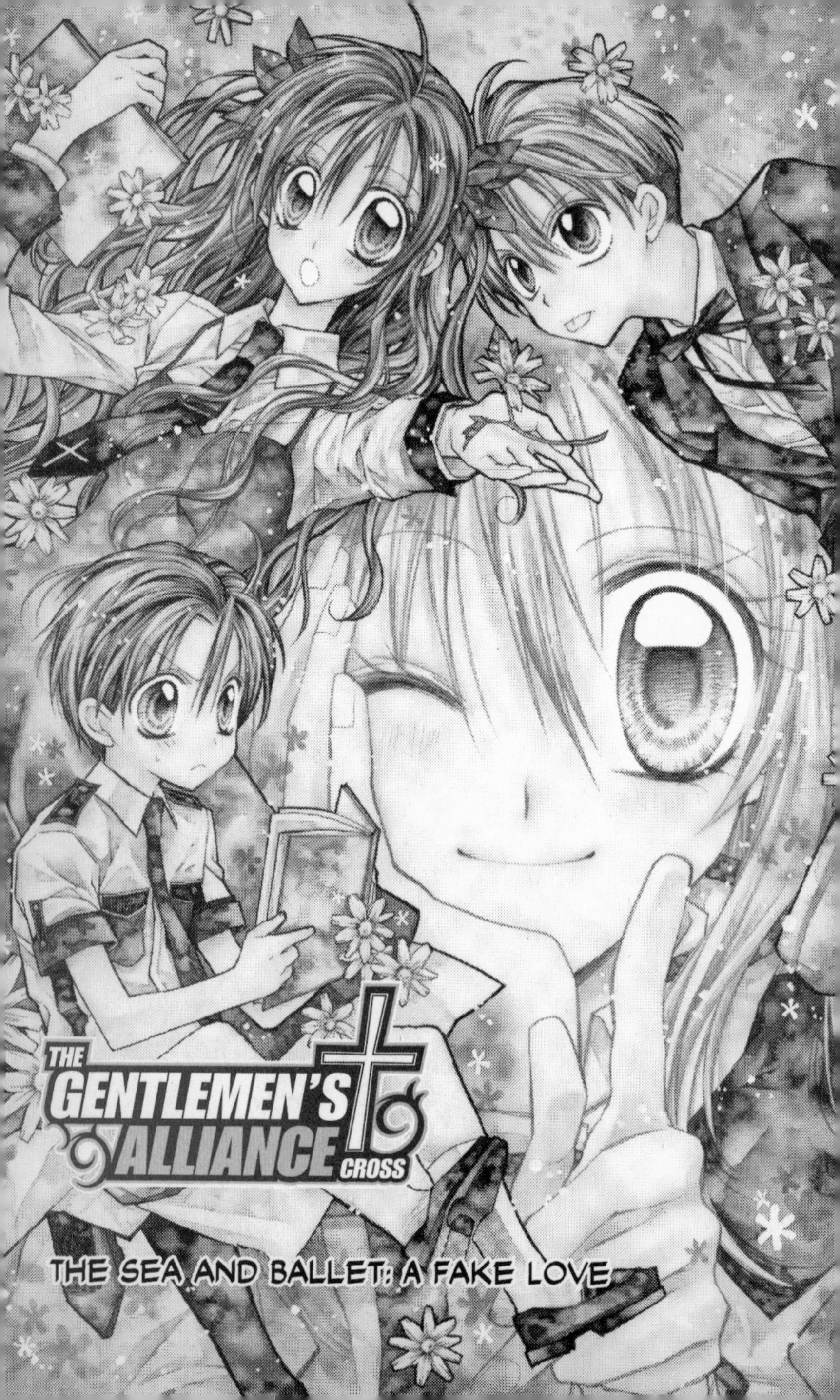
THE GENTLEMEN'S ALLIANCE CROSS
THE SEA AND BALLET: A FAKE LOVE

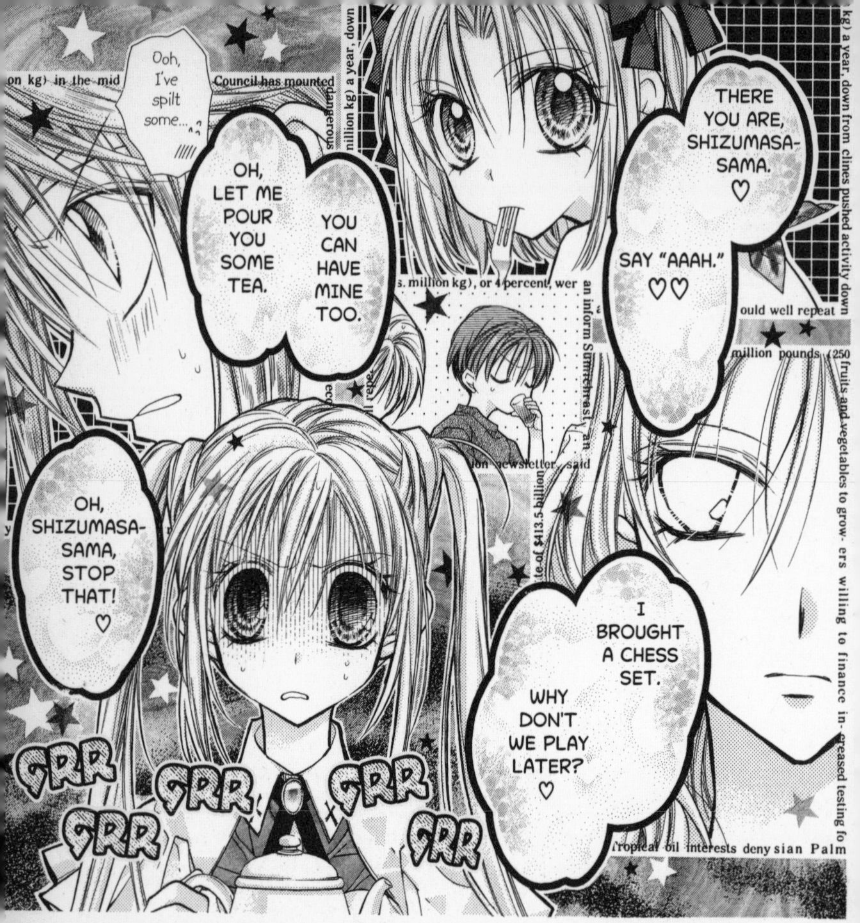
THERE YOU ARE, SHIZUMASA-SAMA. ♡
SAY "AAAH." ♡♡
YOU CAN HAVE MINE TOO.
OH, LET ME POUR YOU SOME TEA.
Ooh, I've spilt some...
I BROUGHT A CHESS SET.
WHY DON'T WE PLAY LATER? ♡
OH, SHIZUMASA-SAMA, STOP THAT! ♡
GRR GRR GRR GRR GRR GRR

Chapter 13: The Sea and Ballet: A Fake Love

Lead-in A request from the Onee-chan! ♡ I want everybody to get along.

I like this chapter very much (and it was popular too). I think I was able to successfully draw Haine-chan's clothes and hair...

As I draw the rough outlines for the manga, I often get the feeling that the fake guy smiles a lot more often now... That's a good thing.

Though I'm getting a little off-topic, I like snake fireworks a lot. I watch it burn with a sober look and a smile on my face. And the sea... I had a lot of fun drawing the sea (or pasting the screen tones?)... You know, it's the seeeeea!

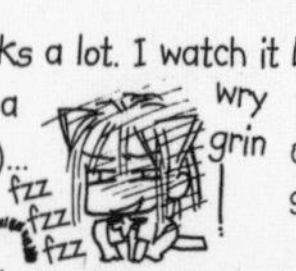
wry grin
fzz fzz fzz
Okay, I'm a gloomy person.

I tend to have less to talk about with chapters I was able to draw successfully. That's the case for ShinKuro. And once I turn it in, I zone out completely.

I'm utterly burnt out...

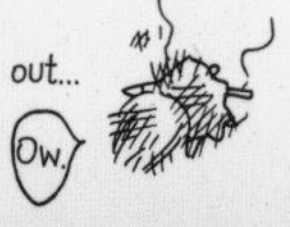
Ow.

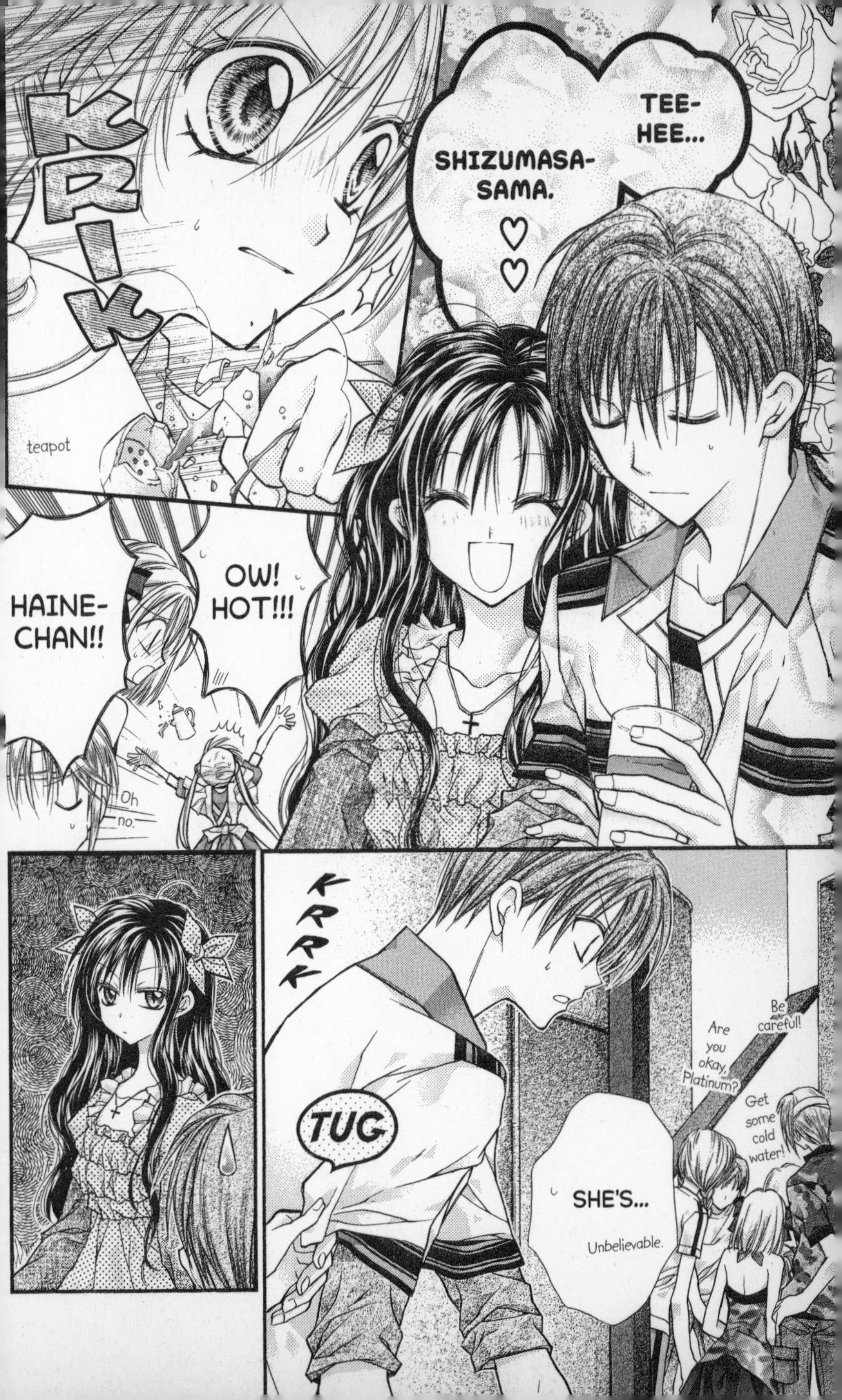
TEE-HEE...
SHIZUMASA-SAMA. ♡ ♡
KRIK
teapot
OW! HOT!!!
HAINE-CHAN!!
Oh no.
KRRRK
Be careful!
Are you okay, Platinum?
Get some cold water!
TUG
SHE'S...
Unbelievable.

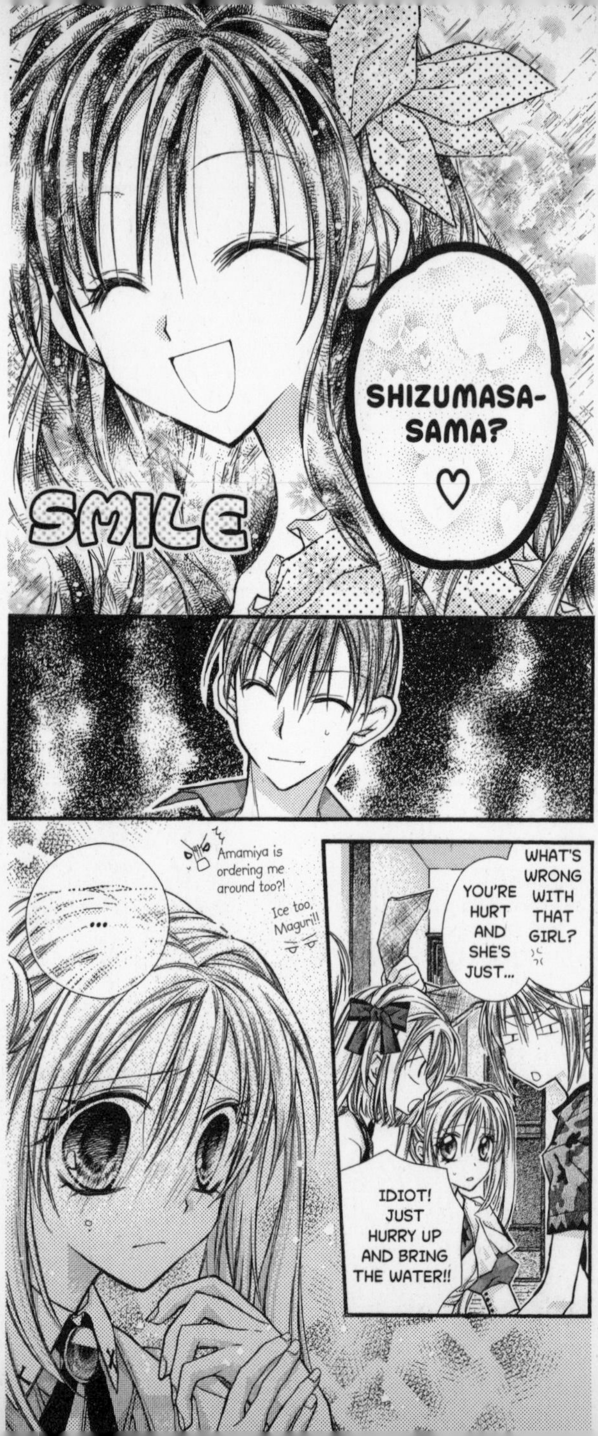

SHIZUMASA-SAMA? ♡
SMILE
WHAT'S WRONG WITH THAT GIRL?
YOU'RE HURT AND SHE'S JUST...
IDIOT! JUST HURRY UP AND BRING THE WATER!!
Amamiya is ordering me around too?!
Ice too, Maguri!!
...

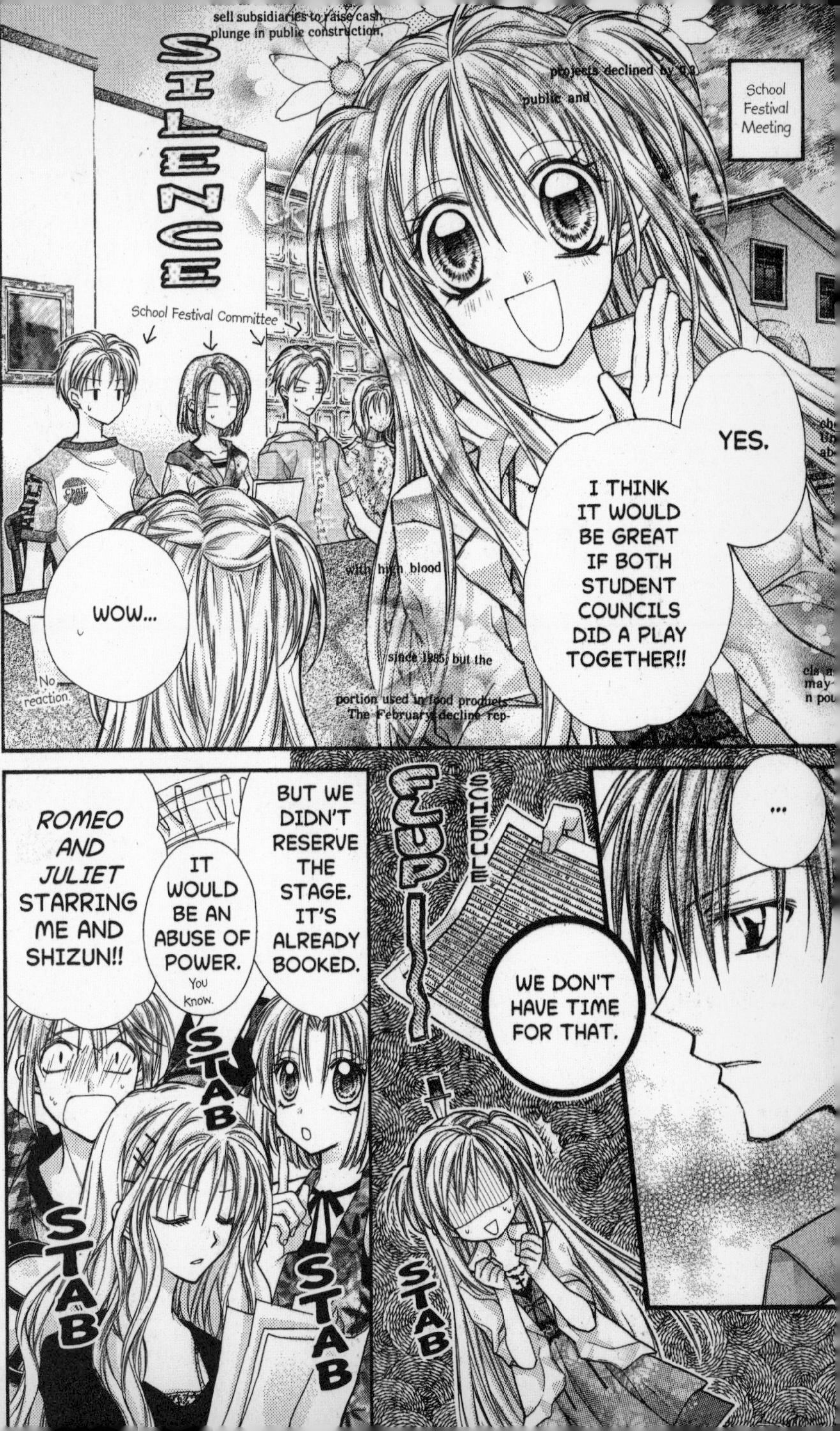

School Festival Meeting
YES.
I THINK IT WOULD BE GREAT IF BOTH STUDENT COUNCILS DID A PLAY TOGETHER!!
SILENCE
School Festival Committee
Chair
WOW...
No reaction.
...
WE DON'T HAVE TIME FOR THAT.
SCHEDULE
FLUP
STAB
BUT WE DIDN'T RESERVE THE STAGE. IT'S ALREADY BOOKED.
IT WOULD BE AN ABUSE OF POWER.
You know.
ROMEO AND JULIET STARRING ME AND SHIZUN!!
STAB
STAB
STAB

Games 2

I apologize to those who aren't interested.

Fatal Frame 3: The Tormented

It's a Japanese-style, horror/action (?) game. I couldn't defeat the last boss in *Crimson Butterfly*, so I never finished it... (And I played it on easy mode too.)

The third in the series, *The Tormented* is easier to play (or maybe I just got used to it??), I've been able to clear it!! ← Asano-san cleared it, and I watched.

※ I'll do my best not to talk too much about the story, but if you don't want to know anything about it, please don't read the rest.

It's nice that you come back to the real world pretty quickly in this game, so you get to have some time to give a little "phew." But slowly the things that happen inside the dream come out into reality, and that part was very stressful, but it was great at the same time. It's so scary!! It's so fun!! I loved the ending!! (I've seen it like 10 times in the gallery mode!!) It still brings tears to my eyes when I watch it!! Tsukiko Amano-san's song, "Koe" matched the game perfectly, making the ending even more moving! Every time I hear it, it feels as if something is seeping out of my heart!! I recommend this song even to those who haven't played the game!! (And "Chou" as well.)

I really recommend *Legendia* too, but it's a complete album, so...

But I recommend it nevertheless.

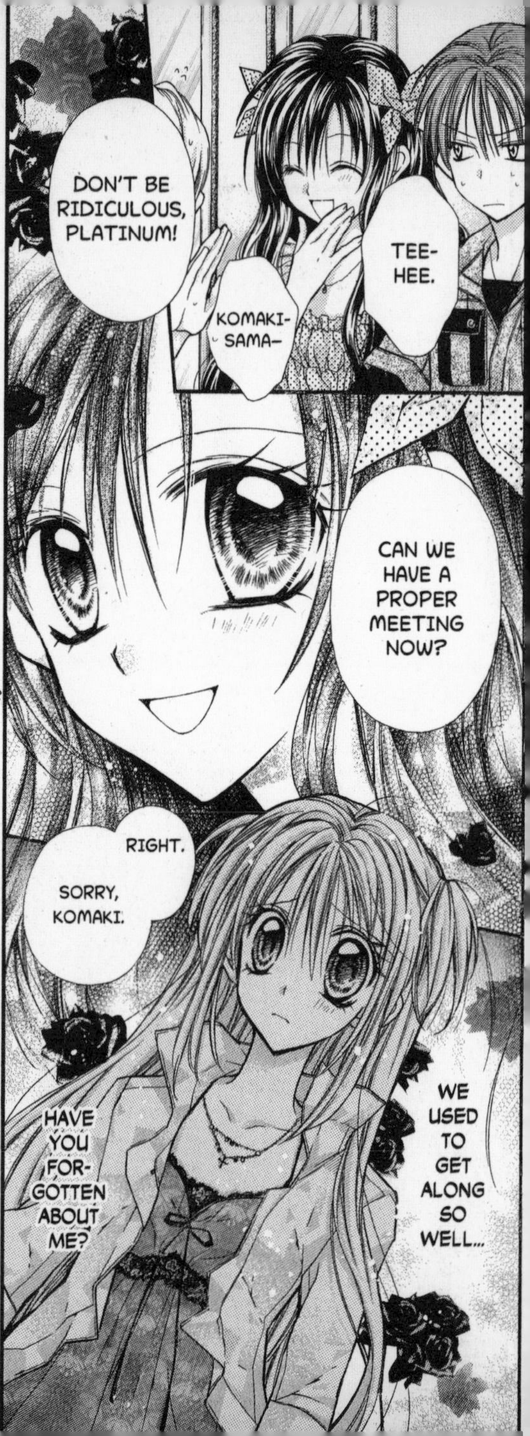
TEE-HEE.
DON'T BE RIDICULOUS, PLATINUM!
KOMAKI-SAMA—
CAN WE HAVE A PROPER MEETING NOW?
RIGHT.
SORRY, KOMAKI.
WE USED TO GET ALONG SO WELL...
HAVE YOU FORGOTTEN ABOUT ME?

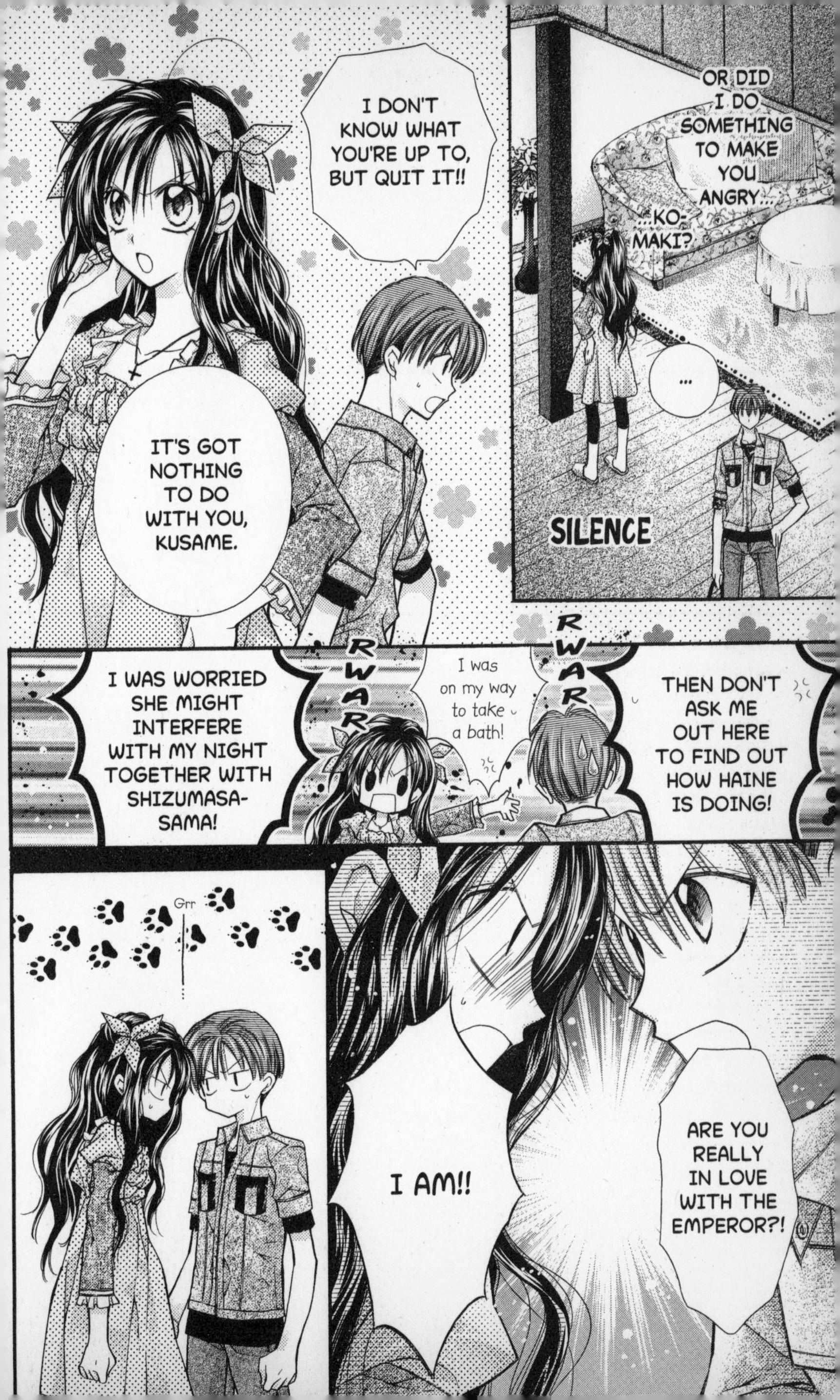
OR DID I DO SOMETHING TO MAKE YOU ANGRY...
...KO-MAKI?
...
SILENCE
I DON'T KNOW WHAT YOU'RE UP TO, BUT QUIT IT!!
IT'S GOT NOTHING TO DO WITH YOU, KUSAME.
THEN DON'T ASK ME OUT HERE TO FIND OUT HOW HAINE IS DOING!
RWAR
I was on my way to take a bath!
RWAR
I WAS WORRIED SHE MIGHT INTERFERE WITH MY NIGHT TOGETHER WITH SHIZUMASA-SAMA!
ARE YOU REALLY IN LOVE WITH THE EMPEROR?!
I AM!!
Grr
...

Things I'm Hooked On

- The Tori-Nabe at Family Mart! (It's really good!! You pour ground chili on it and eat it.) Recently, I've been eating this once a day...
- Berryz Koubou They rock. I'm totally into them. I want to go to their concert... (I forgot to pay the money for the fan club, so I can't get tickets...)
- *Margaret* (biweekly) I'm completely hooked... I just seem to be a big Shueisha fan... I especially like *Tail of the Moon* and *Parfait Tic*! (I like all the series. And I collect a lot of them.)

I've been having all the *Margaret* magazines sent to my parents' house, but I like it so much that I asked them to start sending it to the apartment I use as my office. (The nearby convenience store doesn't stock *Margaret*.)

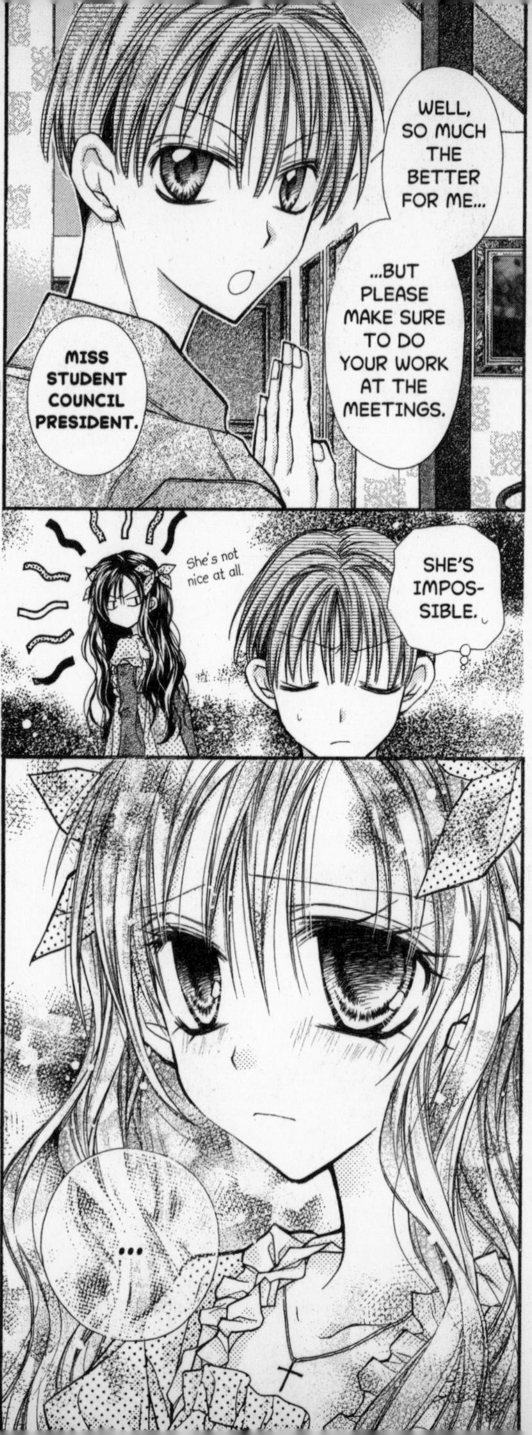
WELL, SO MUCH THE BETTER FOR ME...
...BUT PLEASE MAKE SURE TO DO YOUR WORK AT THE MEETINGS.
MISS STUDENT COUNCIL PRESIDENT.
SHE'S IMPOSSIBLE.
She's not nice at all.
...

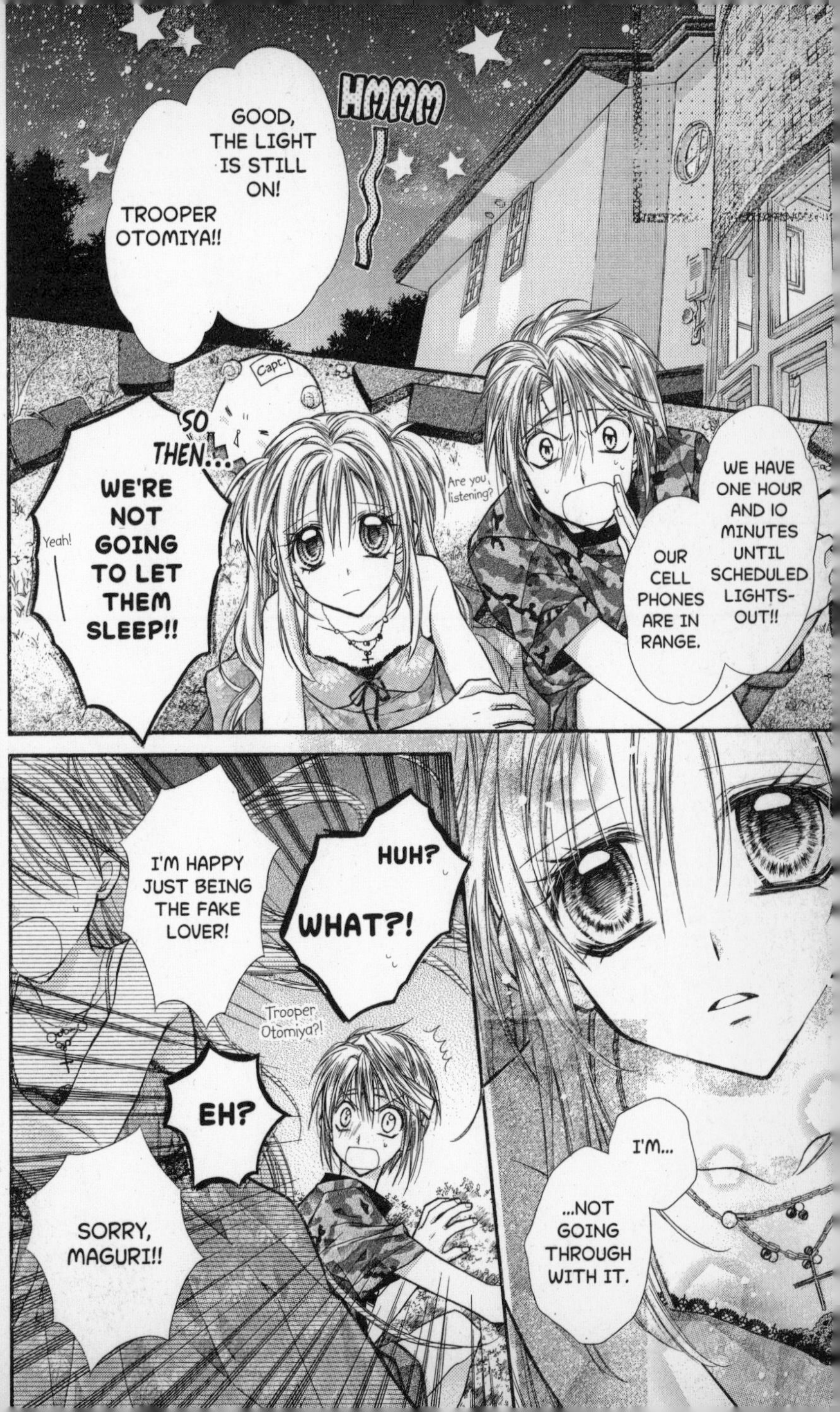
HMMM
GOOD, THE LIGHT IS STILL ON!
TROOPER OTOMIYA!!
Capt.
WE HAVE ONE HOUR AND 10 MINUTES UNTIL SCHEDULED LIGHTS-OUT!!
OUR CELL PHONES ARE IN RANGE.
Are you listening?
SO THEN...
WE'RE NOT GOING TO LET THEM SLEEP!!
Yeah!
I'M...
...NOT GOING THROUGH WITH IT.
HUH?
WHAT?!
I'M HAPPY JUST BEING THE FAKE LOVER!
Trooper Otomiya?!
EH?
SORRY, MAGURI!!

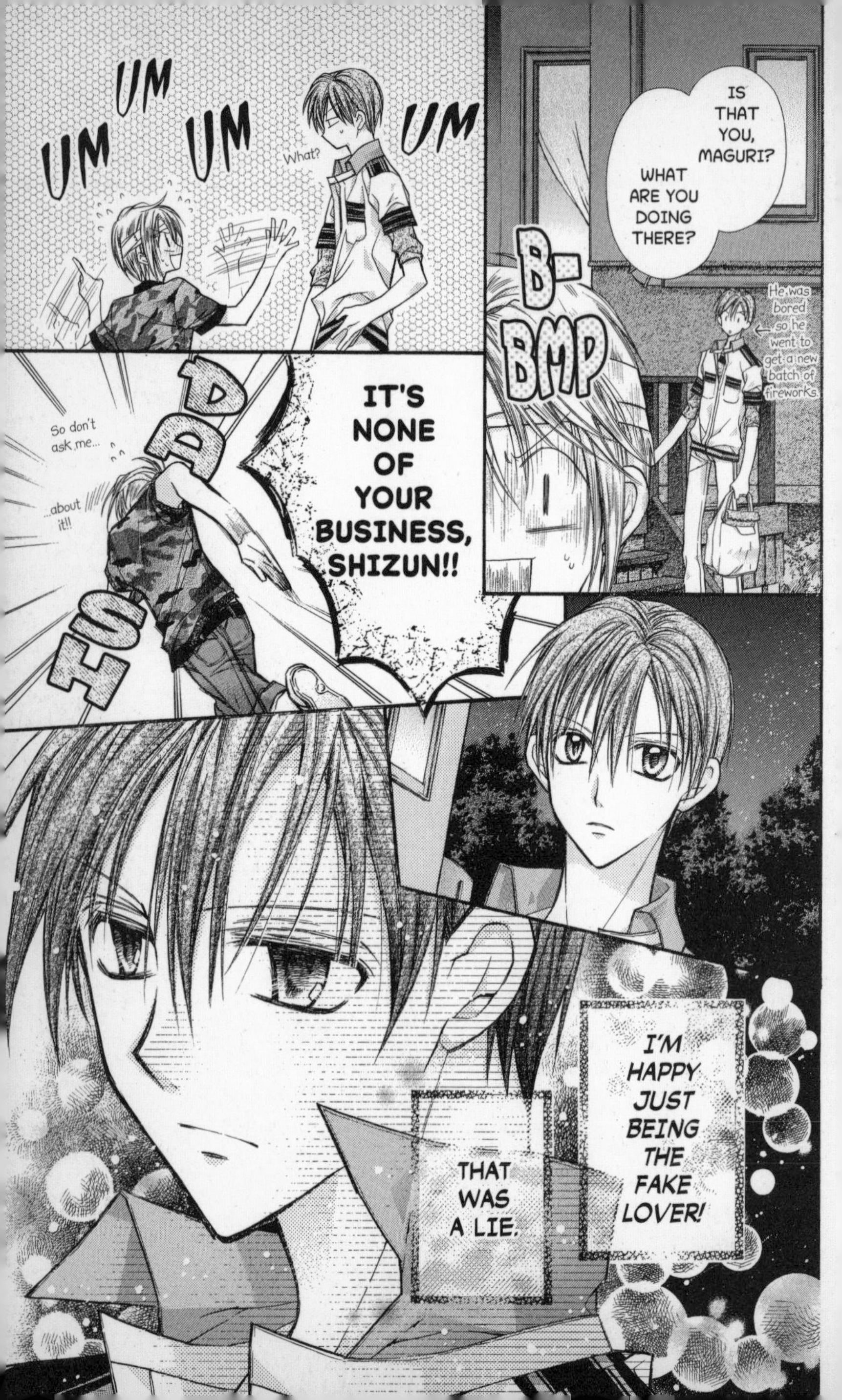

IS THAT YOU, MAGURI?
WHAT ARE YOU DOING THERE?
B-BMP
He was bored so he went to get a new batch of fireworks.
UM UM UM UM
What?
DASH
So don't ask me...
...about it!!
IT'S NONE OF YOUR BUSINESS, SHIZUN!!
I'M HAPPY JUST BEING THE FAKE LOVER!
THAT WAS A LIE.

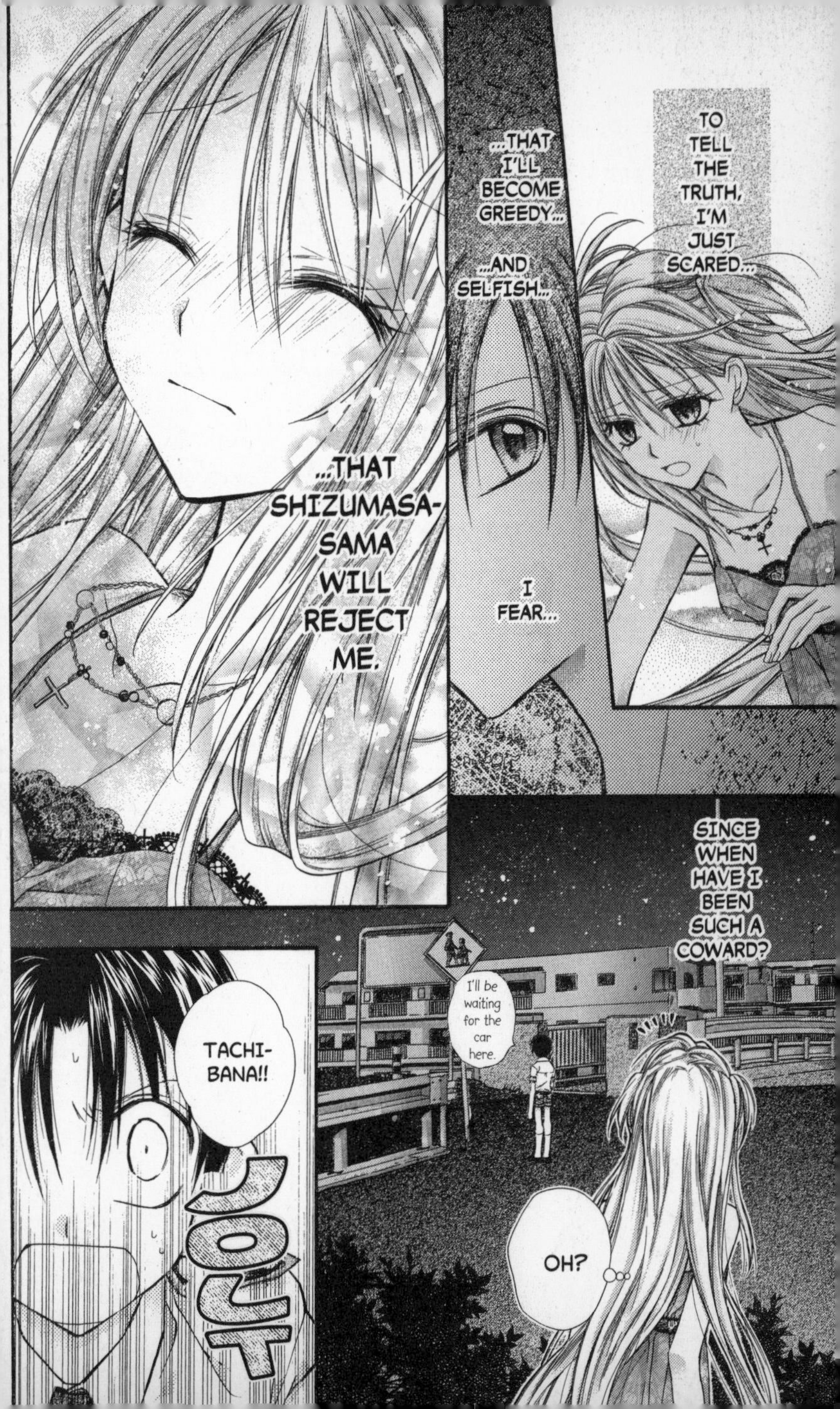

TO TELL THE TRUTH, I'M JUST SCARED...
...THAT I'LL BECOME GREEDY...
...AND SELFISH...
I FEAR...
...THAT SHIZUMASA-SAMA WILL REJECT ME.
SINCE WHEN HAVE I BEEN SUCH A COWARD?
I'll be waiting for the car here.
OH?
TACHI-BANA!!
JOLT

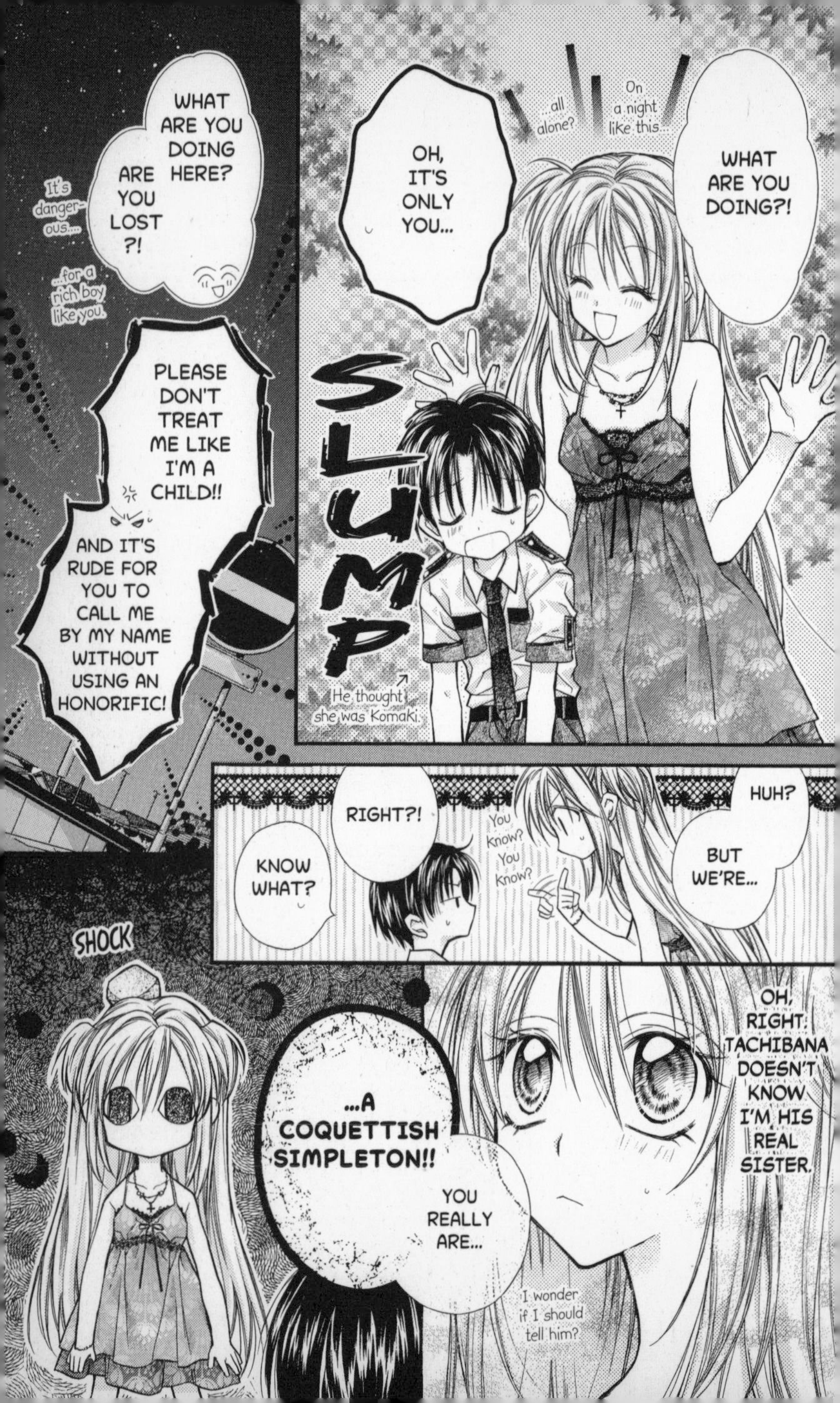
WHAT ARE YOU DOING?!
On a night like this...
...all alone?
OH, IT'S ONLY YOU...
SLUMP
He thought she was Komaki.
WHAT ARE YOU DOING HERE? ARE YOU LOST?!
It's danger-ous....
...for a rich boy like you.
PLEASE DON'T TREAT ME LIKE I'M A CHILD!!
AND IT'S RUDE FOR YOU TO CALL ME BY MY NAME WITHOUT USING AN HONORIFIC!
HUH?
BUT WE'RE...
You Know? You Know?
RIGHT?!
KNOW WHAT?
OH, RIGHT. TACHIBANA DOESN'T KNOW I'M HIS REAL SISTER.
I wonder if I should tell him?
YOU REALLY ARE...
...A COQUETTISH SIMPLETON!!
SHOCK

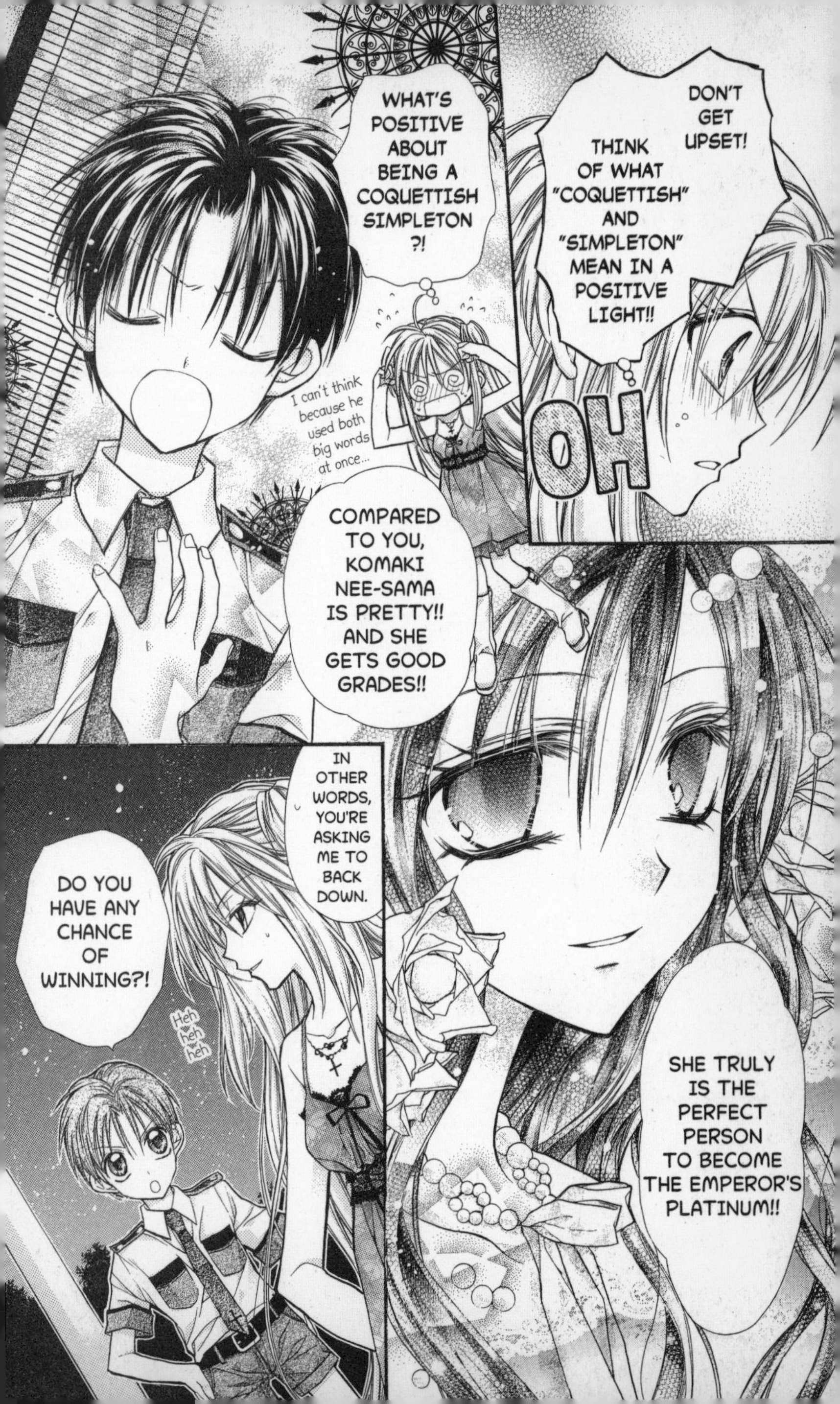
DON'T GET UPSET!
THINK OF WHAT "COQUETTISH" AND "SIMPLETON" MEAN IN A POSITIVE LIGHT!!
OH
WHAT'S POSITIVE ABOUT BEING A COQUETTISH SIMPLETON ?!
I can't think because he used both big words at once...
COMPARED TO YOU, KOMAKI NEE-SAMA IS PRETTY!! AND SHE GETS GOOD GRADES!!
SHE TRULY IS THE PERFECT PERSON TO BECOME THE EMPEROR'S PLATINUM!!
IN OTHER WORDS, YOU'RE ASKING ME TO BACK DOWN.
DO YOU HAVE ANY CHANCE OF WINNING?!
Heh heh heh

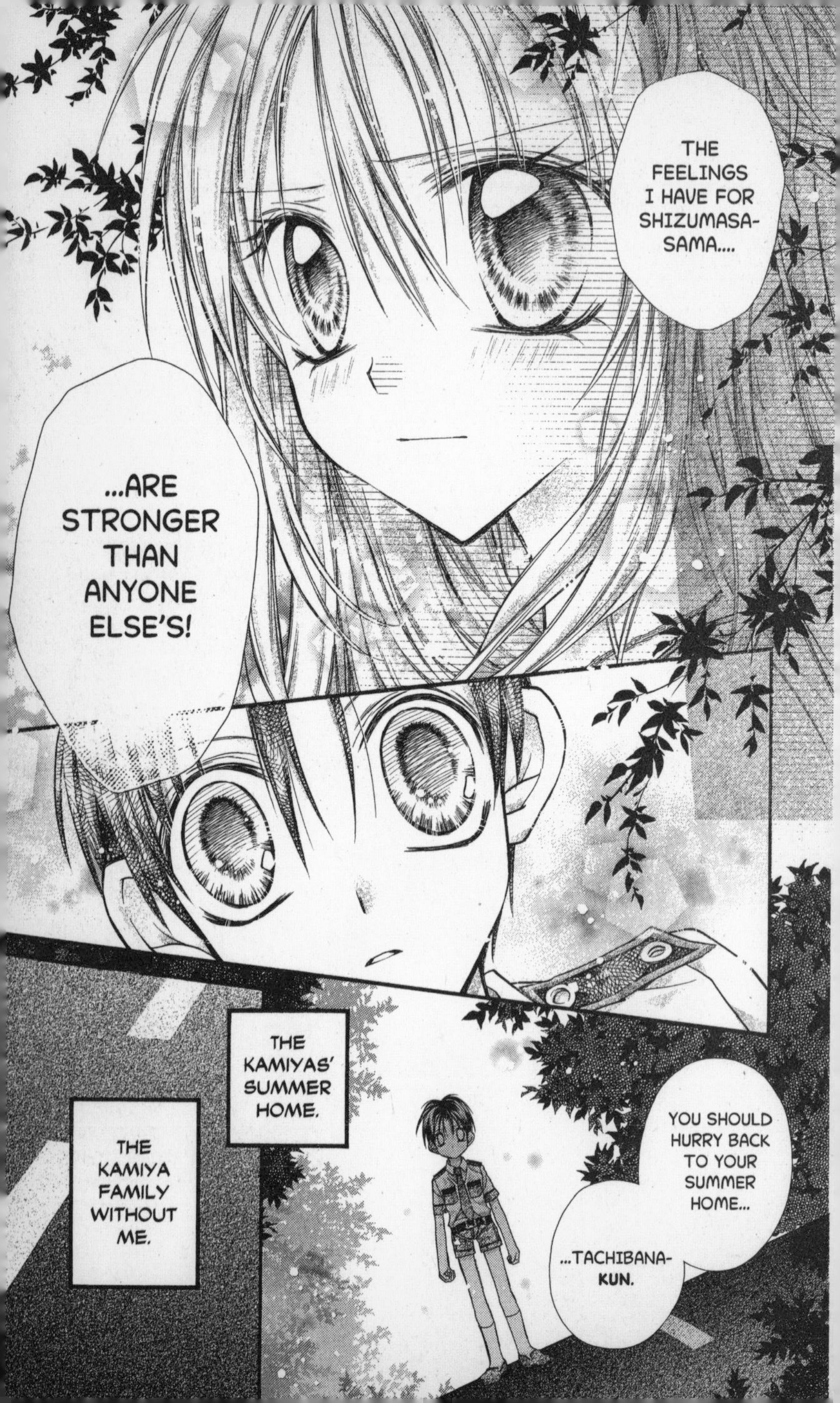
THE FEELINGS I HAVE FOR SHIZUMASA-SAMA....
...ARE STRONGER THAN ANYONE ELSE'S!
YOU SHOULD HURRY BACK TO YOUR SUMMER HOME...
...TACHIBANA-KUN.
THE KAMIYAS' SUMMER HOME.
THE KAMIYA FAMILY WITHOUT ME.

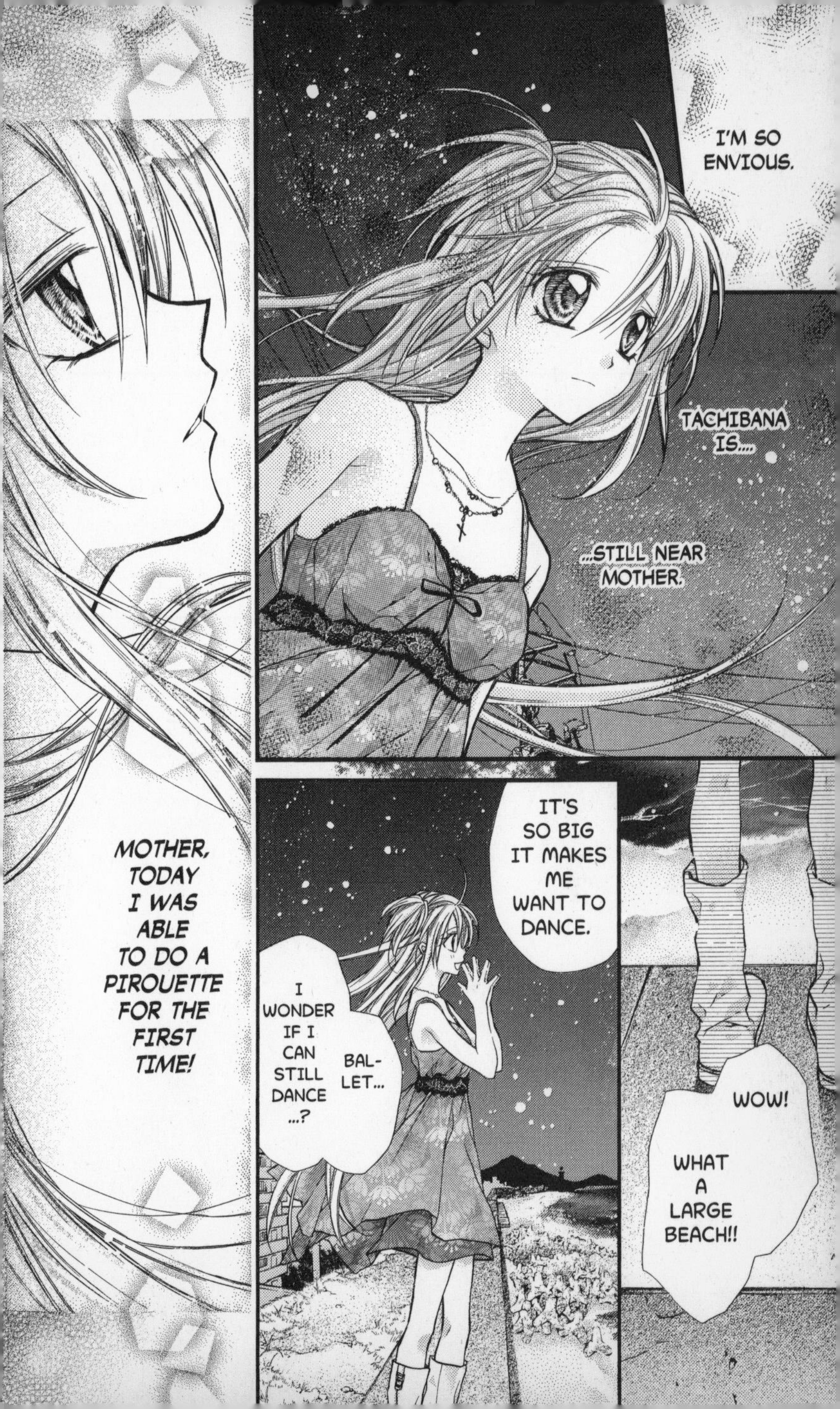
I'M SO ENVIOUS.
TACHIBANA IS....
...STILL NEAR MOTHER.
WOW!
WHAT A LARGE BEACH!!
IT'S SO BIG IT MAKES ME WANT TO DANCE.
I WONDER IF I CAN STILL DANCE ...? BALLET...
MOTHER, TODAY I WAS ABLE TO DO A PIROUETTE FOR THE FIRST TIME!

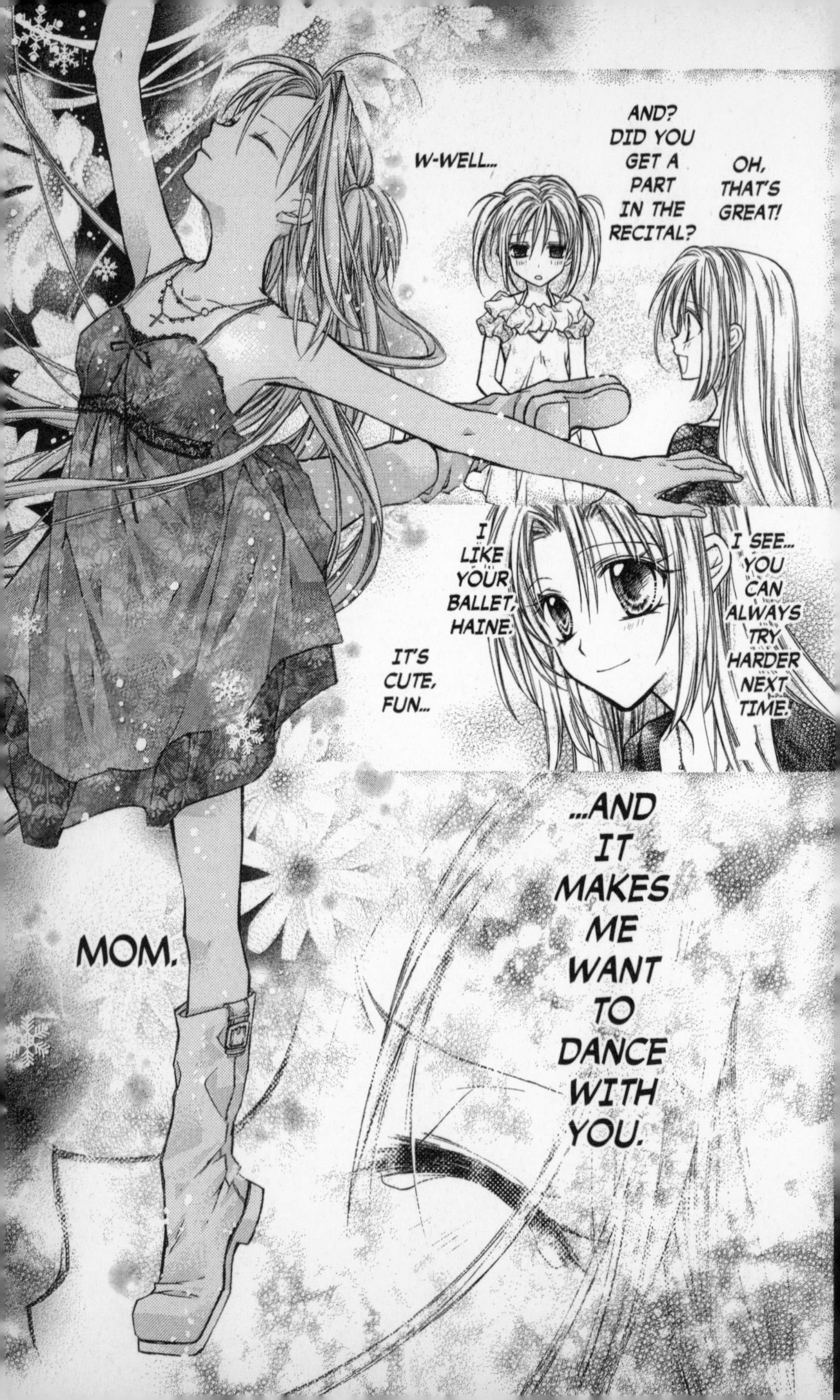
OH, THAT'S GREAT!
AND? DID YOU GET A PART IN THE RECITAL?
W-WELL...
I SEE... YOU CAN ALWAYS TRY HARDER NEXT TIME.
I LIKE YOUR BALLET, HAINE.
IT'S CUTE, FUN...
...AND IT MAKES ME WANT TO DANCE WITH YOU.
MOM.

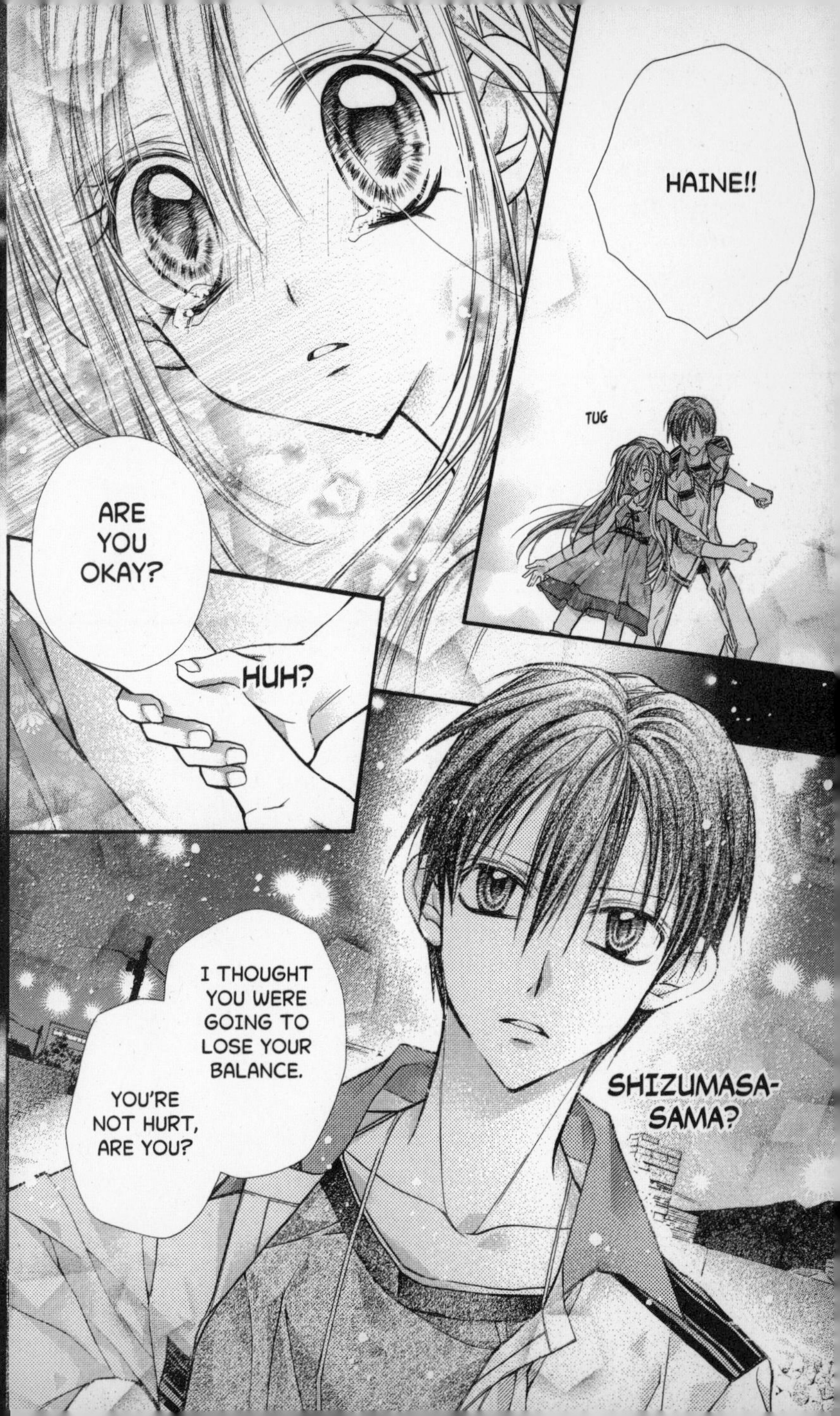
HAINE!!
TUG
ARE YOU OKAY?
HUH?
SHIZUMASA-SAMA?
I THOUGHT YOU WERE GOING TO LOSE YOUR BALANCE.
YOU'RE NOT HURT, ARE YOU?

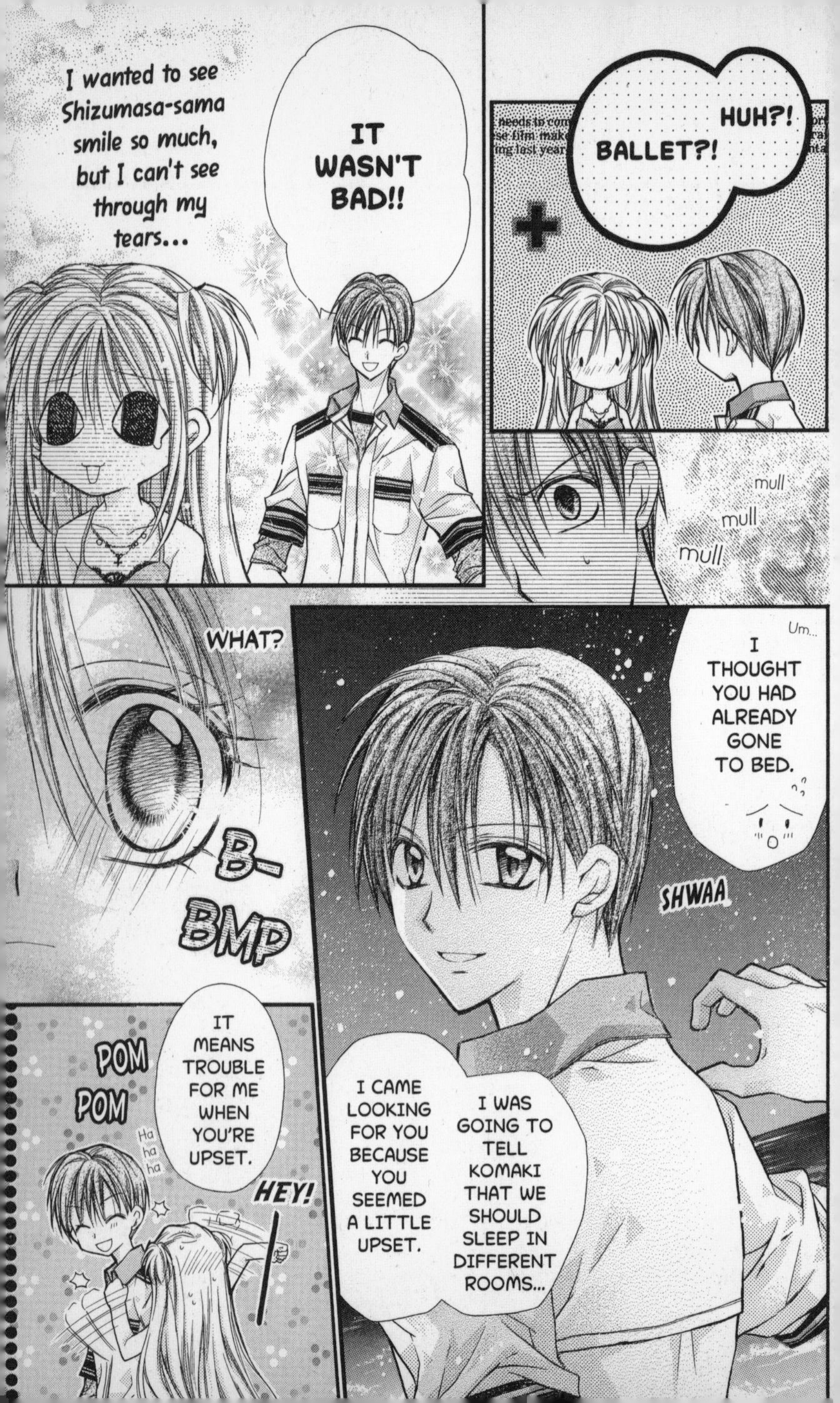
HUH?!
BALLET?!
mull
mull
mull
IT WASN'T BAD!!
I wanted to see Shizumasa-sama smile so much, but I can't see through my tears...
Um...
I THOUGHT YOU HAD ALREADY GONE TO BED.
SHWAA
I WAS GOING TO TELL KOMAKI THAT WE SHOULD SLEEP IN DIFFERENT ROOMS...
I CAME LOOKING FOR YOU BECAUSE YOU SEEMED A LITTLE UPSET.
WHAT?
B-BMP
IT MEANS TROUBLE FOR ME WHEN YOU'RE UPSET.
POM POM
Ha ha ha
HEY!

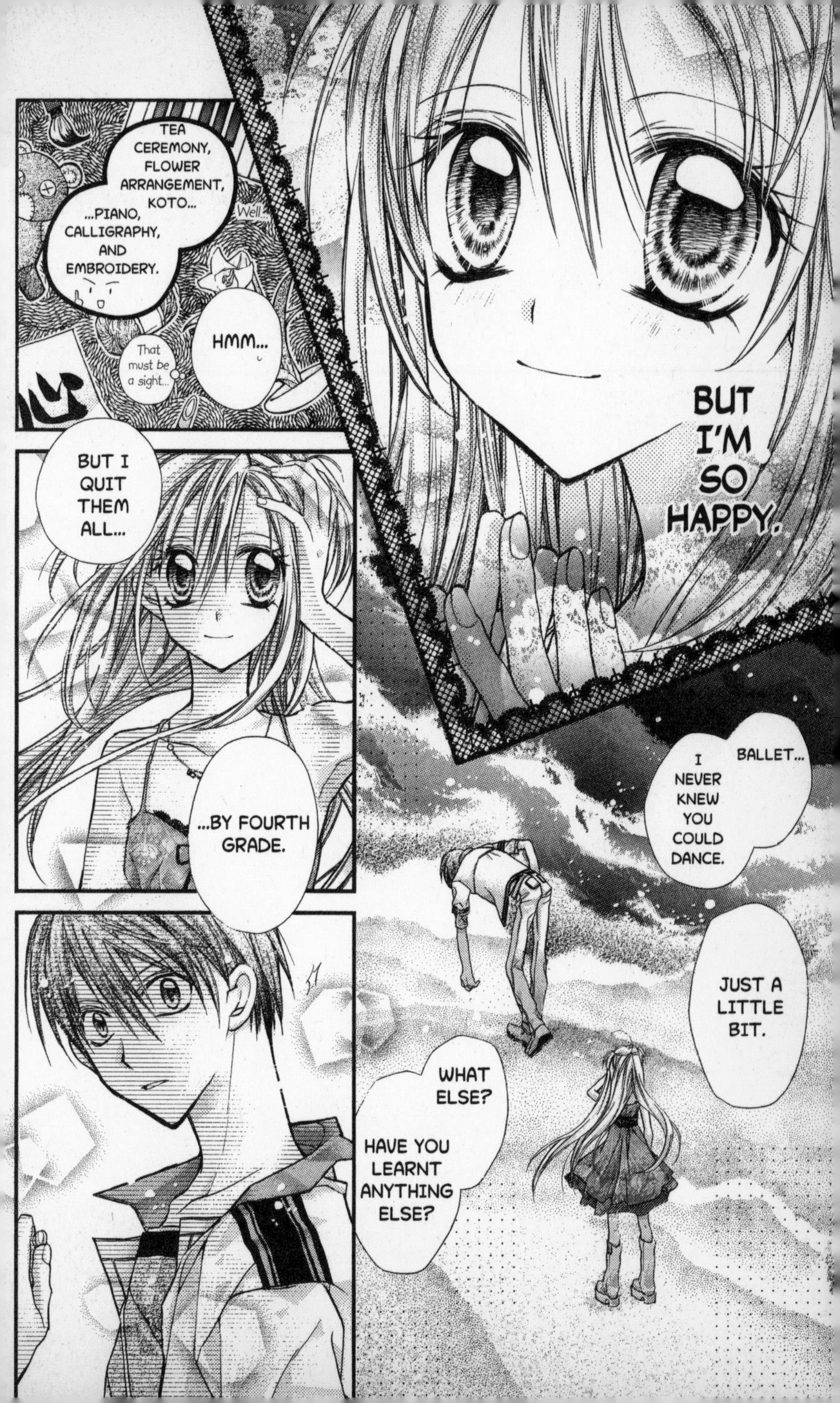
BALLET...
I NEVER KNEW YOU COULD DANCE.
JUST A LITTLE BIT.
WHAT ELSE?
HAVE YOU LEARNT ANYTHING ELSE?
Well...
TEA CEREMONY, FLOWER ARRANGEMENT, KOTO...
...PIANO, CALLIGRAPHY, AND EMBROIDERY.
HMM...
That must be a sight...
BUT I QUIT THEM ALL...
...BY FOURTH GRADE.
BUT I'M SO HAPPY.

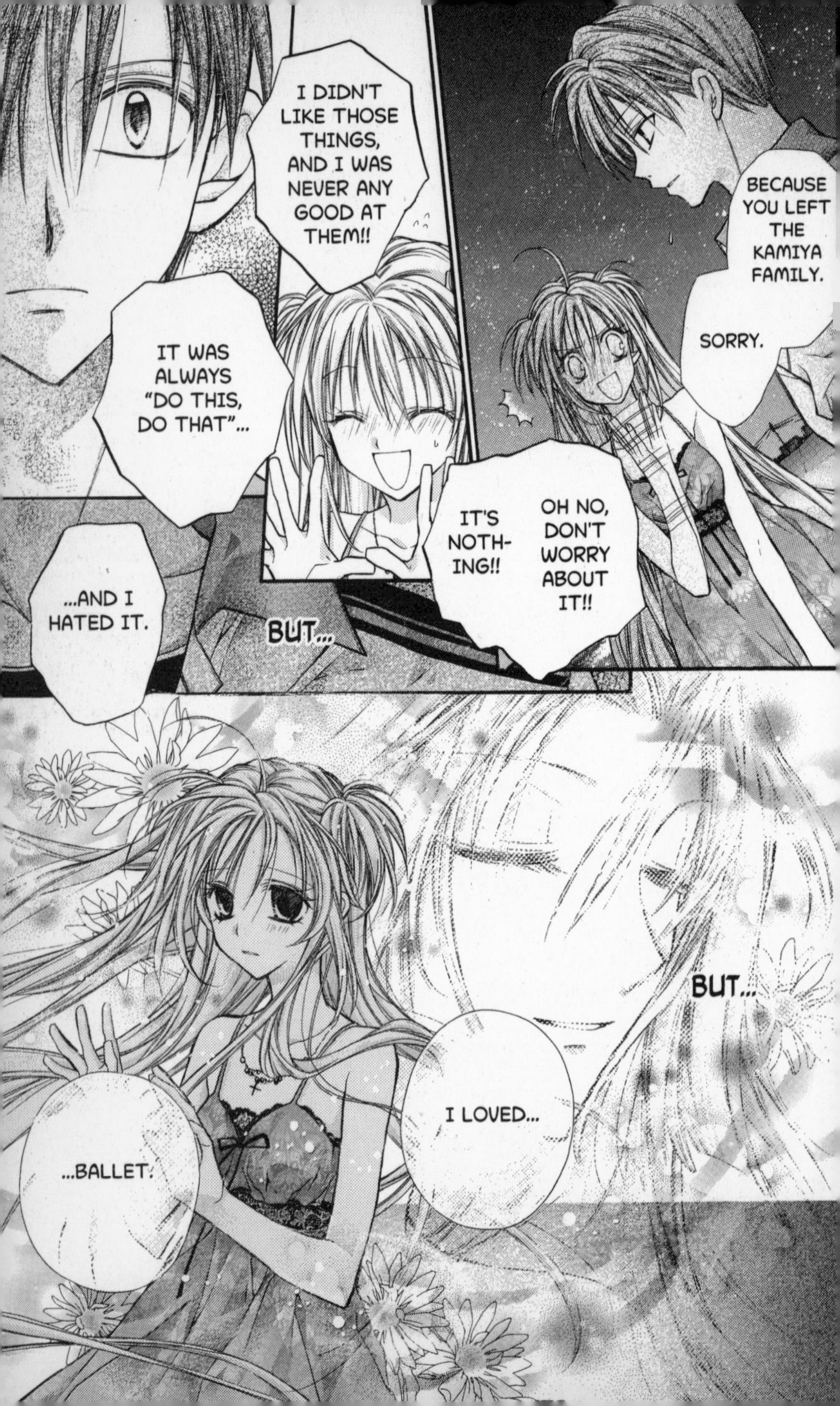
BECAUSE YOU LEFT THE KAMIYA FAMILY.
SORRY.
OH NO, DON'T WORRY ABOUT IT!!
IT'S NOTH-ING!!
I DIDN'T LIKE THOSE THINGS, AND I WAS NEVER ANY GOOD AT THEM!!
IT WAS ALWAYS "DO THIS, DO THAT"...
...AND I HATED IT.
BUT...
BUT...
I LOVED...
...BALLET.

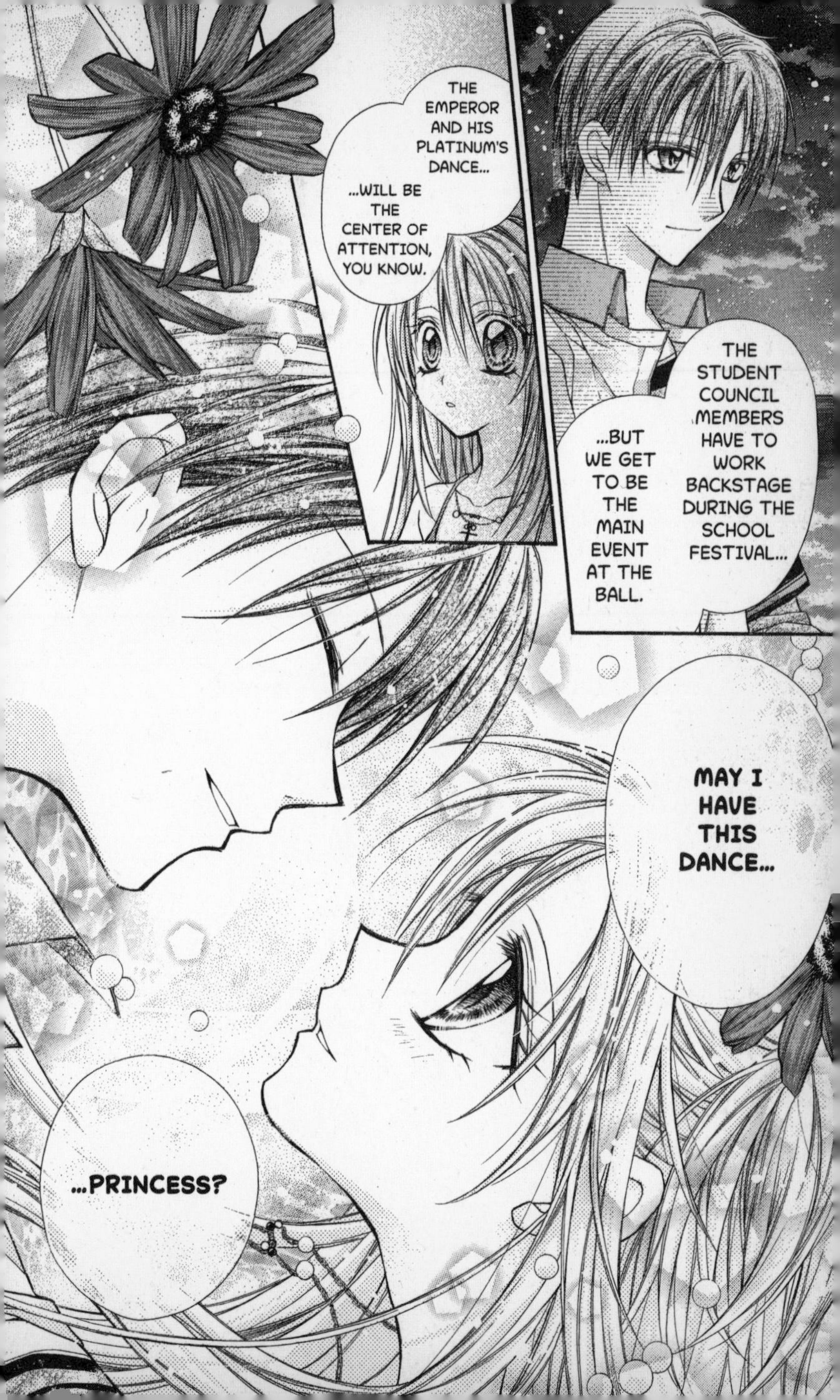
THE STUDENT COUNCIL MEMBERS HAVE TO WORK BACKSTAGE DURING THE SCHOOL FESTIVAL...
...BUT WE GET TO BE THE MAIN EVENT AT THE BALL.
THE EMPEROR AND HIS PLATINUM'S DANCE...
...WILL BE THE CENTER OF ATTENTION, YOU KNOW.
MAY I HAVE THIS DANCE...
...PRINCESS?

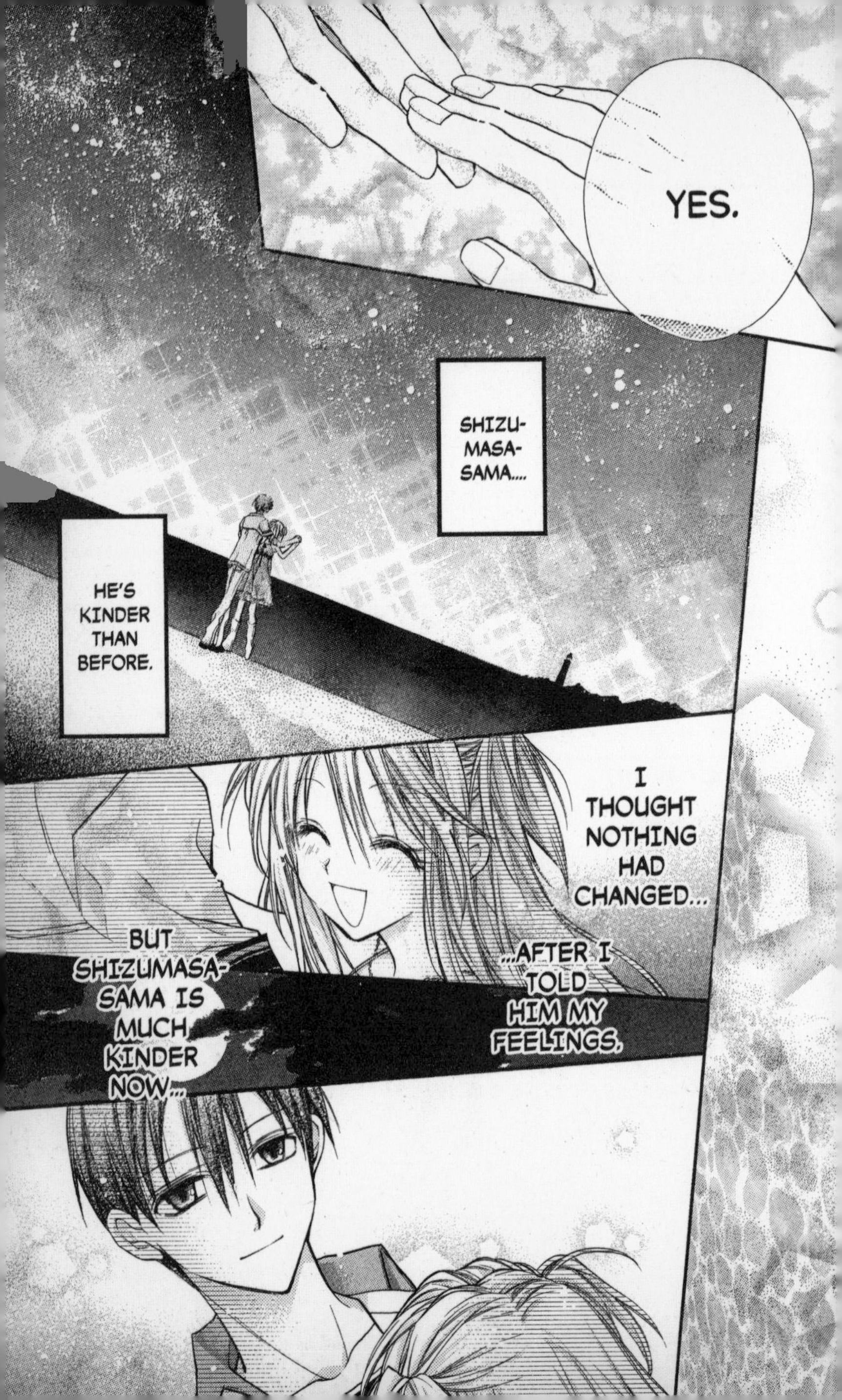
YES.
SHIZU-MASA-SAMA....
HE'S KINDER THAN BEFORE.
I THOUGHT NOTHING HAD CHANGED...
...AFTER I TOLD HIM MY FEELINGS.
BUT SHIZUMASA-SAMA IS MUCH KINDER NOW...

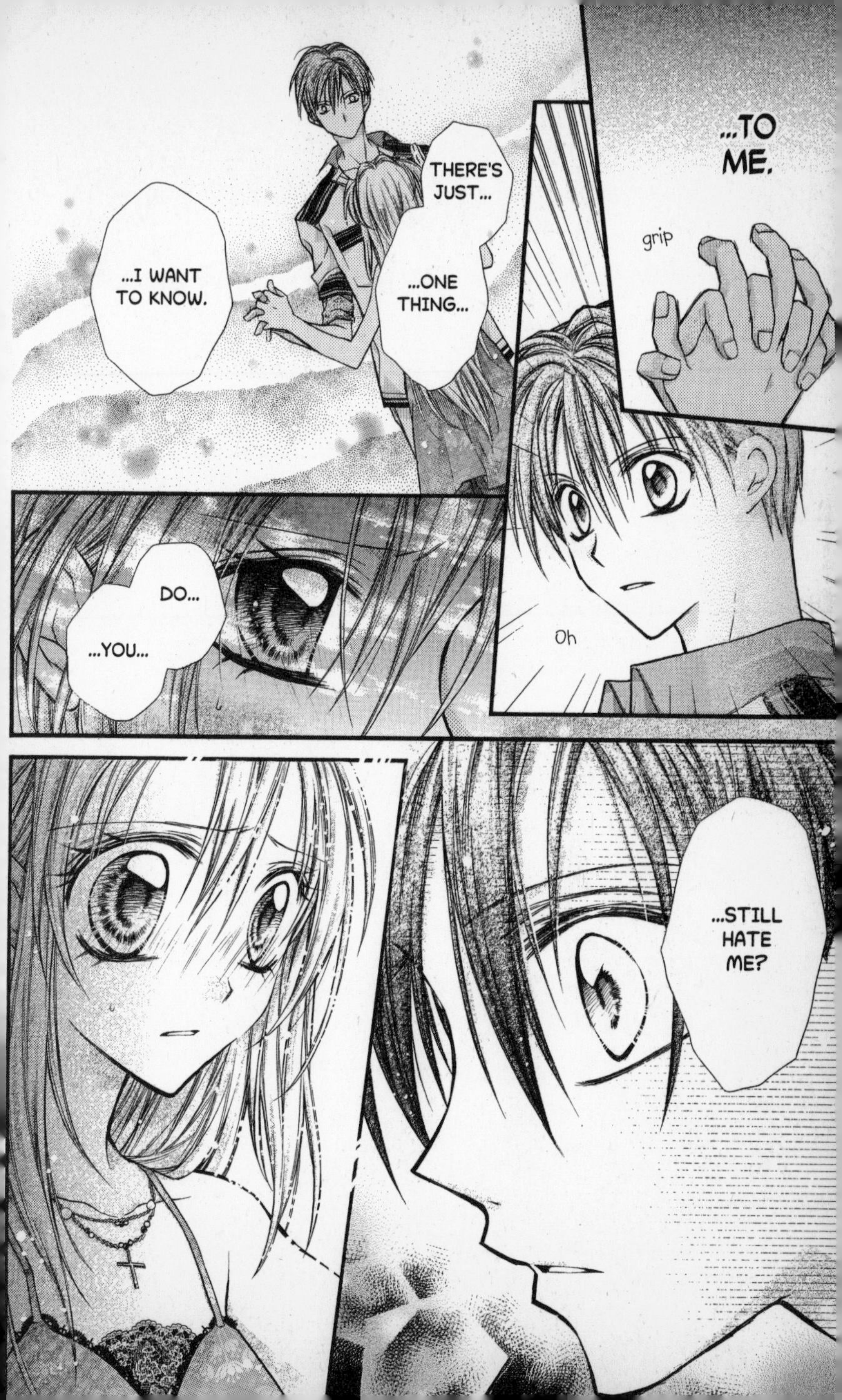
...TO ME.
grip
THERE'S JUST...
...ONE THING...
...I WANT TO KNOW.
Oh
DO...
...YOU...
...STILL HATE ME?

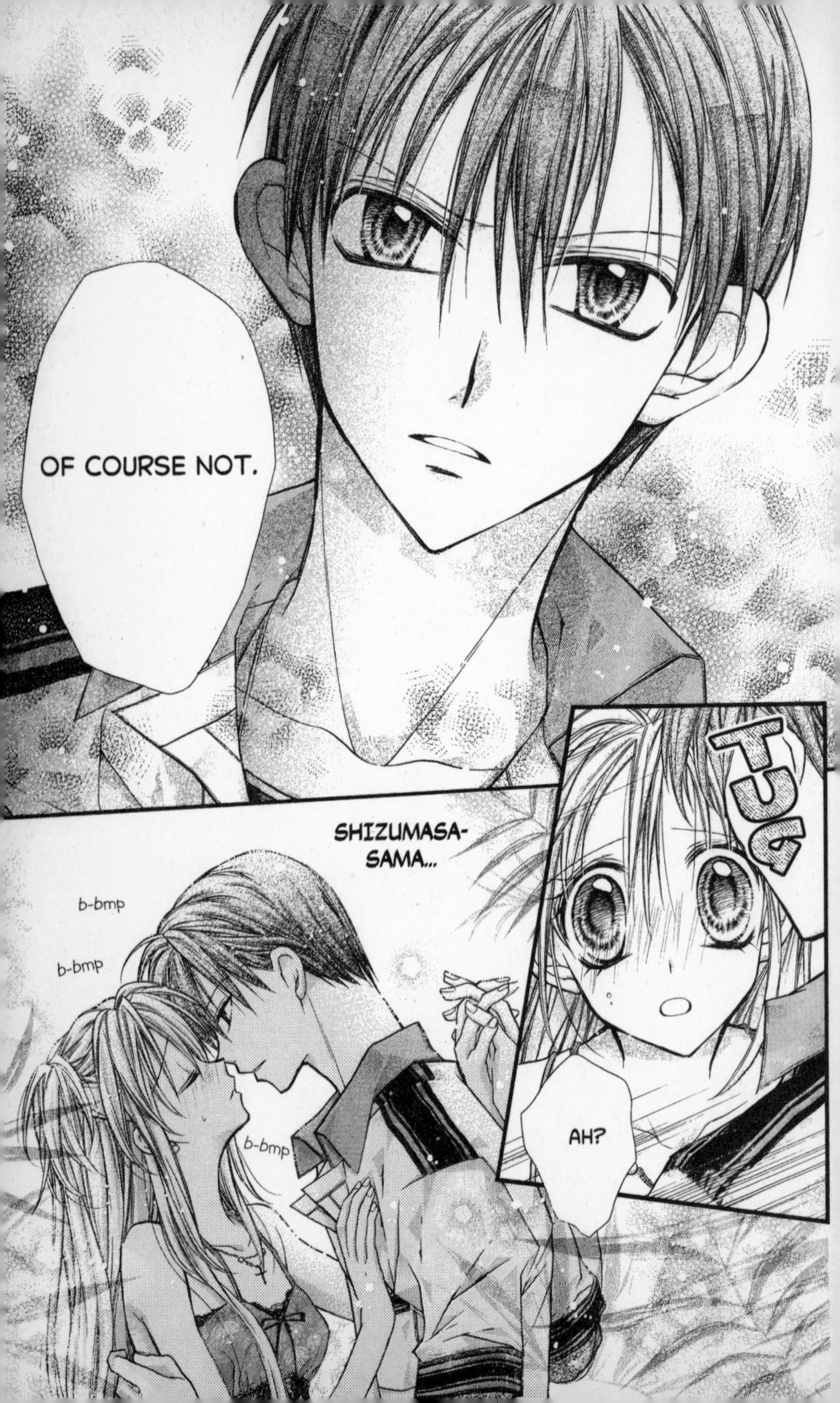

OF COURSE NOT.
TUG
AH?
SHIZUMASA-SAMA...
b-bmp
b-bmp
b-bmp

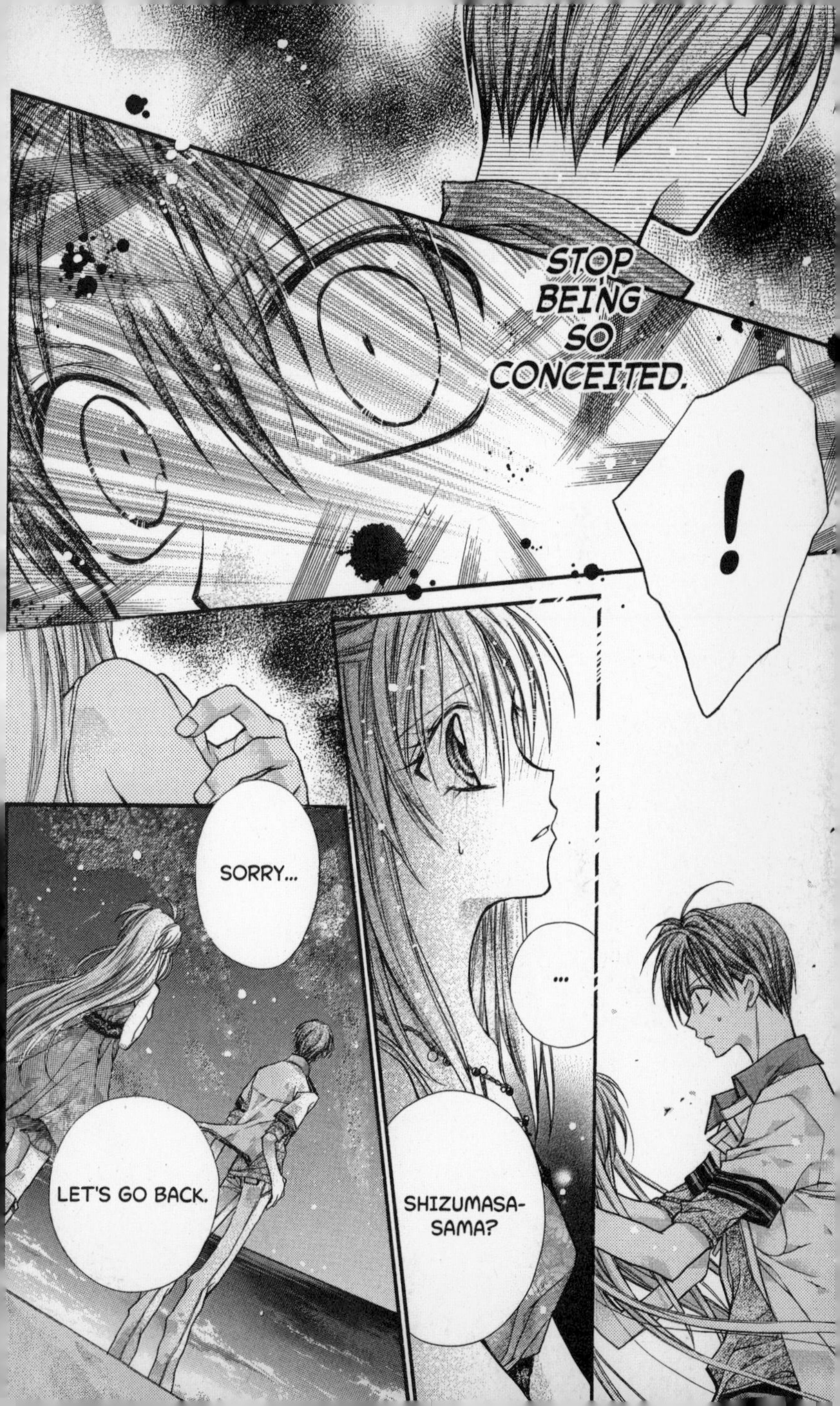
STOP BEING SO CONCEITED.
!
...
SHIZUMASA-SAMA?
SORRY...
LET'S GO BACK.

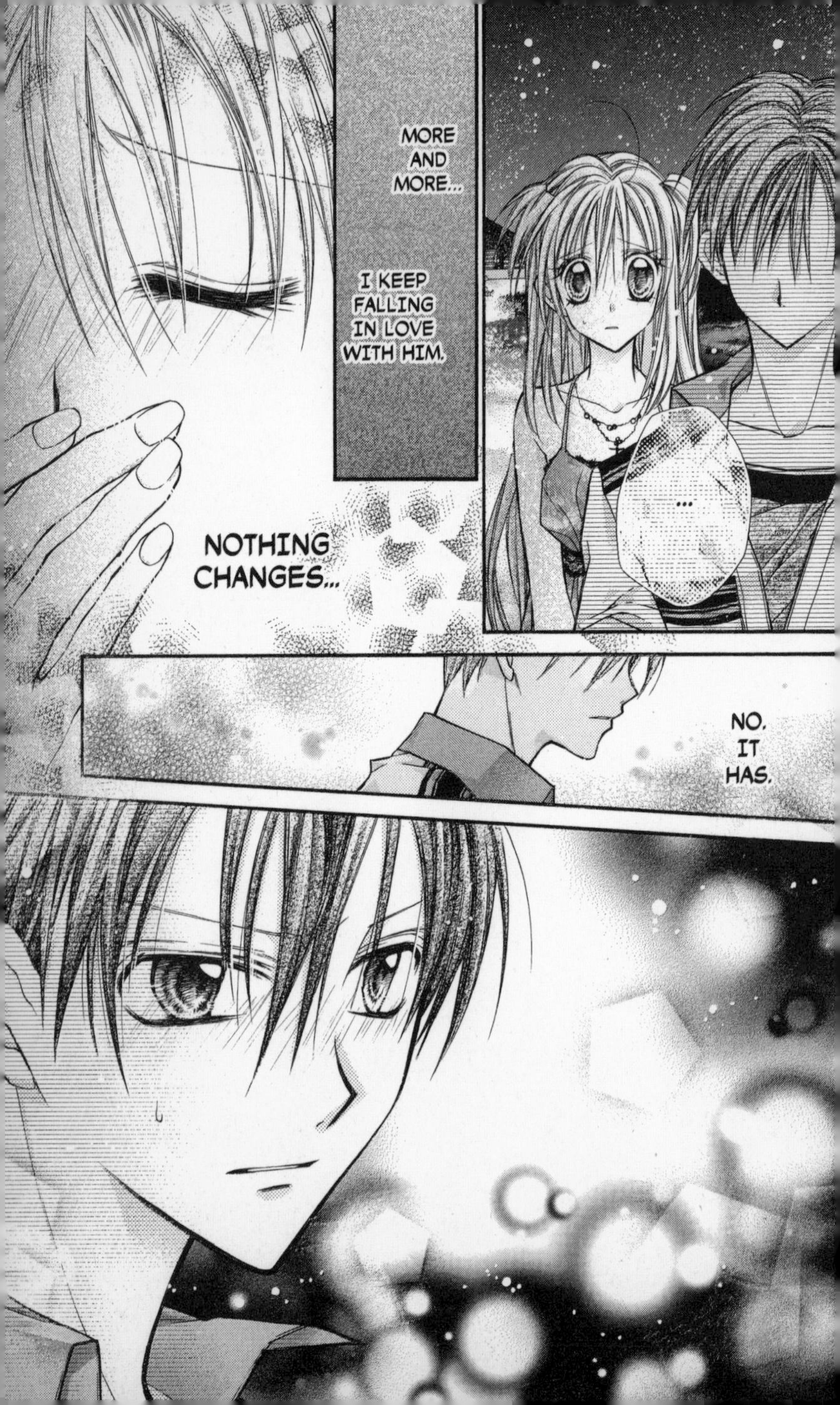
...
MORE AND MORE...
I KEEP FALLING IN LOVE WITH HIM.
NOTHING CHANGES...
NO. IT HAS.

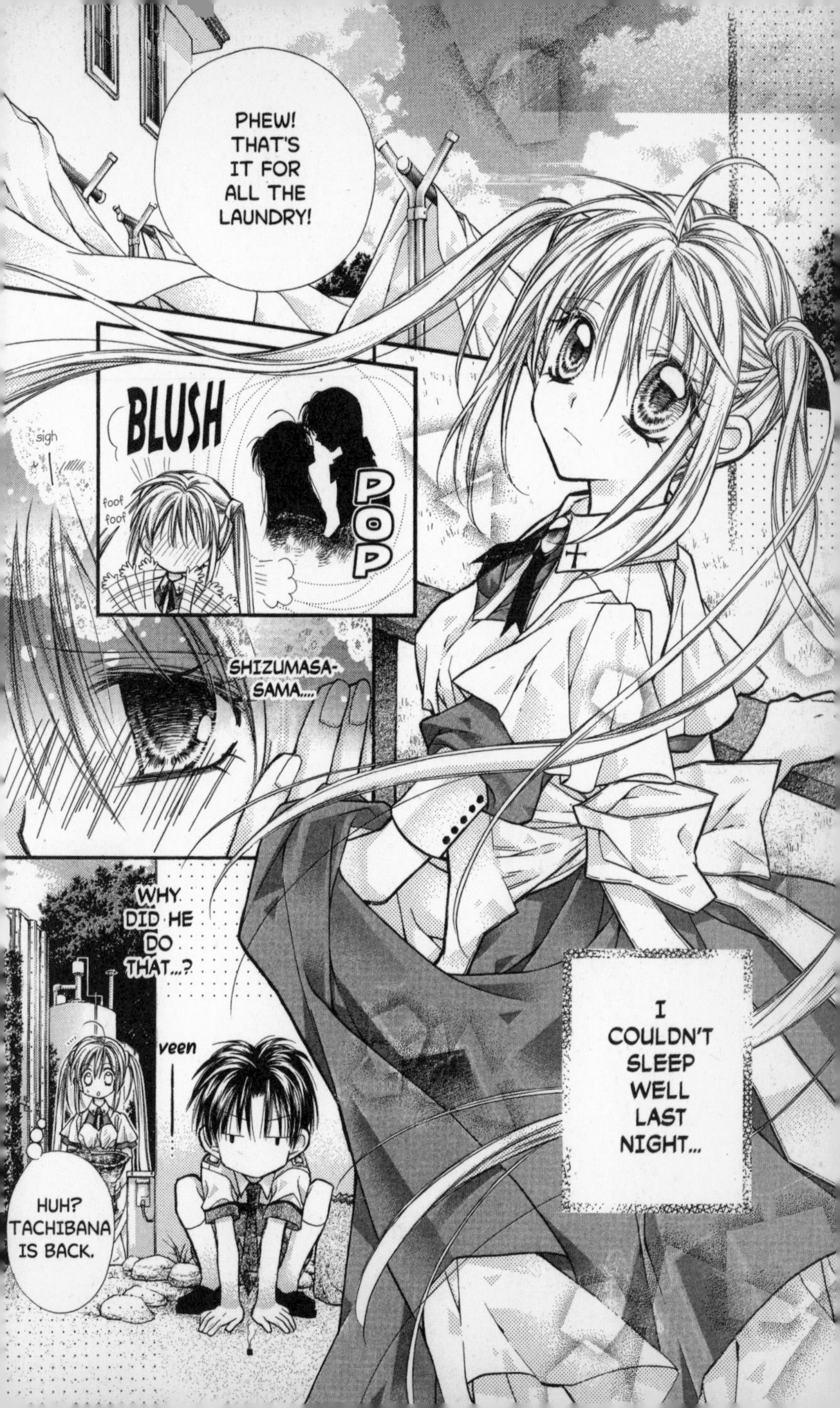
PHEW! THAT'S IT FOR ALL THE LAUNDRY!
I COULDN'T SLEEP WELL LAST NIGHT...
BLUSH
POP
sigh
foof foof
SHIZUMASA-SAMA...
WHY DID HE DO THAT...?
veen
HUH? TACHIBANA IS BACK.

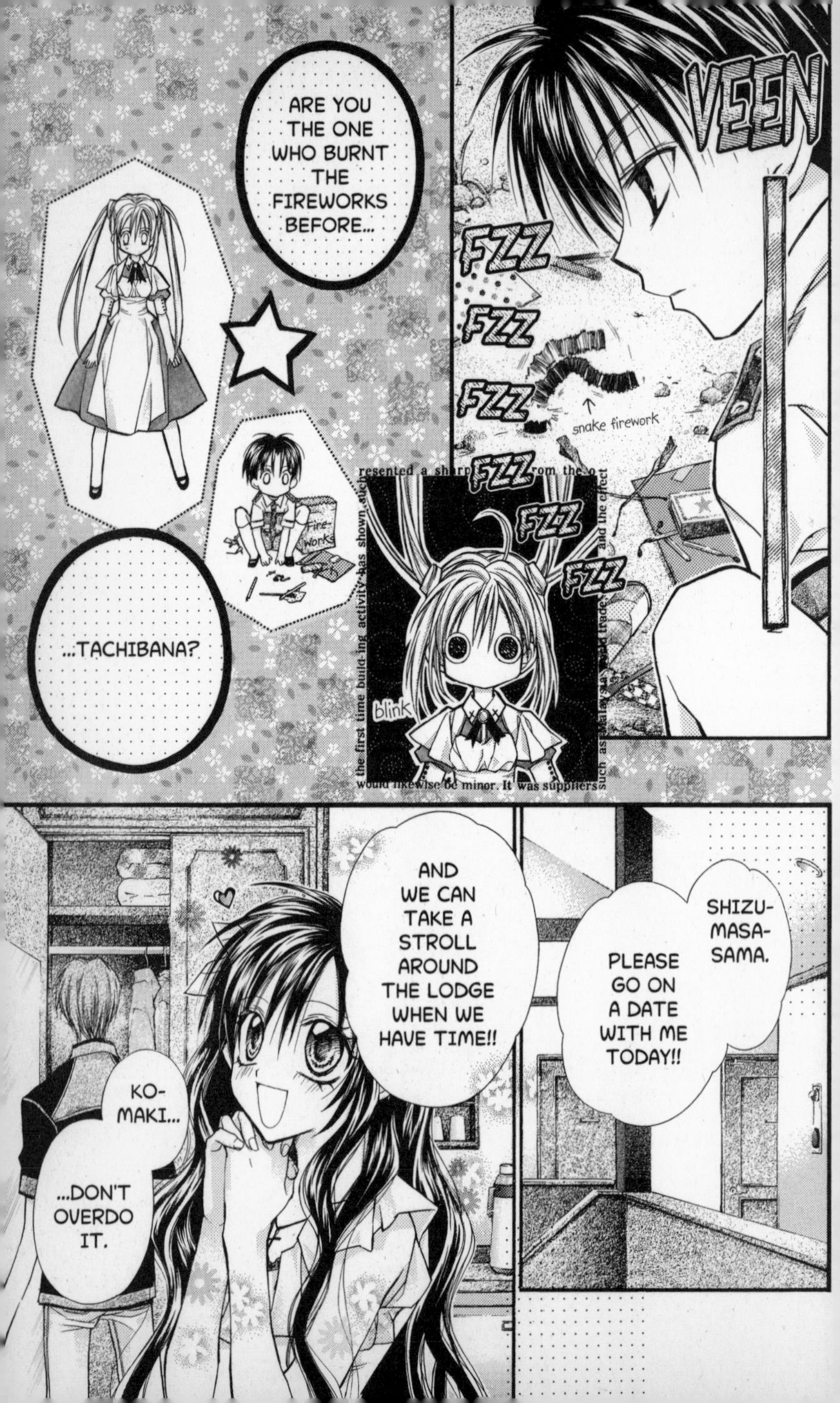
VEEN
FZZ
FZZ
FZZ
snake firework
FZZ
FZZ
FZZ
blink
ARE YOU THE ONE WHO BURNT THE FIREWORKS BEFORE...
Fire-works
...TACHIBANA?
SHIZU-MASA-SAMA.
PLEASE GO ON A DATE WITH ME TODAY!!
AND WE CAN TAKE A STROLL AROUND THE LODGE WHEN WE HAVE TIME!!
KO-MAKI...
...DON'T OVERDO IT.

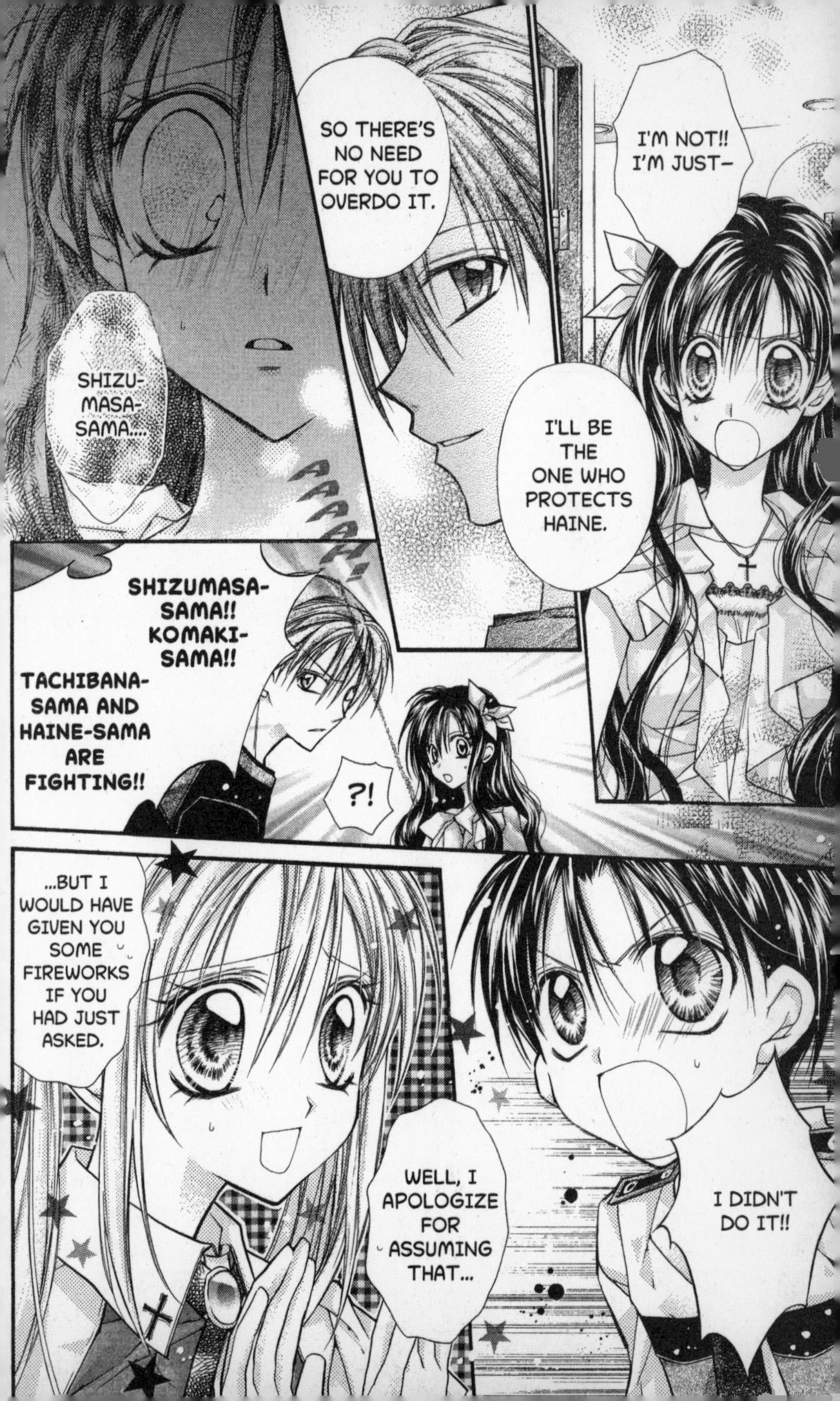

I'M NOT!! I'M JUST–
SO THERE'S NO NEED FOR YOU TO OVERDO IT.
I'LL BE THE ONE WHO PROTECTS HAINE.
SHIZU-MASA-SAMA....
SHIZUMASA-SAMA!! KOMAKI-SAMA!!
TACHIBANA-SAMA AND HAINE-SAMA ARE FIGHTING!!
?!
I DIDN'T DO IT!!
WELL, I APOLOGIZE FOR ASSUMING THAT...
...BUT I WOULD HAVE GIVEN YOU SOME FIREWORKS IF YOU HAD JUST ASKED.

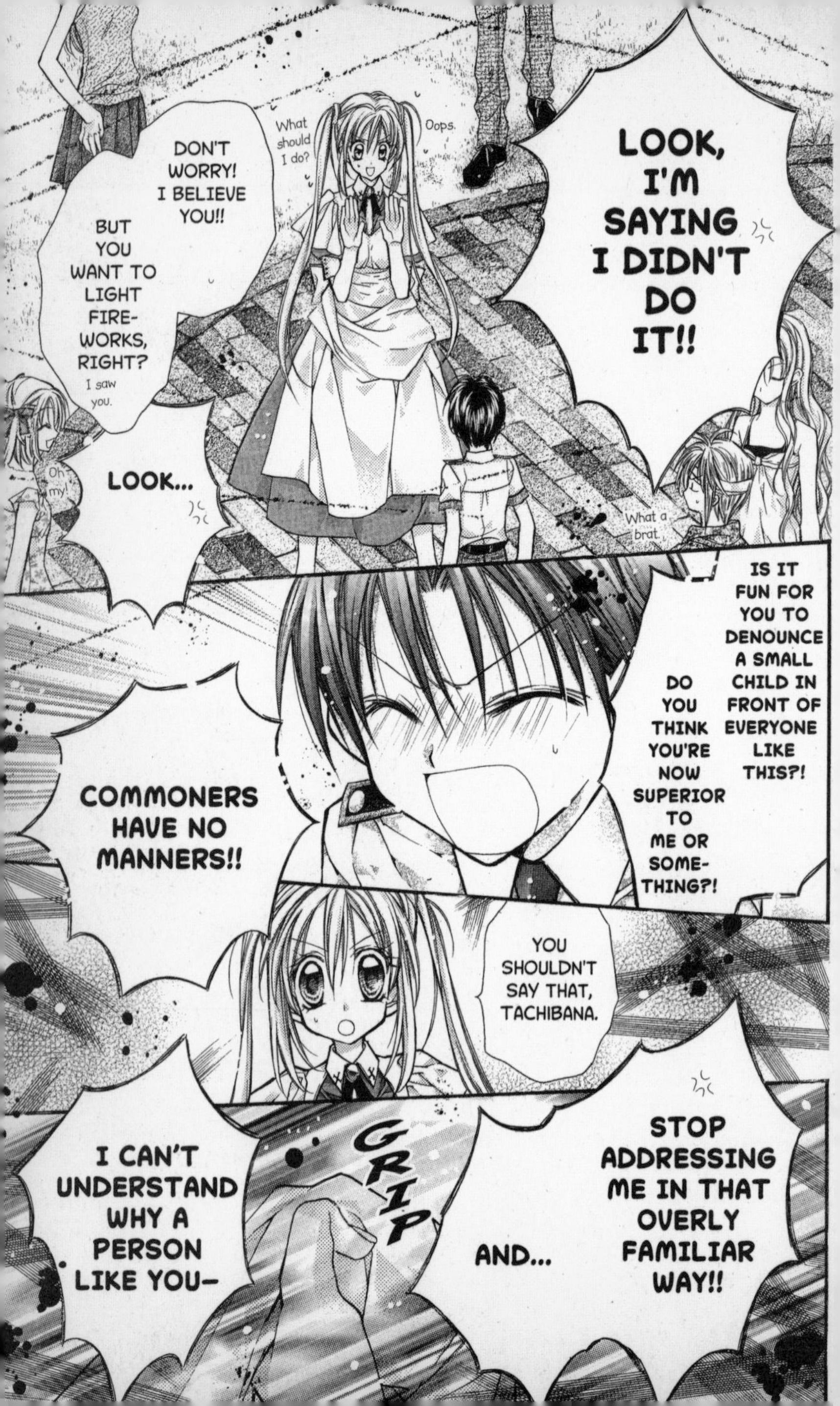

LOOK, I'M SAYING I DIDN'T DO IT!!
Oops.
What should I do?
DON'T WORRY! I BELIEVE YOU!!
BUT YOU WANT TO LIGHT FIRE-WORKS, RIGHT?
I saw you.
What a brat.
LOOK...
Oh my!
IS IT FUN FOR YOU TO DENOUNCE A SMALL CHILD IN FRONT OF EVERYONE LIKE THIS?!
DO YOU THINK YOU'RE NOW SUPERIOR TO ME OR SOME-THING?!
COMMONERS HAVE NO MANNERS!!
YOU SHOULDN'T SAY THAT, TACHIBANA.
STOP ADDRESSING ME IN THAT OVERLY FAMILIAR WAY!!
AND...
GRIP
I CAN'T UNDERSTAND WHY A PERSON LIKE YOU–

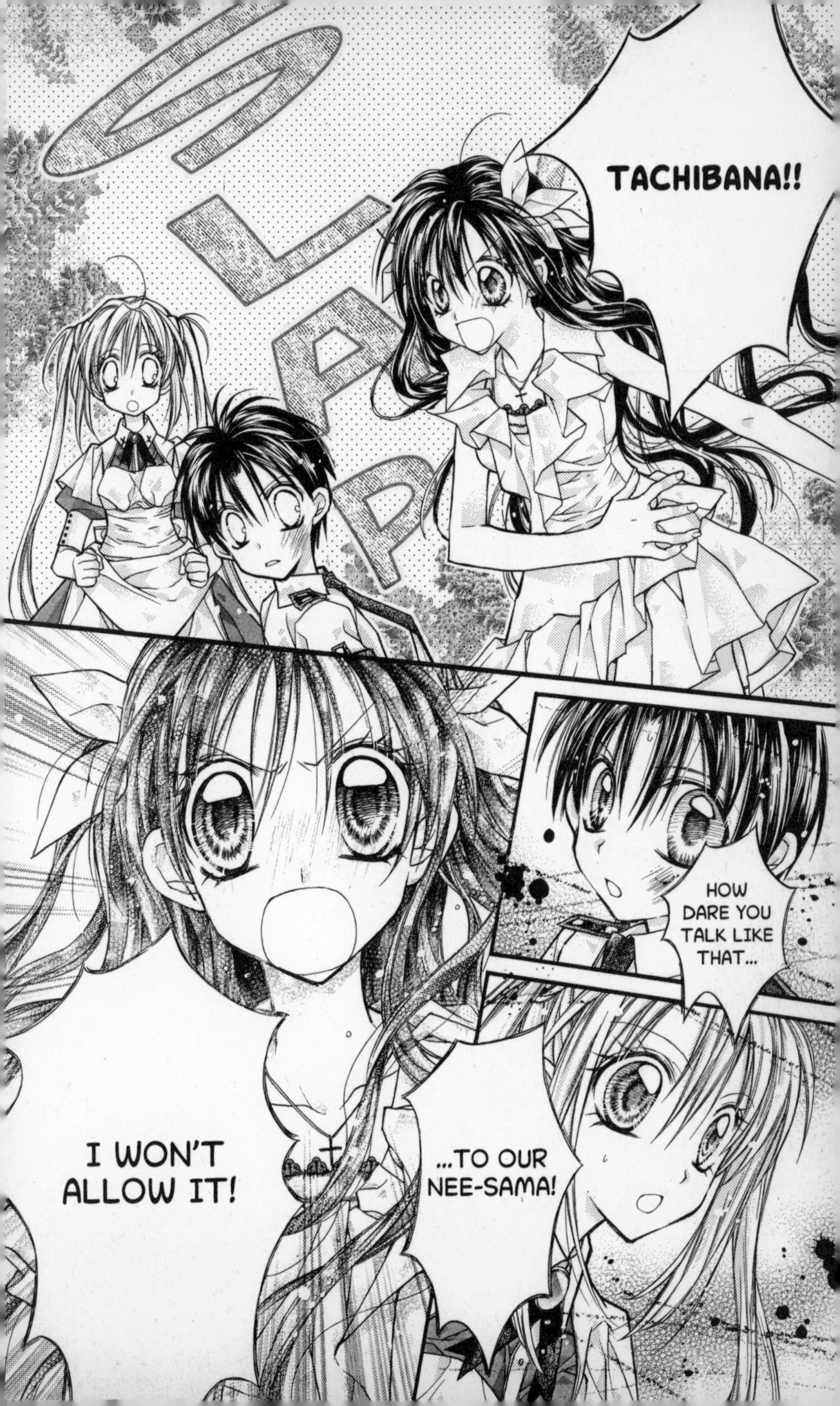
SLAP
TACHIBANA!!
HOW DARE YOU TALK LIKE THAT...
...TO OUR NEE-SAMA!
I WON'T ALLOW IT!

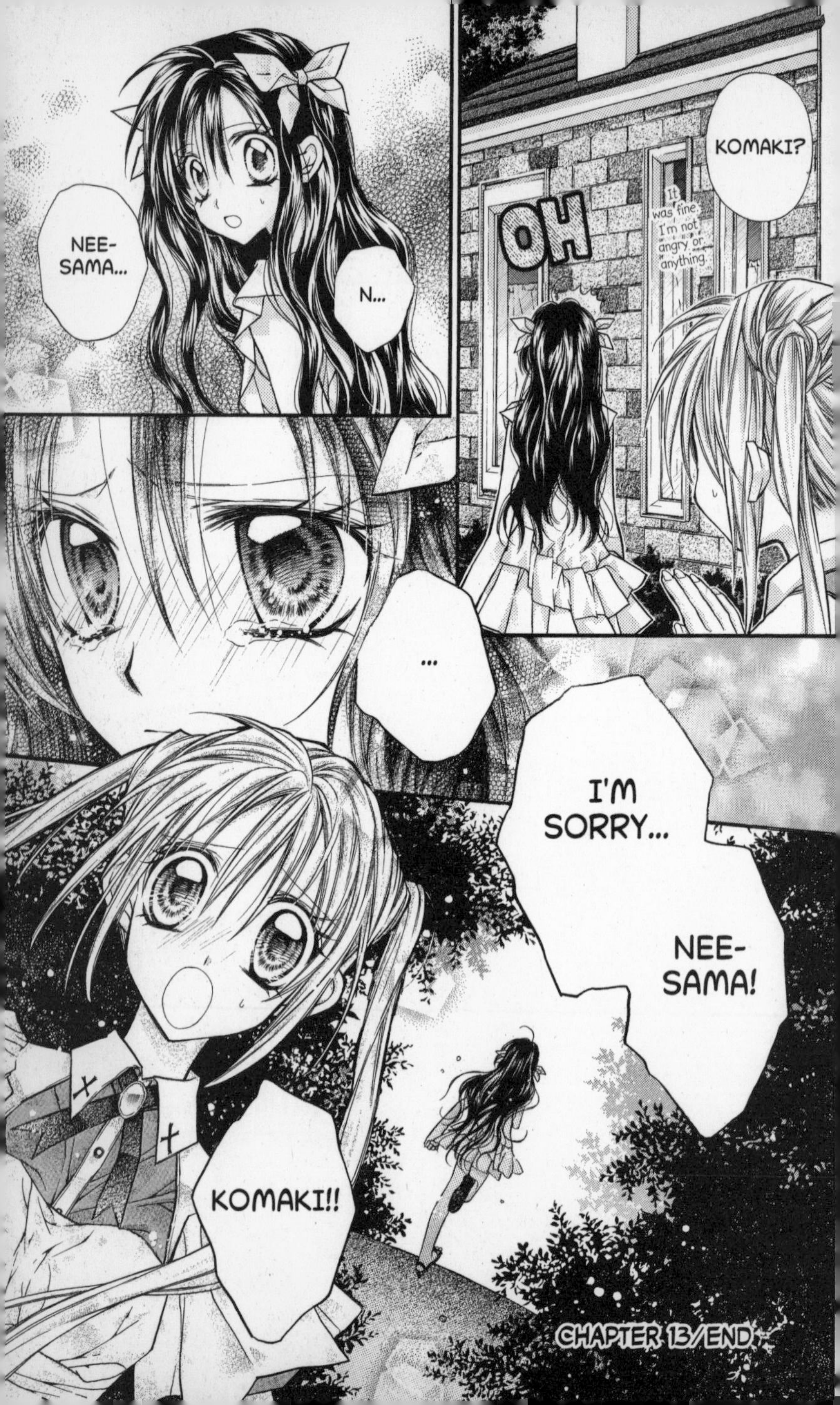
KOMAKI?
OH
It was fine. I'm not angry or anything.
N...
NEE-SAMA...
...
I'M SORRY... NEE-SAMA!
KOMAKI!!
CHAPTER 13/END

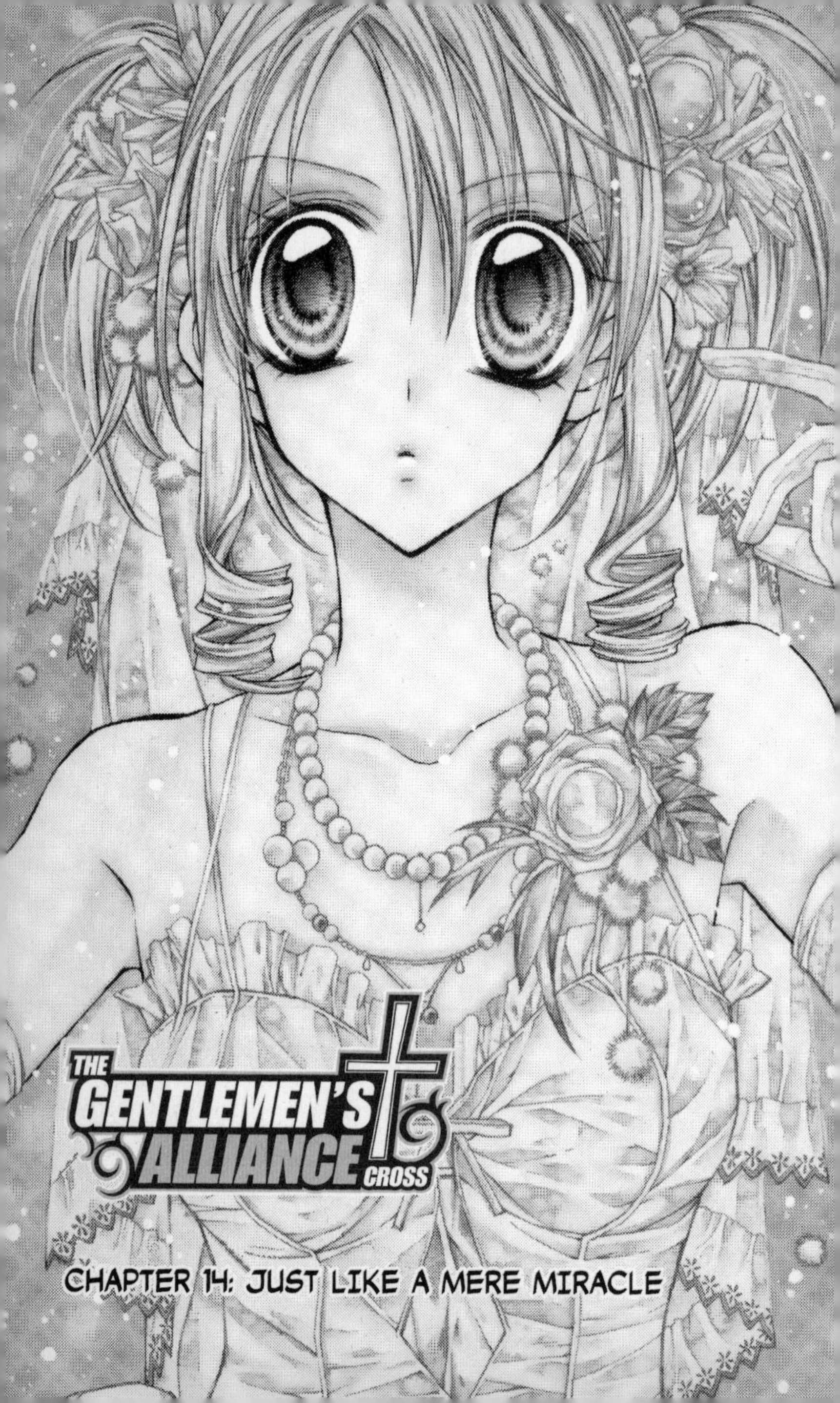
THE GENTLEMEN'S ALLIANCE CROSS
CHAPTER 14: JUST LIKE A MERE MIRACLE

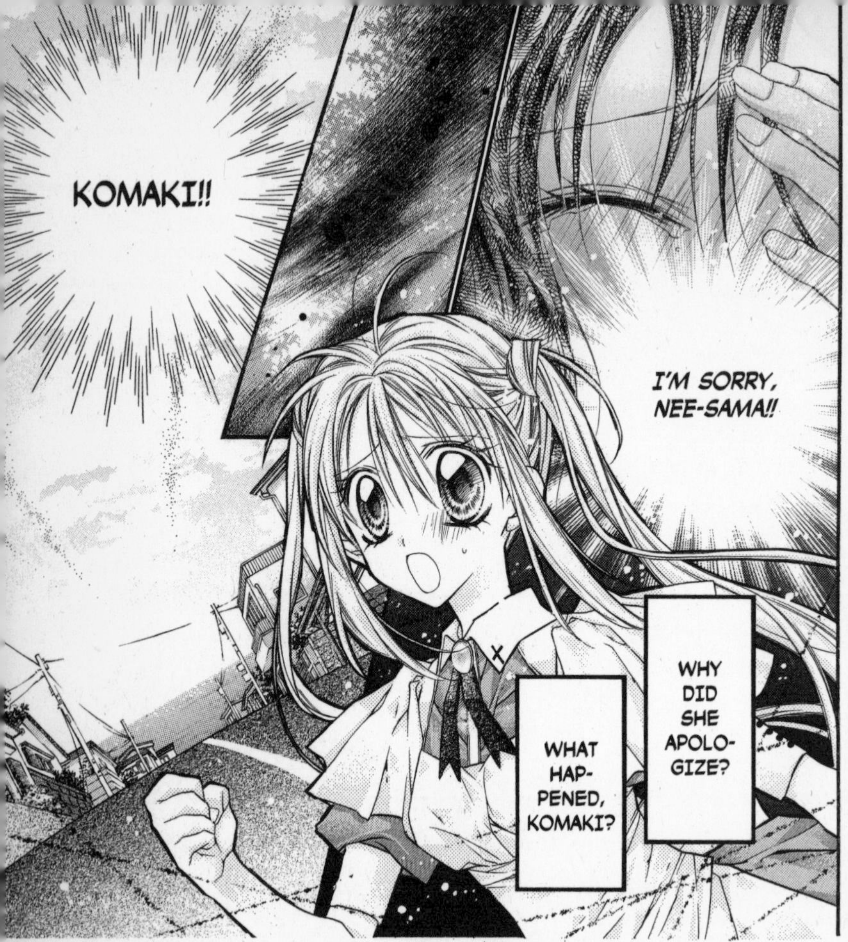
KOMAKI!!
I'M SORRY, NEE-SAMA!!
WHY DID SHE APOLOGIZE?
WHAT HAPPENED, KOMAKI?

Chapter 14: Just Like a Mere Miracle [Lead-in] I'm an invincible☆bride!

↙ I may have said this before, but...

Actually, I'm doing a "let's go ahead and draw the things I'm actually not that good at drawing" campaign for *The Gentleman's Alliance Cross* series. I wasn't very fond of Komaki's black wavy hair because it looked like something from an old manga. I decided to give her a very light wave, and... Tah-dah! Problem solved! Komaki's ribbon...the tip of that bandanna-like object... I didn't like it, but I decided to use it anyway because it would look the same as Mao-chan's if I had drawn an ordinary ribbon. But it turned out pretty nice once I drew it, so... Tah-dah! Problem solved!!

And blond hair... I wasn't confident that I'd be able to draw over the pencil lines that well with a pen, but I didn't want four out of the five main characters to have white hair (in black and white with screentones), so I decided to give it a shot...

I'm still not very good at it, but I don't feel as uncomfortable as I did before drawing it, I think... Ta-dah! Problem solved! There's a lot of other things too, but... I'm trying very hard.

I'm going to overcome my weaknesses.
Yeah!

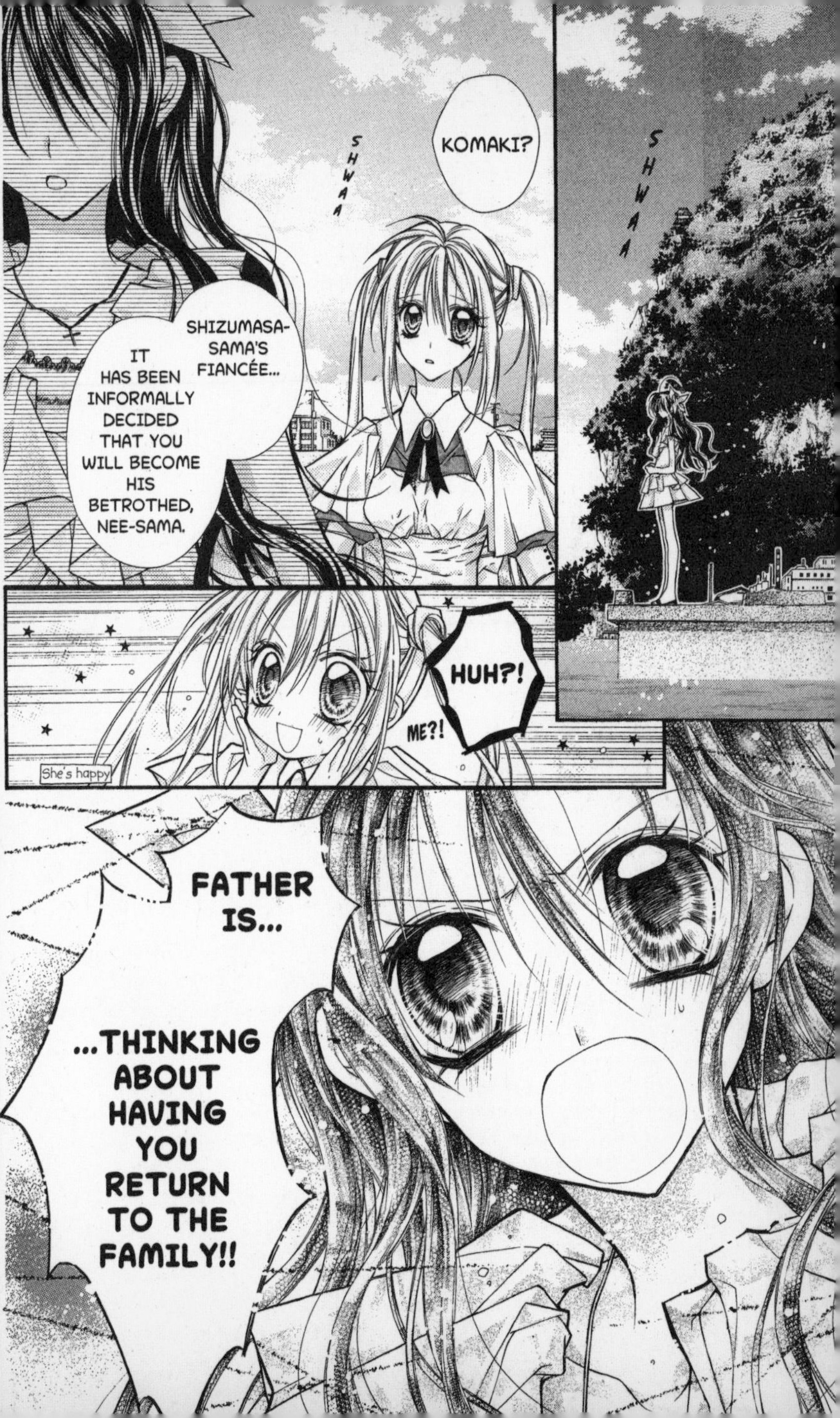
SHWAA
KOMAKI?
SHWAA
SHIZUMASA-SAMA'S FIANCÉE...
IT HAS BEEN INFORMALLY DECIDED THAT YOU WILL BECOME HIS BETROTHED, NEE-SAMA.
HUH?!
ME?!
She's happy
FATHER IS...
...THINKING ABOUT HAVING YOU RETURN TO THE FAMILY!!

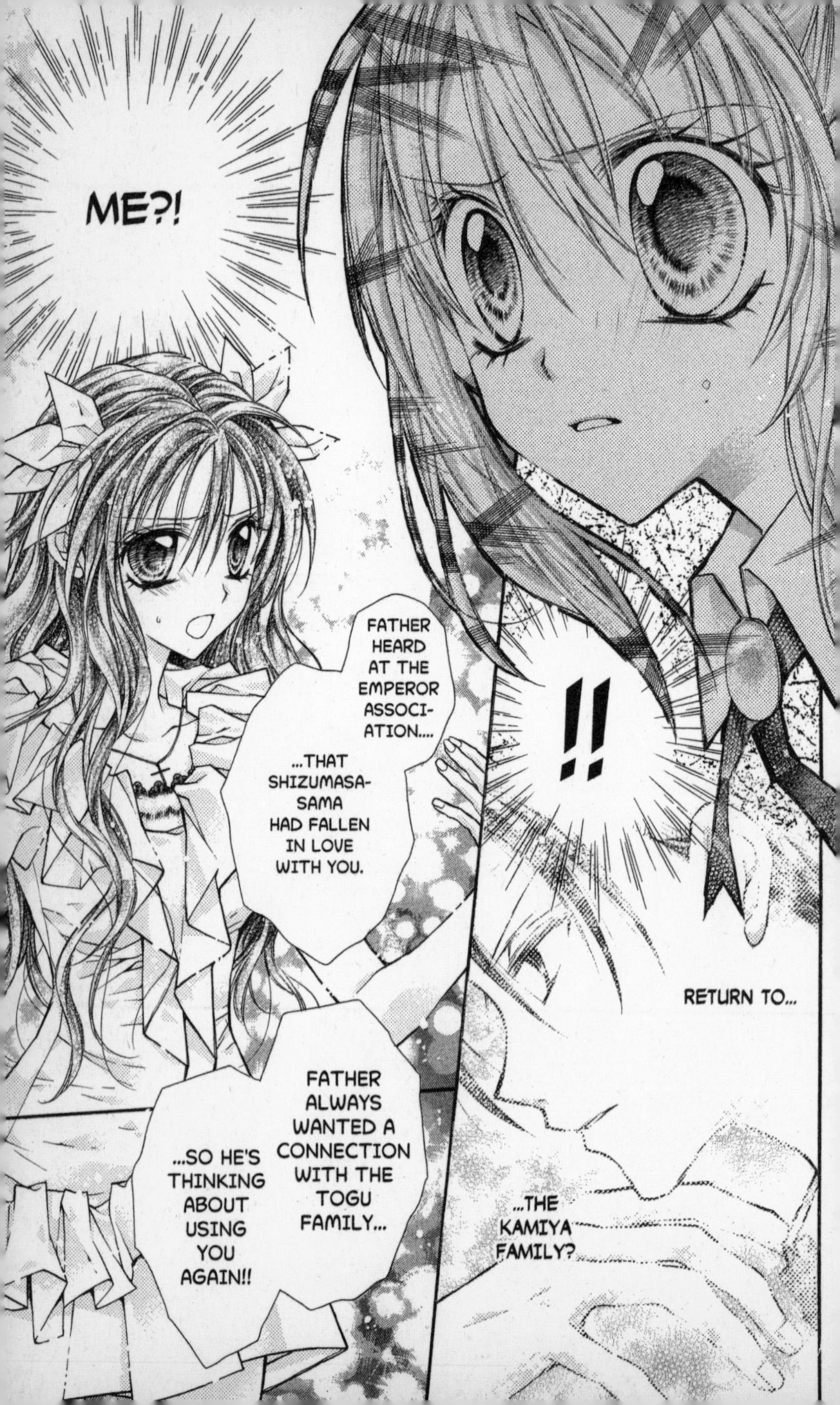
!!
RETURN TO...
...THE KAMIYA FAMILY?
ME?!
FATHER HEARD AT THE EMPEROR ASSOCI-ATION....
...THAT SHIZUMASA-SAMA HAD FALLEN IN LOVE WITH YOU.
FATHER ALWAYS WANTED A CONNECTION WITH THE TOGU FAMILY...
...SO HE'S THINKING ABOUT USING YOU AGAIN!!

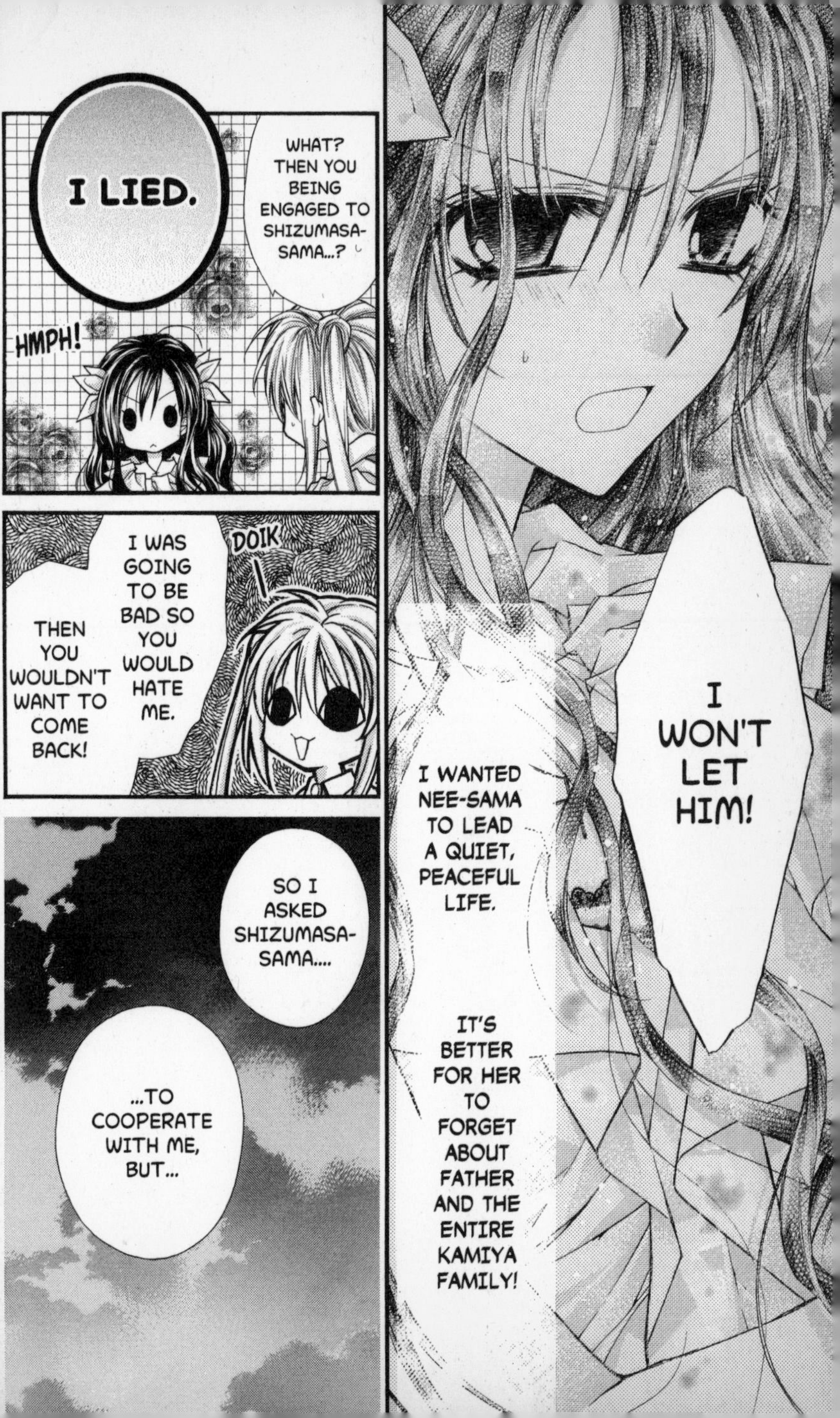
I WON'T LET HIM!
I WANTED NEE-SAMA TO LEAD A QUIET, PEACEFUL LIFE.
IT'S BETTER FOR HER TO FORGET ABOUT FATHER AND THE ENTIRE KAMIYA FAMILY!
WHAT? THEN YOU BEING ENGAGED TO SHIZUMASA-SAMA...?
I LIED.
HMPH!
DOIK
I WAS GOING TO BE BAD SO YOU WOULD HATE ME.
THEN YOU WOULDN'T WANT TO COME BACK!
SO I ASKED SHIZUMASA-SAMA....
...TO COOPERATE WITH ME, BUT...

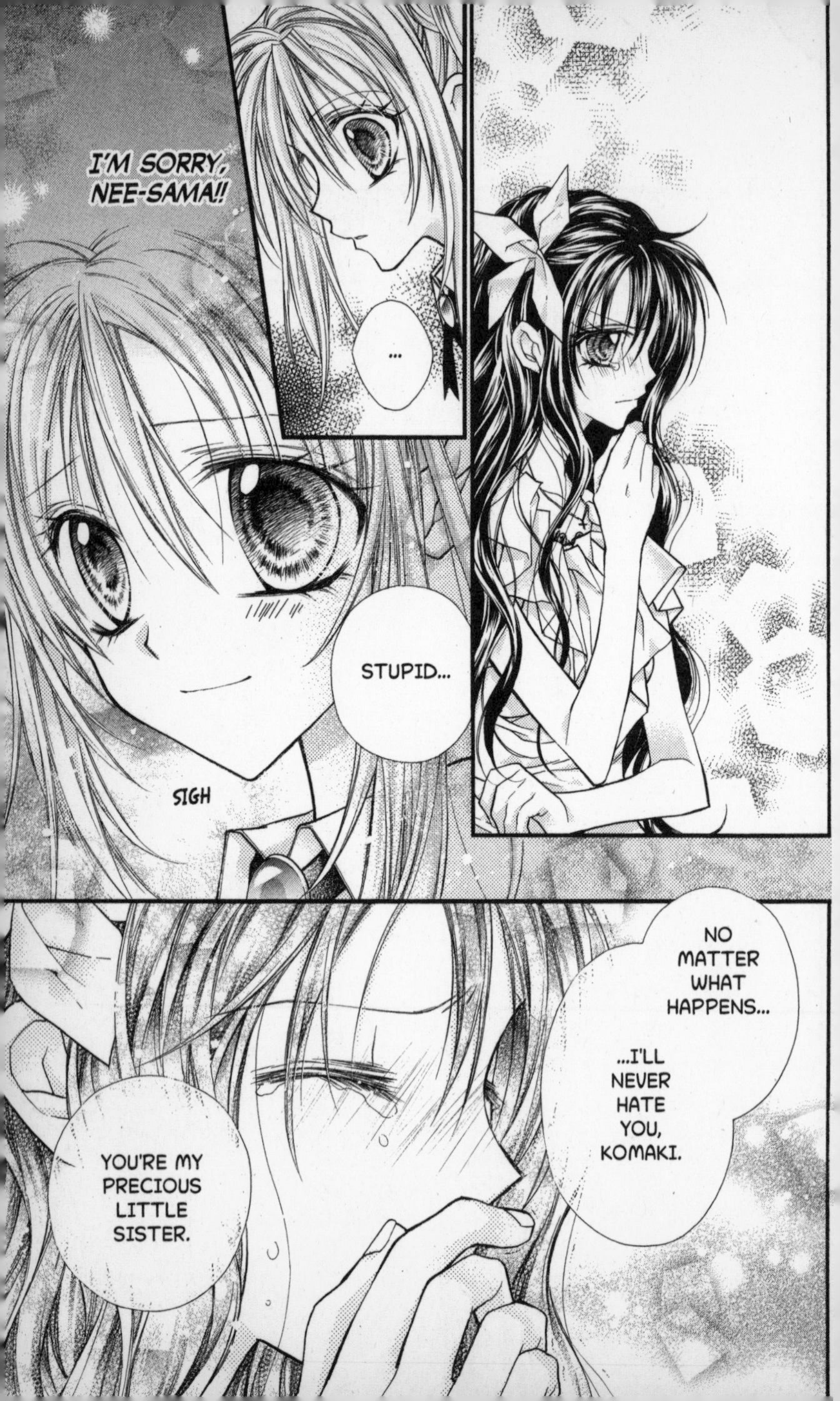
I'M SORRY, NEE-SAMA!!
...
STUPID...
SIGH
NO MATTER WHAT HAPPENS...
...I'LL NEVER HATE YOU, KOMAKI.
YOU'RE MY PRECIOUS LITTLE SISTER.

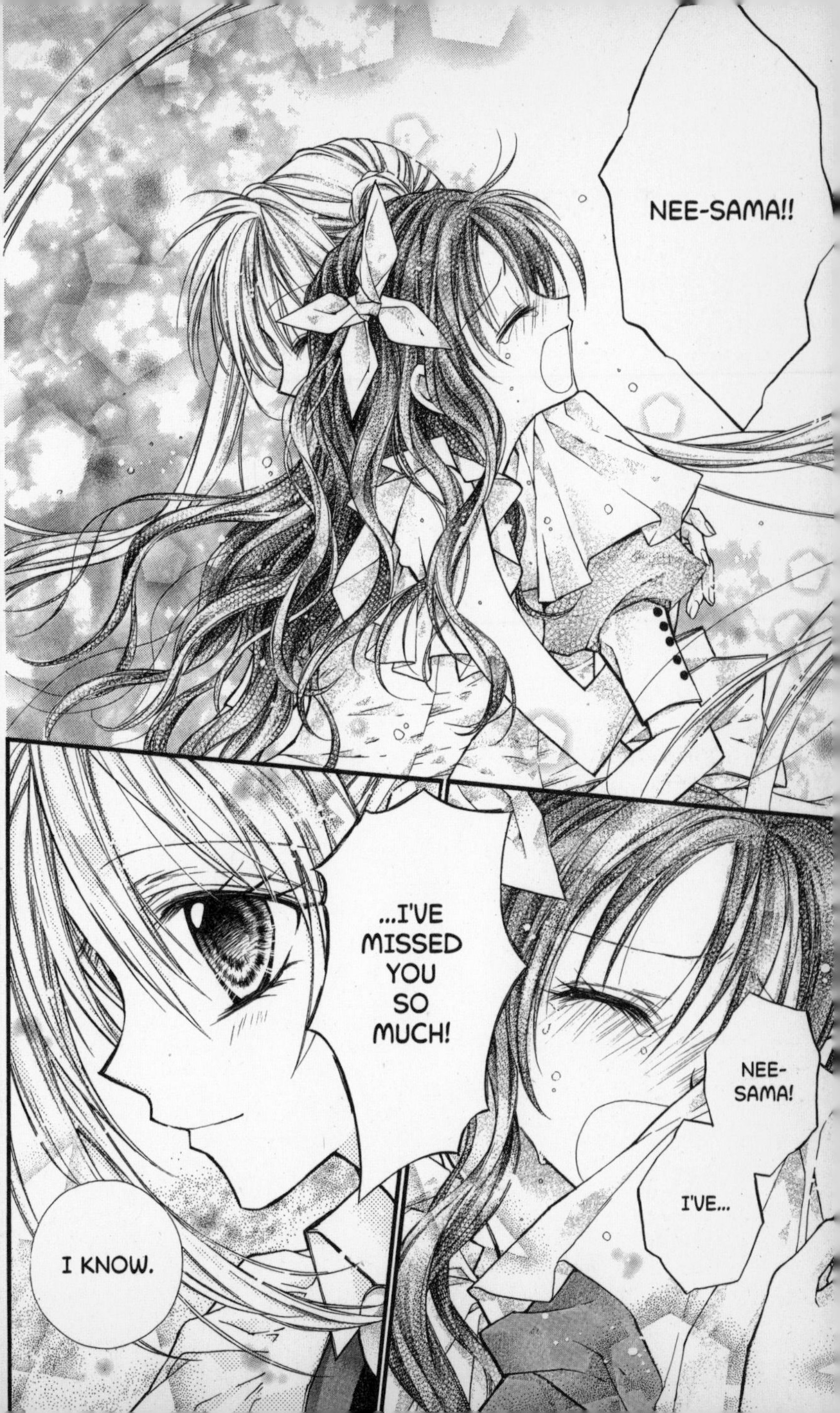

NEE-SAMA!!
NEE-SAMA!
I'VE...
...I'VE MISSED YOU SO MUCH!
I KNOW.

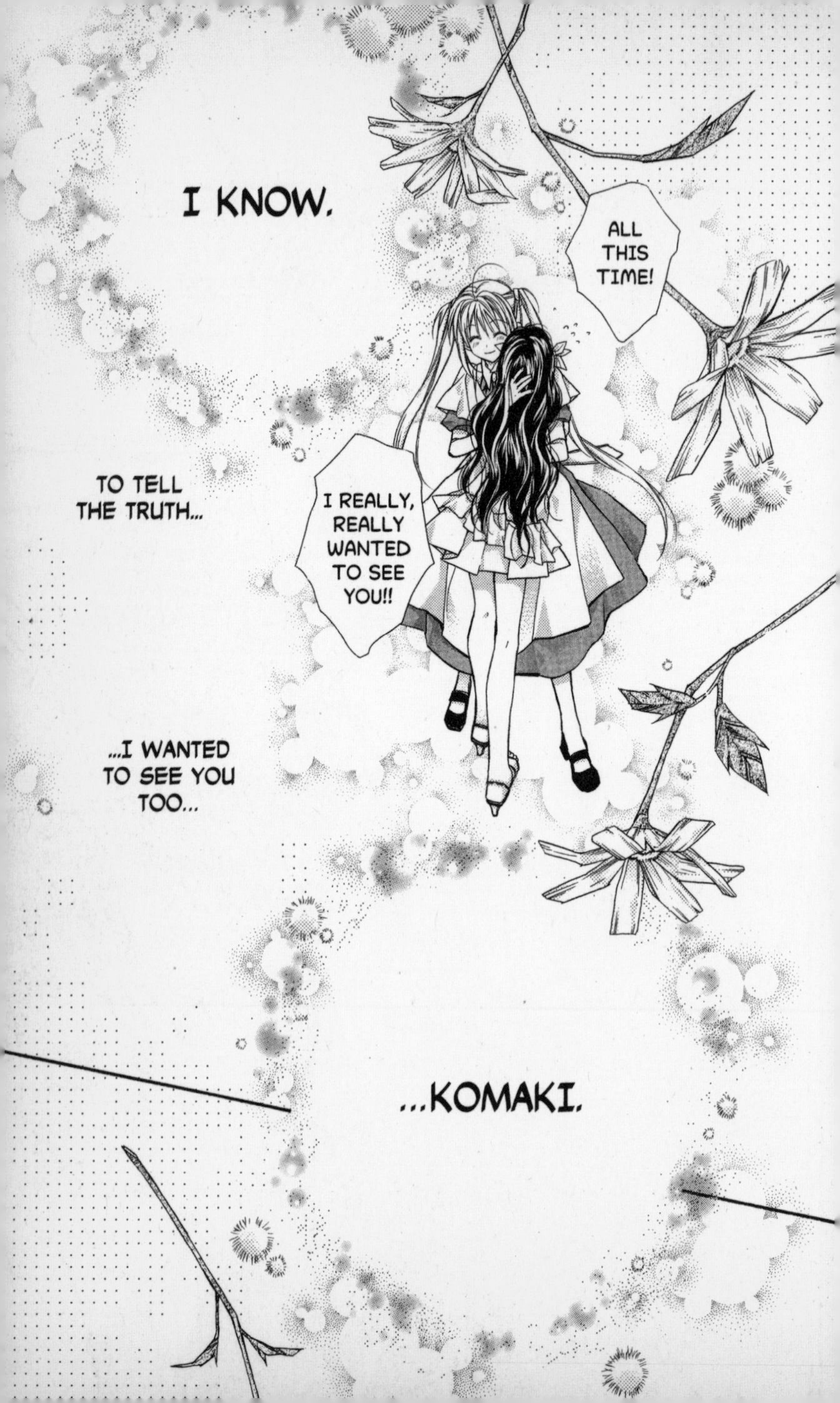
ALL THIS TIME!
I REALLY, REALLY WANTED TO SEE YOU!!
I KNOW.
TO TELL THE TRUTH...
...I WANTED TO SEE YOU TOO...
...KOMAKI.

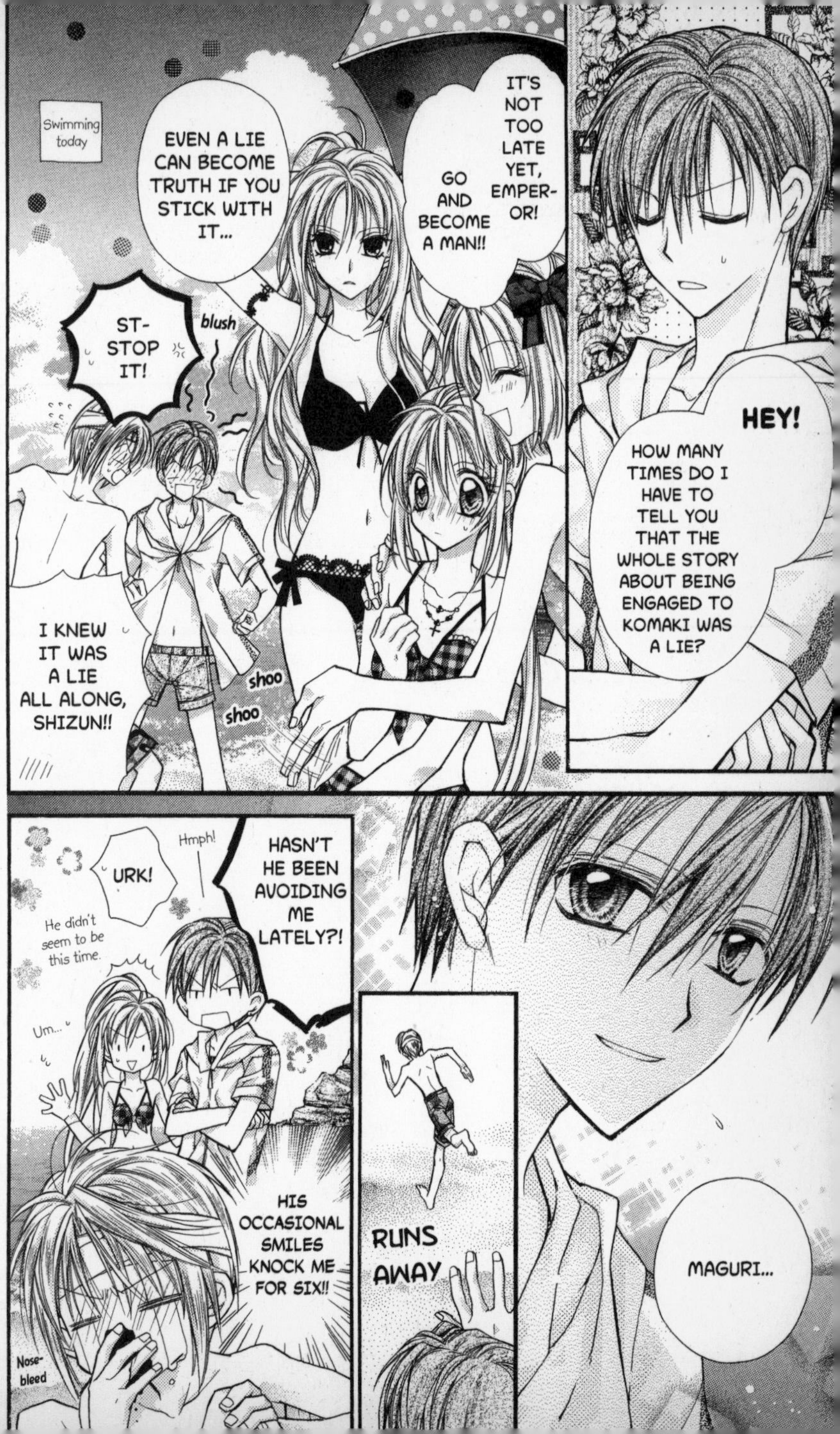
HEY!
HOW MANY TIMES DO I HAVE TO TELL YOU THAT THE WHOLE STORY ABOUT BEING ENGAGED TO KOMAKI WAS A LIE?
IT'S NOT TOO LATE YET, EMPEROR!
GO AND BECOME A MAN!!
EVEN A LIE CAN BECOME TRUTH IF YOU STICK WITH IT...
Swimming today
ST-STOP IT!
blush
I KNEW IT WAS A LIE ALL ALONG, SHIZUN!!
shoo
shoo
MAGURI...
RUNS AWAY
HASN'T HE BEEN AVOIDING ME LATELY?!
Hmph!
URK!
He didn't seem to be this time.
Um...
HIS OCCASIONAL SMILES KNOCK ME FOR SIX!!
Nose-bleed

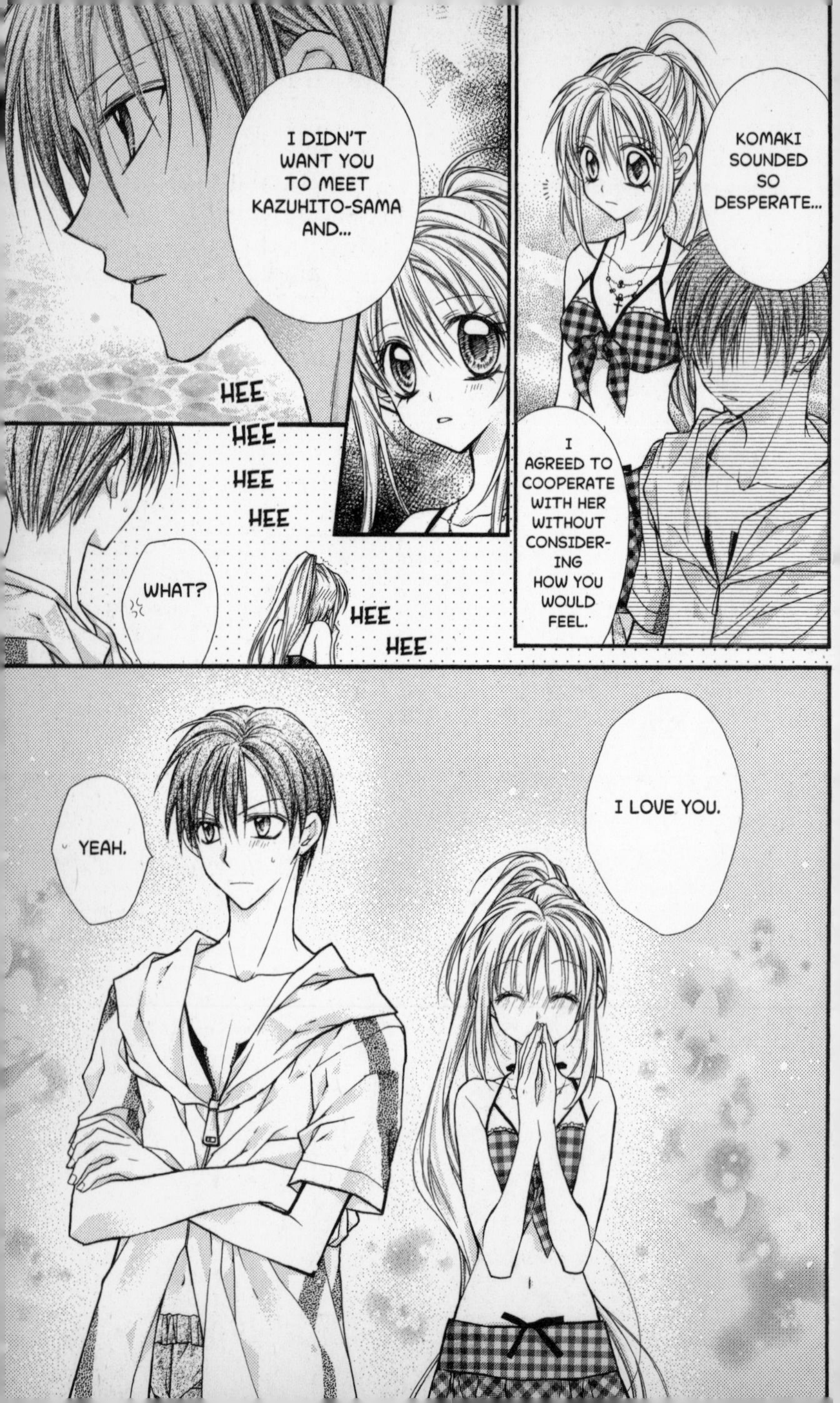
KOMAKI SOUNDED SO DESPERATE...
I AGREED TO COOPERATE WITH HER WITHOUT CONSIDER-ING HOW YOU WOULD FEEL.
I DIDN'T WANT YOU TO MEET KAZUHITO-SAMA AND...
HEE HEE HEE HEE HEE HEE
WHAT?
I LOVE YOU.
YEAH.

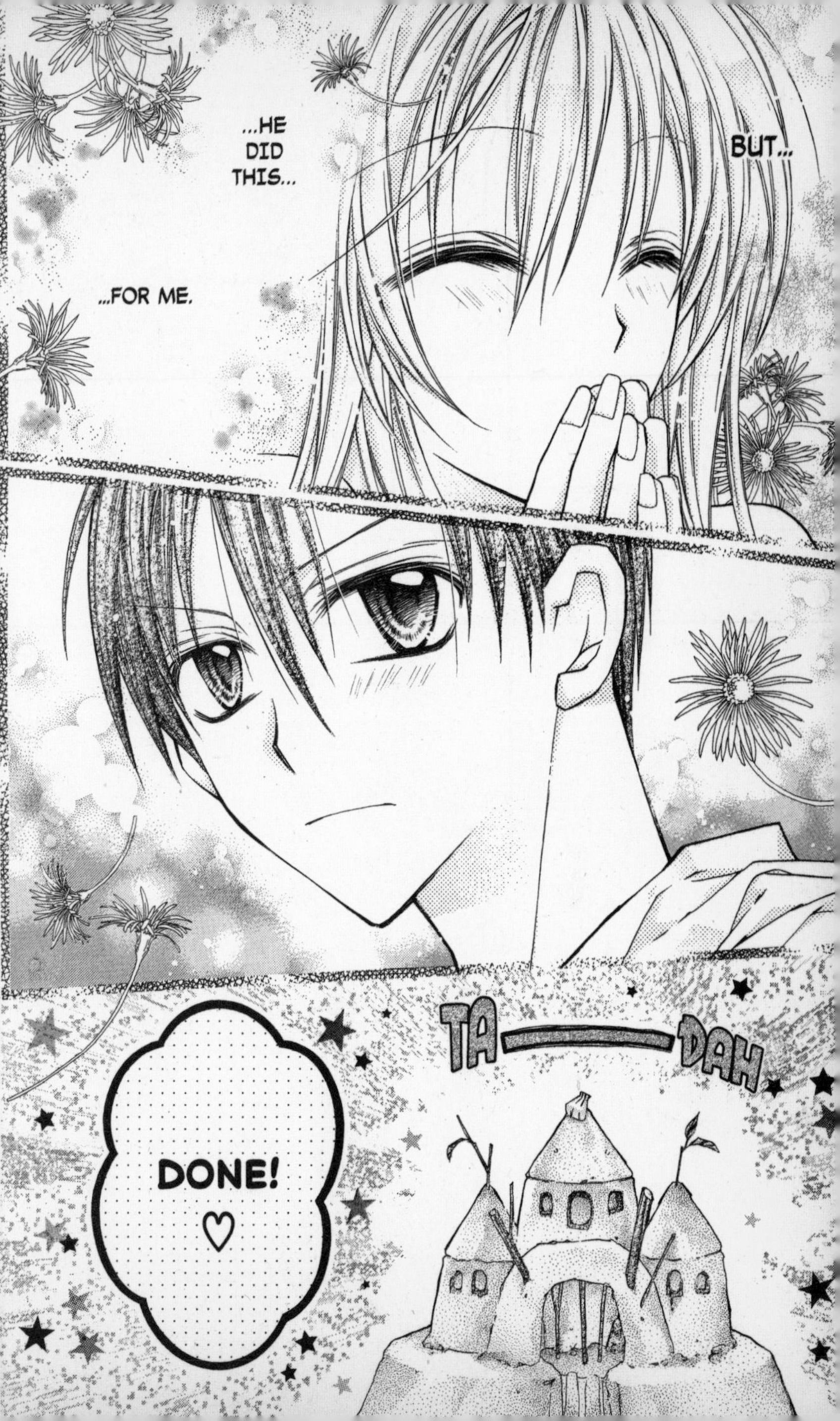
BUT...
...HE DID THIS...
...FOR ME.
TA——DAH
DONE! ♡

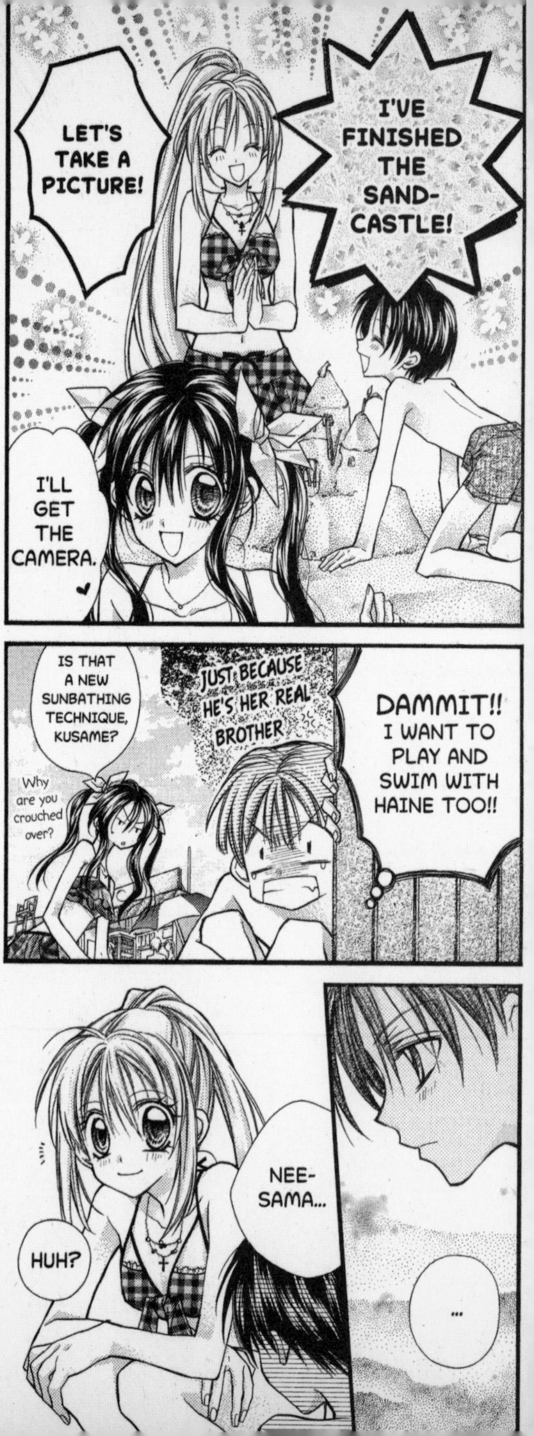
I'VE FINISHED THE SAND-CASTLE!
LET'S TAKE A PICTURE!
I'LL GET THE CAMERA.
DAMMIT!! I WANT TO PLAY AND SWIM WITH HAINE TOO!!
JUST BECAUSE HE'S HER REAL BROTHER
IS THAT A NEW SUNBATHING TECHNIQUE, KUSAME?
Why are you crouched over?
...
NEE-SAMA...
HUH?

Greetings

✿ Some information...

If you get ☆Ribon's January edition (currently on sale) it comes with a bonus scarf! (And it's fleece too. ♥Wow!!)

✿ Maguri is going to be on the cover of volume 4.

I've got some things on my mind... So please look forward to it!!

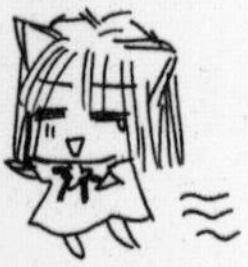

Sorry, I look so tired.

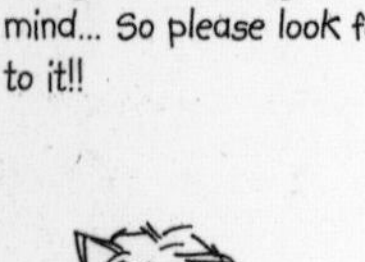
mew
mew

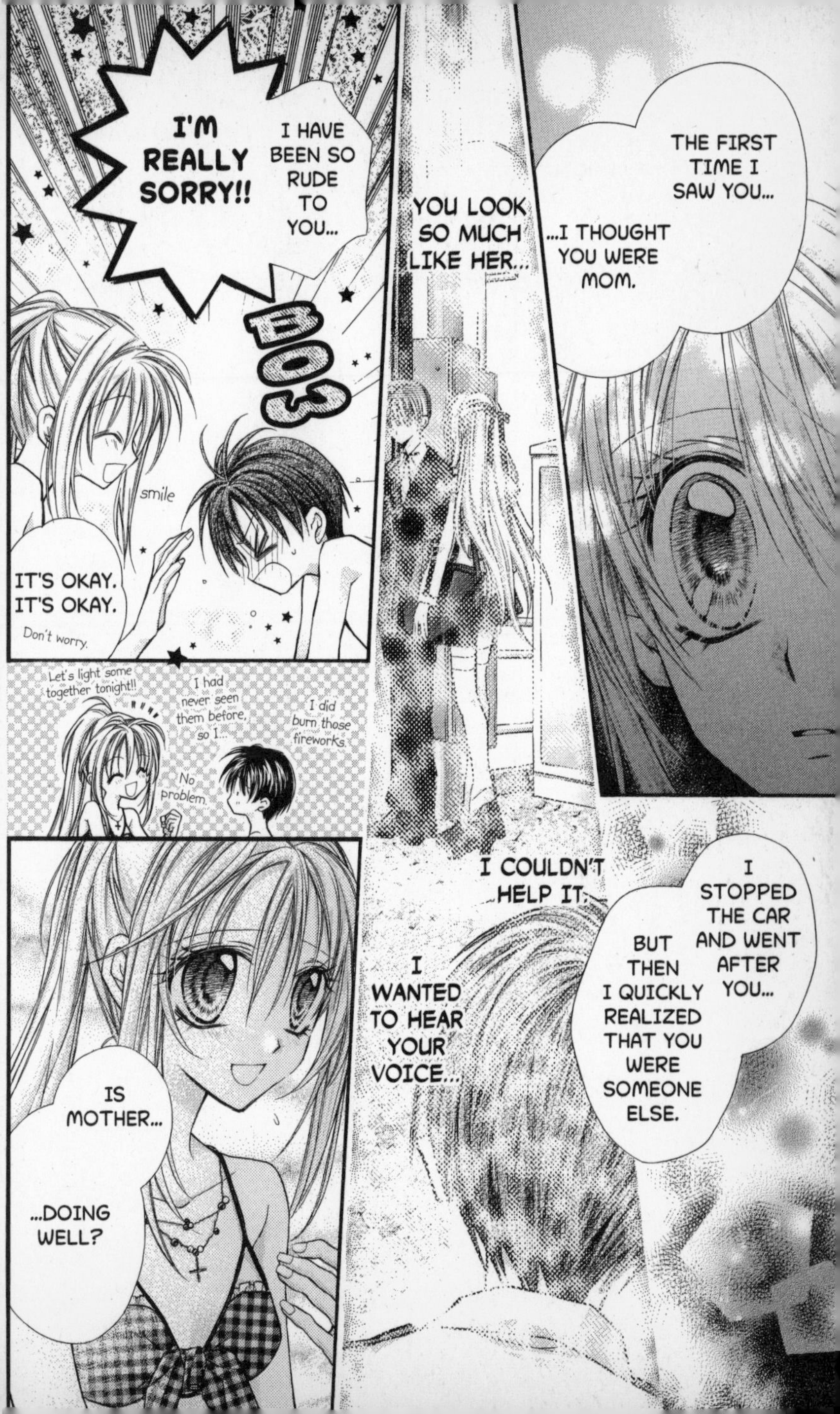
THE FIRST TIME I SAW YOU...
...I THOUGHT YOU WERE MOM.
YOU LOOK SO MUCH LIKE HER...
I STOPPED THE CAR AND WENT AFTER YOU...
BUT THEN I QUICKLY REALIZED THAT YOU WERE SOMEONE ELSE.
I COULDN'T HELP IT.
I WANTED TO HEAR YOUR VOICE...
I HAVE BEEN SO RUDE TO YOU...
I'M REALLY SORRY!!
BOW
smile
IT'S OKAY. IT'S OKAY.
Don't worry.
I did burn those fireworks.
I had never seen them before, so I...
Let's light some together tonight!!
No problem.
IS MOTHER...
...DOING WELL?

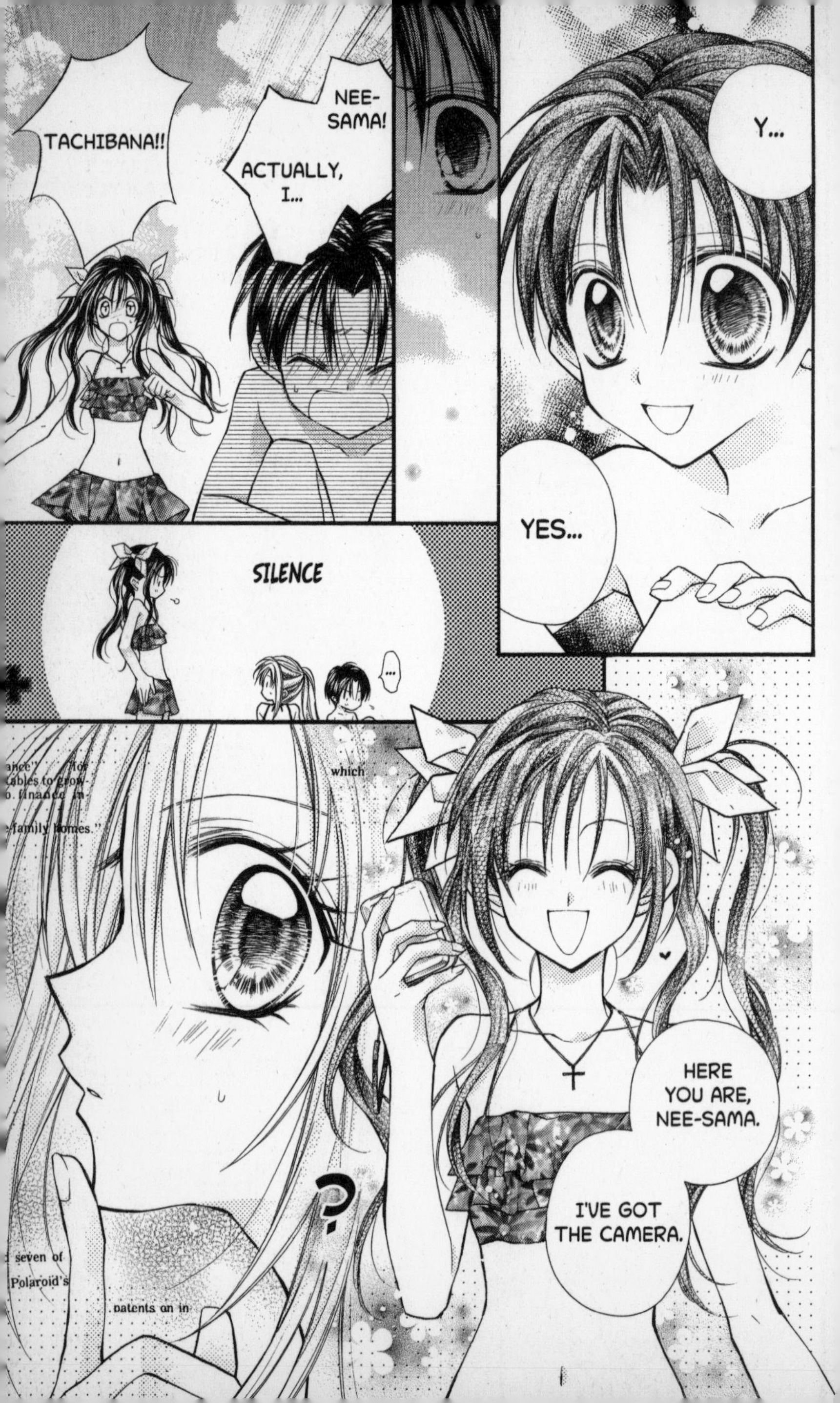
Y...
YES...
NEE-SAMA!
ACTUALLY, I...
TACHIBANA!!
SILENCE
...
HERE YOU ARE, NEE-SAMA.
I'VE GOT THE CAMERA.
?

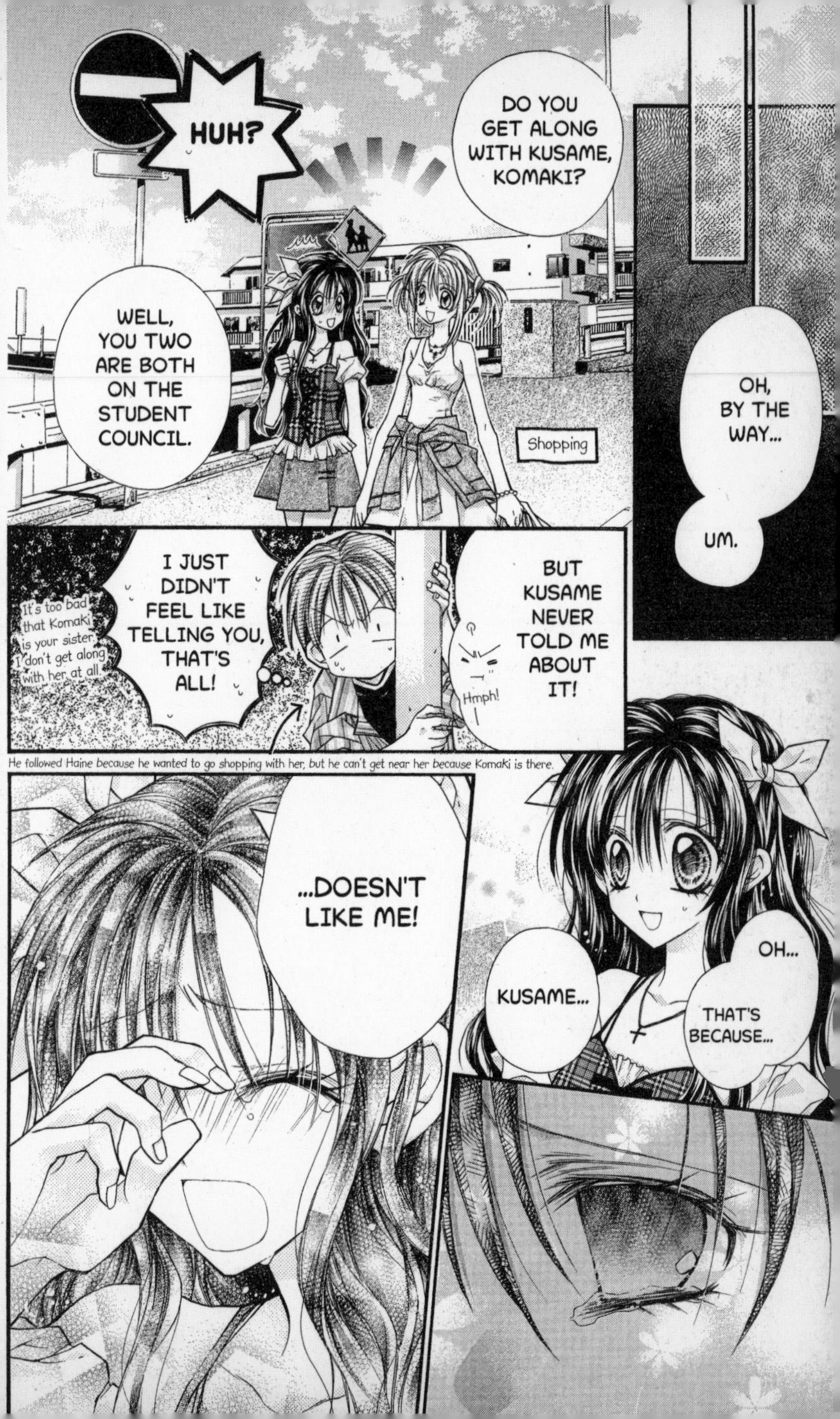
OH, BY THE WAY...
UM.
DO YOU GET ALONG WITH KUSAME, KOMAKI?
HUH?
WELL, YOU TWO ARE BOTH ON THE STUDENT COUNCIL.
Shopping
BUT KUSAME NEVER TOLD ME ABOUT IT!
Hmph!
I JUST DIDN'T FEEL LIKE TELLING YOU, THAT'S ALL!
It's too bad that Komaki is your sister. I don't get along with her at all.
He followed Haine because he wanted to go shopping with her, but he can't get near her because Komaki is there.
OH...
THAT'S BECAUSE...
KUSAME...
...DOESN'T LIKE ME!

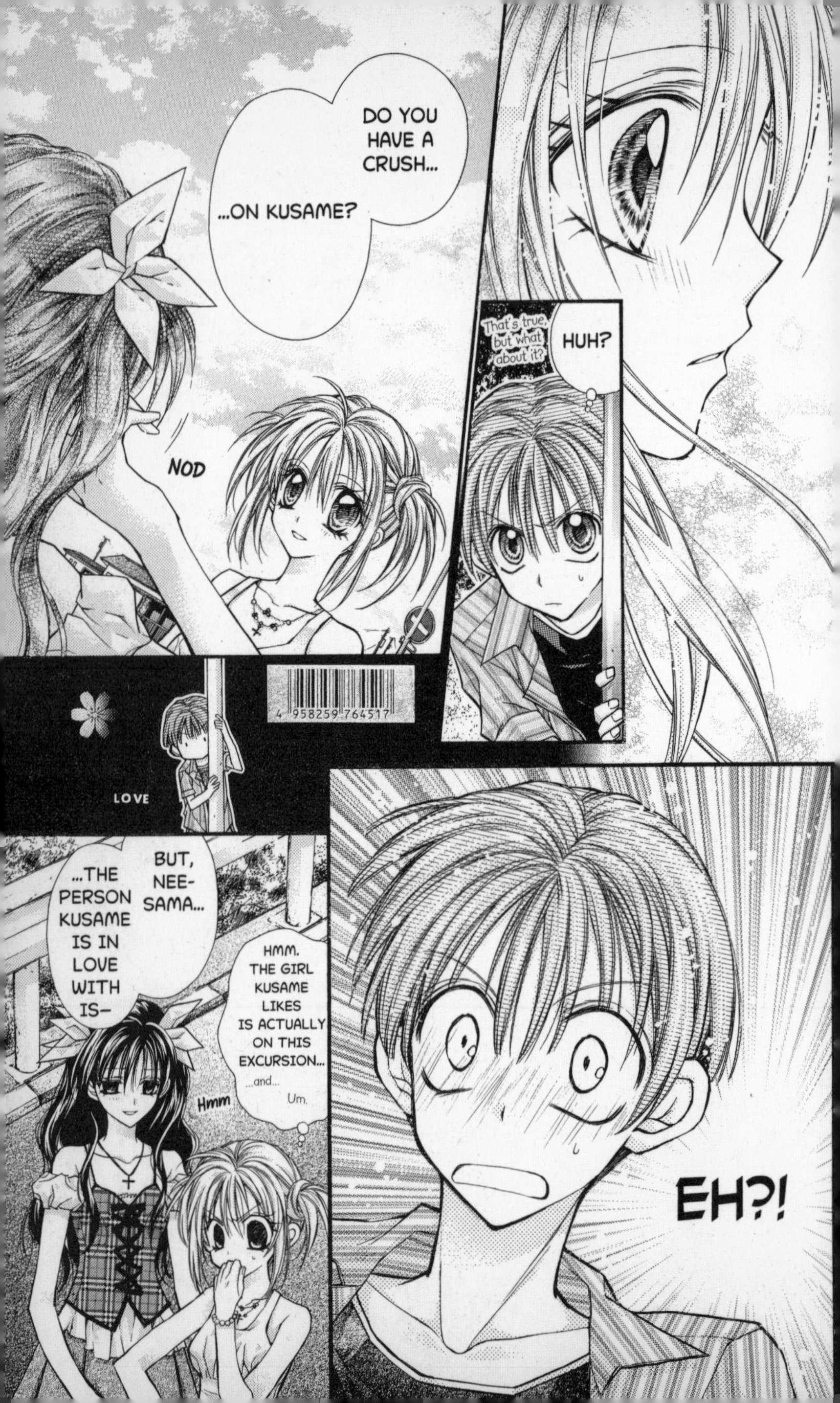
DO YOU HAVE A CRUSH...
...ON KUSAME?
NOD
HUH?
That's true, but what about it?
LOVE
BUT, NEE-SAMA...
...THE PERSON KUSAME IS IN LOVE WITH IS—
HMM. THE GIRL KUSAME LIKES IS ACTUALLY ON THIS EXCURSION...
...and...
Um.
Hmm
EH?!

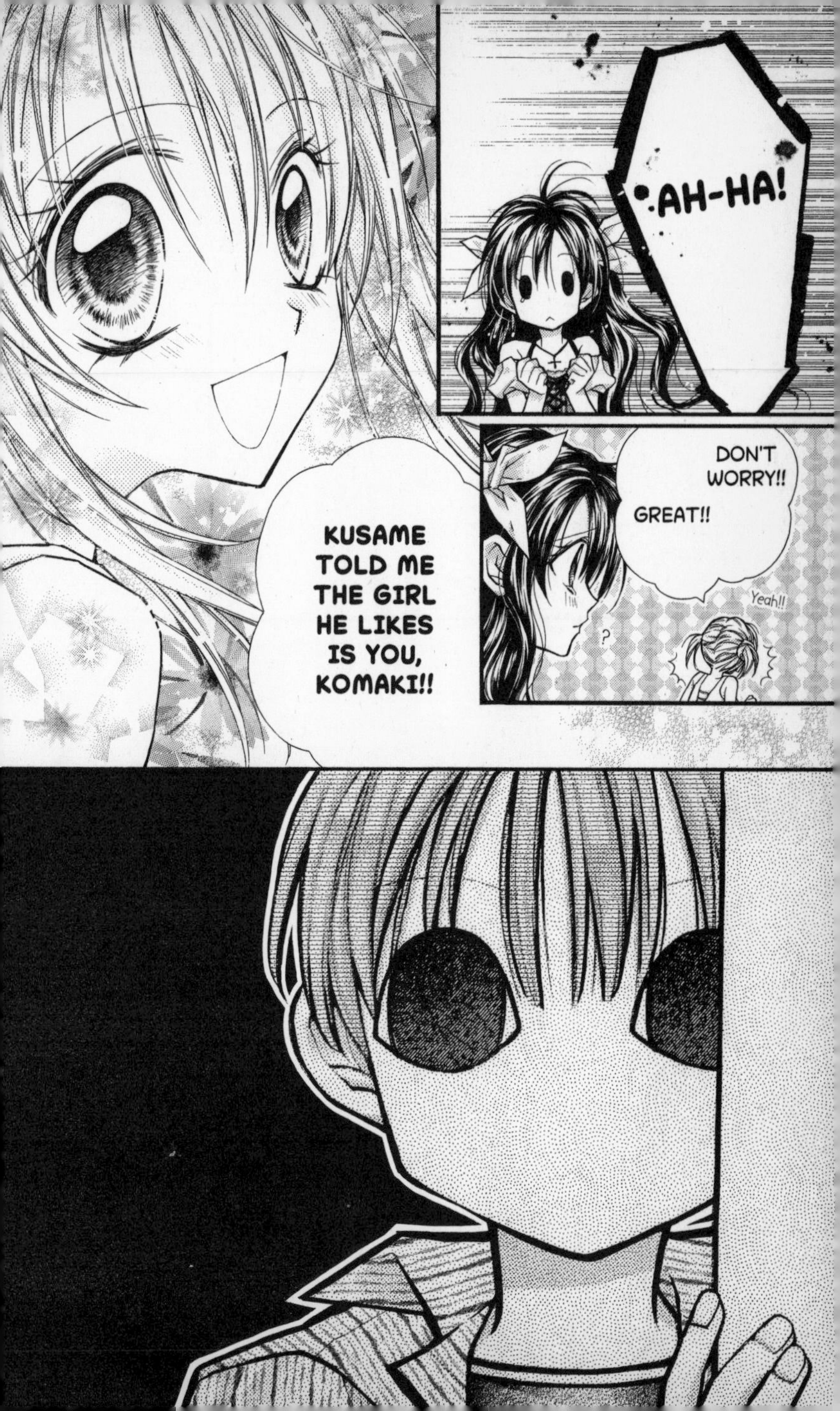
AH-HA!
DON'T WORRY!!
GREAT!!
Yeah!!
KUSAME TOLD ME THE GIRL HE LIKES IS YOU, KOMAKI!!

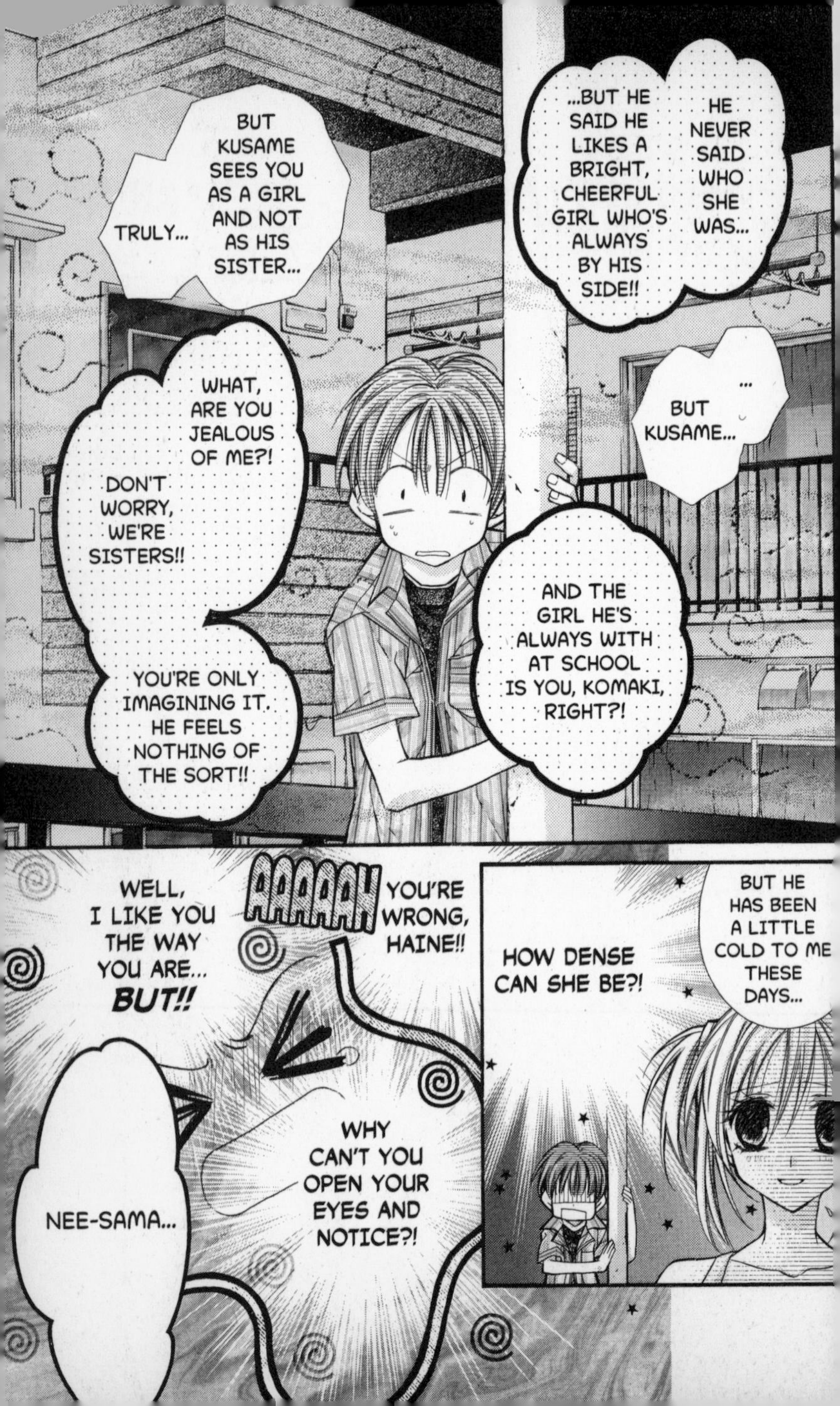
HE NEVER SAID WHO SHE WAS...
...BUT HE SAID HE LIKES A BRIGHT, CHEERFUL GIRL WHO'S ALWAYS BY HIS SIDE!!
...
BUT KUSAME...
AND THE GIRL HE'S ALWAYS WITH AT SCHOOL IS YOU, KOMAKI, RIGHT?!
BUT KUSAME SEES YOU AS A GIRL AND NOT AS HIS SISTER...
TRULY...
WHAT, ARE YOU JEALOUS OF ME?!
DON'T WORRY, WE'RE SISTERS!!
YOU'RE ONLY IMAGINING IT. HE FEELS NOTHING OF THE SORT!!
BUT HE HAS BEEN A LITTLE COLD TO ME THESE DAYS...
HOW DENSE CAN SHE BE?!
YOU'RE WRONG, HAINE!!
AAAAAH
WELL, I LIKE YOU THE WAY YOU ARE... BUT!!
WHY CAN'T YOU OPEN YOUR EYES AND NOTICE?!
NEE-SAMA...

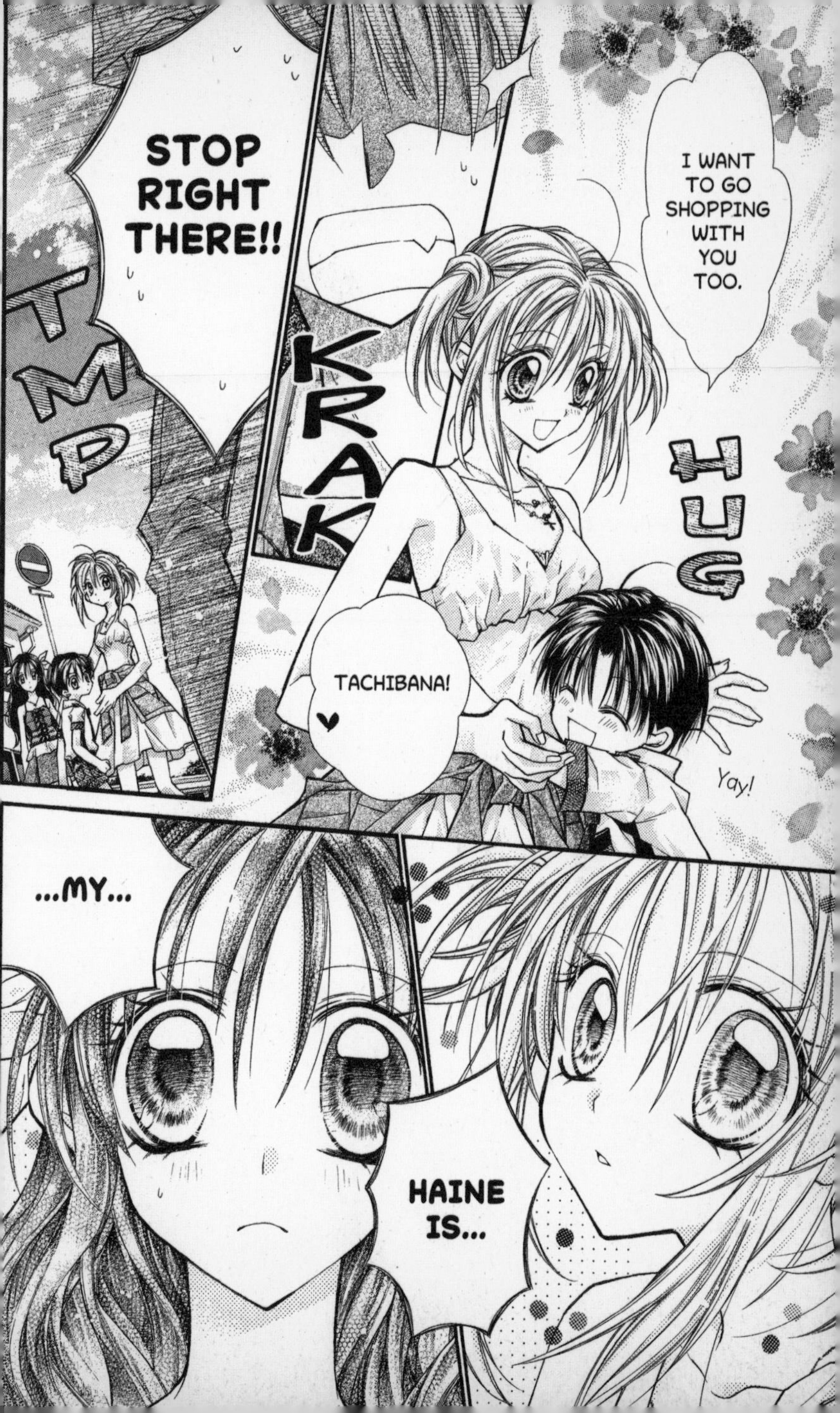
I WANT TO GO SHOPPING WITH YOU TOO.
HUG
TACHIBANA! ♥
Yay!
KRAK
STOP RIGHT THERE!!
TMP
HAINE IS...
...MY...

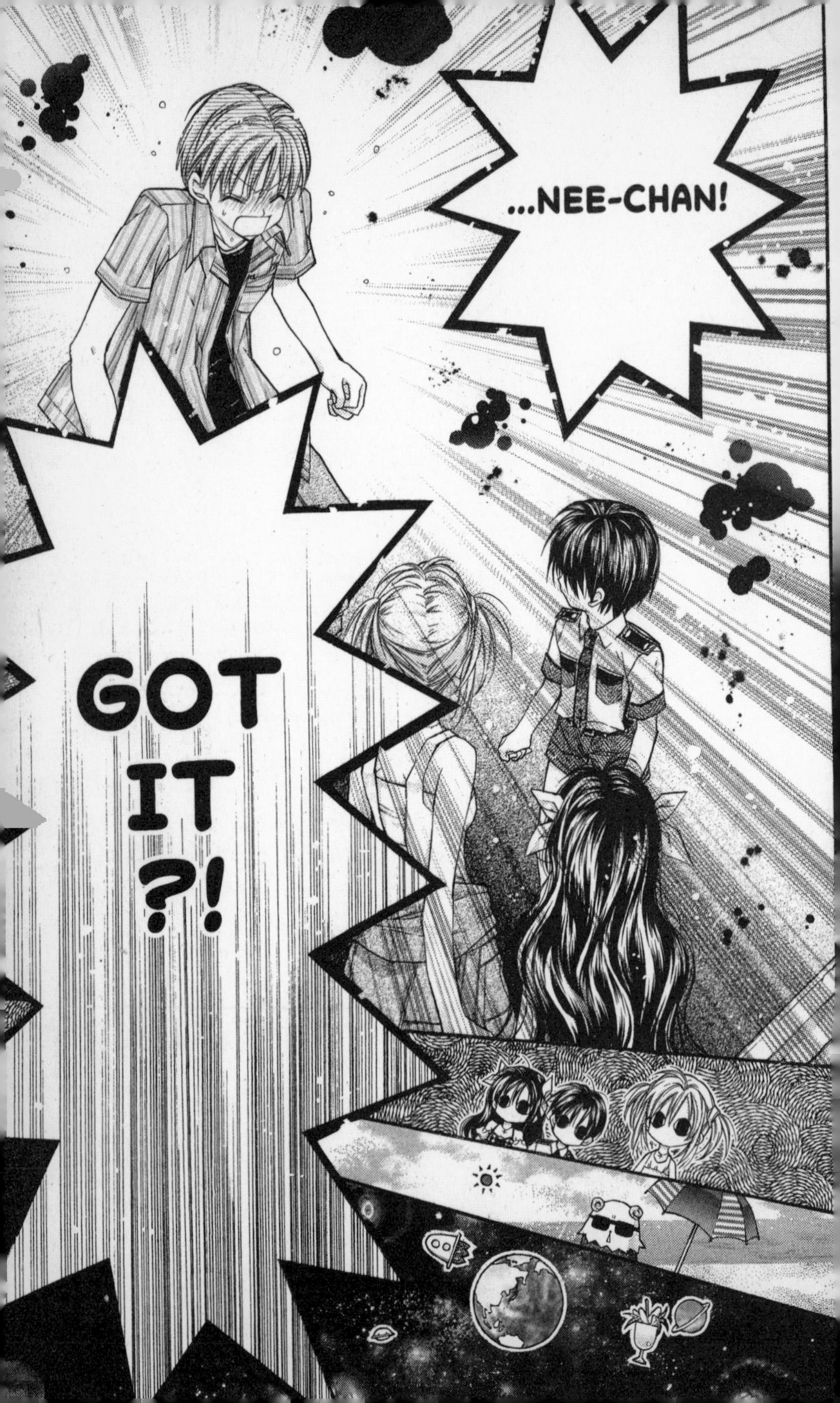
...NEE-CHAN!
GOT IT ?!

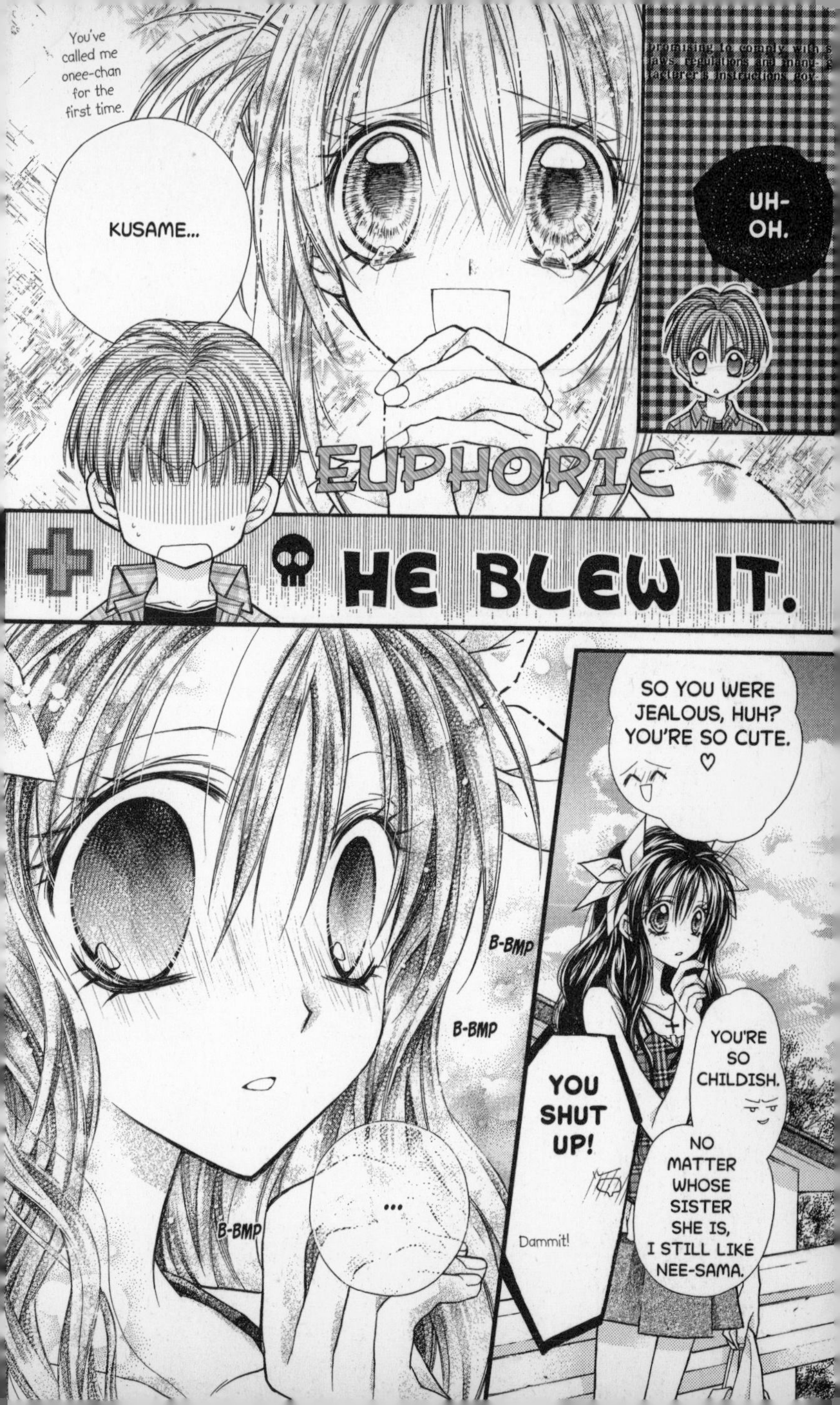
UH-OH.
You've called me onee-chan for the first time.
KUSAME...
EUPHORIC
HE BLEW IT.
SO YOU WERE JEALOUS, HUH? YOU'RE SO CUTE. ♡
YOU'RE SO CHILDISH.
NO MATTER WHOSE SISTER SHE IS, I STILL LIKE NEE-SAMA.
YOU SHUT UP!
Dammit!
B-BMP
B-BMP
B-BMP
...

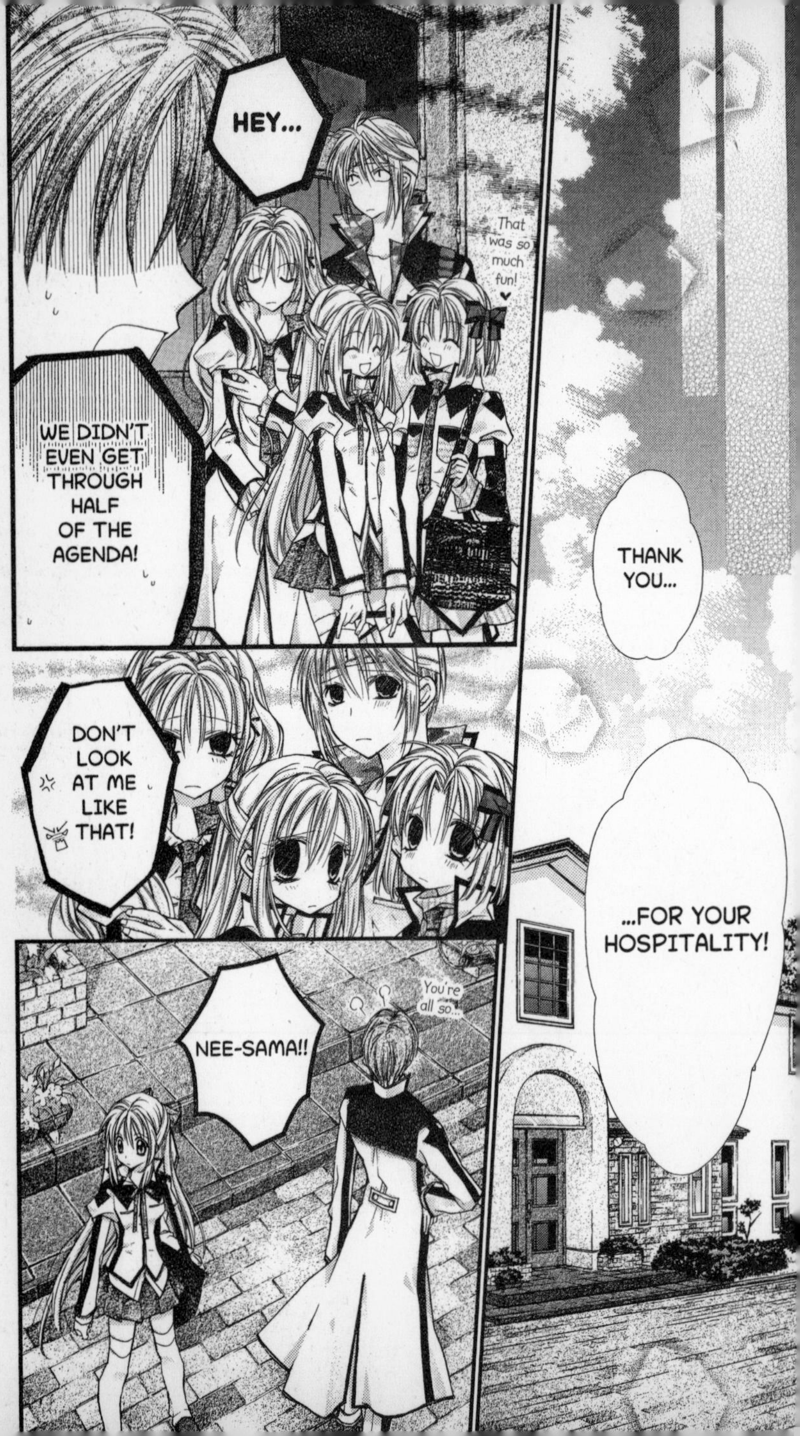

THANK YOU...
...FOR YOUR HOSPITALITY!
HEY...
That was so much fun!
WE DIDN'T EVEN GET THROUGH HALF OF THE AGENDA!
DON'T LOOK AT ME LIKE THAT!
You're all so...
NEE-SAMA!!

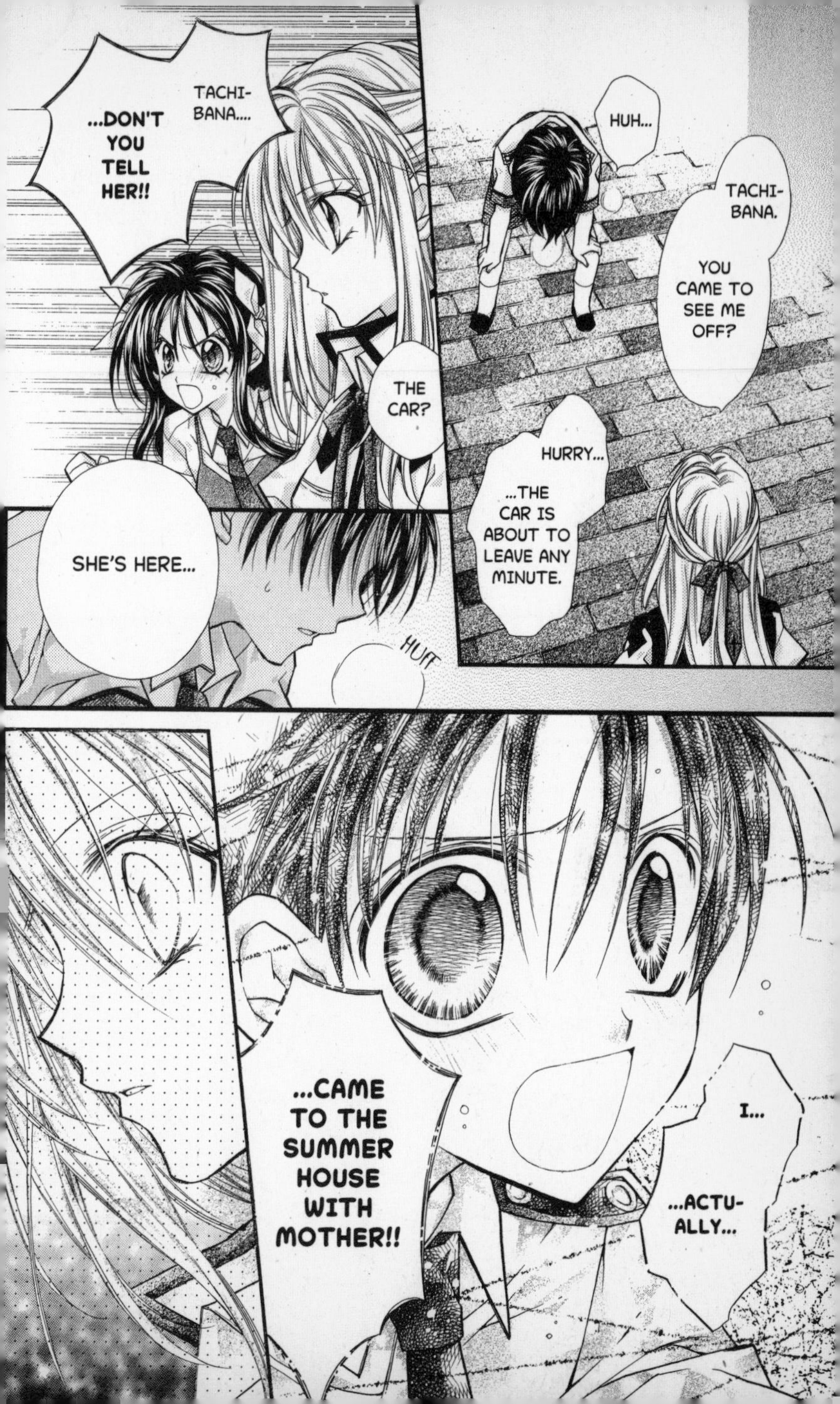
HUH...
TACHI-BANA.
YOU CAME TO SEE ME OFF?
HURRY...
...THE CAR IS ABOUT TO LEAVE ANY MINUTE.
TACHI-BANA....
...DON'T YOU TELL HER!!
THE CAR?
HUFF
SHE'S HERE...
I...
...ACTU-ALLY...
...CAME TO THE SUMMER HOUSE WITH MOTHER!!

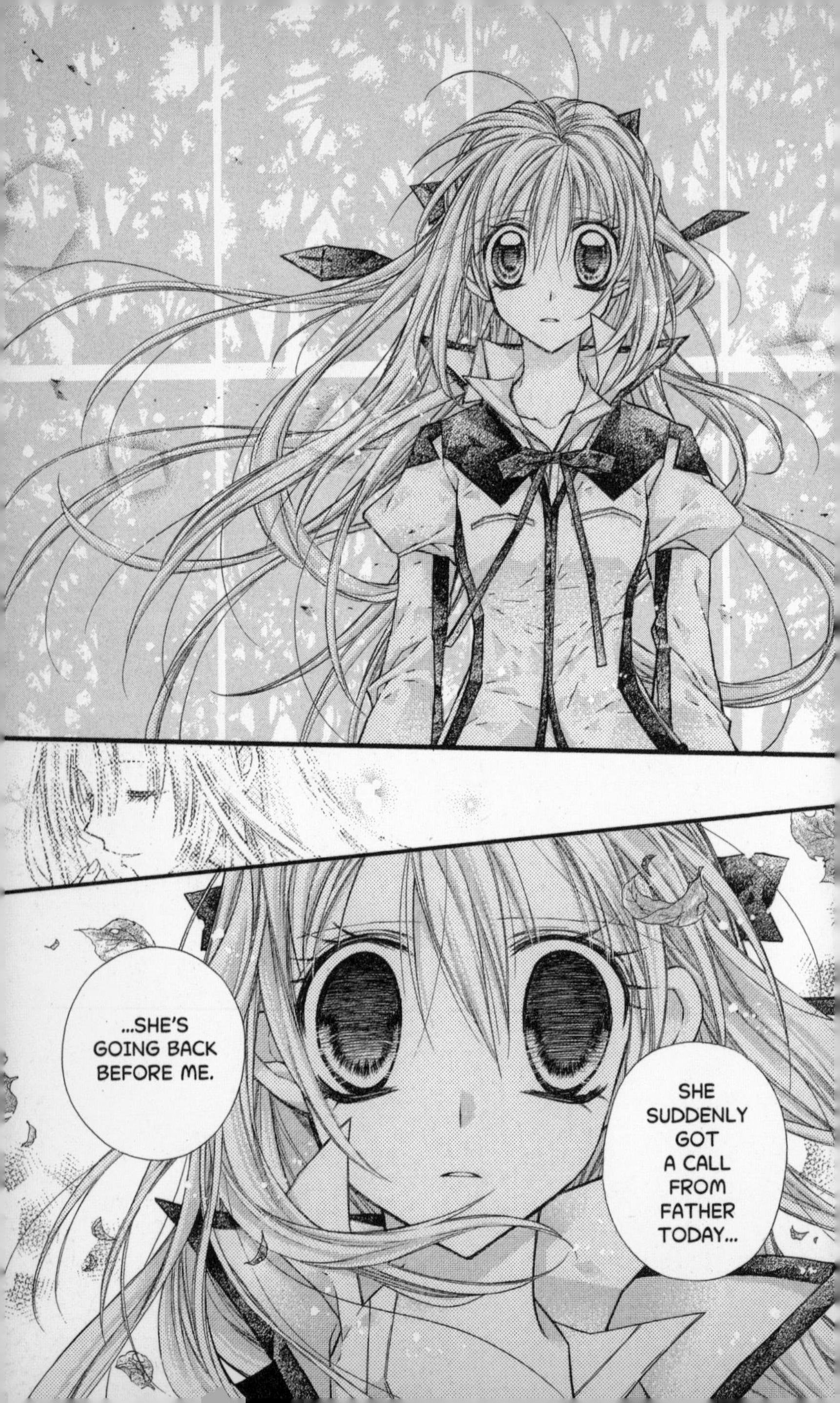
SHE SUDDENLY GOT A CALL FROM FATHER TODAY...
...SHE'S GOING BACK BEFORE ME.

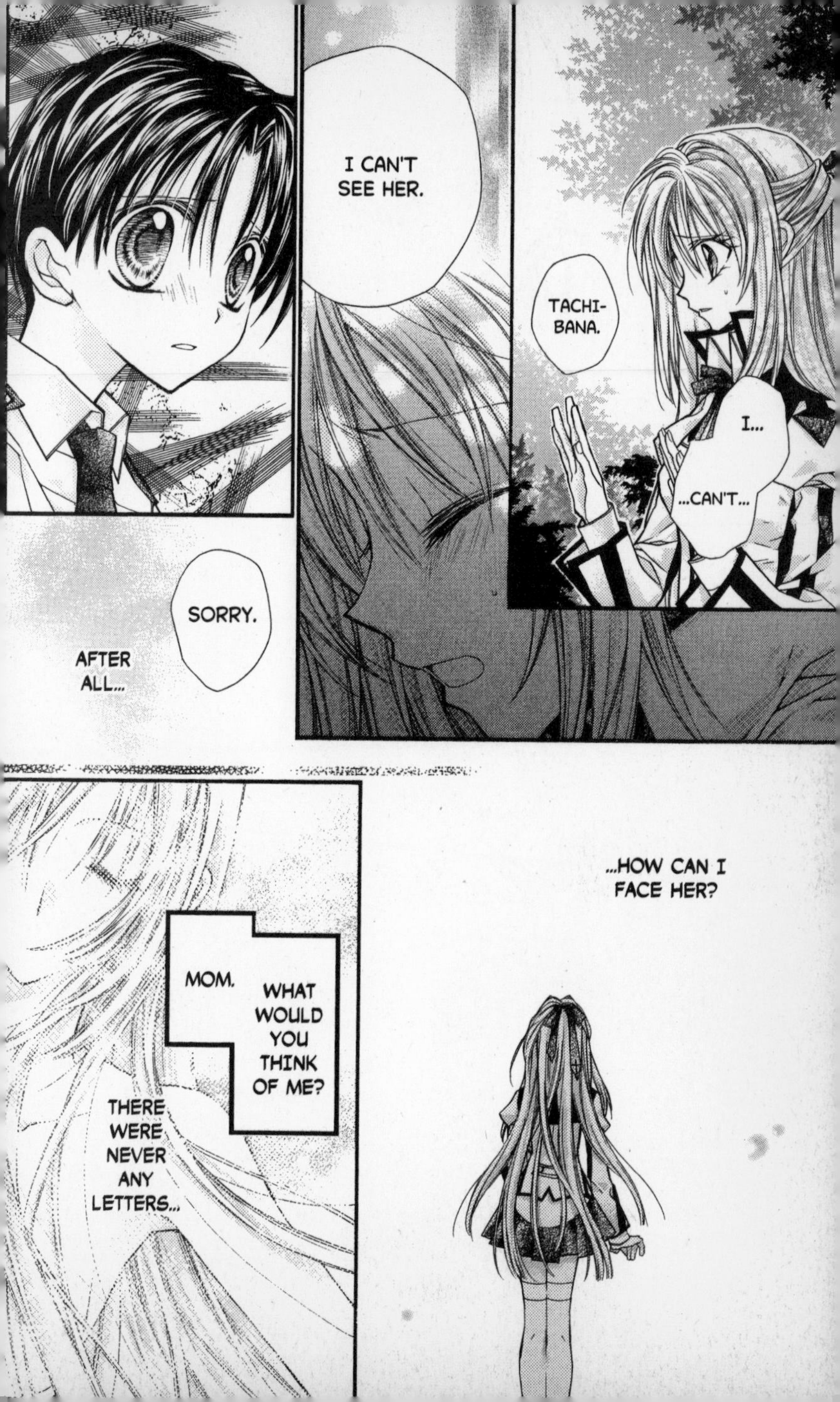
TACHI-BANA.
I...
...CAN'T...
I CAN'T SEE HER.
SORRY.
AFTER ALL...
...HOW CAN I FACE HER?
MOM.
WHAT WOULD YOU THINK OF ME?
THERE WERE NEVER ANY LETTERS...

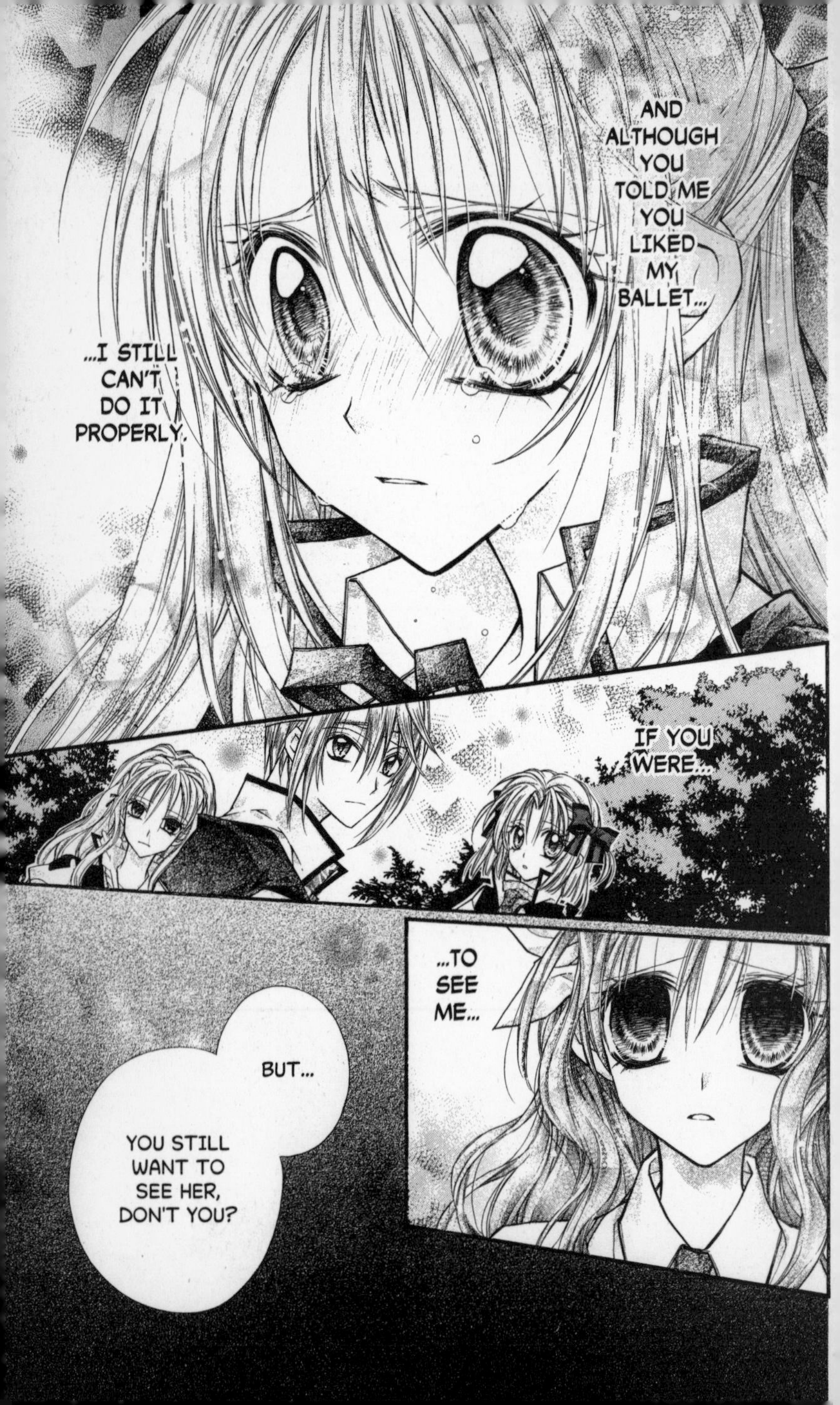
AND ALTHOUGH YOU TOLD ME YOU LIKED MY BALLET...
...I STILL CAN'T DO IT PROPERLY.
IF YOU WERE...
...TO SEE ME...
BUT...
YOU STILL WANT TO SEE HER, DON'T YOU?

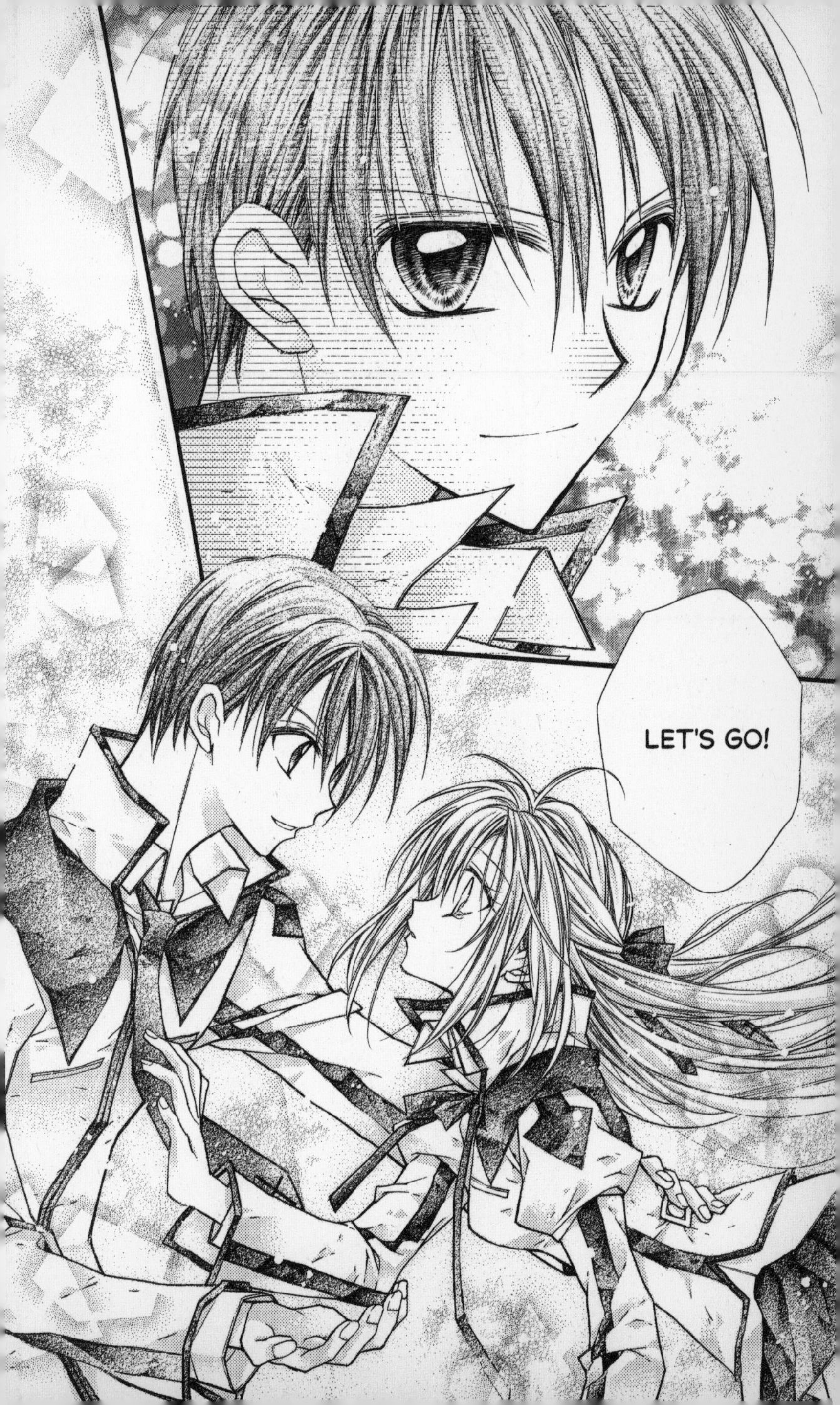
LET'S GO!

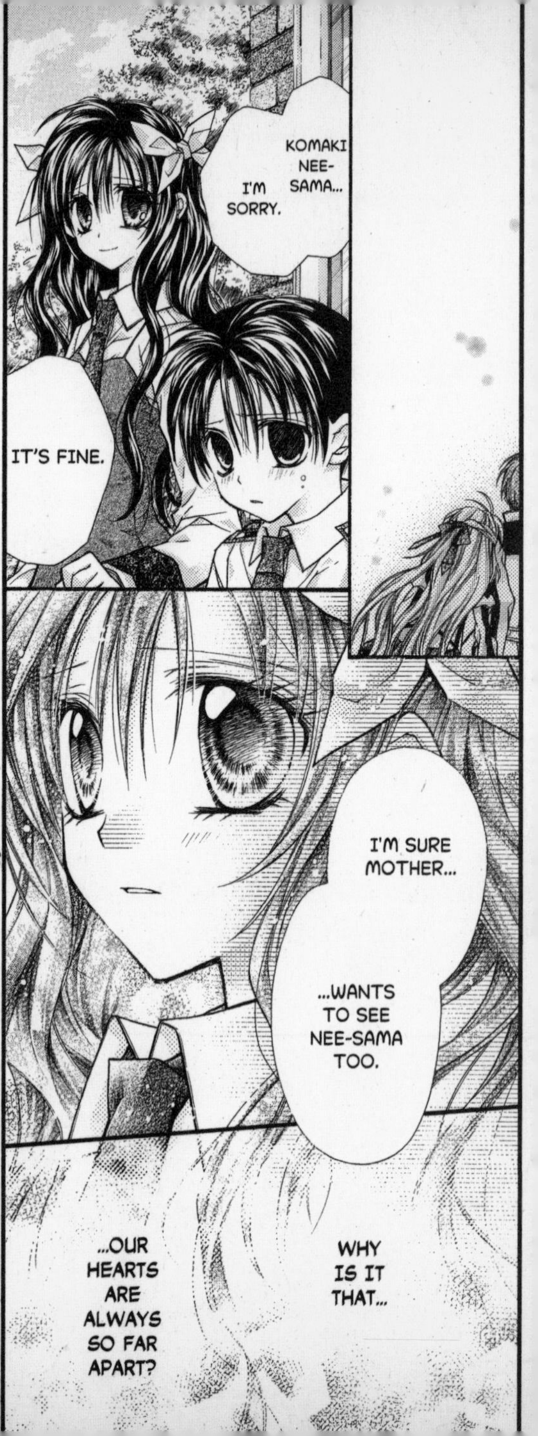
KOMAKI NEE-SAMA... I'M SORRY.
IT'S FINE.
I'M SURE MOTHER...
...WANTS TO SEE NEE-SAMA TOO.
WHY IS IT THAT...
...OUR HEARTS ARE ALWAYS SO FAR APART?

Special Thanks

AI MINASE
KAYORU ASANO
SAORI HINANO
NAKAME
KYAKYA ASANO
NIKI SEISOU

AIRI TEITO
MIWA SAWAKAMI
KANAN KISEKI

HINA MASIRO
SAKURA ARIKAWA
YASUKO HATTORI

Shueisha
Ribon Editorial Department

Ammonite Inc.

RIKU & KAI

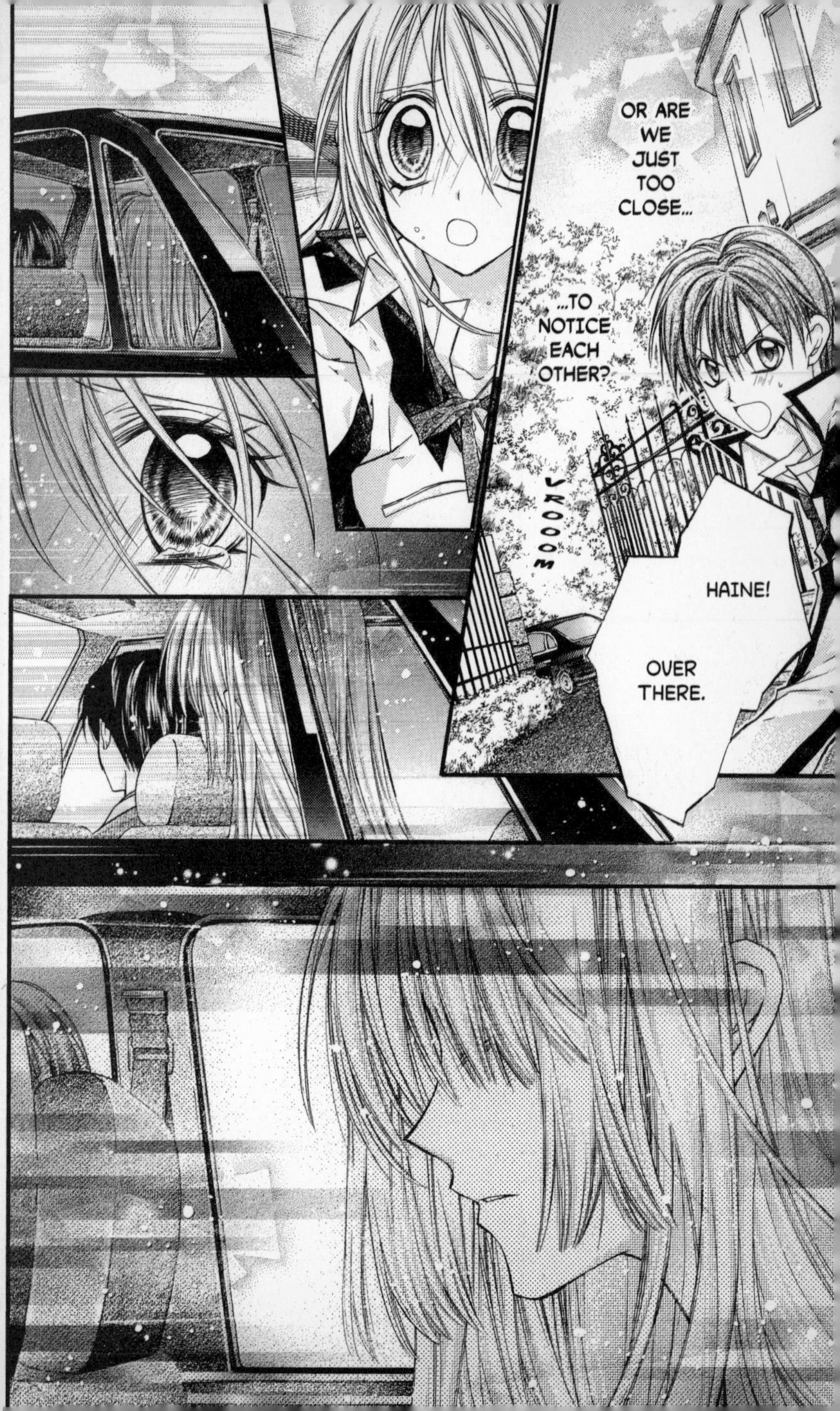
OR ARE WE JUST TOO CLOSE...
...TO NOTICE EACH OTHER?
HAINE!
OVER THERE.
VROOOM

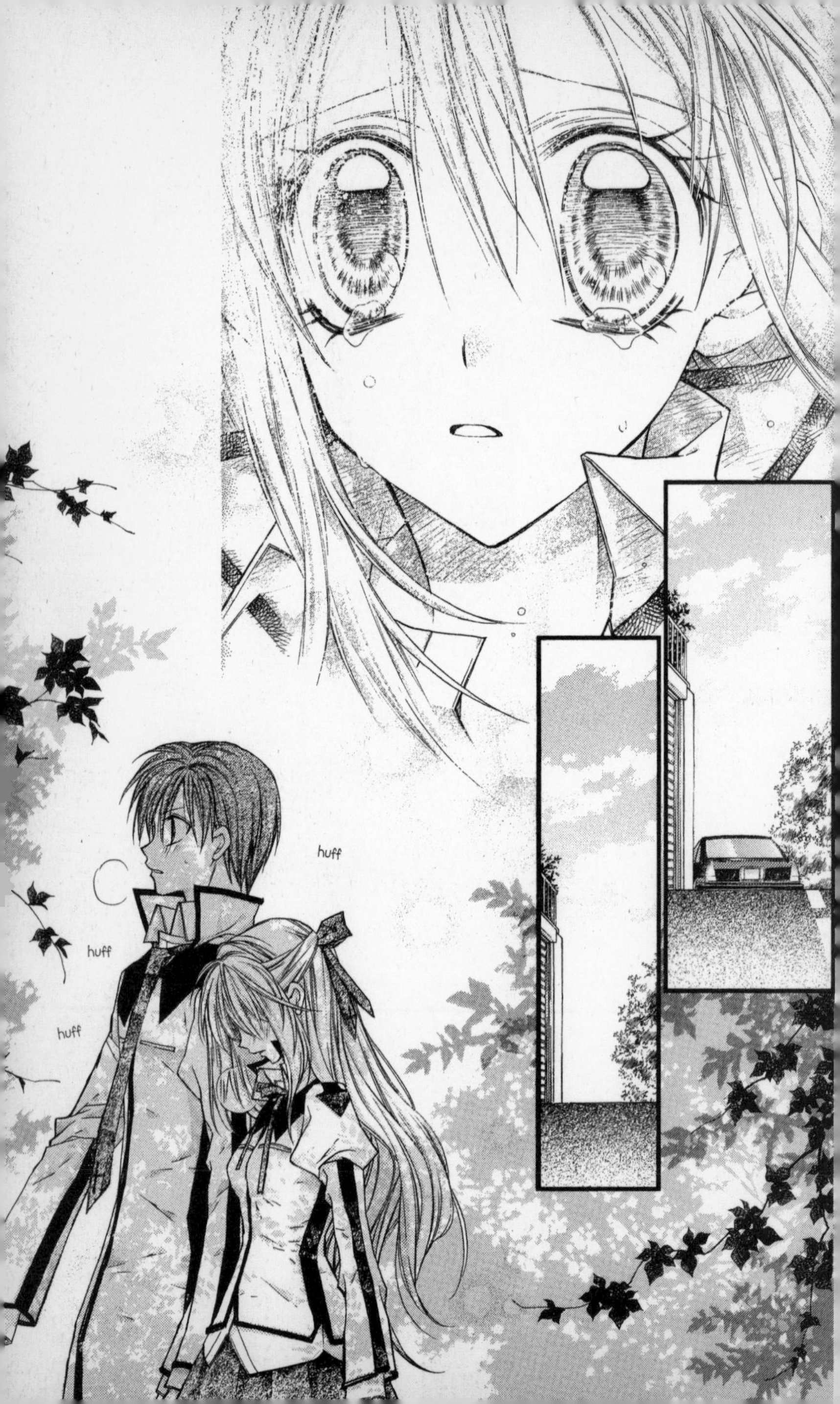
huff
huff
huff

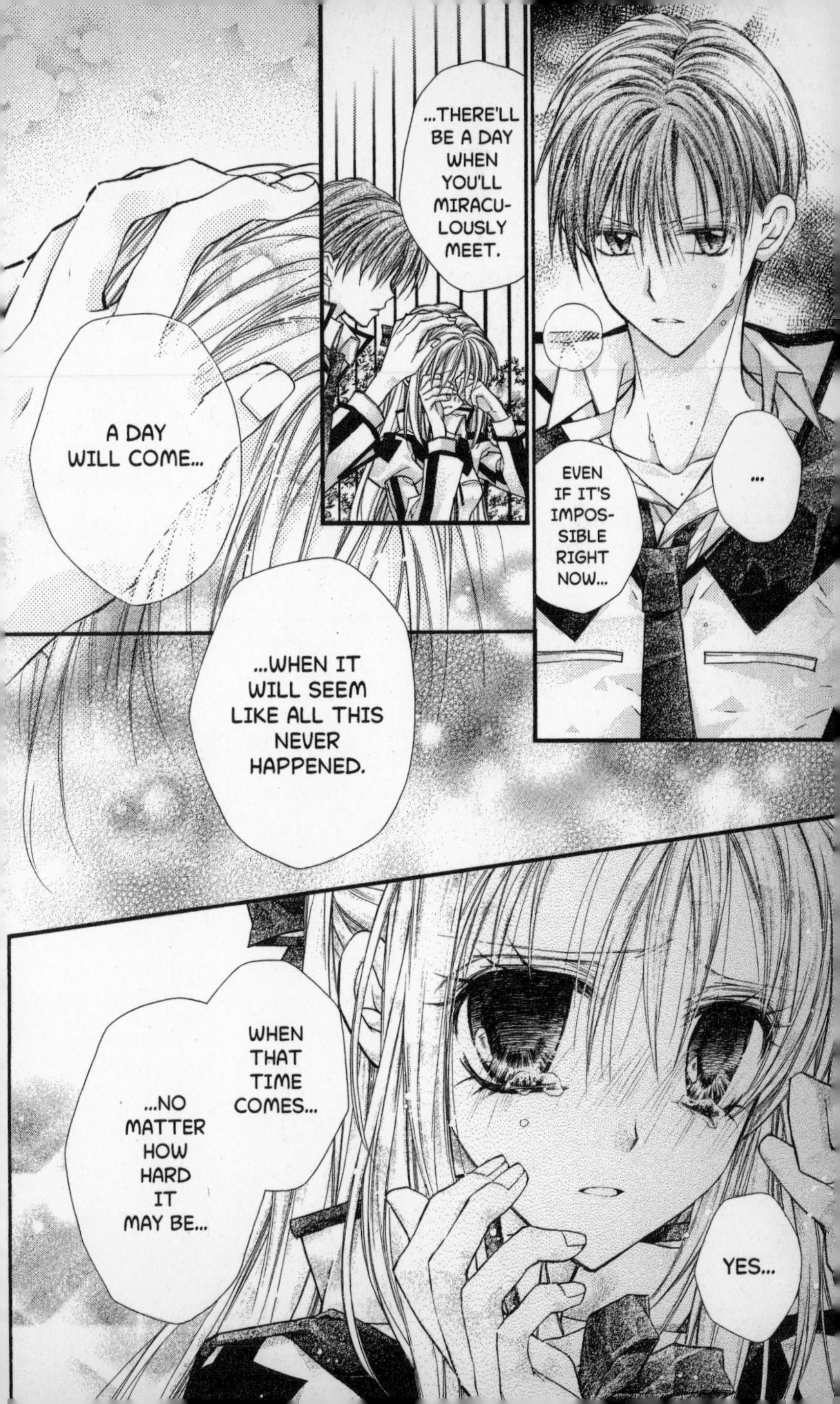
...
EVEN IF IT'S IMPOSSIBLE RIGHT NOW...
...THERE'LL BE A DAY WHEN YOU'LL MIRACULOUSLY MEET.
A DAY WILL COME...
...WHEN IT WILL SEEM LIKE ALL THIS NEVER HAPPENED.
WHEN THAT TIME COMES...
...NO MATTER HOW HARD IT MAY BE...
YES...

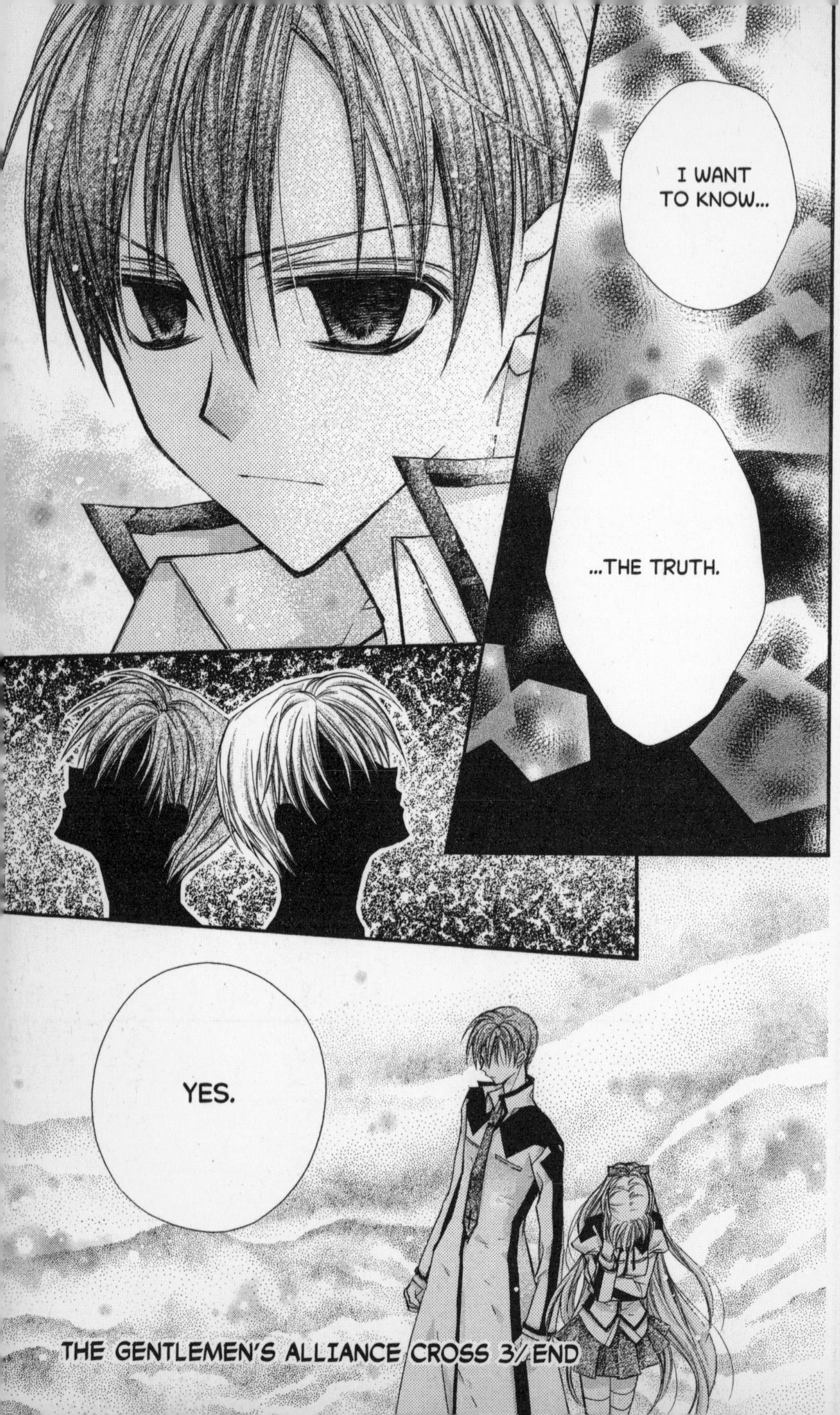
I WANT TO KNOW...
...THE TRUTH.
YES.
THE GENTLEMEN'S ALLIANCE CROSS 3/ END

NOTES ON THE TEXT

PAGE 6:

Fin, Moe-san

Fin (Fin Fish) is a character in *Kamikaze Kaitou Jeanne*. Moe-san, also known as Meroko, is a character in *Full Moon o Sagashite*.

PAGE 11:

Revolution

In the card game *Daihinmin*, or "Big-Time Loser," a revolution is when the strongest cards become the weakest, and vice versa. The current winner of the game then becomes the person with the weakest hand.

myco-chan

This singer/voice actress was in the animated version of *Full Moon o Sagashite*.

SMILE

"SMILE" is a song in the *Full Moon o Sagashite* anime. You can read a translation of the lyrics in *Full Moon* volume 7.

PAGE 25:

Sanction

This type of "sanction" is commonplace among yanki groups. Anybody who wants to quit to start a new life is first beaten up by everyone in the gang.

PAGE 28:

Pine

In Japan, some schools use names rather than numbers for classes. "Plum tree," "Bamboo," and "Pine" are popular class designations.

PAGE 51:

Doting Assistants

In Japanese, "doting assistants" is a play on "doting parents," who think everything their child does is adorable.

PAGE 85:

Changin' My Life

Changin' My Life is the name of myco's band.

PAGE 91:

Watermelon Split

Suika-wari, or "watermelon split," is a Japanese beach game. A blindfolded person will be spun around, and then must crack the watermelon in half with a stick.

Test of Courage!

Kimo-dameshi, or "test of courage" is another popular game played in the summer. People must pass through someplace scary alone or in pairs. Usually other participants try to scare the people to make them abandon the game before they reach the goal.

Ghosts and goblins

This is a pun. *Nanka youkai* can mean either "What do you want?" or "Like a demon."

PAGE 104:

Yeargh!

In the Japanese version, Maguri screams, "Katsu!" This is a cry that Zen monks use to pull themselves together.

PAGE 115:

Tori-nabe

Tori-nabe is a chicken stew.

PAGE 115:

Family Mart
Family Mart is a Japanese convenience store chain.

Berryz Koubou
Berryz Koubou is a group of female pop singers. They have the same producer as Morning Musume.

Margaret
Margaret is a shojo manga magazine.

PAGE 126:

Koto
A *koto* is a traditional Japanese harp. It is usually played by women.

I'm happy to announce that this volume is filled with some of my favorite chapters! I've began to play around with Haine-chan's hairstyle, so you'll probably be able to enjoy the fun even more if you keep your eyes open to the changes...♥

—*Arina Tanemura*

Arina Tanemura was born in Aichi, Japan. She got her start in 1996, publishing *Nibanme no Koi no Katachi* (The Style of the Second Love) in *Ribon Original* magazine. Her early work includes a collection of short stories called *Kanshaku Dama no Yuutsu* (Short-Tempered Melancholic). Two of her titles, *Kamikaze Kaito Jeanne* and *Full Moon*, were made into popular TV series. Tanemura enjoys karaoke and is a huge *Lord of the Rings* fan.

THE GENTLEMEN'S ALLIANCE † vol.3
Shojo Beat Edition

STORY & ART BY
ARINA TANEMURA

English Translation & Adaptation/Tetsuichiro Miyaki
Touch-up Art & Lettering/Elena Diaz
Design/Amy Martin
Editor/Nancy Thistlethwaite

Printed in the U.S.A.

Published by VIZ Media, LLC
P.O. Box 77010
San Francisco, CA 94107

10 9 8 7 6 5 4 3
First printing, September 2007
Third printing, March 2012

www.viz.com

www.shojobeat.com

PARENTAL ADVISORY
THE GENTLEMEN'S ALLIANCE † is rated T+ for Older Teen and is recommended for ages 16 and up. This volume contains suggestive themes.

RATED T+ FOR OLDER TEEN

ratings.viz.com

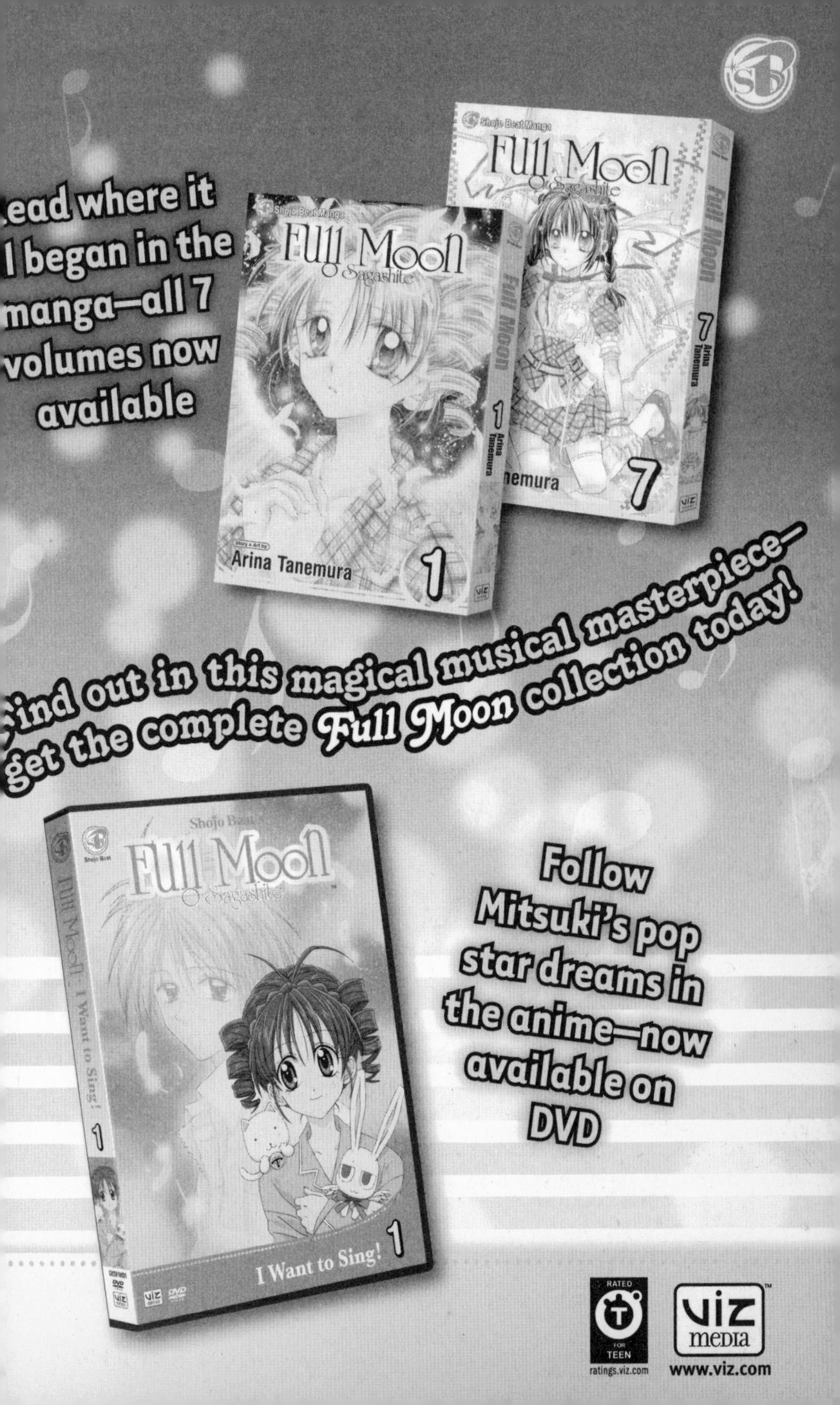
ead where it
l began in the
manga—all 7
volumes now
available
Shojo Beat Manga
Full Moon o Sagashite
Story + Art by
Arina Tanemura
1
Shojo Beat Manga
Full Moon o Sagashite
nemura
7
ind out in this magical musical masterpiece—
get the complete Full Moon collection today!
Shojo Beat
Full Moon o Sagashite
I Want to Sing! 1
Follow
Mitsuki's pop
star dreams in
the anime—now
available on
DVD
RATED
T
FOR
TEEN
ratings.viz.com
VIZ media
www.viz.com